The Sea War of 1812
Volume 1

The Sea War of 1812
A History of the Maritime Conflict
Volume 1

A. T. Mahan

The Sea War of 1812: a History of the Maritime Conflict—Volume 1
A. T. Mahan

originally published under the title
Sea Power in its Relations to the War of 1812

Leonaur is an imprint of Oakpast Ltd

Text in this form and material original to this edition
copyright © 2008 Oakpast Ltd

ISBN: 978-1-84677-548-2 (hardcover)
ISBN: 978-1-84677-547-5 (softcover)

http://www.leonaur.com

Publisher's Notes
The opinions expressed in this book are those of the author
and are not necessarily those of the publisher.

Contents

Preface	7
Colonial Conditions	11
From Independence to Jay's Treaty, 1794	49
From Jay's Treaty to the Orders in Council, 1794-1807	93
From the Orders in Council to War, 1807-1812	143
The Theatre of Operations	274
Early Cruises and Engagements	302
Operations on the Northern Frontier	341
Privateering & Naval Actions	374

Preface

The present work concludes the series of "The Influence of Sea Power upon History," as originally framed in the conception of the author. In the previous volumes he has had the inspiring consciousness of regarding his subject as a positive and commanding element in the history of the world. In the War of 1812, also, the effect is real and dread enough; but to his own country, to the United States, as a matter of national experience, the lesson is rather that of the influence of a negative quantity upon national history. The phrase scarcely lends itself to use as a title; but it represents the truth which the author has endeavoured to set forth, though recognizing clearly that the victories on Lake Erie and Lake Champlain do illustrate, in a distinguished manner, his principal thesis, the controlling influence upon events of naval power, even when transferred to an inland body of fresh water. The lesson there, however, was the same as in the larger fields of war heretofore treated. Not by rambling operations, or naval duels, are wars decided, but by force massed, and handled in skilful combination. It matters not that the particular force be small. The art of war is the same throughout; and may be illustrated as really, though less conspicuously, by a flotilla as by an armada; by a corporal's guard, or the three units of the Horatii, as by a host of a hundred thousand.

The interest of the War of 1812, to Americans, has commonly been felt to lie in the brilliant evidence of high professional tone and efficiency reached by their navy, as shown by the single-ship actions, and by the two decisive victories achieved by little squadrons upon the lakes. Without in the least overlooking the permanent value of such examples and such traditions, to the nation, and to the military service which they illustrate, it nevertheless appears to the writer that the effect may be even harmful to the people at large, if it be permitted to conceal the deeply mortifying condition to which the country was reduced by parsimony in preparation, or to obscure the lessons thence to be drawn for practical application now. It is perhaps useless to quarrel with the tendency of mankind to turn its eyes from disagreeable subjects, and to dwell complacently upon those which minister to self-content. We mostly read the newspapers in which we find our views reflected, and dispense ourselves easily with the less pleasing occupation of seeing them roughly disputed; but a writer on a subject of national importance may not thus exempt himself from the unpleasant features of his task.

The author has thought it also essential to precede his work by a somewhat full exposition of the train of causes, which through a long series of years led to the war. It may seem at first far-fetched to go back to 1651 for the origins of the War of 1812; but without such preliminary consideration it is impossible to understand, or to make due allowance for, the course of Great Britain. It will be found, however, that the treatment of the earlier period is brief, and only sufficient for a clear comprehension of the five years of intense international strain preceding the final rupture; years the full narrative of which is indispensable to appreciating the grounds and development of the quarrel,—to realize what they fought each other for.

That much of Great Britain's action was unjustifiable, and at times even monstrous, regarded in itself alone, must be admitted; but we shall ill comprehend the necessity of preparation for war, if we neglect to note the pressure of emergency, of deadly peril, upon a state, or if we fail to recognize that traditional habits of thought constitute with nations, as with individuals, a compulsive moral force which an opponent can control only by the display of adequate physical power. Such to the British people was the conviction of their right and need to compel the service of their native seamen, wherever found on the high seas. The conclusion of the writer is, that at a very early stage of the French Revolutionary Wars the United States should have obeyed Washington's warnings to prepare for war, and to build a navy; and that, thus prepared, instead of placing reliance upon a system of commercial restrictions, war should have been declared not later than 1807, when the news of Jena, and of Great Britain's refusal to relinquish her practice of impressing from American ships, became known almost coincidently. But this conclusion is perfectly compatible with a recognition of the desperate character of the strife that Great Britain was waging; that she could not disengage herself from it, Napoleon being what he was; and that the methods which she pursued did cause the Emperor's downfall, and her own deliverance, although they were invasions of just rights, to which the United States should not have submitted.

If war is always avoidable, consistently with due resistance to evil, then war is always unjustifiable; but if it is possible that two nations, or two political entities, like the North and South in the American Civil War, find the question between them one which neither can yield without sacrificing conscientious conviction, or national welfare, or the interests of posterity, of which each generation in its day is the trustee, then war is not justifiable only; it is imperative. In these days of glorified arbitration it cannot be affirmed too distinctly that bodies of men—nations—have convictions binding on their consciences, as well as interests which are vital in character; and that nations, no more than individuals, may surrender conscience to another's keeping. Still less may they rightfully pre-engage so to do. Nor is this conclusion invalidated by a triumph of the unjust in war. Subjugation to wrong is not acquiescence in wrong. A beaten nation is not necessarily a disgraced nation; but the nation or man is disgraced who shirks an obligation to defend right.

From 1803 to 1814 Great Britain was at war with Napoleon, without intermission; until 1805 single handed, thenceforth till

1812 mostly without other allies than the incoherent and disorganized mass of the Spanish insurgents. After Austerlitz, as Pitt said, the map of Europe became useless to indicate distribution of political power. Thenceforth it showed a continent politically consolidated, organized and driven by Napoleon's sole energy, with one aim, to crush Great Britain; and the Continent of Europe then meant the civilized world, politically and militarily. How desperate the strife, the author in a previous work has striven fully to explain, and does not intend here to repeat. In it Great Britain laid her hand to any weapon she could find, to save national life and independence. To justify all her measures at the bar of conventional law, narrowly construed, is impossible. Had she attempted to square herself to it she would have been overwhelmed; as the United States, had it adhered rigidly to its Constitution, must have foregone the purchase of the territories beyond the Mississippi. The measures which overthrew Napoleon grievously injured the United States; by international law grievously wronged her also. Should she have acquiesced? If not, war was inevitable. Great Britain could not be expected to submit to destruction for another's benefit.

The author has been indebted to the Officers of the Public Records Office in London, to those of the Canadian Archives, and to the Bureau of Historical Research of the Carnegie Institution of Washington, for kind and essential assistance in consulting papers. He owes also an expression of personal obligation to the Marquis of Londonderry for permission to use some of the Castlereagh correspondence, bearing on the peace negotiations, which was not included in the extensive published Memoirs and Correspondence of Lord Castlereagh; and to Mr. Charles W. Stewart, the Librarian of the United States Navy Department, for inexhaustible patience in searching for, or verifying, data and references, needed to make the work complete on the naval side.

A. T. Mahan
September, 1905

CHAPTER 1

Colonial Conditions

The head waters of the stream of events which led to the War of 1812, between the United States and Great Britain, must be sought far back in the history of Europe, in the principles governing commercial, colonial, and naval policy, accepted almost universally prior to the French Revolution. It is true that, before that tremendous epoch was reached, a far-reaching contribution to the approaching change in men's ideas on most matters touching mercantile intercourse, and the true relations of man to man, of nation to nation, had been made by the publication, in 1776, of Adam Smith's *Inquiry into the Nature and Causes of the Wealth of Nations*; but, as is the case with most marked advances in the realm of thought, the light thus kindled, though finding reflection here and there among a few broader intellects, was unable to penetrate at once the dense surface of prejudice and conservatism with which the received maxims of generations had incrusted the general mind. Against such obstruction even the most popular of statesmen—as the younger Pitt soon after this became—cannot prevail at once; and, before time permitted the British people at large to reach that wider comprehension of issues, whereby alone radical change is made possible, there set in an era of reaction consequent upon the French Revolution, the excesses of which involved in one universal discredit all the more liberal ideas that were leavening the leaders of mankind.

The two principal immediate causes of the War of 1812 were the impressment of seamen from American merchant ships, upon the high seas, to serve in the British Navy, and the interference with the carrying trade of the United States by the naval power of Great Britain. For a long time this interference was confined by the British Ministry to methods which they thought themselves able to defend—as they did the practice of impressment—upon the ground of rights, prescriptive and established, natural or belligerent; although the American Government contended that in several specific measures no such right existed,—that the action was illegal as well as oppressive. As the war with Napoleon increased in intensity, however, the exigencies of the struggle induced the British cabinet to formulate and enforce against neutrals a restriction of trade which it confessed to be without sanction in law, and justified only upon the plea of necessary retaliation, imposed by the unwarrantable course of the French Emperor. These later proceedings, known historically as the Orders in Council,[1] by their enormity dwarfed all previous causes of complaint, and with the question of impressment constituted the vital and irreconcilable body of dissent which dragged the two states into armed collision. Undoubtedly, other matters of difficulty arose from time to time, and were productive of dispute; but either they were of comparatively trivial importance, easily settled by ordinary diplomatic methods, or there was not at bottom any vital difference as to principle, but only as to the method of adjustment. For instance, in the flagrant and unpardonable outrage of taking men by force from the United States frigate *Chesapeake*, the British Government, although permitted by the American to spin out discussion over a period of four years, did not pretend to sustain the act itself; the act, that is, of searching a neutral ship of war. Whatever the motive of the Ministry in postponing redress, their pretexts turned upon points of detail, accessory to the main transaction, or upon the subsequent course of the United States Government, which showed con-

---

1. Order in Council was a general term applied to all orders touching affairs, internal as well as external, issued by the King in Council. The particular orders here in question, by their extraordinary character and wide application, came to have a kind of sole title to the expression in the diplomatic correspondence between the two countries.

scious weakness by taking hasty, pettish half-measures; instead of abstaining from immediate action, and instructing its minister to present an ultimatum, if satisfaction were shirked.

In the two causes of the war which have been specified, the difference was fundamental. Whichever was right, the question at stake was in each case one of principle, and of necessity. Great Britain never claimed to impress American seamen; but she did assert that her native-born subjects could never change their allegiance, that she had an inalienable right to their service, and to seize them wherever found, except within foreign territory. From an admitted premise, that the open sea is common to all nations, she deduced a common jurisdiction, in virtue of which she arrested her vagrant seamen. This argument of right was reinforced by a paramount necessity. In a life and death struggle with an implacable enemy, Great Britain with difficulty could keep her fleet manned at all; even with indifferent material. The deterioration in quality of her ships' companies was notorious; and it was notorious also that numerous British seamen sought employment in American merchant ships, hoping there to find refuge from the protracted confinement of a now dreary maritime war. Resort to impressment was not merely the act of a high-handed Government, but the demand of both parties in the state, coerced by the sentiment of the people, whose will is ultimately irresistible. No ministry could hope to retain power if it surrendered the claim to take seamen found under a neutral flag. This fact was thoroughly established in a long discussion with United States plenipotentiaries, five years before the war broke out.

On the other hand, the United States maintained that on the sea common the only jurisdiction over a ship was that of its own nation. She could not admit that American vessels there should be searched, for other purposes than those conceded to the belligerent by international law; that is, in order to determine the nature of the voyage, to ascertain whether, by destination, by cargo, or by persons carried, the obligations of neutrality were being infringed. If there was reasonable cause for suspicion, the vessel, by accepted law and precedent, might be sent to a port of the belligerent, where the question was adjudicated by legal process; but the actual captor could not decide it on the spot. On the contrary, he was bound, to the utmost possible, to preserve from molestation everything on board the seized vessel; in order that, if cleared, the owner might undergo no damage beyond the detention. So deliberate a course was not suited to the summary methods of impressment, nor to the urgent needs of the British Navy. The boarding officer, who had no authority to take away a bale of goods, decided then and there whether a man was subject to impressment, and carried him off at once, if he so willed.

It is to the credit of the American Government under Jefferson, that, though weak in its methods of seeking redress, it went straight back of the individual sufferer, and rested its case unswervingly on the broad principle.[2] That impressment, thus practised, swept in American seamen, was an incident only, although it grievously aggravated the injury. Whatever the native allegiance of individuals on board any vessel on the open ocean, their rights were not to be regulated by the municipal law of the belligerent, but by that of the nation to which the ship belonged, of whose territory she was constructively a part, and whose flag therefore was dishonoured, if acquiescence were yielded to an infringement of personal liberty, except as conceded by obligations of treaty, or by the general law of nations. Within British waters, the United States suffered no wrong by the impressment of British subjects—the enforcement of local municipal law—on board American vessels; and although it was suggested that such visits should not be made, and that an arriving crew should be considered to have the nationality of their ship, this concession, if granted, would have been a friendly limitation by Great Britain of her own municipal jurisdiction. It therefore could not be urged upon the British Government by a nation which took its stand resolutely upon the supremacy of its own municipal rights, on board its merchant shipping on the high seas.

---

2. Instructions of Madison, Secretary of State, to Monroe, Minister to Great Britain, January 5, 1804. Article I. American State Papers, vol. iii. p. 82.

It is to be noted, furthermore, that the voice of the people in the United States, the pressure of influence upon the Government, was not as unanimous as that exerted upon the British Ministry. The feeling of the country was divided; and, while none denied the grievous wrong done when an American was impressed, a class, strong at least in intellectual power, limited its demands to precautions against such mistakes and to redress when they occurred. The British claim to search, with the object of impressing British subjects, was considered by these men to be valid. Thus Gouverneur Morris, who on a semi-official visit to London in 1790 had had occasion to remonstrate upon the impressment of Americans in British ports, and who, as a pamphleteer, had taken strong ground against the measures of the British Government injurious to American commerce, wrote as follows in 1808 about the practice of seizing British subjects in American ships:

> That we, the people of America, should engage in ruinous warfare to support a rash opinion, that foreign sailors in our merchant ships are to be protected against the power of their sovereign, is downright madness.

In 1813, while the war was raging, he wrote again:

> Why not, waiving flippant debate, lay down the broad principle of national right, on which Great Britain takes her native seamen from our merchant ships? Let those who deny the right pay, suffer, and fight, to compel an abandonment of the claim. Men of sound mind will see, and men of sound principle will acknowledge, its existence.

In his opinion, there was but one consistent course to be pursued by those who favoured the war with Great Britain, which was to insist that she should, without compensation, surrender her claim. "If that ground be taken," he wrote, "the war (on our part) will be confessedly, as it is now impliedly, unjust."[3] Morris was a man honourably distinguished in our troubled national

---

3. Diary and Letters of Governor Morris, vol. ii. pp. 508, 546.

GOVERNOR MORRIS
FROM THE PAINTING BY MARCHANT, AFTER SULLY
IN INDEPENDENCE HALL, PHILADELPHIA

history—a member of the Congress of the Revolution and of the Constitutional Convention, a trained lawyer, a practised financier, and an experienced diplomatist; one who throughout his public life stood high in the estimation of Washington, with whom he was in constant official and personal correspondence. It is to be added that those to whom he wrote were evidently in sympathy with his opinions.

So again Representative Gaston, of North Carolina, a member of the same political party as Morris, speaking from his seat in the House in February, 1814,[4] maintained the British doctrine of inalienable allegiance. "Naturalization granted in another country has no effect whatever to destroy the original primary allegiance." Even Administration speakers did not deny this, but they maintained that the native allegiance could be enforced only within its territorial limits, not on the high seas. While perfectly firm and explicit as to the defence of American seamen,—even to the point of war, if needful,—Gaston spoke of the British practice as a right. "If you cannot by substitute obtain an abandonment of the right, or practice, to search our vessels, regulate it so as to prevent its abuse; waiving for the present, not relinquishing, your objections to it." He expressed sympathy, too, for the desperate straits in which Great Britain found herself. "At a time when her floating bulwarks were her whole safeguard against slavery, she could not view without alarm and resentment the warriors who should have manned those bulwarks pursuing a more gainful occupation in American vessels. Our merchant ships were crowded with British seamen, most of them deserters from their ships of war, and all furnished with fraudulent protections to prove them Americans. To us they were not necessary." On the contrary, "they ate the bread and bid down the wages of native seamen, whom it was our first duty to foster and encourage." This competition with native seamen was one of the pleas likewise of the New England opposition, too much of which was obstinately and reprehensibly factious. "Many thousands of British seamen," said Governor Strong of Massachusetts, in ad-

---

4. Annals of Congress. Thirteenth Congress, vol. ii. pp. 1563; 1555-1558.

dressing the Legislature, May 28, 1813, "deserted that service for a more safe and lucrative employment in ours." Had they not, "the high price for that species of labour would soon have induced a sufficient number of Americans to become seamen. It appears, therefore, that British seamen have been patronized at the expense of our own; and should Great Britain now consent to relinquish the *right of taking her own subjects*, it would be no advantage to our native seamen; it would only tend to reduce their wages by increasing the numbers of that class of men."[5] Gaston further said, that North Carolina, though not a commercial state, had many native seamen; but, "at the moment war was declared, though inquiry was made, I could not hear of a single native seaman detained by British impressment."

It is desirable, especially in these days, when everything is to be arbitrated, that men should recognize both sides of this question, and realize how impossible it was for either party to acquiesce in any other authority than their own deciding between them. "As I never had a doubt," said Morris, "so I thought it a duty to express my conviction that British ministers would not, *dared not*, submit to mediation a question of essential right."[6] "The way to peace is open and clear," he said the following year. "Let the right of search and impressment be acknowledged as maxims of public law."[7]

These expressions, uttered in the freedom of private correspondence, show a profound comprehension of the constraint under which the British Government and people both lay. It was impossible, at such a moment of extreme national peril, to depart from political convictions engendered by the uniform success of a policy followed consistently for a hundred and fifty years. For Great Britain, the time had long since passed into a

---

5. Niles' Register, vol. iv. p. 234. Author's italics.
6. Diary and Letters, vol. ii. p. 553.
7. Ibid., p. 560. Those unfamiliar with the subject should be cautioned that the expression "right of search" is confined here, not quite accurately, to searching for British subjects liable to impressment. This right the United States denied. The "right of search" to determine the nationality of the vessel, and the character of the voyage, was admitted to belligerents then, as it is now, by all neutrals.

dim distance, when the national appreciation of the sea to her welfare was that of mere defence, as voiced by Shakespeare:

England, hedged in with the main, That water-walled bulwark, still secure And confident from foreign purposes.[8]

This little world, This precious stone set in the silver sea, Which serves it in the office of a wall, Or as a moat defensive to a house Against the envy of less happier lands.[9]

By the middle of the seventeenth century, the perception of Great Britain's essential need to predominate upon the sea had dawned upon men's minds, and thence had passed from a vague national consciousness to a clearly defined national line of action, adopted first through a recognition of existing conditions of inferiority, but after these had ceased pursued without any change of spirit, and with no important changes of detail. This policy was formulated in a series of measures, comprehensively known as the Navigation Acts, the first of which was passed in 1651, during Cromwell's Protectorate. In 1660, immediately after the Restoration, it was reaffirmed in most essential features, and thenceforward continued to and beyond the times of which we are writing. In form a policy of sweeping protection, for the development of a particular British industry,—the carrying trade,—it was soon recognized that, in substance, its success had laid the foundations of a naval strength equally indispensable to the country. Upon this ground it was approved even by Adam Smith, although in direct opposition to the general spirit of his then novel doctrine. While exposing its fallacies as a commercial measure, he said it exemplified one of two cases in which protective legislation was to be justified. "The defence of Great Britain, for example, depends very much upon the number of its sailors and shipping. The Act of Navigation therefore very properly endeavours to give the sailors and shipping of Great Britain the monopoly of the trade of their own country.... It is not impossible that some of the regulations of this famous Act may have proceeded from national animosity. They are as wise, however,

---

8. King John, Act II. Scene 1.
9. King Richard II., Act II. Scene 1.

as though they had all been dictated by the most deliberate wisdom.... The Act is not favourable to foreign commerce, nor to the opulence which can arise from that; but defence is of much more importance than opulence. The Act of Navigation is perhaps the wisest of all the commercial regulations of England."[10] It became a dominant prepossession of British statesmen, even among Smith's converts, in the conduct of foreign relations, that the military power of the state lay in the vast resources of native seamen, employed in its merchant ships. Even the wealth returned to the country, by the monopoly of the imperial markets, and by the nearly exclusive possession of the carrying trade, which was insured to British commerce by the elaborate regulations of the Act, was thought of less moment. "Every commercial consideration has been repeatedly urged," wrote John Adams, the first United States Minister to Great Britain, "but to no effect; seamen, the Navy, and power to strike an awful blow to an enemy at the first outbreak of war, are the ideas which prevail."[11] This object, and this process, are familiar to us in these

---

10. Inquiry into the Nature and Causes of the Wealth of Nations. Edited by J.E. Thorold Rogers. Oxford, 1880, pp. 35-38. In a subsequent passage (p. 178), Smith seems disposed somewhat to qualify the positive assertion here quoted, on the ground that the Navigation Act had not had time to exert much effect, at the period when some of the most decisive successes over the Dutch were won. It is to be observed, however, that a vigorous military government, such as Cromwell's was, can assert itself in the fleet as well as in the army, creating an effective organization out of scanty materials, especially when at war with a commercial state of weak military constitution, like Holland. It was the story of Rome and Carthage repeated. Louis XIV. for a while accomplished the same. But under the laxity of a liberal popular government, which England increasingly enjoyed after the Restoration, naval power could be based securely only upon a strong, available, and permanent maritime element in the civil body politic; that is, on a mercantile marine. As regards the working of the Navigation Act to this end, whatever may be argued as to the economical expediency of protecting a particular industry, there is no possible doubt that such an industry can be built up, to huge proportions, by sagacious protection consistently enforced. The whole history of protection demonstrates this, and the Navigation Act did in its day. It created the British carrying trade, and in it provided for the Royal Navy an abundant and accessible reserve of raw material, capable of being rapidly manufactured into naval seamen in an hour of emergency.

11. Works of John Adams, vol. viii. pp. 389-390.

later days under the term "mobilization;" the military value of which, if rapidly effected, is well understood.

In this light, and in the light of the preceding experience of a hundred and fifty years, we must regard the course of the British Ministry through that period, extremely critical to both nations, which began when our War of Independence ended, and issued in the War of 1812. We in this day are continually told to look back to our fathers of the Revolutionary period, to follow their precepts, to confine ourselves to the lines of their policy. Let us then either justify the British ministries of Pitt and his successors, in their obstinate adherence to the traditions they had received, or let us admit that even ancestral piety may be carried too far, and that venerable maxims must be brought to the test of existing conditions.

The general movement of maritime intercourse between countries is commonly considered under two principal heads: Commerce and Navigation. The first applies to the interchange of commodities, however effected; the second, to their transportation from port to port. A nation may have a large commerce, of export and import, carried in foreign vessels, and possess little shipping of its own. This is at present the condition of the United States; and once, in far gone days, it was in great measure that of England. In such case there is a defect of navigation, consequent upon which there will be a deficiency of native seamen; of seamen attached to the country and its interests, by ties of birth or habit. For maritime war such a state will have but small resources of adaptable naval force; a condition dangerous in proportion to its dependence upon control of the sea. Therefore the attention of British statesmen, during the period in which the Navigation Act flourished, fastened more and more upon the necessity of maintaining the navigation of the kingdom, as distinguished from its commerce. Subsidiary to the movement of commerce, there is a third factor, relatively stationary, the consideration of which is probably less familiar now than it was to the contemporaries of the Navigation Act, to whom it was known under the name *entrepôt*. This term was applied to those commercial centres—in this connection maritime centres—where goods accumulate on their way to market; where they are handled, stored, or transhipped. All these processes involve expenditure, which inures to the profit of the port, and of the nation; the effect being the exact equivalent of the local gains of a railroad centre of the present day. It was a dominant object with statesmen of the earlier period to draw such accumulations of traffic to their own ports, or nations; to force trade, by ingenious legislation, or even by direct coercion, to bring its materials to their own shores, and there to yield to them the advantages of the *entrepôt*. Thus the preamble to one of the series of Navigation Acts states, as a direct object, the "making this Kingdom a staple[12] (emporium), not only of the commodities of our plantations, but also of the commodities of other countries, and places, for the supply of the plantations."[13] An instructive example of such indirect effort was the institution of free ports; ports which, by exemption from heavy customary tolls, or by the admission of foreign ships or goods, not permitted entrance to other national harbours, invited the merchant to collect in them, from surrounding regions, the constituents of his cargoes. On the other hand, the Colonial System, which began to assume importance at the time of the Navigation Act, afforded abundant opportunity for the compulsion of trade. Colonies being part of the mother country, and yet transoceanic with reference to her, maritime commerce between them and foreign communities could by direct legislation be obliged first to seek the parent state, which thus was made the distributing centre for both their exports and imports.

For nearly three centuries before the decisive measures taken by the Parliament of the Commonwealth, the development and increase of English shipping, by regulation of English trade, had been recognized as a desirable object by many English rulers. The impulse had taken shape in various enactments, giving to English vessels privileges, exclusive or qualified, in the import

---

12. This primary meaning of the word "staple" seems to have disappeared from common use, in which it is now applied to the commercial articles, the concentration of which at a particular port made that port a "staple."
13. Bryan Edwards, West Indies, vol. ii. p. 448.

or export carriage of the kingdom; and it will readily be understood that the matter appeared of even more pressing importance, when the Navy depended upon the merchant service for ships, as well as for men; when the war fleets of the nation were composed of impressed ships, as well as manned by impressed sailors. These various laws had been tentative in character. Both firmness of purpose and continuity of effort were lacking to them; due doubtless to the comparative weakness of the nation in the scale of European states up to the seventeenth century. During the reigns of the first two Stuarts, this weakness was emphasized by internal dissensions; but the appreciation of the necessity for some radical remedy to the decay of English naval power remained and increased. To this conviction the ship-money of Charles the First bears its testimony; but it was left to Cromwell and his associates to formulate the legislation, upon which, for two centuries to come, the kingdom was thought to depend, alike for the growth of its merchant shipping and for the maintenance of the navy. All that preceded has interest chiefly as showing the origin and growth of an enduring national conviction, with which the United States came into collision immediately after achieving independence.

The ninth of October, 1651, is the date of the passing of the Act, the general terms of which set for two hundred years the standard for British legislation concerning the shipping industry. The title of the measure, "Goods from foreign ports, by whom to be imported," indicated at once that the object in view was the carrying trade; navigation, rather than commerce. Commerce was to be manipulated and forced into English bottoms as an indispensable agency for reaching British consumers. At this time less than half a century had elapsed since the first English colonists had settled in Massachusetts and Virginia. The British plantation system was still in its beginnings, alike in America, Asia, and Africa. When the then recent Civil War ended, in the overthrow of the royal power, it had been "observed with concern that the merchants of England had for several years usually freighted Dutch ships for fetching home their merchandise, because the freights were lower than in English ships. Dutch ships, therefore, were used for importing our own American products, while English ships lay rotting in harbour."[14] "Notwithstanding the regulations made for confining that branch of navigation to the mother country, it is said that in the West India Islands there used, at this time, out of forty ships to be thirty-eight ships Dutch bottoms."[15] English mariners also, for want of employment, went into the Dutch service. In this way seamen for the navy disappeared, just as, at a later day, they did into the merchant shipping of the United States.

The one great maritime rival of England, Holland, had thus engrossed, not only the carrying trade of Europe at large, most of which, from port to port, was done by her seamen, but that of England as well. Even of the English coasting trade much was done by Dutch ships. Under this competition, the English merchant marine was dwindling, and had become so inadequate that, when the exclusion of foreigners was enforced by the Act, the cry at once arose in the land that the English shipping was not sufficient for the work thus thrust upon it. "Although our own people have not shipping enough to import from all parts what they want, they are needlessly debarred from receiving new supplies of merchandise from other nations, who alone can, and until now did, import it."[16] The effect of this decadence of shipping upon the resources of men for the navy is apparent.

The existence of strained relations between England and Holland facilitated the adoption of the first Navigation Act, which, as things were, struck the Dutch only; they being the one great carrying community in Europe. Although both the letter and the purpose of the new law included in its prohibitions all foreign countries, the commercial interests of other states were too slight, and their commercial spirit too dull, to take note of the future effect upon themselves; whether absolutely, or in relation to the maritime power of Great Britain, the cornerstone of which was then laid. This first Act directed that no merchandise from Asia,

---

14. Macpherson, Annals of Commerce, vol. ii. p. 443.
15. Reeves, History of the Law of Navigation, Dublin, 1792, p. 37.
16. Macpherson, vol. ii. p. 444.

Africa, or America, including therein English "plantations," as the colonies were then styled,[17] should be imported into England in other than English-built ships, belonging to English subjects, and of which "the master and mariners are also, for the most part of them, of the people of this commonwealth." This at once reserved a large part of the external trade to English ships; and also, by the regulation of the latter, constituted them a nursery for English seamen. To the general tenor of this clause, confining importation wholly to English vessels, an exception was made for Europe only; importations from any part of which was permitted to "such foreign ships and vessels as do truly and properly belong to the people of that country or place of which the said goods are the growth, production, or manufacture."[18] Foreign merchantmen might therefore import into England the products of their own country; but both they and English vessels must ship such cargoes in the country of origin, not at any intermediate port. The purpose of these provisos, especially of the second, was to deprive Holland of the profit of the middleman, or the *entrepôt*, which she had enjoyed hitherto by importing to herself from various regions, warehousing the goods, and then re-exporting. The expense of these processes, pocketed by Dutch handlers, and the exaction of any dues levied by the Dutch Treasury, reappeared in increased cost to foreign consumers. This appreciation of the value of the *entrepôt* underlay much of the subsequent colonial regulation of England, and actuated the famous Orders in Council of 1807, which were a principal factor in causing the War of 1812. A second effect of these restrictions, which in later

---

17. Reeves, writing in 1792, says that there seemed then no distinction of meaning between "plantation" and "colony." Plantation was the earlier term; "'colony' did not come much into use till the reign of Charles II., and it seems to have denoted the political relation." (p. 109.) By derivation both words express the idea of cultivating new ground, or establishing a new settlement; but "plantation" seems to associate itself more with the industrial beginnings, and "colony" with the formal regulative purpose of the parent state.

18. The Navigation Acts of 1651, 1660, 1662, and 1663, as well as other subsequent measures of the same character, can be found, conveniently for American readers, in MacDonald's Select Charters Illustrative of American History. Macmillan, New York. 1899.

times was deemed even more important than the pecuniary gain, was to compel English ships to go long voyages, to the home countries of the cargoes they sought, instead of getting them nearby in Dutch depots. This gave a corresponding development to the carrying trade—the navigation—of the Commonwealth; securing greater employment for ships and seamen, increasing both their numbers and experience, and contributing thereby to the resources of the navy in men.

A considerable carrying trade would be lost to us, and would remain with the merchants of Holland, of Hamburg, and other maritime towns, if our merchants were permitted to furnish themselves by short voyages to those neighbouring ports, and were not compelled to take upon themselves the burden of bringing these articles from the countries where they were produced.[19]

The Act of 1660, officially known as that of 12 Charles II., modified the provisos governing the European trade. The exclusion of goods of European origin from all transportation to England, save in ships of their own nation, was to some extent removed. This surrender was censured by some, explicitly, because it again enabled the Dutch to collect foreign articles and send them to England, thereby "permitting competition with this country in the longer part of the voyage;" to the injury, therefore, of British navigation. The remission, though real, was less than appeared; for the prohibitions of the Commonwealth were still applied to a large number of specified articles, the produce chiefly of Russia and Turkey, which could be imported only in their national ships, or those of England. As those countries had substantially no long voyage shipping, trade with them was to all practical purposes confined to English vessels.[20] The concession to foreign vessels, such as it was, was further qualified by heavier duties, called aliens' duties, upon their cargoes; and by the requirement that three-fourths of their crew, entering

---

19. Reeves, History of the Law of Navigation, p. 162.
20. For instance, in 1769, eighteen hundred and forty vessels passed the Sound in the British trade. Of these only thirty-five were Russian. Considerably more than half of the trade of St. Petersburg with Europe at large was done in British ships. Macpherson, vol. iii. p. 493.

English ports, should be of the same nationality as the ship. The object of this regulation was to prevent the foreign state from increasing its tonnage, by employing seamen other than its own. This went beyond mere protection of English vessels, and was a direct attack, though by English municipal law, upon the growth of foreign shipping.

This purpose indeed was authoritatively announced from the bench, construing the Act in the decision of a specific case.

Parliament had wisely foreseen that, if they restrained the importation or exportation of European goods, unless in our own ships, and manned with our own seamen, other states would do the same; and this, in its consequences, would amount to a prohibition of all such goods, which would be extremely detrimental to trade, and in the end defeat the very design of the Act. It was seen, however, that many countries in Europe, as France, Spain, and Italy, could more easily buy ships than build them; that, on the other hand, countries like Russia, and others in the North, had timber and materials enough for building ships, but wanted sailors. It was from a consideration of this inaptness in most countries to accomplish a complete navigation, that the Parliament prohibited the importation of most European goods, unless in ships owned and navigated by English, or in ships of the *build of* and manned by sailors of that country of which the goods were the growth. The consequence would be that foreigners could not make use of ships they bought, though English subjects might. This would force them to have recourse to our shipping, and the general intent of the Act, to secure the carrying trade to the English, would be answered as far as it possibly could.[21]

It was therefore ruled that the tenor of the Act forbade foreigners to import to England in ships not of their own building; and, adds the reporter, "This exposition of the Act of Navigation is certainly the true one.

Having thus narrowed foreign competition to the utmost extent possible to municipal statutes, Parliament made the carrying industry even more exclusively than before a preserve

---

21. Opinion of Chief Baron Parker, quoted by Reeves, pp. 187-189.

for native seamen. The Commonwealth's requirement, that "the most" of the crew should be English, was changed to a definite prescription that the master and three-fourths of the mariners should be so.

Under such enactments, with frequent modification of detail, but no essential change of method, British shipping and seamen continued to be "protected" against foreign competition down to and beyond the War of 1812. In this long interval there is no change of conception, nor any relaxation of national conviction. The whole history affords a remarkable instance of persistent policy, pursued consecutively for five or six generations. No better evidence could be given of its hold upon the minds of the people, or of the serious nature of the obstacle encountered by any other state that came into collision with it; as the United States during the Napoleonic period did, in matters of trade and carriage, but especially in the closely related question of impressment.

Whether the Navigation Act, during its period of vigour, was successful in developing the British mercantile marine and supporting the British Navy has been variously argued. The subsequent growth of British navigation is admitted; but whether this was the consequence of the measure itself has been disputed. It appears to the writer that those who doubt its effect in this respect allow their convictions of the strength of economical forces to blind them to the power of unremitting legislative action. To divert national activities from natural channels into artificial may be inexpedient and wasteful; and it may be reasonable to claim that ends so achieved are not really successes, but failures. Nevertheless, although natural causes, till then latent, may have conspired to further the development which the Navigation Act was intended to promote, and although, since its abolition, the same causes may have sufficed to sustain the imposing national carrying trade built up during its continuance, it is difficult to doubt the great direct influence of the Act itself; having in view the extent of the results, as well as the corroborative success of modern states in building up and maintaining other distinctly artificial industries, sometimes to the injury of the natural industries of other peoples, which the Navigation Act also in its day was meant to effect.

The condition of British navigation in 1651 has been stated. The experience of the remaining years of the Protectorate appears to have confirmed national opinion as to the general policy of the Act, and to have suggested the modifications of the Restoration. To trace the full sequence of development, in legislation or in shipping, is not here permissible; the present need being simply to give an account, and an explanation, of the strength of a national prepossession, which in its manifestation was a chief cause of the events that are the theme of this book. A few scattered details, taken casually, seem strikingly to sustain the claims of the advocates of the system, bearing always in mind the depression of the British shipping industry before the passage of the law. In 1728 there arrived in London from all parts beyond sea 2052 ships, of which only 213 were under foreign flags; less than one in nine. In Liverpool, in 1765, of 1533 entered and cleared, but 135 were foreign; in Bristol, the same year, of 701 but 91 foreign. Of the entire import of that year only 28 per cent, in money value, came from Europe; the carriage of the remaining 72 per cent was confined to British ships. It may, of course, be maintained that this restriction of shipping operated to the disadvantage of the commerce of the kingdom; that there was direct pecuniary loss. This would not be denied, for the object of the Act was less national gain than the up-building of shipping as a resource for the navy. Nevertheless, at this same period, in 1764, of 810 ships entering the great North German commercial centre, Hamburg, 267—over one-third—were British; the Dutch but 146, the Hamburgers themselves 157. A curious and suggestive comparison is afforded by the same port in 1769. From the extensive, populous, and fruitful country of France, the *entrepôt* of the richest West Indian colony, Santo Domingo, there entered Hamburg 203 ships, of which not one was French; whereas from Great Britain there came a slightly larger total, 216, of which 178 were British.

Such figures seem to substantiate the general contemporary opinion of the efficacy of the Navigation Act, and to support the particular claim of a British writer of the day, that the naval weakness of Holland and France was due to the lack of similar measures.

> The Dutch have indeed pursued a different policy, but they have thereby fallen to a state of weakness, which is now the object of pity, or of contempt. It was owing to the want of sailors, and not to the fault of their officers, that the ten ships of the line, which during their late impudent quarrel with Britain had been stipulated to join the French fleet, never sailed.[22]

> The French Navy, which at all times depended chiefly upon the West India trade for a supply of seamen, must have been laid up, if the war (of American Independence) had continued another year.[23]

Whatever the accuracy of these statements,[24]—and they are those of a well-informed man,—they represented a general conviction, not in Great Britain only but in Europe, of the results of the Navigation legislation. A French writer speaks of it as the source of England's greatness,[25] and sums up his admiration in words which recognize the respective shares of natural advantages and sagacious supervision in the grand outcome.

Called to commerce by her situation, it became the spirit of her government and the lever of her ambition. In other monar-

---

22. Chalmers, Opinions on Interesting Subjects of Public Law and Commercial Policy Arising from American Independence, p. 32.
23. Ibid., p. 55.
24. A French naval historian supports them, speaking of the year 1781: "The considerable armaments made since 1778 had exhausted the resources of personnel. To remedy the difficulty the complements were filled up with coast-guard militia, with marine troops until then employed only to form the guards of the ships, and finally with what were called *novices volontaires*, who were landsmen recruited by bounties. It may be imagined what crews were formed with such elements."—Troude, Batailles Navales, vol. ii. p. 202.
25. Raynal, Histoire Philosophique des deux Indes, vol. vii. p. 287 (Edition 1820). Raynal's reputation is that of a plagiarist, but his best work is attributed to far greater names of his time. He died in 1796.

chies, it is private individuals who carry on commerce; but in that happy constitution it is the state, or the nation in its entirety.

In Great Britain itself there was substantial unanimity. This coloured all its after policy towards its lately rebellious and now independent children, who as carriers had revived the once dreaded rivalry of the Dutch. To quote one writer, intimately acquainted with the whole theory and practice of the Navigation Acts, they—

> . . . . tend to the establishment of a monopoly; but our ancestors. . . . considered the defence of this island from foreign invasion as the first law in the national policy. Judging that the dominion of the land could not be preserved without possessing that of the sea, they made every effort to procure to the nation a maritime power of its own. They wished that the merchants should own as many ships, and employ as many mariners as possible. To induce, and sometimes to force, them to this application of their capital, restrictions and prohibitions were devised. The interests of commerce were often sacrificed to this object.

Yet he claims that in the end commerce also profited, for "the increase in the number of ships became a spur to seek out employment for them." In 1792, British registered shipping amounted to 1,365,000 tons, employing 80,000 seamen. Of these, by common practice, two-thirds—say 50,000—were available for war, during which it was the rule to relax the Act so far as to require only one-fourth of the crew to be British.

> That the increase in our shipping is to be ascribed to our navigation system appears in the application of it to the trade of the United States. When those countries were part of our plantations, a great portion of our produce was transported to Great Britain and our West India Islands in American bottoms; they had a share in the freight of sugars from those islands to Great Britain; they built annually more than one hundred ships, which were employed in the carrying trade of Great Britain; but since the

Independence of those states, since their ships have been excluded from our plantations, and that trade is wholly confined to British ships, we have gained that share of our carrying trade from which they are now excluded.[26]

In corroboration of the same tendency, it was also noted during the war with the colonies, that "the shipyards of Britain in every port were full of employment, so that new yards were set up in places never before so used."[27]

That is, the war, stopping the intrusion of American colonists into the British carrying trade, just as the Navigation Act prohibited that of foreign nations, created a demand for British ships to fill the vacancy; a result perfectly in keeping with the whole object of the navigation system. But when hostilities with France began again in 1793, and lasted with slight intermission for twenty years, the drain of the navy for seamen so limited the development of the British navigation as to afford an opening for competition, of which American maritime aptitude took an advantage, threatening British supremacy and arousing corresponding jealousy.

Besides the increase of national shipping, the idea of *entrepôt* received recognition in both the earlier and later developments of the system. Numerous specified articles, produced in English colonies, could be carried nowhere but to England, Ireland, or another colony, where they must be landed before going farther. Because regularly listed, such articles were technically styled "enumerated;" "enumerated commodities being such as must first be landed in England before being taken to foreign parts."[28] From this privilege Ireland was soon after excepted; enumerated goods for that country having first to be landed in England.[29] Among such enumerated articles, tobacco and rice held prominent places and illustrate the system. Of the former, in the first half of the eighteenth century, it was estimated that on an aver-

---

26. Reeves, pp. 430-434.
27. Macpherson, vol. iv. p. 10.
28. Macpherson, Annals of Commerce, vol. i. p. 485-486.
29. Bryan Edwards, West Indies, vol. ii. p. 450.

age seventy-two million pounds were sent yearly to England, of which fifty-four million were re-exported; an export duty of sixpence per pound being then levied, besides the cost of handling. Rice, made an enumerated article in 1705, exemplifies aptly the ideas which influenced the multifold manipulation of the nation's commerce in those days. The restriction was removed in 1731, so far as to permit this product to be sent direct from South Carolina and Georgia to any part of Europe south of Cape Finisterre; but only in British ships navigated according to the Act. In this there is a partial remission of the *entrepôt* exaction, while the nursing of the carrying trade is carefully guarded. The latter was throughout the superior interest, inseparably connected in men's minds with the support of the navy. At a later date, West India sugar received the same indulgence as rice; it being found that the French were gaining the general European market, by permitting French vessels to carry the products of their islands direct to foreign continental ports. Rice and sugar for northern Europe, however, still had to be landed in England before proceeding.

The colonial trade in general was made entirely subservient to the support and development of English shipping, and to the enrichment of England, as the half-way storehouse. Into England foreign goods could be imported in some measure by foreign vessels, though under marked restrictions and disabilities; but into the colonies it was early forbidden to import any goods, whatever their origin, except in English-built ships, commanded and manned in accordance with the Act. Further, even in such ships they must be imported from England itself, not direct; not from the country of origin. The motive for this statute of 1663[30] is avowed in the preamble: to be with a view of maintaining a greater correspondence and kindness between them and the mother country, keeping the former in a firmer dependence upon the latter, and to make this kingdom the staple both of the commodities of the plantations, and of other countries in order to supply them. Further, it was alleged that

---

30. Officially, Statute of 15 Charles II

it was the usage of nations to keep their plantation trade to themselves.[31] In compensation for this subjection of their trade to the policy of the mother country, the supplying of the latter with West India products was reserved to the colonists.

Thus, goods for the colonies, as well as those from the colonies, from or to a foreign country,—from or to France, for example,—must first be landed in England before proceeding to the ultimate destination. Yet even this cherished provision, enforced against the foreigner, was made to subserve the carrying trade—the leading object; for, upon re-exportation to the colonies, there was allowed a drawback of duties paid upon admission to England, and permanent upon residents there. The effect of this was to make the articles cheaper in the colonies than in England itself, and so to induce increased consumption. It was therefore to the profit of the carrier; and the more acceptable, because the shipping required to bring home colonial goods was much in excess of that required for outward cargoes, to the consequent lowering of outward freights. "A regard to the profits of freights," writes a contemporary familiar with the subject, "as much as the augmentation of seamen, dictated this policy."[32] From the conditions, it did not directly increase the number of seamen; but by helping the shipping merchant it supported the carrying industry as a whole.

Upon the legislative union of Scotland with England, in 1707, this *entrepôt* privilege, with all other reserved advantages of English trade and commerce, was extended to the northern kingdom, and was a prominent consideration in inducing the Scotch people to accept a political change otherwise distasteful, because a seeming sacrifice of independence. Before this time they had had their own navigation system, modelled on the English; the Acts of the two parliaments embodying certain relations of reciprocity. Thenceforward, the Navigation Act is to be styled more properly a British, than an English, measure; but its benefits, now common to all Great Britain, were denied still to Ireland.

---

31. Reeves, p. 50.
32. Chalmers, Opinions on Interesting Subjects, p. 28.

It will be realized that the habit of receiving exclusive favours at the expense of a particular set of people—the colonist and the foreigner—readily passed in a few generations into an unquestioning conviction of the propriety, and of the necessity, of such measures. It should be easy now for those living under a high protective tariff to understand that, having built up upon protection a principal national industry,—the carrying trade,—involving in its ramifications the prosperity of a large proportion of the wealth-producers of the country, English statesmen would fear to touch the fabric in any important part; and that their dread would be intensified by the conviction, universally held, that to remove any of these artificial supports would be to imperil at the same time the Royal Navy, the sudden expansion of which, from a peace to a war footing, depended upon impressment from the protected merchant ships. It will be seen also that with such precedents of *entrepôt*, for the nourishing of British commerce, it was natural to turn to the same methods,—although in a form monstrously exaggerated,—when Napoleon by his decrees sought to starve British commerce to death. In conception and purpose, the Orders in Council of 1807 were simply a development of the *entrepôt* system. Their motto, "No trade save through England,"—the watchword of the ministry of Canning, Castlereagh, and Perceval, 1807-12,—was merely the revival towards the United States, as an independent nation, of the methods observed towards her when an assemblage of colonies, forty years before; the object in both cases being the welfare of Great Britain, involved in the monopoly of an important external commerce, the material of which, being stored first in her ports, paid duty to her at the expense of continental consumers.

Nor was there in the thought of the age, external to Great Britain, any corrective of the impressions which dominated her commercial policy. "Commercial monopoly," wrote Montesquieu, "is the leading principle of colonial intercourse;" and an accomplished West Indian, quoting this phrase about 1790, says: "The principles by which the nations of Europe were influenced were precisely the same: (1) to secure to themselves respectively the most important productions of their colonies, and (2) to retain to themselves exclusively the advantage of supplying the colonies with European goods and manufactures."[33] "I see," wrote John Adams from France, in 1784, "that the French merchants regard their colonies as English merchants considered us twenty years ago." The rigor of the French colonial trade system had been relaxed during the War of American Independence, as was frequently done by all states during hostilities; but when Louis XVI., in 1784, sought to continue this, though in an extremely qualified concession, allowing American vessels of under sixty tons a limited trade between the West Indies and their own country, the merchants of Marseilles, Bordeaux, Rochelle, Nantes, St. Malo, all sent in excited remonstrances, which found support in the provincial parliaments of Bordeaux and Brittany.[34]

A further indication of the economical convictions of the French people, and of the impression made upon Europe generally by the success of the British Navigation Act, is to be seen in the fact that in 1794, under the Republic, the National Convention issued a decree identical in spirit, and almost identical in terms, with the English Act of 1651. In the latter year, said the report of the Committee to the Convention:

> .... one-half the navigation of England was carried on by foreigners. She has imperceptibly retaken her rights. Towards the year 1700 foreigners possessed no more than the fifth part of this navigation; in 1725 only a little more than the ninth; in 1750 a little more than a twelfth; and in 1791 they possessed only the fourteenth part of it.[35]

It is perhaps unnecessary to add that the colonial system of Spain was as rigid as that of Great Britain, though far less capably administered. So universal was the opinion of the day as

---

33. Bryan Edwards, West Indies, vol. ii. p. 443-444 (3rd Edition).
34. Works of John Adams, vol. viii. p. 228.
35. Compare with Sheffield, Observations on the Commerce of the American States (Edition February, 1784), p. 137, note; from which, indeed, these figures seem to have been taken, or from some common source.

to the relation of colonies to navigation, that a contemporary American, familiar with the general controversy, wrote:

> Though speculative politicians have entertained doubts in regard to favourable effects from colonial possessions, taking into view the expenses of their improvement, defence, and government, no question has been made but that the monopoly of their trade greatly increases the commerce of the nations to which they are appurtenant.[36]

Very soon after the adoption of the Constitution, the Congress of the United States, for the development of the carrying trade, enacted provisions analogous to the Navigation Act, so far as applicable to a nation having no colonies, but with large shipping and coasting interests to be favoured.

To such accepted views, and to such traditional practice, the independence of the thirteen British colonies upon the American continent came not only as a new political fact, but as a portentous breach in the established order of things. As such, it was regarded with uneasy jealousy by both France and Spain; but to Great Britain it was doubly ominous. Not only had she lost a reserved market, singly the most valuable she possessed, but she had released, however unwillingly, a formidable and recognized rival for the carrying trade, the palladium of her naval strength. The market she was not without hopes of regaining, by a compulsion which, though less direct, would be in effect as real as that enforced by colonial regulation; but the capacity of the Americans as carriers rested upon natural conditions not so easy to overcome. The difficulty of the problem was increased by the fact that the governments of the world generally were awaking to the disproportionate advantages Great Britain had been reaping from them for more than a century, during which they had listlessly acquiesced in her aggressive absorption of the carriage of the seas. America could count upon their sympathies, and possible co-operation, in her rivalry with the British carrier. "It is manifest," wrote Coxe in 1794, "that a prodigious and al-

---

36. Coxe's View of the United States of America, Philadelphia, 1794, p. 330.

most universal revolution in the views of nations has taken place with regard to the carrying trade." When John Adams spoke of the United States retaliating upon Great Britain, by enacting a similar measure of its own, the minister of Portugal, then a country of greater weight than now, replied: "Not a nation in Europe would suffer a Navigation Act to be made by any other at this day. That of England was made in times of ignorance, when few nations cultivated commerce, and no country but she understood or cared anything about it, but now all courts are attentive to it;"[37] so much so, indeed, that it has been said this was the age of commercial treaties. It was the age also of commercial regulation, often mistaken and injurious, which found its ideals largely in the Navigation Act of Great Britain, and in the resultant extraordinary processes of minute and comprehensive interference, with every species of commerce, and every article of export or import; for, while the general principles of the Navigation Act were few and simple enough, in application they entailed a watchful and constant balancing of advantages by the Board of Trade, and a consequent manipulation of the course of commerce,—a perfectly idealized and sublimated protection. The days of its glory, however, were passing fast. Great Britain was now in the position of one who has been first to exploit a great invention, upon which he has an exclusive patent. Others were now entering the field, and she must prepare for competition, in which she most of all feared those of her own blood, the children of her loins; for the signs of the menacing conditions following the War of Independence had been apparent some time before the revolt of the colonies gained for them liberty of action, heretofore checked in favour of the mother country. In these conditions, and in the national sentiment concerning them, are to be found the origin of a course of action which led to the War of 1812.

Under the Navigation Act, and throughout the colonial pe-

---

37. Works of John Adams, vol. viii. p. 341. Adams says again, himself: "It is more and more manifest every day that there is, and will continue, a general scramble for navigation. Carrying trade, ship-building, fisheries, are the cry of every nation."—Vol. viii. p. 342.

riod, the transatlantic colonies of Great Britain had grown steadily; developing a commercial individuality of their own, depending in each upon local conditions. The variety of these, with the consequent variety of occupations and products, and the distance separating all from the mother country, had contributed to develop among them a certain degree of mutual dependence, and consequent exchange; the outcome of which was a commercial system interior to the group as a whole, and distinct from the relations to Great Britain borne by them individually and collectively. There was a large and important inter-colonial commerce,[38] consistent with the letter of the Navigation Act, as well as a trade with Great Britain; and although each of these exerted an influence upon the other, it was indirect and circuitous. The two were largely separate in fact, as well as in idea; and the interchange between the various colonies was more than double that with the mother country. It drew in British as well as American seamen, and was considered thus to entail the disadvantage that, unless America were the scene of war, the crews there were out of reach of impressment; that measure being too crude and unsystematic to reach effectively so distant a source of supply. Curiously enough, also, by an act passed in the reign of Queen Anne, seamen born in the American colonies were exempted from impressment.[39] "During the late Civil War (of American Independence) it has been found difficult sufficiently to man our fleet, from the seamen insisting that, since they had been born in America, they could not be pressed to serve in the British navy."[40] In these conditions, and especially in the difficulty of distinguishing the place of birth by the language

---

38. From an official statement, made public in 1784, it appears that in the year 1770 the total trade, inward and outward, of the colonies on the American Continent, amounted to 750,546 tons. Of this 32 per cent was coastwise, to other members of the group; 30 with the West Indies; 27 with Great Britain and Ireland; and 11 with Southern Europe. Bermuda and the Bahamas, inconsiderable as to trade, were returned among continental colonies by the Custom House.—Sheffield, Commerce of the American States, Table VII.
39. Chalmers, Opinions, p. 73.
40. Ibid., p. 18.

spoken, is seen the foreshadowing of the troubles attending the practice of Impressment, after the United States had become a separate nation.

The British American colonies were divided by geographical conditions into two primary groups: those of the West India Islands, and those of the Continent. The common use of the latter term, in the thought and speech of the day, is indicated by the comprehensive adjective "Continental," familiarly applied to the Congress, troops, currency, and other attributes of sovereignty, assumed by the revolted colonies after their declaration of independence. Each group had special commercial characteristics—in itself, and relatively to Great Britain. The islands, whatever their minor differences of detail, or their mutual jealousies, or even their remoteness from one another,—Jamaica being a thousand miles from her eastern sisters,—were essentially a homogeneous body. Similarity of latitude and climate induced similarity of social and economical conditions; notably in the dependence on slave labour, upon which the industrial fabric rested. Their products, among which sugar and coffee were the most important, were such as Europe did not yield; it was therefore to their advantage to expend labour upon these wholly, and to depend upon external sources for supplies of all kinds, including food. Their exports, being directed by the Navigation Act almost entirely upon Great Britain, were, in connection with Virginia tobacco, the most lucrative of the "enumerated" articles which rendered tribute to the *entrepôt* monopoly of the mother country. It was in this respect particularly, as furnishing imports to be handled and re-exported, that the islands were valuable to the home merchants. To the welfare of the body politic they contributed by their support of the carrying trade; for the cargoes, being bulky, required much tonnage, and the entire traffic was confined to British ships, manned three-fourths by British seamen. As a market also the islands were of consequence; all their supplies coming, by law, either from or through Great Britain, or from the continental colonies. Intercourse with foreign states was prohibited, and that with foreign colonies allowed only under rare and disabling conditions. But although the West Indies thus maintained a large part of the mother country's export trade, the smallness of their population, and the simple necessities of the slaves, who formed the great majority of the inhabitants, rendered them as British customers much inferior to the continental colonies; and this disparity was continually increasing, for the continent was growing rapidly in numbers, wealth, and requirements. In the five years 1744-48, the exports from Great Britain to the two quarters were nearly equal; but a decade later the continent took double the amount that the islands demanded. The figures quoted for the period 1754-58 are: to the West Indies, £3,765,000; to North America, £7,410,000.[41] In the five years ending 1774 the West Indies received £6,748,095; the thirteen continental colonies, £13,660,180.[42]

Imports from the continent also supported the carrying trade of Great Britain, but not to an extent proportionate to those from the islands; for many of the continental colonies were themselves large carriers. The imports to them, being manufactured articles, less bulky than the exports of the islands, also required less tonnage. The most marked single difference between the West India communities and those of the continent was that the latter, being distributed on a nearly north and south line, with consequent great divergences of climate and products, were essentially not homogeneous. What one had, another had not. Such differences involve of course divergence of interests, with consequent contentions and jealousies, the influence of which was felt most painfully prior to the better Union of 1789, and never can wholly cease to act; but, on the other hand, it tends also to promote exchange of offices, where need and facility of transport combine to make such exchange beneficial to both. That the intercourse between the continental colonies required a tonnage equal to

---

41. Macpherson, vol. iii. p. 317.
42. Report of Committee of Privy Council, Jan. 28, 1791, pp. 21-23.

that employed between them and the West Indies,—testified by the return of 1770 before quoted,[43]—shows the existence of conditions destined inevitably to draw them together. The recognition of such mutual dependence, when once attained, furthers the practice of mutual concession for the purpose of combined action. Consequently, in the protracted struggle between the centripetal and centrifugal forces in North America, the former prevailed, though not till after long and painful wavering.

While thus differing greatly among themselves in the nature of their productions, and in their consequent wants, the continental colonists as a whole had one common characteristic. Recent occupants of a new, unimproved, and generally fertile country, they turned necessarily to the cultivation of the soil as the most remunerative form of activity, while for manufactured articles they depended mainly upon external supplies, the furnishing of which Great Britain reserved to herself. For these reasons they afforded the great market which they were to her, and which by dint of habit and of interest they long continued to be. But, while thus generally agricultural by force of circumstances, the particular outward destinations of their surplus products varied. Those of the southern colonies, from Maryland to Georgia, were classed as "enumerated," and, with the exception of the rice of South Carolina and Georgia, partially indulged as before mentioned, must be directed upon Great Britain. Tobacco, cotton, indigo, pitch, tar, turpentine, and spars of all kinds for ships, were specifically named, and constituted much the larger part of the exports of those colonies. These were carried also chiefly by British vessels, and not by colonial. The case was otherwise in the middle colonies, Pennsylvania, New York, New Jersey, and in Connecticut and Rhode Island of the eastern group. They were exporters of provisions,—of grain, flour, and meat, the latter both as live stock and salted; of horses also. As the policy of the day protected the British farmer, these articles were not required to be sent to

---

43. Ante, p. 31 (note).

Great Britain; on the contrary, grain was not allowed admission except in times of scarcity, determined by the price of wheat in the London market. The West Indies, therefore, were the market of the middle colonies; the shortness of the voyage, and the comparatively good weather, after a little southing had been gained, giving a decisive advantage over European dealers in the transportation of live animals. Flour also, because it kept badly in the tropics, required constant carriage of new supplies from sources near at hand. Along with provisions the continental vessels took materials for building and cooperage, both essential to the industry of the islands,—to the housing of the inhabitants, and to the transport of their sugar, rum, and molasses. In short, so great was the dependence of the islands upon this trade, that a well-informed planter of the time quotes with approval the remark of "a very competent judge," that, "if the continent had been wholly in foreign hands, and England wholly precluded from intercourse with it, it is very doubtful whether we should now have possessed a single acre in the West Indies."[44]

Now this traffic, while open to all British shipping, was very largely in the hands of the colonists, who built ships decidedly cheaper than could be done in England, and could distribute their tonnage in vessels too small to brave the Atlantic safely, but, from their numbers and size, fitted to scatter to the numerous small ports of distribution, which the badness of internal communications rendered advantageous for purposes of supply. A committee of the Privy Council of Great Britain, constituted soon after the independence of the United States to investigate the conditions of West India trade, reported that immediately before the revolt the carriage between the islands and the continent had occupied 1610 voyages, in vessels aggregating 115,634 tons, navigated by 9718 men. These transported what was then considered "the vast" American cargo, of £500,000 outward and £400,000 inward. But the ominous feature from the point of view of the Navigation Act was

---

44. Bryan Edwards, West Indies, vol. ii. p. 486.

that this was carried almost wholly in American bottoms.[45] In short, not to speak of an extensive practice of smuggling, facilitated by a coast line too long and indented to be effectually watched,—mention of which abounds in contemporary annals,[46]—a very valuable part of the British carrying trade was in the hands of the middle colonists, whose activity, however, did not stop even there; for, not only did they deal with foreign West Indies,[47] but the cheapness of their vessels, owing to the abundance of the materials, permitted them to be used also to advantage in a direct trade with southern Europe, their native products being for the most part "not enumerated." As early as 1731, Pennsylvania employed eight thousand tons of shipping, while the New England colonies at the same time owned forty thousand tons, distributed in six hundred vessels, manned by six thousand seamen.

The New Englanders, like their countrymen farther south, were mostly farmers; but the more rugged soil and severer climate gave them little or no surplus for export. For gain by traffic, for material for exchange, they therefore turned to the sea, and became the great carriers of America, as well as its great fishers. An English authority, writing of the years immediately preceding the War of Independence, states that most of the seamen sailing out of the southern ports were British; from the middle colonies, half British and half American; but in the New England shipping he admits three-fourths were natives.[48] This tendency of British seamen to take employment in colonial ships is worthy of note, as foreshadowing the impressment difficulties of a later day. These, like most of the disagreements which led

---

45. Chalmers, Opinions, p. 133.
46. See, for instance, the Colden Papers, Proceedings N.Y. Historical Society, 1877. There is in these much curious economical information of other kinds.
47. A comparison of the figures just quoted, as to the British West Indies, with Sheffield's Table VII., indicates that the trade of the Continent with the foreign islands about equalled that with the British. The trade with the French West Indies, "open or clandestine, was considerable, and wholly in American vessels."—Macpherson, vol. iii. p. 584.
48. Sheffield, Commerce of the American States, p. 108.

to the War of 1812, had their origin in ante-revolutionary conditions. For example, Commodore Palliser, an officer of mark, commanding the Newfoundland station in 1767, reported to the Admiralty the "cruel custom," long practised by commanders of fishing ships, of leaving many men on the desert coast of Newfoundland, when the season was over, whereby "these men were obliged to sell themselves to the colonists, or piratically run off with vessels, which they carry to the continent of America. By these practices the Newfoundland fishery, supposed to be one of the most valuable nurseries for seamen,[49] has long been an annual drain."[50] In the two years, 1764-65, he estimates that 2,500 seamen thus went to the colonies; in the next two years, 400. The difference was probably due to the former period being immediately after a war, the effects of which it reflected.

The general conditions of 1731 remained thirty years later, simply having become magnified as the colonies grew in wealth and population. In 1770 twenty-two thousand tons of shipping were annually built by the continental colonists. They even built ships for Great Britain; and this indulgence, for so it was considered, was viewed jealously by a class of well-informed men, intelligent, but fully imbued with the ideas of the Navigation Act, convinced that the carrying trade was the corner-stone of the British Navy, and realizing that where ships were cheaply built they could be cheaply sailed, even if they paid higher wages. It is true, and should be sedulously remembered, especially now in the United States, that the strength of a merchant shipping lies in its men even more than in its ships; and therefore that the policy of a country which wishes a merchant marine should be to allow its ships to be purchased where they most cheaply can, in order that the owner may be able to spend more on his crew, and the nation consequently to keep more seamen under its flag. But in 1770 the relative conditions placed Great Britain under serious disadvantages towards America in the matter of ship-building; for the heavy

---

49. That is, for the navy.
50. Macpherson, Annals of Commerce, vol. iii. p. 472.

drafts upon her native oak had caused the price to rise materially, and even the forests of continental Europe felt the strain, while the colonies had scarcely begun to touch their resources. In 1775, more than one-third of the foreign trade of Great Britain was carried in American-built ships; the respective tonnage being, British-built, 605,545; American, 373,618.[51]

British merchants and ship-owners knew also that the colonial carriers were not ardent adherents of the Navigation Act, but conducted their operations in conformity with it only when compelled.[52] They traded with the foreigner as readily as with the British subject; and, what was quite unpardonable in the ideas of that time, after selling a cargo in a West Indian port, instead of reloading there, they would take the hard cash of the island to a French neighbour, buying of him molasses to be made into rum at home. In this commercial shrewdness the danger was not so much in the local loss, or in the single transaction, for in the commercial supremacy of England the money was pretty sure to find its way back to the old country. The sting was that the sharp commercial instinct, roving from port to port, with a keen scent for freight and for bargains, maintained a close rivalry for the carrying trade, which was doubly severe from the natural advantages of the shipping and the natural aptitudes of the ship-owners. Already the economical attention of the New Englanders to the details of their shipping business had been noted, and had earned for them the name of the Dutchmen of North America; an epithet than

---

51. Macpherson, vol. iv. p. 11. The great West India cargo of 1772, an especial preserve of the Navigation Act, was carried to England in 679 ships, of which one-third were built in America.

52. "The contraband trade carried on by plantation ships in defiance of the Act of Navigation was a subject of repeated complaint." "The laws of Navigation were nowhere disobeyed and contemned so openly as in New England. The people of Massachusetts Bay were from the first disposed to act as if independent of the mother country."—Reeves, pp. 54, 58. The particular quotations apply to the early days of the measure, 1662-3; but the complaint continued to the end. In 1764-5, "one of the great grievances in the American trade was, that great quantities of foreign molasses and syrups were clandestinely run on shore in the British Colonies."—p. 79.

which there was then none more ominous to British ears, and especially where with the carrying trade was associated the twin idea of a nursery of seamen for the British Navy.

A fair appreciation of the facts and relations, summarized in the preceding pages from an infinitude of details, is necessary to a correct view of the origin and course of the misunderstandings and disagreements which finally led to the War of 1812. In 1783, the restoration of peace and the acknowledgment of the independence of the former colonies removed from commerce the restrictions incident to hostilities, and replaced in full action, essentially unchanged, the natural conditions which had guided the course of trade in colonial days. The old country, retaining all the prepossessions associated with the now venerable and venerated Navigation Act, saw herself confronted with the revival of a commercial system, a commercial independence, of which she had before been jealous, and which could no longer be controlled by political dependence. It was to be feared that supplying the British West Indies would increase American shipping, and that British seamen would more and more escape into it, with consequent loss to British navigation, both in tonnage and men, and discouragement to British maritime industries. Hence, by the ideas of the time, was to be apprehended weakness for war, unless some effective check could be devised.

What would have been the issue of these anxieties, and of the measures to which they gave rise, had not the French Revolution intervened to aggravate the distresses of Great Britain, and to constrain her to violent methods, is bootless to discuss. It remains true that, both before and during the conflict with the French Republic and Empire, the general character of her actions, to which the United States took exception, was determined by the conditions and ideas that have been stated, and can be understood only through reference to them. No sooner had peace been signed, in 1783, than disagreements sprang up again from the old roots of colonial systems and ideals. To these essentially was due the detailed sequence of events which, influenced by such traditions of opinion and policy as have been indicated, brought on the War of 1812, which has not inaptly been styled the second War of Independence. Madison, who was contemporary with the entire controversy, and officially connected with it from 1801 to the end of the war, first as Secretary of State, and later as President, justly summed up his experience of the whole in these words:

> To have shrunk from resistance, under such circumstances, would have acknowledged that, on the element which forms three-fourths of the globe which we inhabit, and where all independent nations have equal and common rights, the American People were not an independent people, but colonists and vassals. With such an alternative war was chosen.[53]

The second war was closely related to the first in fact, though separated by a generation in time.

---

53. American State Papers, Foreign Relations, vol. i. p. 82.

CHAPTER 2

From Independence to Jay's Treaty, 1794

The colonial connection between Great Britain and the thirteen communities which became the original States of the American Union was brought to a formal conclusion in 1776, by their Declaration of Independence. Substantially, however, it had already terminated in 1774. This year was marked by the passage of the Boston Port Bill, with its accessory measures, by the British Parliament, and likewise by the renewal, in the several colonies, of the retaliatory non-importation agreements of 1765.

The fundamental theory of the eighteenth century concerning the relations between a mother country and her colonies, that of reciprocal exclusive benefit, had thus in practice yielded to one of mutual injury; to coercion and deprivation on the one side, and to passive resistance on the other. On September 5 the representatives of twelve colonies assembled in Philadelphia; Georgia alone sending no delegates, but pledging herself in anticipation to accept the decisions taken by the others. One of the first acts of this Congress of the Continental Colonies was to indorse the resolutions by which Massachusetts had placed herself in an attitude of contingent rebellion against the Crown, and to pledge their support to her in case of a resort to arms.

These several steps were decisive and irrevocable, except by an unqualified abandonment, by one party or the other, of the principles which underlay and dictated them. The die was cast.

To use words attributed to George the Third, "the colonies must now either submit or triumph."

The period which here began, viewed in the aggregate of the national life of the United States, was one of wavering transition and uncertain issue in matters political and commercial. Its ending, in these two particulars, is marked by two conspicuous events: the adoption of the Constitution and the Commercial Treaty with Great Britain. The formation of the Federal Government, 1788-90, gave to the Union a political stability it had hitherto lacked, removing elements of weakness and dissensions, and of consequent impotence in foreign relations; the manifestation of which since the acknowledgment of independence had justified alike the hopes of enemies and the forebodings of friends. Settled conditions being thus established at home, with institutions competent to regulate a national commerce, internal and external, as well as to bring the people as a whole into fixed relations with foreign communities, there was laid the foundations of a swelling prosperity to which the several parts of the country jointly contributed. The effects of these changes were soon shown in a growing readiness on the part of other nations to enter into formal compacts with us. Of this, the treaty negotiated by John Jay with Great Britain, in 1794, is the most noteworthy instance; partly because it terminated one long series of bickerings with our most dangerous neighbour, chiefly because the commercial power of the state with which it was contracted had reached a greater eminence, and exercised wider international effect, than any the modern world had then seen.

Whatever the merits of the treaty otherwise, therefore, the willingness of Great Britain to enter into it at all gave it an epochal significance. Since independence, commercial intercourse between the two peoples had rested on the strong compelling force of natural conditions and reciprocal convenience, the true foundation, doubtless, of all useful relations; but its regulation had been by municipal ordinance of either state, changeable at will, not by mutual agreement binding on both for a prescribed period. Since the separation, this condition had seemed preferable to Great Britain, which, as late as 1790, had evaded overtures towards a commercial arrangement.[54] Her consenting now to modify her position was an implicit admission that in trade, as in political existence, the former mother country recognized at last the independence of her offspring. The latter, however, was again to learn that independence, to be actual, must rest on something stronger than words, and surer than the acquiescence of others. This was to be the lesson of the years between 1794 and 1815, administered to us not only by the preponderant navy of Great Britain, but by the petty piratical fleets of the Barbary powers.

From the Boston Port Bill to Jay's Treaty was therefore a period of transition from entire colonial dependence, under complete regulation of all commercial intercourse by the mother country, to that of national commercial power, self-regulative and efficient, through the adoption of the Constitution. Upon this followed international influence, the growing importance of which Great Britain finally recognized by formal concessions, hitherto refused or evaded. During these years the policy of her government was undergoing a process of adjustment, conditioned on the one hand by the still vigorous traditional prejudices associated with the administration of dependencies, and on the other by the radical change in political relations between her remaining colonies in America and the new states which had broken from the colonial bond. This change was the more embarrassing, because the natural connection of specific mutual usefulness remained, although the tie of a common allegiance had been loosed. The old order was yielding to the new, but the process was signalized by the usual slowness of men to accept events in their full significance. Hitherto, all the western hemisphere had been under a colonial system of complete monopoly by mother countries, and had been generally excluded from direct communication with Europe, except the respective parent states. In the comprehensive provisions of the British Navigation Act, America was associated with Asia and Africa. Now had

---

54. American State Papers, Foreign Relations, vol. i. p. 121.

arisen there an independent state, in political standing identical with those of Europe, yet having towards colonial America geographical and commercial relations very different from theirs. Consequently there was novelty and difficulty in the question, What intercourse with the remaining British dominions, and especially with the American colonies, should be permitted to the new nation? Notwithstanding the breach lately made, it continued a controlling aim with the British people, and of the government as determined by popular pressure, to restore the supremacy of British trade, by the subjection of America, independent as well as colonial, to the welfare of British commerce. Notably this was to be so as regards the one dominant interest called Navigation, under which term was comprised everything relating to shipping,—ship-building, seafaring men, and the carrying trade. Independence had deprived Great Britain of the right she formerly had to manipulate the course of the export and import trade of the now United States. It remained to try whether there did not exist, nevertheless, the ability effectually to control it to the advantage of British navigation, as above defined. "Our remaining colonies on the Continent, and the West India Islands," it was argued, "with the favourable state of English manufactures, may still give us almost exclusively the trade of America;" provided these circumstances were suitably utilized, and their advantages rigorously enforced, where power to do so still remained, as it did in the West Indies.

Although by far the stronger and more flourishing part of her colonial dominions had been wrested from Great Britain, there yet remained to her upon the continent, in Canada and the adjacent provinces, a domain great in area, and in the West India Islands another of great productiveness. Whatever wisdom had been learned as regards the political treatment of colonies, the views as to the nature of their economical utility to the mother country, and their consequent commercial regulation, had undergone no enlargement, but rather had been intensified in narrowness and rigor by the loss of so valuable a part of the whole. No counteractive effect to this prepossession was to be found in contemporary opinion in Europe. The French Revolution itself, subversive as it was of received views in many respects, was at the first characterized rather by an exaggeration of the traditional exclusive policy of the eighteenth century relating to colonies, shipping, and commerce. In America, the unsettled commercial and financial conditions which succeeded the peace, the divergence of interests between the several new states, the feebleness of the confederate government, its incompetency to deal assuredly with external questions, and lack of all power to regulate commerce, inspired a conviction in Great Britain that the continent could not offer strong, continued resistance to commercial aggression, carried on under the peaceful form of municipal regulation. It was generally thought that the new states could never unite, but instead would drift farther apart.

The belief was perfectly reasonable; a gift of prophecy only could have foretold the happy result, of which many of the most prominent Americans for some time despaired. "It will not be an easy matter," wrote Lord Sheffield,[55] "to bring the American States to act as a nation; they are not to be feared as such by us. It must be a long time before they can engage, or will concur, in any material expense.... We might as reasonably dread the effects of combinations among the German as among the American states, and deprecate the resolves of the Diet, as those of Congress." "No treaty can be made that will be binding on the whole of them." "A decided cast has been given to public opinion here," wrote John Adams from London, in November, 1785, "by two presumptions. One is, that the American states are not, and cannot, be united."[56] Two years later Washington wrote:

> The situation of the General Government, if it can be called a government, is shaken to its foundation, and liable to be overturned at every blast. In a word, it is at an end... The primary cause of all our disorders lies in the different state governments, and in the tenacity of that power which underlies the whole of their systems. Independent

---

55. Commerce of the American States (Edition February, 1784), pp. 198-199.
56. Works of John Adams, vol. viii. p. 290.

sovereignty is so ardently contended for." "At present, under our existing form of confederation, it would be idle to think of making commercial regulations on our part. One state passes a prohibitory law respecting one article; another state opens wide the avenue for its admission. One assembly makes a system, another assembly unmakes it."[57]

Under such conditions it was natural that a majority of Englishmen should see power and profit for Great Britain in availing herself of the weakness of her late colonists, to enforce upon them a commercial dependence as useful as the political dependence which had passed away. Were this realized, she would enjoy the emoluments of the land without the expense of its protection. This gospel was preached at once to willing ears, and found acceptance; not by the strength of its arguments, for these, though plausible, were clearly inferior in weight to the facts copiously adduced by those familiar with conditions, but through the prejudices which the then generation had received from the three or four preceding it. The policy being adopted, the instrument at hand for enforcing it was the relation of colonies to mother countries, as then universally maintained by the governments of the day. The United States, like other independent nations, was to be excluded wholly from carrying trade with the British colonies, and as far as possible from sending them supplies. It was urged that Canada, and the adjacent British dominions, encouraged by this reservation of the West India market for their produce, would prove adequate to furnishing the provisions and lumber previously derived from the old continental colonies. The prosperity once enjoyed by the latter would be transferred, and there would be reconstituted the system of commercial intercourse, interior to the empire, which previously had commanded general admiration. The new states, acting commercially as separated communities, could oppose no successful rivalry to this combination, and would revert to isolated commercial dependence; tributary to the financial supremacy of

---

[57]. Washington's Correspondence, 1787, edited by W.C. Ford, vol. viii. pp. 159, 160, 254.

Great Britain, as they recently had been to her political power. In debt to her for money, and drawing from her manufactures, returns for both would compel their exports to her ports chiefly, whence distribution would be, as of old, in the hands of British middlemen and navigators. Just escaped from the fetters of the carrying trade and *entrepôt* regulations, the twin monopolies in which consisted the value of a colonial empire, it was proposed to reduce them again under bondage by means for which the West India Islands furnished the leverage; for "the trade carried on by Great Britain with the countries now become the United States was, and still is, so connected with the trade carried on to the remaining British colonies in America, and the British islands in the West Indies, that it is impossible to form a true judgment of the past and present of the first, without taking a comprehensive view of all, as they are connected with, and influence, each other."[58]

Before the peace of 1783, the writings of Adam Smith had gravely shaken belief in the mercantile system of extraordinary trade regulation and protection as conducive to national prosperity. Though undermined, however, it had not been overthrown; and even to doubters there remained the exception, which Smith himself admitted, of the necessity to protect navigation as a nursery for the navy, and consequently as a fundamental means of national defence. Existence takes precedence of prosperity; the life is more than the meat. Commercial regulation, though unfitted to increase wealth, could be justified as a means to promote ship-building; to retain ship-builders in the country; to husband the raw materials of their work; to force the transport of merchandise in British-built ships and by British seamen; and thus to induce capital to invest, and men to embark their lives, in maritime trade, to the multiplication of ships and seamen, the chief dependence of the nation in war. "Keeping ships for freight," said Sheffield, "is not the most profitable branch of trade. It is necessary, for the sake of our marine, to force or encourage it by exclusive advantages." "Comparatively

---

58. Report of the Committee of the Privy Council, Jan. 28, 1791, p. 20.

with the number of our people and the extent of our country, we are doomed almost always to wage unequal war; and as a means of raising seamen it cannot be too often repeated that it is not possible to be too jealous on the head of navigation." He proceeds then at once to draw the distinction between the protection of navigation and that of commerce generally. "This jealousy should not be confounded with that towards neighbouring countries as to trade and manufactures; nor is the latter jealousy in many instances reasonable or well founded. Competition is useful, forcing our manufacturers to act fairly, and to work reasonably." Sheffield was the most conspicuous, and probably the most influential, of the controversialists on this side of the question at this period; the interest of the public is shown by his pamphlet passing through six editions in a twelvemonth. He was, however, far from singular in this view. Chalmers, a writer of much research, said likewise:

> In these considerations of nautical force and public safety we discover the fundamental principle of Acts of Navigation, which, though established in opposition to domestic and foreign clamours, have produced so great an augmentation of our native shipping and sailors, and which therefore should not be sacrificed to any projects of private gain, (that is, of commercial advantage). There are intelligent persons who suggest that the imposing of alien duties on alien ships, rather than on alien merchandise, would augment our naval strength.[59]

Colonies therefore were esteemed desirable to this end chiefly. To use the expression of a French officer,[60] they were the fruitful nursery of seamen. French writers of that day considered their West India islands the chief nautical support of the state. But in order to secure this, it was necessary to exercise complete control of their trade inward and outward; of the supplies they needed as well as of the products they raised, and especially to

---

59. Chalmers, Opinions, p. 32.
60. Jurien de la Gravière, Guerres Maritimes, Paris, 1847, vol. ii. p. 238.

confine the carriage of both to national shipping. "The only use and advantage of the (remaining) American colonies[61] or West India islands to Great Britain," says Sheffield, "are the monopoly of their consumption and the carriage of their produce. It is the advantage to our navigation which in any degree countervails the enormous expense of protecting our islands. Rather than give up their carrying trade it would be better to give up themselves." The *entrepôt* system herein found additional justification, for not only did it foster navigation by the homeward voyage, confined to British ships, and extort toll in transit, but the re-exportation made a double voyage which was more than doubly fruitful in seamen; for from the nearness of the British Islands to the European continent, which held the great body of consumers, this second carriage could be done, and actually was done, by numerous small vessels, able to bear a short voyage but not to brave an Atlantic passage. Economically, trade by many small vessels is more expensive than by a few large, because for a given aggregate tonnage it requires many more men; but this economical loss was thought to be more than compensated by the political gain in multiplying seamen. It was estimated in 1795 that there was a difference of from thirty-five to forty men in carrying the same quantity of goods in one large or ten small vessels. This illustrates aptly the theory of the Navigation Act, which sought wealth indeed, but, as then understood, subordinated that consideration distinctly to the superior need of increasing the resources of the country in ships and seamen. Moreover, the men engaged in these short voyages were more immediately at hand for impressment in war, owing to the narrow range of their expeditions and their frequent returns to home ports.

In 1783, therefore, the Navigation Act had become in general acceptance a measure not merely commercial, but military. It was defended chiefly as essential to the naval power of Great Britain, which rested upon the sure foundation of maritime resources thus laid. Nor need this view excite derision to-day, for it compelled then the adhesion of an American who of all in

---

61. Canada, Newfoundland, Bermuda, etc.

his time was most adverse to the general commercial policy of Great Britain. In a report on the subject made to Congress in 1793, by Jefferson, as Secretary of State, he said:

> Our navigation involves still higher considerations than our commerce. As a branch of industry it is valuable, but as a resource of defence essential. It will admit neither neglect nor forbearance. The position and circumstances of the United States leave them nothing to fear on their land-board;. . . . but on their seaboard they are open to injury, and they have there too a commerce (coasting) which must be protected. This can only be done by possessing a respectable body of citizen-seamen, and of artists and establishments in readiness for ship-building.[62]

The limitations of Jefferson's views appear here clearly, in the implicit relegation of defence, not to a regular and trained navy, but to the occasional unskilled efforts of a distinctly civil force; but no stronger recognition of the necessities of Great Britain could be desired, for her nearness to the great military states of the world deprived her land-board of the security which the remoteness of the United States assured. With such stress laid upon the vital importance of merchant seamen to national safety, it is but a step in thought to perceive how inevitable was the jealousy and indignation felt in Great Britain, when she found her fleets, both commercial and naval, starving for want of seamen, who had sought refuge from war in the American merchant service, and over whom the American Government, actually weak and but yesterday vassal, sought to extend its protection from impressment.

Up to the War of American Independence, the singular geographical situation of Great Britain, inducing her to maritime enterprise and exempting her from territorial warfare, with the financial and commercial pre-eminence she had then maintained for three-fourths of a century, gave her peculiar advantages for enforcing a policy which until that time had thriven conspicu-

---

62. American State Papers, Foreign Relations, vol. i. p. 303.

ously, if somewhat illusively, in its commercial results, and had substantially attained its especial object of maritime preponderance. Other peoples had to submit to the compulsion exerted by her overweening superiority. The obligation upon foreign shipping to be three-fourths manned by their own citizens, for instance, rested only upon a British law, and applied only in a British port; but the accumulations of British capital, with the consequent facility for mercantile operations and ability to extend credits, the development of British manufactures, the extent of the British carrying trade, the enforced storage of colonial products in British territory, with the correlative obligation that foreign goods for her numerous and increasing colonists must first be brought to her shores and thence transhipped,—all these circumstances made the British islands a centre for export and import, towards which foreign shipping was unavoidably drawn and so brought under the operation of the law. The nation had so far out-distanced competition that her supremacy was unassailable, and remained unimpaired for a century longer. To it had contributed powerfully the economical distribution of her empire, greatly diversified in particulars, yet symmetrical in the capacity of one part to supply what the other lacked. There was in the whole a certain self-sufficiency, resembling that claimed in this age for the United States, with its compact territory but wide extremes of boundary, climates, and activities.

This condition, while it lasted, in large degree justified the Navigation Act, which may be summarily characterized as a great protective measure, applied to the peculiar conditions of a particular maritime empire, insuring reciprocal and exclusive benefit to the several parts. It was uncompromisingly logical in its action, not hesitating at rigid prohibition of outside competition. Protection, in its best moral sense, may be defined as the regulation of all the business of the nation, considered as an interrelated whole, by the Government, for the best interests of the entire community, likewise regarded as a whole. This the Navigation Act did for over a century after its enactment; and it may be plausibly argued that, as a war resort at least, it afterwards measurably strengthened the hands of Great Britain during the wars of the French Revolution. No men suffered more than did the West India planters from its unrelieved enforcement after 1783; yet in their vehement remonstrance they said:

> The policy of the Act is justly popular. Its regulations, until the loss of America, under the various relaxations which Parliament has applied to particular events and exigencies as they arose, have guided the course of trade without oppressing it; for the markets which those regulations left open to the consumption of the produce of the colonies were sufficient to take off the whole, and no foreign country could have supplied the essential part of their wants materially cheaper than the colonies of the mother country could supply one another.

Thus things were, or were thought to be, up to the time when the revolt of the continental colonies made a breach in the wall of reciprocal benefit by which the whole had been believed to be enclosed. The products of the colonies sustained the commercial prosperity of the mother country, ministering to her export trade, and supplying a reserve of consumers for her monopoly of manufactures, which they were forbidden to establish for themselves, or to receive from foreigners. She on her part excluded from the markets of the empire foreign articles which her colonies produced, constituting for them a monopoly of the imperial home market, as well in Great Britain as in the sister colonies. The carriage of the whole was confined to British navigation, the maintenance of which by this means raised the British Navy to the mastery of the seas, enabling it to afford to the entire system a protection, of which convincing and brilliant evidence had been afforded during the then recent Seven Years' War. As a matter of political combination and adjustment, for peace or for war, the general result appeared to most men of that day to be consummate in conception and in development, and therefore by all means to be perpetuated. In that light men of to-day must realize it, if they would adequately understand the influence exercised by this prepossession upon the course of events which for the United States issued in the War of 1812.

In this picture, so satisfactory as a whole, there had been certain shadows menacing to the future. Already, in the colonial period, these had been recognized by some in Great Britain as predictive of increasing practical independence on the part of the continental colonies, with results injurious to the empire at large, and to the particular welfare of the mother kingdom. In the last analysis, this danger arose from the fact that, unlike the tropical West Indies, these children were for the most part too like their parent in political and economical character, and in permanent natural surroundings. There was, indeed, a temporary variation of activities between the new communities, where the superabundance of soil kept handicrafts in abeyance, and the old country, where agriculture was already failing to produce food sufficient for the population, and men were being forced into manufactures and their export as a means of livelihood. There was also a difference in their respective products which ministered to beneficial exchange. Nevertheless, in their tendencies and in their disposition, Great Britain and the United States at bottom were then not complementary, but rivals. The true complement of both was the West Indies; and for these the advantage of proximity, always great, and especially so with regard to the special exigencies of the islands, lay with the United States. Hence it came to pass that the trade with the West Indies, which then had almost a monopoly of sugar and coffee production for the world, became the most prominent single factor in the commercial contentions between the two countries, and in the arbitrary commercial ordinances of Great Britain, which step by step led the two nations into war. The precedent struggle was over a market; artificial regulation and superior naval power seeking to withstand the natural course of things, and long successfully retarding it.

The suspension of intercourse during the War of Independence had brought the economical relations into stronger relief, and accomplished independence threatened the speedy realization of their tendencies. There were two principal dangers dreaded by Great Britain. The West India plantation industry had depended upon the continental colonies for food supplies, and to a considerable extent also financially; because these alone were the consumers of one important product—rum. Again, ship-building and the carrying trade of the empire had passed largely into the hands of the continental colonists, keeping on that side of the Atlantic, it was asserted, a great number of British-born seamen. While vessels from America visited many parts of the world, the custom-house returns showed that of the total inward and outward tonnage of the thirteen colonies, over sixty per cent had been either coastwise or with the West Indies; and this left out of account the considerable number engaged in smuggling. Of the remainder, barely twenty-five per cent went to Great Britain or Ireland. In short, there had been building upon the western side of the ocean, under the colonial connection, a rival maritime system, having its own products, its own special markets, and its own carrying trade. The latter also, being done by very small vessels, adapted to the short transit, had created for itself, or absorbed from elsewhere, a separate and proportionately large maritime population, rivalling that of the home country, while yet remaining out of easy reach of impressment and remote from immediate interest in European wars. One chief object of the Navigation Act was thus thwarted; and indeed, as might be anticipated from quotations already made, it was upon this that British watchfulness more particularly centred. As far as possible all interchange was to be internal to the empire, a kind of coasting trade, which would naturally, as well as by statute, fall to British shipping. Protective regulation therefore should develop in the several parts those productions which other parts needed,—the material of commerce; but where this could not be done, and supplies must be sought outside, they should go and come in British vessels, navigated according to the Act. "Our country," wrote Sheffield, in concluding his work, "does not entirely depend upon the monopoly of the commerce of the thirteen

American states, and it is by no means necessary to sacrifice any part of our carrying trade for imaginary advantages never to be attained."[63]

A further injury was done by the cheapness with which the Americans built and sold ships, owing to their abundance of timber. They built them not only to order, but as it were for a market. Although acceptable to the mercantile interest, and even indirectly beneficial by sparing the resources for building ships of war, this was an invasion of the manufacturing industry of the kingdom, in a particular peculiarly conducive to naval power. The returns of the British underwriters for twenty-seven shipping ports of Great Britain and Ireland, during a series of years immediately preceding the American revolt, no ship being counted twice, showed the British-built vessels entered to be 3,908, and the American 2,311.[64] The tonnage of the latter was more than one-third of the total. The intercourse between the American continent and the West Indies, not included in this reckoning, was almost wholly in American bottoms. The proportion of American-built shipping in the total of the empire is hence apparent, as well as the growth of the ship-building industry. This of course was accompanied by a tendency of mechanics, as well as seamen, to remove to a situation so favourable for employment. But the maintenance of home facilities for building ships was as essential to the development of naval power as was the fostering of a class of seamen. In this respect, therefore, the ship-building of America was detrimental to the objects of the Navigation Act; and the evil threatened to increase, because of a discernible approaching shortness of suitable timber in the overtaxed forests of Europe.

Such being the apparent tendency of things, owing to circumstances relatively permanent in character, the habit of mind traditional with British merchants and statesmen, formed by the accepted colonial and mercantile systems, impelled them at once to prohibitory measures of counteraction, as soon as the colonies,

---

63. p. 288.
64. Coxe, View of the United States, p. 346.

naturally rival, had become by independence a foreign nation. For a moment, indeed, it appeared that broader views might prevail, based upon a sounder understanding of actual conditions and of the principles of international commerce. The second William Pitt was Chancellor of the Exchequer at the time the provisional articles of peace with the United States were signed, in November, 1782; and in March, 1783, he introduced into the House of Commons a bill for regulating temporarily the intercourse between the two nations, so far as dependent upon the action of Great Britain, until it should be possible to establish a mutual arrangement by treaty. This measure reflected not only a general attitude of good will towards America, characteristic of both father and son, but also the impression which had been made upon the younger man by the writings of Adam Smith. Professing as its objects "to establish intercourse on the most enlarged principles of reciprocal benefit," and "to evince the disposition of Great Britain to be on terms of most perfect amity with the United States of America," the bill admitted the ships and vessels of the United States, with the merchandise on board, into all the ports of Great Britain in the same manner as the vessels of other independent states; that is, manned three-fourths by American seamen. This preserved the main restrictions of the Navigation Act, protective of British navigation; but the merchandise, even if brought in American ships, was relieved of all alien duties. These, however, wherever still existing for other nations, were light, and this remission slight;[65] a more substantial concession was a rebate upon all exports from Great Britain to the United States, equal to that allowed upon goods exported to the colonies. As regarded intercourse with the West Indies, there was to be made in favour of the thirteen states a special and large remission in the rigor of the Act; one affecting both commerce and navigation. To British colonies, by long-standing proscription, no ships except British had been admitted to export or import. By the proposed measure, the United States,

---

65. Reeves, p. 381. Nevertheless, foreign nations frequently complained of this as a distinction against them (Report of the Committee of the Privy Council, Jan. 28, 1791, p. 10).

alone among the nations of the world, were to be allowed to import freely any goods whatsoever, of their own growth, produce, or manufacture, in their own ships; on the same terms exactly as British vessels, if these should engage in the traffic between the American continent and the islands. Similarly, freedom to export colonial produce was granted to American bottoms from the West Indies to the United States. Both exports and imports, thus to be authorized, were to be "liable to the same duties and charges only as the same merchandise would be subject to, if it were the property of British native-born subjects, and imported in British ships, navigated by British seamen."[66] In short, while the primary purpose doubtless was the benefit of the islands, the effect of the measure, as regarded the West India trade, was to restore the citizens of the now independent states to the privileges they had enjoyed as colonists. The carrying trade between the islands and the continent was conceded to them, and past experience gave ground to believe it would be by them absorbed.

It was over this concession that the storm of controversy arose and raged, until the outbreak of the French Revolution, by the conservative reaction it provoked in other governments, arrested for the time any change of principle in regard to colonial administration, whatever modifications might from time to time be induced by momentary exigencies of policy. The question immediately argued was probably on all hands less one of principle than of expediency. Superior as commercial prosperity and the preservation of peace were to most other motives in the interest of Pitt's mind, he doubtless would have admitted, along with his most earnest opponents, that the fostering of the national carrying trade, as a nursery to the navy and so contributory to national defence, took precedence of purely commercial legislation. With all good-will to America, his prime object necessarily was the welfare of Great Britain; but this he, contrary to the mass of public opinion, conceived to lie in the restoration of the old intercourse between the two peoples, modified as little as possible by the new condition of independence. He trusted

---

66. Bryan Edwards, West Indies, vol. ii. p. 494 (note).

that the habit of receiving everything from England, the superiority of British manufactures, a common tongue, and commercial correspondences only temporarily interrupted by the war, would tend to keep the new states customers of Great Britain chiefly, as they had been before; and what they bought they must pay for by sending their own products in return. This constraint of routine and convenience received additional force from the scarcity of capital in America, and its abundance in Great Britain, relatively to the rest of Europe. The wealthiest nation could hold the Americans by their need of accommodations which others could not extend.

In so far there probably was a general substantial agreement in Great Britain. The Americans had been consumers to over double the amount of the West Indies before the war, and it was desirable to retain their custom. Nor was the anticipation of success deceived. Nine years later, despite the rejection of Pitt's measure, an experienced American complained "that we draw so large a proportion of our manufactures from one nation. The other European nations have had the eight years of the war (of Independence) exclusively, and the nine years of peace in fair competition, and do not yet supply us with manufactures equivalent to half of the stated value of the shoes made by ourselves."[67] In the first year of the government under the Constitution, from August, 1789, to September 30, 1790, after seven years of independence, out of a total of not quite $20,000,000 imports to the United States, over $15,000,000 were from the dominions of Great Britain;[68] and nearly half the exports went to the same destination, either as raw material for manufactures, or as to the distributing centre for Europe. The commercial dependence is evident; it had rather increased than diminished since the Peace. As regards American navigation, the showing was somewhat better; but even here 217,000 tons British had entered

---

67. Coxe's View, p. 318.
68. American State Papers, Foreign Affairs, vol. i. p. 301. Jefferson added, "These imports consist mostly of articles on which industry has been exhausted,"—*i.e.*, completed manufactures. The State Papers, Commerce and Navigation, give the tabulated imports and exports for many succeeding years.

United States ports, against a total of only 355,000 American. As of the latter only 50,000 had sailed from Great Britain, it is clear that the empire had retained its hold upon its carrying trade, throughout the years intervening between the Peace and the adoption of the Constitution.

As regards the commercial relations between the two nations, these results corresponded in the main with the expectations of those who frustrated Pitt's measure. He had conceived, however, that it was wise for Great Britain not only to preserve a connection so profitable, but also to develop it; to multiply the advantage by steps which would promote the prosperity and consequent purchasing power of the communities involved. This was the object of his proposed concession. During the then recent war, no part of the British dominions—save besieged Gibraltar—had suffered so severely as the West Indies. Though other causes concurred, this was due chiefly to the cessation of communications with the revolted colonies, entailing failure of supplies indispensable to their industries. Despite certain alleviations incidental to the war, such as the capture of American vessels bound to foreign islands, and the demand for tropical products by the British armies and fleets, there had been great misery among the population, as well as financial loss. The restoration of commercial intercourse would benefit the continent as well as the islands; but the latter more. The prosperity of both would redound to the welfare of Great Britain; for the one, though now politically independent, was chained to her commercial system by imperative circumstances, while of the trade of the other she would have complete monopoly, except for this tolerance of a strictly local traffic with the adjoining continent. As for British navigation, the supreme interest, Pitt believed that it would receive more enlargement from the increase of productiveness in the islands, and of consequent demand for British manufactures, than it would suffer loss by American navigation. More commerce, more ships. Then, as at the present day, the interests of Great Britain and of the United States, in their relations to a matter of common external concern, were not opposed, but complementary; for the prosperity of the islands through America would make for the prosperity of Great Britain through the islands.

This, however, was just the point disputed; and, in default of the experience which the coming years were to furnish, fears not wholly unreasonable, from the particular point of view of sea power, as then understood, were aroused by the known facts of American shipping enterprise, both as ship-builders and carriers, even under colonial trammels. John Adams, who was minister to Great Britain from 1785 to 1788, had frequent cause to note the deep and general apprehension there entertained of the United States as a rival maritime state. The question of admission to the colonial trade, as it presented itself to most men of the day, was one of defence and of offence, and was complicated by several considerations. As a matter of fact, there was no denying the existence of that transatlantic commercial system, in which the former colonies had been so conspicuous a factor, the sole source of certain supplies to an important market, reflecting therein exactly Great Britain's own position relatively to the consumers of the European continent. The prospect of reviving what had always been an *imperium in imperio*, but now uncontrolled by the previous conditions of political subjection, seemed ominous; and besides, there was cherished the hope, ill-founded and delusive though it was, that the integrity of the empire as a self-sufficing whole, broken by recent revolt, might be restored by strong measures, coercive towards the commerce of the United States, and protective towards Canada and the other remaining continental colonies. It was believed by some that the agriculture, shipping, and fisheries of Canada, Nova Scotia, and Newfoundland, despite the obstacles placed by nature, could be so fostered as to supply the needs of the West Indies, and to develop also a population of consumers bound to take off British manufactures, as the lost colonists used to do. This may be styled the constructive idea, in Sheffield's series of propositions, looking to the maintenance of the British carrying trade at the expense of that of the United States. This expectation proved erroneous.

Up to and through the War of 1812, the British provinces, so far from having a surplus for export, had often to depend upon the United States for much of the supplies which Sheffield expected them to send to the West Indies.

The proposition was strongly supported also by a wish to aid the American loyalists, who, to the number of many thousands, had fled from the old colonies to take refuge in the less hospitable North. These men, deprived of their former resources, and having a new start in life to make, desired that the West India market should be reserved for them, to build up their local industries. Their influence was exerted in opposition to the planters, and the mother country justly felt itself bound to their relief by strong obligation. Conjoined to this was doubtless the less worthy desire to punish the successful rebellion, as well as to hinder the growth of a competitor. "If I had not been here and resided here some time," wrote John Adams, in 1785, "I should not have believed, nor could have conceived, such an union of all Parliamentary factions against us, which is a demonstration of the unpopularity of our cause."[69]

> Their direct object is not so much the increase of their own wealth, ships, or sailors, as the diminution of ours. A jealousy of our naval power is the true motive, the real passion which actuates them. They consider the United States as their rival, and the most dangerous rival they have in the world. I can see clearly they are less afraid of the augmentation of French ships and sailors than American. They think they foresee that if the United States had the same fisheries, carrying trade, and same market for ready-built ships, they had ten years ago, they would be in so respectable a position, and in so happy circumstances, that British seamen, manufacturers, and merchants too, would hurry over to them.[70]

These statements, drawn from Adams's association with many men, reflect so exactly the line of argument in the best known of

---
69. Works of John Adams, vol. viii. p. 333.
70. Works of John Adams, vol. viii. p. 291.

the many controversial pamphlets published about that time,—Lord Sheffield's "Observations on the Commerce of the American States,"—as to prove that it represented correctly a preponderant popular feeling, not only adverse to the restoration of the colonial privileges contemplated by Pitt, but distinctly inimical to the new nation; a feeling born of past defeat and of present apprehension.

Inextricably associated with this feeling was the conviction that the navigation supported by the sugar islands, being a monopoly always under the control of the mother country, and ministering to the *entrepôt* on which so much other shipping depended, was the one sure support of the general carrying trade of the nation. "Considering the bulk of West India commodities," Sheffield had written, "and the universality and extent of the consumption of sugar, a consumption still in its infancy even in Europe, and still more in America, it is not improbable that in a few ages the nation which may be in possession of the most extensive and best cultivated sugar islands, *subject to a proper policy*,[71] will take the lead at sea." Men of all schools concurred in this general view, which is explanatory of much of the course pursued by the British Government, alike in military enterprise, commercial regulation, and political belligerent measures, during the approaching twenty years of war with France. It underlay Pitt's subsequent much derided, but far from unwise, care to get the whole West India region under British control, by conquering its sugar islands. It underlay also the other measures, either instituted or countenanced by him, or inherited from his general war policy, which led through ever increasing exasperation to the war with the United States. The question, however, remained, "What is the proper policy conducive to the end which all desire?" Those who thought with Pitt in 1783 urged that to increase the facilities of the islands, by abundant supplies from the nearest and best source, in America, would so multiply the material of commerce as most to promote the necessary navigation. The West India planters pressed this view with forcible logic. "Navigation and naval power are not the parents of commerce, but its happy fruits. If mutual wants did not

---

71. My italics.

furnish the subject of intercourse between distant countries, there would soon be an end of navigation. The carrying trade is of great importance, but it is of greater still to have trade to carry." To this the reply substantially was that if the trade were thrown open to Americans, by allowing them to carry in their own vessels, the impetus so given to their navigation, with the cheapness of their ships, owing to the cheapness of materials, would make them carriers to the whole world, breaking up the monopoly of British merchants, and supplanting the employment of British ships.

A few statesmen, more far seeing and deeper reasoning,—notably Edmund Burke,—came to Pitt's support, and the West India proprietors, largely resident in England, by their knowledge of details contributed much to elucidate the facts; but their efforts were unavailing. Their argument ran thus:

> Only the American continent can furnish at reasonable rates the animals required for the agriculture of the islands, the food for the slaves, the lumber for buildings and for packing produce. Only the continent will take the rum which Europe refuses, and with which the planter pays his running expenses. Owing to irreversible currents of trade, neither British nor island shipping can carry this traffic at a profit to themselves, except by ruinously overcharging the planter. Americans only can do it. Concede the exchange by this means, and the development of sugar and coffee raising, owing to their bulk as freight, will enlarge British shipping to Europe by an amount much beyond that lost in the local transport. Of the European carriage you will retain a monopoly, as you will of the produce, which goes into your storehouses alone; whence you reap the advantage of brokerage and incidental handling, at the expense of the continental consumer, while your home navigation is enlarged by its export. Refuse this privilege, and your islands sink under French and Spanish competition. French Santo Domingo, especially, exceeds by far all your possessions, both in the extent of soil and quality of product.

Very shortly they were able also to say that the French allowed ships to be bought from Americans; and, although in their treaty with the United States they had refused free intercourse to American vessels, a royal ordinance of 1784 permitted it to vessels of under sixty tons' burden.

Within a month of the introduction of Pitt's bill the ministry to which he then belonged fell. The one which followed refrained from dealing at all with the subject, except by recourse to an expedient not uncommon with party leaders, dealing with a new question of admitted intricacy. They passed a bill leaving the whole matter to the Crown for executive action. Accordingly, in July, 1783, a proclamation was issued permitting intercourse between the islands and the American continent, in a long list of specified articles, but only by British ships, owned and navigated as required by the Navigation Act. American vessels were excluded by omission, and while most necessaries for food, agriculture, and commerce were admitted, one staple article, salt fish, urgently requested by the planters, was forbidden. This was partly to encourage the Newfoundland fisheries and those of Great Britain, and partly to injure American. Both objects were in the line of the Navigation Act, to foster home navigation and impede that of foreigners; fisheries being considered a prime support of each. A generation before, the elder Pitt had inveighed against the Peace of Paris, in 1763, on account of the concession of the cod fisheries. "You leave to France," he said, "the opportunity of reviving her navy." Before the separation, the near and great market of the West India negro population had consumed one-third of the American catch of fish. So profitable a condition could no longer be continued. Salt provisions also, butter, and cheese, were not allowed, being reserved for Irish producers.[72]

The next December the enabling bill was renewed and the proclamation re-issued. At this moment Pitt returned to office. A few months later, in the spring of 1784, Parliament was dissolved, and the ensuing elections carried him into power at the

---

72. Chalmers, Opinions, p. 65.

head of a great majority. He made no immediate attempt to resume legislation favouring the American trade with the West Indies. The disposition of the majority of Englishmen in the matter had been plainly shown, and other more urgent commercial reforms engaged his attention. Soon after the receipt of the news in America, some of the states passed retaliatory measures, on their own account, or authorized the Continental Congress so to act for them. The bad feeling already caused by the non-fulfilment, on both sides, of certain stipulations of the treaty of peace was particularly exasperated by this proclamation; for anticipation, aroused by Pitt's proposed measure, had been nursed into confident expectation during the four months' interval, in which intercourse had been openly or tacitly allowed. It was at this period that Nelson first came conspicuously into public notice, by checking the connivance of the West Indian governors in the infractions of the Navigation Laws; the Act authorizing commanders of Kings' ships to seize offending vessels, and bring them before the Court of Admiralty.[73] It is said also that his experience had much to do with shaping subsequent legislation upon the same prohibitory lines. In America disappointment was bitter. Little concern was felt in England. Concerted action by several states was thought most unlikely, and a more perfect union impossible. While Massachusetts, for example, in 1785 forbade import or export in any vessel belonging in whole or in part to British subjects, the state then next to her in maritime importance, Pennsylvania, in 1786 repealed laws imposing extra charges on British ships, and admitted all nations on equal terms with her sister states. "The ministry in England," wrote Adams, "build all their hopes and schemes upon the supposition of such divisions in America as will forever prevent a combination of the States, either in prohibition or in retaliatory duties."[74]

Effective retaliation consequently was not feared, and as for results otherwise, it was doubtless thought best to await the test of experience. Proclamation, annually authorized and re-

---

73. Reeves, pp. 47, 57.
74. Works of John Adams, vol. viii. p. 281.

issued, remained therefore the mode of regulating commerce between the British dominions and the United States up to the date of Jay's treaty. Once only, in 1788, Parliament interfered so far as to pass a law, confining the trade with the West Indies to British-built ships and to certain enumerated articles, in the strict spirit of the Navigation system. Otherwise, intercourse with the United States was throughout this period subject at any moment to be modified or annulled by the single will of the Executive; whereas that with other nations, fixed by statute,—the Navigation Act,—could be altered only by the legislature.[75]

Of this British commercial policy, following immediately upon the recognition of independence, Americans had not the slightest reason to complain. They had insisted upon being independent, and it would be babyish to fret about the consequences, when unpalatable. It was unpleasant to find that Great Britain, satisfied that the carrying trade was the first of her interests, upon which depended her naval supremacy, rigorously excluded Americans from branches of that trade before permitted to them; but in so doing she was simply seeking her own advantage by means of her own laws, as a nation does, for instance, when it imposes heavy protective duties. It is quite as legitimate to protect the carrying trade as any other form of industry; and the Navigation Act was no new device, for the special annoyance of Americans. It is very possible that the action of Great Britain at this time was so stupid, that, to use words of Jefferson's, the only way to prophesy what she would do was to ascertain what she ought to do, and infer the contrary. The rule, he said, never failed. This particular stupidity, if such it were,—and there was at least partial ground for the charge,—was simply another case of a most common form of human dullness of perception, preoccupation with a fixed idea. But were the policy wise or foolish, as regards herself, towards the Americans it was not a wrong, but an injury; and, consequently, what the newly independent people had to do was

---

75. American State Papers, Foreign Relations, vol. i. p. 307.

not to complain, but to strike back with retaliatory commercial measures. Jefferson, no friend generally to coercive action, wrote concerning this particular situation:

> It is not to the moderation or justice of others we are to trust for fair and equal access to market with our productions, or for our due share in the transportation of them; but to our own means of independence, and the firm will to use them.[76]

Equally, when Great Britain, under the emergencies of the French Revolution, resorted to measures that overpassed her rights, either municipal or international, and infringed our own, the resort should have been to the remedy with which nations defend their rights, as distinct from their interest. The American people, then poor, and habituated to colonial dependence, failed to create for themselves in due time the power necessary to self-assertion; nor did they as a nation realize, what men like John Adams and Gouverneur Morris saw and preached, that in the complicated tangle of warring interests which constitutes every contemporary situation, the influence of any single factor depends, not merely upon its own value, but upon that value taken in connection with other conditions. A pound is but a pound; but when the balance is nearly equal, a pound may turn a scale. Because America could not possibly put afloat the hundred—or two hundred—ships-of-the-line which Great Britain had in commission, therefore, many argued, as many do to-day, it was vain to have any navy. Morris wrote in 1794,[77] and few men better understood financial conditions:

> I believe that we could now maintain twelve ships-of-the-line, perhaps twenty, with a due proportion of frigates and smaller vessels. And I am tolerably certain that, while the United States of America pursue a just and liberal con-

---

76. American State Papers, Foreign Relations, vol. i. p. 304.
77. Morris to Randolph (Secretary of State), May 31, 1794. American State Papers, Foreign Relations, vol. i. p. 409. The italics are Morris's.

duct, *with twenty sail-of-the-line at sea*, no nation on earth will dare to insult them. I believe also, that, not to mention individual losses, five years of war would involve more national expense than the support of a navy for twenty years. One thing I am thoroughly convinced of, that, if we do not render ourselves respectable, we shall continue to be insulted.

A singular, and too much disregarded, instance of the insults to which the United States was exposed, by the absence of naval strength, is found in the action of the Barbary Powers towards our commerce, which scarcely dared to enter the Mediterranean. It is less known that this condition of things was eminently satisfactory to British politicians of the old-fashioned school, and as closely linked as was the Navigation system itself to the ancient rivalry with Holland. the Dutch statesman De Witt, who died in 1672, wrote:

> Our ships should be well guarded by convoy against the Barbary pirates. Yet it would by no means be proper to free that sea of those pirates, because we should hereby be put upon the same footing with East-landers, (*i.e.*, Baltic nations, Denmark, Sweden, etc.) English, Spaniards, and Italians; wherefore it is best to leave that thorn in the sides of those nations, whereby they will be distressed in that trade, while we by convoy engross all the European traffic and navigation.[78]

This cynical philosophy was echoed in 1784 by the cultured English statesman, Lord Sheffield, the intimate friend of the historian Gibbon, and editor of his memoirs.

> If the great maritime powers know their interests," he wrote, "they will not encourage the Americans to be carriers. That the Barbary States are an advantage to the maritime powers is obvious. If they were suppressed, the little states of Italy, etc., would have much more of the carrying

---

78. Quoted from De Witt's Interest of Holland, in Macpherson's Annals of Commerce, vol. ii. p. 472.

trade. The Armed Neutrality would be as hurtful to the great maritime powers as the Barbary States are useful.[79]

It may be a novel thought to many Americans, that at that time American commerce in the Mediterranean depended largely for protection upon Portuguese cruisers; its own country extending none. When peace was unexpectedly made between Portugal and Algiers in 1793, through the interposition of a British consular officer, a wail of dismay went up to heaven from American shipmen. "The conduct of the British in this business," wrote the American consul at Lisbon, "leaves no room to doubt or mistake their object, which was evidently aimed at us, and that they will leave nothing unattempted to effect our ruin." It proved, indeed, that the British consul's action was not that of his Government, but taken on his own initiative; but the incident not only recalls the ideas of the time, long since forgotten, but in its indications, both of British commercial security and American exposure, illustrates the theory of the Navigation Act as to the reciprocal influence of the naval and merchant services. There was then nothing, in the economical conditions of the United States, to forbid a navy stronger than the Portuguese; yet the consul, in his pitiful appeal to the Portuguese Court, had to write:

> My countrymen have been led into their present embarrassment by confiding in the friendship, power, and protection of her Most Faithful Majesty.... (which) lulled our citizens into a fatal security.[80]

Our lamentable dependence upon others, for the respect we should have extorted ourselves, is shown in the instructions issued to Jay, on his mission to England in 1794.

> It may be represented to the British Ministry, how productive of perfect conciliation it might be to the people of

---

79. Observations on the Commerce of the American States, 1783, p. 115. Concerning this pamphlet, Gibbon wrote, "The Navigation Act, the palladium of Britain, was defended, perhaps saved, by his pen."
80. American State Papers, Foreign Relations, vol. i. pp. 296-299.

the United States, if Great Britain would use her influence with the Dey of Algiers for the liberation of the American citizens in captivity, and for a peace upon reasonable terms. It has been communicated from abroad, to be the fixed policy of Great Britain to check our trade in grain to the Mediterranean. This is too doubtful to be assumed, but fit for inquiry.[81]

The Dey had declared war in 1785, this being with the Barbary rulers the customary method of opening piratical action. "If the Dey makes peace with everyone," said one of his captains to Nelson, "what is he to do with his ships?"

The experience of the succeeding fifteen years was to give ample demonstration of the truth of Morris's prophecy; but what is interesting now to observe is, that he, who certainly did not imagine twenty ships to be equal to a hundred, accurately estimated the deterrent force of such a body, prepared to act upon an enemy's communications,—or interests,—at a great distance from the strategic centre of operations. A valuable military lesson of the War of 1812 is just this: that a comparatively small force—a few frigates and sloops—placed as the United States Navy was, can exercise an influence utterly disproportionate to its own strength. Instances of Great Britain's extremity, subsequent to Morris's prediction, are easily cited. In 1796, her fleet was forced to abandon the Mediterranean. In 1799, a year after the Nile, Nelson had to implore a small Portuguese division not to relinquish the blockade of Malta, which he could not otherwise maintain. Under such conditions, apprehension of even a slight additional burden of hostility imposes restraint. Had Morris's navy existed in 1800, we probably should have had no War of 1812; that is, if Jefferson's passion for peace, and abhorrence of navies, could have been left out of the account. War, as Napoleon said, is a business of positions. The commercial importance of the United States, and the position of its navy relatively to the major interests of Great Britain, would together have produced an effect, to which, under the political emergency of the time,

---

81. American State Papers, Foreign Relations, vol. i. p. 474.

the mere commercial retaliation then attempted was quite inadequate. This distressed the enemy, but did not reduce him; and it bitterly alienated a large part of our own community, so that we went into the war a discordant, almost a disunited, nation.

During the years of American impotence under the early confederation, the trade regulations of the British Government, framed on the lines advocated by Lord Sheffield, met with a measure of success which was perhaps more apparent than real; due attention being scarcely paid to the actual loss entailed upon British planters by the heightened cost of supplies, and the consequent effect upon British commerce and navigation. "Under the present limited intercourse with America," wrote the planter, Edwards, "the West Indies are subject to three sets of devouring monopolies: 1, the British ship-owners; 2, their agents in American ports; 3, their agents in the ports of the islands; all of whom exact an unnatural profit of the planters."[82] Chalmers, looking only to the navigation of the kingdom, which these culprits represented, admits that in the principal supplies Great Britain cannot compete with America; but, "whatever may be the difference in price to the West Indians, this is but a small equivalent which they ought to pay to the British consumer, for enjoying the exclusive supply of sugar, rum, and other West India products."[83] A few figures show conclusively that under all disadvantages the islands increased in actual prosperity, although they fell behind their French competitors, favoured by a more liberal policy. In the quiet year 1770, before the revolt of the continent, the British West Indies shipped to the home country produce amounting to £3,279,204;[84] in 1787 this had risen to £4,839,145,[85] a gain of over 30 per cent. Between the same years, exports to the United States, limited after the peace to British ships, had fallen from £481,407 to £196,461. American produce, confined to British bottoms for admission to British colonies,

---

82. West Indies, vol. ii. page 522, note.
83. Opinions, p. 89.
84. Macpherson, vol. iii. p. 506.
85. Ibid., vol. iv. p. 158.

had gone largely to the French islands, with which before the Revolution they could have only surreptitious intercourse. The result was that the British planter had to pay much more for his plantation supplies than did the French, who were furnished by American vessels, built and run much cheaper than British.[86] He was rigidly forbidden also to seek stores in the French islands. Such circuitous intercourse with America, by depriving British ships of the long voyage to the continent, would place the French islands in the obnoxious relation of *entrepôt* to their neighbours, which Holland had once occupied towards England. In all legislation minute care was taken to prevent such injury to navigation. Direct trade with British dominions was the *fetich* of British policy; circuitous trade its abomination.

Despite drawbacks, a distinct advance was observable also in British navigation; in the development of the British-American colonies, continental and island; and in the inter-colonial intercourse and shipping. Immediately after the institution of the new government, the United States enacted laws protective of her own navigation; notably by an alien duty laid upon all foreign tonnage. To consider the probable effects of this legislation, and of the new American institutions, upon British commerce and navigation, a committee of the Privy Council was appointed, to which we owe a digested and authoritative summary of the change of conditions effected by the British measures, between 1783 and 1790. From its report, based upon averages of several years, it appears that in the direct trade between Great Britain and the United States, in which American ships stood on equal terms with British, there had been little variation in value of imports or exports, with the

---

86. Bryan Edwards, himself a planter of the time, says (vol. ii. p. 522) that staves and lumber had risen 37 per cent in the British islands, which he attributes to the extortions of the navigation monopoly, "under the present limited intercourse with America." Coxe (View, etc., p. 134) gives lists of comparative prices, in 1790, June to November, in the neighbouring islands of Santo Domingo and Jamaica, which show forcibly the burdens under which the latter laboured.

single exception of tobacco and rice. These two articles, which formerly had to pass through Great Britain as an *entrepôt*, now went direct to their destination. The American shipping—navigation—employed in the trade with Great Britain herself, was only one-third of the British; the respective tonnage being 26,564 and 52,595. As this was nearly the proportion of American to British built ships in the colonial period, American shipping before the adoption of the Constitution had not gained at all, under the most favourable treatment conceded to it in British dominions. The Report, indeed, estimated that it had lost by nearly 20 per cent.[87]

In the colonial trade, on the other hand, very marked British gains could be reported. The commercially backward communities of Canada, etc., forbidden now to admit American ships, or to import many articles from the United States, and given special privileges in the West Indies, had more than doubled their imports from the mother country; the amount rising from £379,411 to £829,088. These sums are not to be regarded in their own triviality, but as harbingers of a development, which it was hoped would fill the void in the British imperial system caused by the loss of the former colonies. The West Indies showed a more gradual increase, though still satisfactory; their exports since 1774 had risen 20 per cent. It was, however, in navigation, avowedly the chief aim of the protective legislation, that the inter-colonial results were most encouraging. Through the exclusion of American competition, British tonnage to Canada and the neighbouring colonies had enlarged fourfold, from 11,219 to 46,106. The national tonnage engaged between the West Indies and the mother country had grown from 80,482 to 133,736; 60 per cent. More encouraging still, from the ideal point of view of a restored system of mutual support, embracing both sides of the Atlantic, the tonnage employed between Canada and the West Indies had risen from 996 only in 1774, to 14,513 in 1789. In brief, after a careful

---

87. Chalmers, in one of his works quoted by Macpherson (vol. iii. p. 559), estimates the annual entries of American-built ships to British ports, 1771-74, to be 34,587 tons. From this figure the falling off was marked.

and systematic examination of the whole field, the committee considered that British navigation had gained 111,638 tons by excluding Americans from branches of trade they had once shared, and still eagerly desired.

The effects of the system were most conspicuous in the trade between the West Indies and the United States. The tonnage here employed had fallen from 107,739, before the war, to 62,738. The reflections of the Committee upon this particular are so characteristic of national convictions as to be worth quoting.[88]

This decrease is rather less than half what it was before the war;[89] but before the war five-eighths belonged to merchants, permanent inhabitants of the countries now under the dominion of the United States, and three-eighths to British merchants residing occasionally in the said countries. At that time, very few vessels belonging to British merchants, resident in the British European dominions, or in the British Islands in the West Indies, had a share in this trade. The vessels employed in this trade can now only belong to British subjects *residing* in the present British dominions. Many vessels now go from the ports of Great Britain, carrying British manufactures to the United States, there load with lumber and provisions for the British Islands in the West Indies, and return with the produce of these islands to Great Britain. The whole of this branch of freight may also be considered as a new acquisition, and was obtained by your Majesty's Order in Council before mentioned,[90] which has operated to the increase of British Navigation, compared to that of the United States in a double ratio; *but it has taken from the navigation of the United States more than it has added to that of Great Britain.*

The last sentence emphasizes the fact, which John Adams had noted, that the object of the Navigation system was scarcely more defensive than offensive, in the military sense of the

---

88. Report of the Committee of the Privy Council, Jan. 28, 1791, p. 39.
89. This awkward expression means that the amount of decrease was rather less than half the before-the-war total.
90. June 18, 1784, substantially the re-issue of that of Dec. 26, 1783, which Reeves (p. 288) considers the standard exemplar.

word. The Act carried provisions meant distinctly to impede the development of foreign shipping, as far as possible to do so by municipal regulation. The prohibition of entrance to a port of Great Britain by a foreign trader, unless three-fourths manned by citizens of the country whose flag she bore, was distinctly offensive in intent. But for this, other states might increase their tonnage by employing seamen not their own, which Great Britain could not do without weakening the reserves available for her navy, and imperative to her defence. Rivalry was thus engendered, and became bitter and apprehensive in proportion to the national interests involved; but at no time had such considerations persuaded the country to depart from its purpose.

The foreign war which those measures first brought upon us, and the odium which they have never ceased to cause, to the present day (1792) among neighbouring nations, have not induced the legislature to give up any one of its principles.[91]

In the case of the United States, the exasperation aroused was very great. It perpetuated the national animosity surviving from the War of Independence, and provoked retaliation. Before the formation of the better Union this was too desultory and divided to have much effect, and the artificial system of which Sheffield was the chief public champion had the appearance of success which has been described; but as soon as the thirteen states could wield their power as one whole, under a system at once consistent and permanent, American navigation began to make rapid headway. In 1790 there entered American ports from abroad 355,000 tons of American shipping and 251,000 foreign, of which 217,000 were British.[92] After one year of the discriminating tonnage dues laid by the national Congress, the American tonnage entering home ports from Great Britain had risen, from the 26,564 average of the three years, 1787 to 1789, ascertained by the British committee, to 43,580.[93] In 1801 there

---

91. Reeves, p. 431.
92. American State Papers, Commerce and Navigation, vol. x. p. 389.
93. Ibid., Foreign Relations, vol. i. p. 301.

entered 799,304 tons of native shipping,[94] and but 138,000 foreign.[95] The amount of British among the latter is not stated; but in the year 1800 there cleared from Great Britain, under her own flag, for the United States, but 14,381 tons.[96] This reversal of the conditions in 1787-89, before quoted,[97] was the result of a gradual progress, noticeable immediately after the American imposition of tonnage duties, and increasing up to 1793, when it was accelerated by the war between Great Britain and France.

It is carefully to be remembered that the British committee, representing strictly the prepossessions of the body by which it was constituted, looked primarily to the development of national carrying trade.

As the security of the British dominions principally depends on the greatness of your Majesty's naval power, it has ever been the policy of the British Government to watch with a jealous eye every attempt that has been made by foreign nations to the detriment of its navigation; and even in cases where the interests of commerce and those of navigation could not be wholly reconciled, the Government of Great Britain has always given the preference to the interests of navigation; and it has never yet submitted to the imposition of any tonnage duties by foreign nations on British ships trading to their ports, without proceeding immediately to retaliation.[98]

It had, however, submitted to several such measures, retaliatory for the exclusion from the West India trade, enacted by the separate states in the years 1783 to 1789; as well as to other legislation, taxing British shipping by name much above that of other foreigners. This quiescence was due to confidence, that the advantages possessed by Great Britain would enable her to overcome all handicaps. It was therefore with satisfaction that, after six years of commercial antagonism, the committee was able, not only to report the growth of British shipping, already quoted, but to show

---

94. Ibid., Commerce and Navigation, vol. x. p. 528.
95. Ibid., p. 584.
96. Macpherson, Annals of Commerce, vol. iv. p. 535.
97. Ante, pp. 77, 78.
98. Report of the Committee, p. 85.

by the first official statement of entries issued by the American Government,[99] for the first year of its own existence, that for every five American tons entering American ports from over sea, there entered also three British; and that of the whole foreign tonnage there were six British to one of all other nations together.

Upon the whole, therefore, while regretting the evidence in the American statement which showed increasing activity by American shipping over that ascertained by themselves for the previous years,—to be accounted for, as was believed, by transient circumstances,—the committee, after consultation with the leading merchants in the American trade, thought better to postpone retaliation for the new tonnage duties, which contained no invidious distinction in favour of other foreign shipping against British. The system of trade regulation so far pursued had given good results, and its continuance was recommended; though bitterly antagonizing Americans, and maintaining ill-will between the two countries. Upon one point, especially desired by the United States, the committee was particularly firm. It considered that its Government might judiciously make one proposition—and one only—for a commercial treaty; namely, that there should be entire equality of treatment, as to duties and tonnage, towards the ships of both nations in the home ports of each other.

> But if Congress should propose (as they certainly will) that this principle of equality should be extended to the ports of our Colonies and Islands, and that the ships of the United States should there be treated as British ships, it should be answered that this demand cannot be admitted even as a subject of negotiation. . . . This branch of freight is of the same nature with the freight from one American state to another (that is, trade internal to the empire is essentially a coasting trade). Congress has made regulations to confine the freight, employed between the different states, to the ships of the United States, and Great Britain does not object to this restriction.[100]

---

99. Ibid., p. 52.
100. Report, p. 96.

The great advantages which have resulted from excluding American ships appear in the accounts given in this report; many of the merchants and planters of the West Indies, who formerly resisted this advice, now acknowledge the wisdom of it.[101]

The committee recognized that exclusion from the carrying trade of the British West Indies was in some degree compensated to the American carrier, by the permission given by the Government of France for vessels not exceeding sixty tons to trade with her colonies, actually much greater producers, and therefore larger customers. Santo Domingo in particular, in the period following the American war, had enjoyed a heyday of prosperity, far eclipsing that of all the British islands together. This was due partly to natural advantages, and partly to social conditions,—the planters being generally resident, which the British were not; but cheaper supplies through free intercourse with the American continent also counted for much. From the French West Indies there entered the United States in 1790, 101,417 tons of shipping, of which only 3,925 were French.[102] From the British Islands there came 90,375, but of these all but 4,057 were British.[103] Returning, the exports from the United States to the two were respectively, $3,284,656 and $2,077,757.[104] The flattering testimony borne by these figures to the meagreness of French navigation, in the particular quarter, needed doubtless to be qualified by reference to their home trade from the West Indies, borne in French ships. This amounted in 1788 to 296,435 tons from Santo Domingo alone;[105] whereas the British trade from all their islands employed but 133,736.[106] This, however, was the sole great carrying trade of France; to the United States she sent from her home ports less than 13,000 tons.

It was the opinion of the British committee that the privilege conceded to American shipping in the French islands was

---

101. Ibid., p. 94.
102. American State Papers, Commerce and Navigation, vol. x. p. 47.
103. Ibid., p. 45.
104. Ibid., p. 24.
105. Coxe, p. 171.
106. Committee's estimate; Report, p. 43.

so contrary to established colonial policy as to be of doubtful continuance. Still, in concluding its report with a summary of American commercial conditions, which it deemed were in a declining way, it took occasion to utter a warning, based upon these relations of America with the foreign colonies. In case of a commercial treaty, "Should it be proposed to treat on maritime regulations, any article allowing the ships of the United States to protect the property of the enemies of Great Britain in time of war" (that is, the flag to cover the goods), "should on no account be admitted. It would be more dangerous to concede this privilege to the United States than to any other foreign country. From their situation, the ships of these states would be able to cover the whole trade of France and Spain with their islands and colonies, in America and the West Indies, whenever Great Britain shall be engaged with either of those Powers; and the navy of Great Britain would, in such case, be deprived of the means of distressing the enemy, by destroying his commerce and thereby diminishing his resources." It is well to note in these words the contemporary recognition of the importance of the position of the United States; of the value of the colonial trade; of the bearing of commerce destruction on war, by "diminishing the resources" of an enemy; and of the opportunity of the United States, "from their situation," to cover the carriage of colonial produce to Europe; for upon these several points turned much of the troubles, which by their accumulation caused mutual exasperation, and established an antagonism that inevitably lent itself to the war spirit when occasion arose. The specific warning of the committee was doubtless elicited by the terms of the then recent British commercial treaty with France, in 1786, by which the two nations had agreed that, in case of war to which one was a party, the vessels of the other might freely carry all kinds of goods, the property of any person or nation, except contraband. Such a concession could be made safely to France,—was in fact perfectly one-sided in favouring Great Britain; but to America it would open unprecedented opportunity.

To the state of things so far described came the French Revolution; already begun, indeed, when the committee sat, but the course of which could not yet be foreseen. Its coincidence with the formation of the new government of the United States is well to be remembered; for the two events, by their tendencies, worked together to promote the antagonism between the United States and Great Britain, which was already latent in the navigation system of the one and the maritime aptitudes of the other. Washington, the first American President, was inaugurated in March, 1789; in May, the States General of France met. In February, 1793, the French Republic declared war against Great Britain, and in March Washington entered on his second term. In the intervening four years the British Government had persisted in maintaining the exclusion of American carrying trade from her colonial ports. During the same period the great French colony Santo Domingo had undergone a social convulsion, which ended in the wreck of its entire industrial system by the disappearance of slavery, and with it of all white government. The huge sugar and coffee product of the island vanished as a commercial factor, and with it the greater part of the colonial carriage of supplies, which had indemnified American shippers and agriculturists for their exclusion from British ports. Of 167,399 American tonnage entering American ports from the West Indies in 1790, 101,417 had been from French islands.

The removal of so formidable a competitor as Santo Domingo of course inured to the advantage of the British sugar and coffee planter, who was thus more able to bear the burden laid upon him to maintain the navigation of the empire, by paying a heavy percentage on his supplies. This, however, was not the only change in conditions affecting commerce and navigation. By 1793 it had become evident that Canada, Nova Scotia, and their neighbours, could not fill the place in an imperial system which it had been hoped they would take, as producers of lumber and food stuffs. This increased the relative importance of the West India Islands to the empire, just when the rise in price of sugar and coffee made it more desirable to develop their production. Should war come, the same reason would make it expedient to extend by conquest British productive territory in the Caribbean, and at the same time to cut off the supplies of such enemy's possessions as could not be subdued; thus crippling them, and removing their competition by force, as that of Santo Domingo had been by industrial ruin. These considerations tended further to fasten the interest of Great Britain upon this whole region, as particularly conducive to her navigation system. That cheapening supplies would stimulate production, to meet the favourable market and growing demands of the world, had been shown by the object-lesson of the French colonies; though as yet the example had not been followed.

At this time also Great Britain had to recognize her growing dependence upon the sea, because her home territory had ceased to be self-sufficing. Her agriculture was becoming inadequate to feeding her people, in whose livelihood manufactures and commerce were playing an increasing part. Both these, as well as food from abroad, required the command of the sea, in war as in peace, to import raw materials and export finished products; and control of the sea required increase of naval resources, proportioned to the growing commercial movement. According to the ideas of the age, the colonial monopoly was the surest means to this. It was therefore urgent to resort to measures which should develop the colonies; and the question was inevitable whether reserving to British navigation the trade by which they were supplied was not more than compensated by the diminished production, with its effect in lessening the cargoes employing shipping for the homeward voyage.

Thus things were when war broke out. The two objects, or motives, which have been indicated, came then at once into play. The conquest of the French West Indies, a perfectly legitimate move, was speedily undertaken; and meanwhile orders passing the bounds of recognized international law were issued, to suppress, by capture, their intercourse with the United States, alike in import and export. The blow of course fell upon American shipping, by which this traffic was almost wholly maintained. This was the beginning of a long series of arbitrary measures,

John Jay From the painting by Gilbert Stuart in Bedford (Jay) House, Katonah, N.Y.

dictated by a policy uniform in principle, though often modified by dictates of momentary expediency. It lasted for years in its various manifestations, the narration of which belongs to subsequent chapters. Complementary to this was the effort to develop production in British colonies, by extending to them the neutral carriage denied to their enemies. This was effected by allowing direct trade between them and the United States to American vessels of not over seventy tons; a limit substantially the same as that before imposed by France, and designed to prevent their surreptitiously conveying the cargoes to Europe, to the injury of British monopoly of the continental supply, effected by the *entrepôt* system, and doubly valuable since the failure of French products.

This concession to American navigation, despite the previous opposition, had become possible to Pitt, partly because its advisability had been demonstrated and the opportunity recognized; partly, also, because the immense increase of the active navy, caused by the war, created a demand for seamen, which by impressment told heavily upon the merchant navigation of the kingdom, fostered for this very purpose. To meet this emergency, it was clearly politic to devolve the supply of the British West Indies upon neutral carriers, who would enjoy an immunity from capture denied to merchant ships of a belligerent, as well as relieve British navigation of a function which it had never adequately fulfilled. The measure was in strict accord with the usual practice of remitting in war the requirement of the Navigation Act, that three-fourths of all crews should be British subjects; by which means a large number of native seamen became at once released to the navy. To throw open a reserved trade to foreign ships, and a reserved employment to foreign seamen, are evidently only different applications of the one principle, *viz.*: to draw upon foreign aid, in a crisis to which the national navigation was unequal.

Correlative to these measures, defensive in character, was the determination that the enemy should be deprived of these benefits; that, so far as international law could be stretched, neutral ships should not help him as they were encouraged to help the British. The welfare of the empire also demanded that native seamen should not be allowed to escape their liability to impressment, by serving in neutral vessels. The lawless measures taken to insure these two objects were the causes avowed by the United States in 1812 for declaring war. The impressment of American seamen, however, although numerous instances had already occurred, had not yet made upon the national consciousness an impression at all proportionate to the magnitude of the wrong; and the instructions given to Jay,[107] as special envoy in 1794, while covering many points at issue, does not mention this, which eventually overtopped all others.

---

107. American State Papers, Foreign Relations, vol. i. p. 472.

CHAPTER 3

From Jay's Treaty to the Orders in Council, 1794-1807

While there were many matters in dispute between the two countries, the particular occasion of Jay's mission to London in 1794 was the measures injurious to the commerce of the United States, taken by the British Government on the outbreak of war with France, in 1793. Neutrals are certain to suffer, directly and indirectly, from every war, and especially in maritime wars; for then the great common of all nations is involved, under conditions and regulations which by general consent legalize interference, suspension, and arrest of neutral voyages, when conflicting with acknowledged belligerent rights, or under reasonable suspicion of such conflict. It was held in the United States that in the treatment of American ships Great Britain had transcended international law, and abused belligerent privilege, by forced construction in two particulars. First, in June, 1793, she sent into her own ports American vessels bound to France with provisions, on the ground that under existing circumstance these were contraband of war. She did indeed buy the cargoes, and pay the freight, thus reducing the loss to the shipper; but he was deprived of the surplus profit arising from extraordinary demand in France, and it was claimed besides that the procedure was illegal. Secondly, in November of the same year, the British Government directed the seizure of "all ships laden with goods the produce of any colony belonging to France, or carrying provisions or other supplies for the use of any such colony." Neutrals were thus forbidden either to go to, or to sail from, any French colony for purposes of commercial intercourse. For the injuries suffered under these measures Jay was to seek compensation.

The first order raised only a question of contraband, of frequent recurrence in all hostilities. It did not affect the issues which led to the War of 1812, and therefore need not here be further considered. But the second turned purely on the question of the intercourse of neutrals with the colonies of belligerents, and rested upon those received opinions concerning the relations of colonies to mother countries, which have been related in the previous chapters. The British Government founded the justification of its action upon a precedent established by its own Admiralty courts, which, though not strictly new, was recent, dating back only to the Seven Years' War, 1756-63, whence it had received the name of the Rule of 1756. At that time, in the world of European civilization, all the principal maritime communities were either mother countries or colonies. A colonial system was the appendage of every maritime state; and among all there obtained the invariable rule, the formulation of which by Montesquieu has been already quoted, that "commercial monopoly is the leading principle of colonial intercourse," from which foreign states were rigorously excluded. Dealing with such a recognized international relation, at a period when colonial production had reached unprecedented proportions, the British courts had laid down the principle that a trade which a nation in time of peace forbade to foreigners could not be extended to them, if neutrals, in time of war, at the will and for the convenience of the belligerent; because by such employment they were "in effect incorporated in the enemy's navigation, having adopted his commerce and character, and identified themselves with his interests and purposes."[108]

During the next great maritime war, that of American Independence, the United States were involved as belligerents, and the only maritime neutrals were Holland and the Baltic States. These drew together in a league known historically as

---

108. Wheaton's International Law, p. 753.

the Armed Neutrality of 1780, in opposition to certain British interpretations of the rights of neutrals and belligerents; but in their formulated demands that of open trade with the colonies of belligerents does not appear, although there is found one closely cognate to it,—an asserted right to coasting trade, from port to port, of a country at war. The Rule of 1756 therefore remained, in 1793, a definition of international maritime law laid down by British courts, but not elsewhere accepted; and it rested upon a logical deduction from a system of colonial administration universal at that period. The logical deduction may be stated thus. The mother country, for its own benefit, reserves to itself both the inward and outward trade; the products of the colony, and the supplying of it with necessaries. The carriage of these commodities is also confined to its own ships. Colonial commerce and navigation are thus each a national monopoly. To open to neutrals the navigation, the carriage of products and supplies, in time of war, is a war measure simply, designed to preserve a benefit endangered by the other belligerent. As a war measure, it tends to support the financial and naval strength of the nation employing it; and therefore, to an opponent whose naval power is capable of destroying that element of strength, the stepping in of a neutral to cover it is clearly an injury. The neutral so doing commits an unfriendly act, partial between the two combatants; because it aids the one in a proceeding, the origin and object of which are purely belligerent.

When the United States in 1776 entered the family of nations, she came without colonies, but in the war attendant upon her liberation she had no rights as a neutral. In the interval of peace, between 1783 and 1793, she had endeavoured, as has been seen, to establish between herself and the Caribbean region those conditions of open navigation which were indicated as natural by the geographical relations of the two and their several products. This had been refused by Great Britain; but France had conceded it on a restricted scale, plainly contrived, by the limitation of sixty tons on the size of vessels engaged, to counteract any attempt at direct carriage from the islands to Europe, which was not permitted. Under these circumstances the United States was brought into collision with the Rule of 1756, for the first time, by the Order in Council of November 6, 1793. A people without colonies, and with a rapidly growing navigation, could have no sympathy with a system, coextensive with Europe, which monopolized the carriage of colonial products. The immediate attitude assumed was one of antagonism; and the wrong as felt was the greater, because the direct intercourse between the United States and the then great French colonies was not incidental to war, but had been established in peace. In principle, the Rule rested for its validity upon an exception made in war, for the purposes of war.

The British Government in fact had overlooked that the Rule had originated in European conditions; and, if applicable at all to the new transatlantic state, it could only be if conditions were the same, or equivalent. Till now, by universal usage, trade from colonies had been only to the mother country; the appearance of an American state with no colonies introduced two factors hitherto non-existent. Here was a people not identified with a general system of colonial exclusiveness; and also, from their geographical situation, it was possible for a European government to permit them to trade with its colonies, without serious trespass on the privileges reserved to the mother country. The monopoly of the latter consisted not only in the commerce and carrying trade of the colony, but in the *entrepôt*; that is, in the receipt and storage of the colonial produce, and its distribution to less favoured European communities,—the profit, in short, of the middleman, or broker. France had recognized, though but partially, this difference of conditions, and in somewhat grudging manner had opened her West Indian ports to American vessels, for intercourse with their own country. This trade, being permitted in peace, did not come under the British Rule; therefore by its own principle the seizures under it were unlawful. Accordingly, on January 8, 1794, the order was revoked, and the application limited to vessels bound from the West Indies direct to Europe.

This further Order in Council preserved the principle of the Rule of 1756, but it removed the cause of a great number of the seizures which had afflicted American shipping. There were nevertheless, among these, some cases of vessels bound direct to France from French colonies, laden with colonial produce; one of which was the first presented to Jay on his arrival in London. In writing to the Secretary of State he says, "It unfortunately happens that this is not among the strongest of the cases;" and in a return made three years later to Congress, of losses recovered under the treaty, this vessel's name does not appear. In the opinion of counsel, submitted to Jay, it was unlikely that the case would be reversed on appeal, because it unequivocally fell under the Rule.[109] It is therefore to be inferred that this principle, the operation of which was revived so disastrously in 1805, was not surrendered by the British Government in 1794. In fact, in the discussions between Mr. Jay and the British Minister of Foreign Affairs, there seems to have been on both sides a disposition to avoid pronouncements upon points of abstract right. It remained the constant policy of British negotiators, throughout this thorny period, to seek modes of temporary arrangement, which should obviate immediate causes of complaint; leaving principles untouched, to be asserted, if desirable, at a more favourable moment. This was quite contrary to the wishes of the United States Government, which repeatedly intimated to Jay that in the case of the Rule of 1756 it desired to settle the question of principle, which it denied. To this it had attached several other topics touching maritime neutral rights, such as the flag covering the cargo, and matters of contraband.[110]

Jay apparently satisfied himself, by his interviews and observation of public feeling in England, that at the moment it was vain for a country without a navy to expect from Great Britain any surrender of right, as interpreted by her jurists; that the most to be accomplished was the adoption of measures which should as far as possible extend the immediate scope of American com-

---

109. American State Papers, Foreign Relations, vol. i. p. 476.
110. American State Papers, Foreign Relations, vol. i. pp. 472-474.

merce, and remove its present injuries, presenting withal a probability of future further concessions. In his letter transmitting the treaty, he wrote:

> That Britain, at this period, and involved in war, should not admit principles which would impeach the propriety of her conduct in seizing provisions bound to France, and enemy's property on board neutral vessels, does not appear to me extraordinary. The articles, as they now stand, secure compensation for seizures, and leave us at liberty to decide whether they were made in such cases as to be warranted by the *existing* law of nations.[111]

The italics are Jay's, and the expression is obscure; but it seems to imply that, while either nation, in their respective claims for damages, would be bound by the decision of the commissioners provided for their settlement by the treaty, it would preserve the right to its own opinion as to whether the decision was in accordance with admitted law, binding in the future. In short, acceptance of the Rule of 1756 would not be affected by the findings upon the claims. If adverse to Great Britain, she could still assert the Rule in times to come, if expedient; if against the United States, she likewise, while submitting, reserved the right of protest, with or without arms, against its renewed enforcement.

"As to the principles we contend for," continued Jay, "you will find them saved in the conclusion of the twelfth article, from which it will appear that we still adhere to them." This conclusion specifies that after the termination of a certain period, during which Great Britain would open to American vessels the carrying trade between her West India Islands and the United States, there should be further negotiation, looking to the extension of mutual intercourse; "and the said parties will then endeavour to agree whether, in any, and what, cases neutral vessels shall protect enemy's property; and in what cases provisions and other articles, not generally contraband, may become

---

111. Ibid., p. 503.

such. But in the meantime, their conduct towards each other in these respects shall be regulated by the articles hereinafter inserted on those subjects."[112] The treaty therefore was a temporary arrangement, to meet temporary difficulties, and involved no surrender of principle on either side. Although the Rule of 1756 is not mentioned, it evidently shared the same fate as the other American propositions looking to the settlement of principles; the more so that subsequent articles admitted, not only the undoubted rule that the neutral flag did not cover enemy's goods, but also the vehemently disputed claim that naval stores and provisions were, or might be, contraband of war. Further evidence of the understanding of Great Britain in this matter is afforded by a letter of the law adviser of the Crown, transmitted in 1801 by the Secretary for Foreign Affairs to Mr. King, then United States Minister.

> The direct trade between the mother country and its colonies has not during this present war been recognized as legal, either by his Majesty's Government or by his tribunals."[113]

It is to be inferred that the Administration and the Senate, while possibly thinking Jay too yielding as a negotiator, reached the conclusion that his estimate of British feeling, formed upon the spot, was correct as to the degree of concession then to be obtained. At all events, the treaty, which provided for mixed commissions to adjudicate upon the numerous seizures made under the British orders, and, under certain conditions, admitted American vessels to branches of British trade previously closed to them, was ratified with the exception of the twelfth article. This conferred on Americans the privilege, long and urgently desired, of direct trade between their own country and the British West Indies on the same terms as British ships, though in vessels of limited size. Greatly desired as this permission had been, it came coupled with the condition, not only that cargoes

---

112. American State Papers, Foreign Relations, vol. i. p. 522.
113. American State Papers, Foreign Relations, vol. ii. p. 491.

from the islands should be landed in the United States alone, but also, while the concession lasted, American vessels should not carry "molasses, sugar, coffee, cocoa, or cotton" from the United States to any part of the world. By strict construction, this would prevent re-exporting the produce of French or other foreign colonies; a traffic, the extent of which during this war may be conceived by the returns for a single year, 1796, when United States shipping carried to Europe thirty-five million pounds of sugar and sixty-two million pounds of coffee, products of the Caribbean region. This article was rejected by the Senate, and the treaty ratified without it; but the coveted privilege was continued by British executive order, the regulations in the matter being suspended on account of the war, and the trade opened to American as well as British ships. Ostensibly a favour, not resting on the obligations of treaty, but on the precarious ground of the Government's will, its continuance was assured under the circumstances of the time by its practical utility to Great Britain; for the trade of that country, and its vital importance in the prevailing wars, were developing at a rate which outstripped its own tonnage. The numbers of native seamen were likewise inadequate, through the heavy demands of the Navy for men. The concurrence of neutrals was imperative. Under the conditions it was no slight advantage to have the islands supplied and the American market retained, by the services of American vessels, leaving to British the monopoly of direct carrying between the colonies and Europe.

Although vexations to neutrals incident to a state of war continued subsequent to this treaty, they turned upon points of construction and practice rather than upon principle. Negotiation was continuous; and in September, 1800, towards the close of Adams's administration, Mr. John Marshall, then Secretary of State, summed up existing complaints of commercial injury under three heads,—definitions of contraband, methods of blockade, and the unjust decisions of Vice-Admiralty Courts; coupled with the absence of penalty to cruisers making unwarranted captures, which emboldened them to seize on any ground, because certain to escape punishment. But no formal pronouncement further injurious to United States commerce was made by the British Government during this war, which ended in October, 1801, to be renewed eighteen months later. On the contrary, the progress of events in the West Indies, by its favourable effect upon British commerce, assisted Pitt in taking the more liberal measures to which by conviction he was always inclined. The destruction of Haiti as a French colony, and to a great degree as a producer of sugar and coffee, by eliminating one principal source of the world's supply, raised values throughout the remaining Caribbean; while the capture of almost all the French and Dutch possessions threw their commerce and navigation into the hands of Great Britain. In this swelling prosperity the British planter, the British carrier, and the British merchant at home all shared, and so bore without apparent grudging the issuance of an Order, in January, 1798, which extended to European neutrals the concession, made in 1795 to the United States, of carrying West Indian produce direct from the islands to their own country, or to Great Britain; not, however, to a hostile port, or to any other neutral territory than their own.

Although this Order in no way altered the existing status of the United States, it was embraced in a list of British measures affecting commerce,[114] transmitted to Congress in 1808. From the American standpoint this was accurate; for the extension to neutrals to carry to their own country, and to no other, continued the exclusion of the United States from a direct traffic between the belligerent colonies and Europe, which she had steadily asserted to be her right, but which the Rule of 1756 denied. The utmost the United States had obtained was the restitution of privileges enjoyed by them as colonists of Great Britain, in trading with the British West Indies; and this under circumstances of delay and bargain which showed clearly that the temporary convenience of Great Britain was alone consulted. No admission had been made on the point of right, as maintained by America. On the contrary, the Order of 1798 was at pains to

---

114. American State Papers, Foreign Relations, vol. iii. p. 263.

state as its motive no change of principle, but "consideration of the present state of the commerce of Great Britain, as well as of that of neutral countries," which makes it "expedient."[115]

Up to the preliminaries of peace in 1801, nothing occurred to change that state of commerce which made expedient the Order of January, 1798. It was renewed in terms when war again began between France and Great Britain, in May, 1803. In consideration of present conditions, the direct trade was permitted to neutral vessels between an enemy's colony and their own country. The United States remained, as before, excluded from direct carriage between the West Indies and Europe; but the general course of the British Administration of the moment gave hopes of a line of conduct more conformable to American standards of neutral rights. Particularly, in reply to a remonstrance of the United States, a blockade of the whole coast of Martinique and Guadaloupe, proclaimed by a British admiral, was countermanded; instructions being sent him that the measure could apply only to particular ports, actually invested by sufficient force, and that neutrals attempting to enter should not be captured unless they had been previously warned.[116] Although no concession of principle as to colonial trade had been made, the United States acquiesced in, though she did not accept, the conditions of its enforcement. These were well understood by the mercantile community, and were such as admitted of great advantage, both to the merchant and to the carrying trade. In 1808, Mr. Monroe, justifying his negotiations of 1806, wrote that, even under new serious differences which had then arisen:

> The United States were in a prosperous and happy condition, compared with that of other nations. As a neutral Power, they were almost the exclusive carriers of the commerce of the whole world; and in commerce they flourished beyond example, notwithstanding the losses they occasionally suffered.[117]

---

115. American State Papers, Foreign Relations, vol. iii. p. 265.
116. Ibid., p. 266.
117. Ibid., p. 175.

Under such circumstances matters ran along smoothly for nearly two years. In May, 1804, occurred a change of administration in England, bringing Pitt again into power. As late as November 8 of this year, Jefferson in his annual message said:

> With the nations of Europe, in general, our friendship and intercourse are undisturbed; and, from the governments of the belligerent powers, especially, we continue to receive those friendly manifestations which are justly due to an honest neutrality.

Monroe in London wrote at the same time, "Our commerce was never so much favoured in time of war."[118] These words testify to general quietude and prosperity under existing conditions, but are not to be understood as affirming absence of subjects of difference. On the contrary, Monroe had been already some time in London, charged to obtain from Great Britain extensive concessions of principle and practice, which Jefferson, with happy optimism, expected a nation engaged in a life and death struggle would yield in virtue of reams of argument, maintaining views novel to it, advanced by a country enjoying the plenitude of peace, but without organized power to enforce its demands.

About this time, but as yet unknown to the President, the question had been suddenly raised by the British Government as to what constituted a direct trade; and American vessels carrying West Indian products from the United States to Europe were seized under a construction of "direct," which was affirmed by the court before whom the cases came for adjudication. As Jefferson's expressions had reflected the contentment of the American community, profiting, as neutrals often profit, by the misfortunes of belligerents, so these measures of Pitt proceeded from the discontents of planters, shippers, and merchants. These had come to see in the prosperity of American shipping, and the gains of American merchants, the measure of their own losses by a trade which, though of long standing, they now claimed was one of direct carriage, because by continuous voyage, between the hos-

---

118. American State Papers, Foreign Relations, vol. iii. p. 98.

tile colonies and the continent of Europe. The losses of planter and merchant, however, were but one aspect of the question, and not the most important in British eyes. The products of hostile origin carried by Americans to neutral or hostile countries in Europe did by competition reduce seriously the profit upon British colonial articles of the same kind, to the injury of the finances of the kingdom; and the American carriers, the American ships, not only supplanted so much British tonnage, but were enabled to do so by British seamen, who found in them a quiet refuge—relatively, though not wholly, secure—from the impressment which everywhere pursued the British merchant ship. It was a fundamental conviction of all British statesmen, and of the general British public, that the welfare of the navy, the one defence of the empire, depended upon maintaining the carrying trade, with the right of impressment from it; and Pitt, upon his return to office, had noted—

> .... with considerable concern, the increasing acrimony which appears to pervade the representations made to you (the British Minister at Washington) by the American Secretary of State on the subject of the impressment of seamen from on board American ships.[119]

The issue of direct trade was decided adversely to the contention of the United States, in the test case of the ship *Essex*, in May, 1805, by the first living authority in England on maritime international law, Sir William Scott. Resting upon the Rule of 1756, he held that direct trade from belligerent colonies to Europe was forbidden to neutrals, except under the conditions of the relaxing Orders of 1798 and 1803; but the privilege to carry to their own country having been by these extended, it was conceded, in accordance with precedent, that products thus imported, if they had complied with the legal requirements for admission *to use* in the importing country, thenceforth had its nationality. They became neutral in character, and could be exported like native produce to any place open to commerce,

---

119. History of the United States, by Henry Adams, vol. ii. p. 423.

belligerent or neutral. United States shippers, therefore, were at liberty to send even to France French colonial products which had been thus Americanized. The effect of this procedure upon the articles in question was to raise their price at the place of final arrival, by all the expense incident to a broken transit; by the cost of landing, storing, paying duties, and reshipping, together with that of the delay consequent upon entering an American port to undergo these processes. With the value thus enhanced upon reaching the continent of Europe, the British planter, carrier, and merchant might hope that British West India produce could compete; although various changes of conditions in the West Indies, and Bonaparte's efforts at the exclusion of British products from the continent, had greatly reduced their market there from the fair proportions of the former war. In the cases brought before Sir William Scott, however, it was found that the duties paid for admission to the United States were almost wholly released, by drawback, on re-exportation; so that the articles were brought to the continental consumer relieved of this principal element of cost. He therefore ruled that they had not complied with the conditions of an actual importation; that the articles had not lost their belligerent character; and that the carriage to Europe was by direct voyage, not interrupted by an importation. The vessels were therefore condemned.

The immediate point thus decided was one of construction, and in particular detail hitherto unsettled. The law adviser of the Crown had stated in 1801, as an accepted precedent, "that landing the goods and paying the duties in the neutral country breaks the continuity of the voyage;"[120] but the circumstance of drawback, which belonged to the municipal prerogative of the independent neutral state, had not then been considered. The foundation on which all rested was the principle of 1756. The underlying motive for the new action taken—the protection of a British traffic—linked the War of 1812 with the conditions of colonial dependence of the United States, which was a matter of recent memory to men of both countries still in the vig-

---

120. American State Papers, Foreign Relations, vol. ii. p. 491.

our of life. The American found again exerted over his national commerce a control indistinguishable in practice from that of colonial days; from what port his ships should sail, whither they might go, what cargoes they might carry, under what rules be governed in their own ports, were dictated to him as absolutely, if not in as extensive detail, as before the War of Independence. The British Government placed itself in the old attitude of a sovereign authority, regulating the commerce of a dependency with an avowed view to the interest of the mother country. This motive was identical with that of colonial administration; the particular form taken being dictated, of course, then as before, by the exigencies of the moment,—by a "consideration of the present state of the commerce of this country." Messrs. Monroe and Pinkney, who were appointed jointly to negotiate a settlement of the trouble, wrote that "the British commissioners did not hesitate to state that their wish was to place their own merchants on an equal footing in the great markets of the continent with those of the United States, by burthening the intercourse of the latter with severe restrictions."[121] The wish was allowable; but the method, the regulation of American commercial movement by British force, resting for justification upon a strained interpretation of a contested belligerent right, was naturally and accurately felt to be a re-imposition of colonial fetters upon a people who had achieved their independence.

The motive remained; and the method, the regulation of American trade by British orders, was identical in substance, although other in form, with that of the celebrated Orders in Council of 1807 and 1809. Mr. Monroe, who was minister to England when this interesting period began, had gone to Spain on a special mission in October, 1804, shortly after his announcement, before quoted, that "American commerce was never so much favoured in time of war. . . . On no principle or pretext, so far, has more than one of our vessels been condemned." Upon his return in July, 1805, he found in full progress the seizures, the legality of which had been affirmed by Sir William Scott. A

---

121. Ibid., vol. iii. p. 145.

Monroe From the painting by Gilbert Stuart

prolonged correspondence with the then British Government followed, but no change of policy could be obtained. In January, 1806, Pitt died; and the ministry which succeeded was composed largely of men recently opposed to him in general principles of action. In particular, Mr. Fox, between whom and Pitt there had been an antagonism nearly lifelong, became Secretary for Foreign Affairs. His good dispositions towards America were well known, and dated from the War of Independence. To him Monroe wrote that under the recent measures "about one hundred and twenty vessels had been seized, several condemned, all taken from their course, detained, and otherwise subjected to heavy losses and damages."[122] The injury was not confined to the immediate sufferers, but reacted necessarily on the general commercial system of the United States.

In his first conversations with Monroe, Fox appeared to coincide with the American view, both as to the impropriety of the seizures and the general right of the United States to the trade in dispute, under their own interpretation of it; namely, that questions of duties and drawbacks, and the handling of the cargoes in American ports, were matters of national regulation, upon which a foreign state had no claim to pronounce. The American envoy was sanguine of a favourable issue; but the British Secretary had to undergo the experience, which long exclusion from office made novel to him, that in the complications of political life a broad personal conviction has often to yield to the narrow logic of particular conditions. It is clear that the measures would not have been instituted, had he been in control; but, as it was, the American representative demanded not only their discontinuance, but a money indemnity. The necessity of reparation for wrong, if admitted, stood in the way of admitting as a wrong a proceeding authorized by the last Government, and pronounced legal by the tribunals. To this obstacle was added the weight of a strong outdoor public feeling, and of opposition in the Cabinet, by no means in accord upon Fox's general views. Consequently, to Monroe's demands for a concession of prin-

---

122. American State Papers, Foreign Relations, vol. iii. p. 114.

ciple, and for pecuniary compensation, Fox at last replied with a proposition, consonant with the usual practical tone of English statesmanship, never more notable than at this period, that a compromise should be effected; modifying causes of complaint, without touching on principles.

> Can we not agree to suspend our rights, and leave you in a satisfactory manner the enjoyment of the trade? In that case, nothing would be said about the principle, and there would be no claim to indemnity.[123]

The United States Government, throughout the controversy which began here and lasted till the war, clung with singular tenacity to the establishment of principles. To this doubtless contributed much the personality of Madison, then Secretary of State; a man of the pen, clear-headed, logical, incisive, and delighting like all men in the exercise of conscious powers. The discussion of principles, the exposure of an adversary's weakness or inconsistencies, the weighty marshalling of uncounted words, were to him the breath of life; and with happy disregard of the need to back phrases with deeds, there now opened before him a career of argumentation, of logical deduction and exposition, constituting a condition of political and personal enjoyment which only the deskman can fully appreciate. It was not, however, an era in which the pen was mightier than the sword; and in the smooth gliding of the current Niagara was forgotten. Like Jefferson, he was wholly oblivious of the relevancy of Pompey's retort to a contention between two nations, each convinced of its own right: "Will you never have done with citing laws and privileges to men who wear swords?"

To neither President nor Secretary does it seem to have occurred that the provision of force might lend weight to argument; a consideration to which Monroe, intellectually much their inferior, was duly sensible.

> Nothing will be obtained without some kind of pressure, such a one as excites an apprehension that it will be

---

123. Monroe to Madison, April 28, 1806. American State Papers, vol. iii. p. 117.

increased in case of necessity; and to produce that effect it will be proper to put our country in a better state of defence, by invigorating the militia system and increasing the naval force.... Victorious at sea, Great Britain finds herself compelled to concentrate her force so much in this quarter, that she would not only be unable to annoy us essentially in case of war, but even to protect her commerce and possessions elsewhere, which would be exposed to our attacks.[124]

Most true when written, in 1805; the time had passed in 1813.

Harassed as they are already with war, and the menaces of a powerful adversary, a state of hostility with us would probably go far to throw this country into confusion. It is an event which the ministry would find it difficult to resist, and therefore cannot, I presume, be willing to encounter.... There is here an opinion, which many do not hesitate to avow, that the United States are, by the nature of their Government, incapable of any great, vigorous, or persevering exertion.[125]

This impression, for which it must sorrowfully be confessed there was much seeming ground in contemporary events, and the idiosyncrasies of Jefferson and Madison, in their full dependence upon commercial coercion to reduce Great Britain to concede their most extreme demands, contributed largely to maintain the successive British ministries in that unconciliatory and disdainful attitude towards the United States, which made inevitable a war that a higher bearing might have averted.

Monroe had been instructed that, if driven to it, he might waive the practical right to sail direct from a belligerent colony to the mother country, being careful to use no expression that would imply yielding of the abstract principle. But the general insistence of his Government upon obtaining from Great

---

124. American State Papers, Foreign Relations, vol. iii. p. 111.
125. American State Papers, Foreign Relations, vol. iii. pp. 109, 107.

Britain acknowledgment of right was so strong that he could not accept Fox's suggestion. The British Minister, forced along the lines of his predecessors by the logic of the situation, then took higher ground. "He proceeded to insist that," to break the continuity of the voyage, "our vessels which should be engaged in that commerce must enter our ports, their cargoes be landed, and the duties paid."[126] This was the full extent of Pitt's requirements, as of the rulings of the British Admiralty Court; and made the regulation of transactions in an American port depend upon the decisions of British authorities. Monroe unhesitatingly rejected the condition, and their interview ended, leaving the subject where it had been. The British Cabinet then took matters into its own hands, and without further communication with Monroe adopted a practical solution, which removed the particular contention from the field of controversy by abandoning the existing measures, but without any expression as to the question of right or principle, which by this tacit omission was reserved. Unfortunately for the wishes of both parties, this recourse to opportunism, for such it was, however ameliorative of immediate friction, resulted in a further series of quarrels; for the new step of the British Government was considered by the American to controvert international principles as much cherished by it as the right to the colonial trade.

Monroe's interview was on April 25. On May 17 he received a letter from Fox, dated May 16, notifying him that, in consequence of certain new and extraordinary means resorted to by the enemy for distressing British commerce, a retaliatory commercial blockade was ordered of the coast of the continent, from the river Elbe to Brest. This blockade, however, was to be absolute, against all commerce, only between the Seine and Ostend. Outside of those limits, on the coast of France west of the Seine, and those of France, Holland, and Germany east of Ostend, the rights of capture attaching to blockades would be forborne in favour of neutral vessels,

---

126. Ibid., p. 118.

bound in, which had not been laden at a port hostile to Great Britain; or which, going out, were not destined to such hostile port.[127] No discrimination was made against the character of the cargo, except as forbidden by generally recognized laws of war. This omission tacitly allowed the colonial trade by way of American ports, just as the measure as a whole tacitly waived all questions of principle upon which that difference had turned. After this, a case coming before a British court would require from it no concession affecting its previous rulings. By these the vessel still would stand condemned; but she was relieved from the application of them by the new Order, in which the Government had relinquished its asserted right. The direct voyage from the colony to the mother country was from a hostile port, and therefore remained prohibited; but the proceedings in the United States ports, as affecting the question of direct voyage, though held by the Court to be properly liable to interpretation by itself on international grounds, if brought before it, was removed from its purview by the act of its own Government, granting immunity.

The first impressions made upon Monroe by this step were favourable, as it evidently relieved the immediate embarrassments under which American commerce was labouring. There would at least be no more seizures upon the plea of direct voyages. While refraining from expressing to Fox any approbation of the Order of May 16, he wrote home in this general sense of congratulation; and upon his letters, communicated to Congress in 1808, was founded a claim by the British Minister at Washington in 1811, that the blockade thus instituted was not at the time regarded by him "as founded on other than just and legitimate principles." "I have not heard that it was considered in a contrary light when notified as such to you by Mr. Secretary Fox, nor until it suited the views of France to endeavour to have it considered otherwise."[128] Monroe, who was then Secretary of

---

127. For the text of this measure, see American State Papers, Foreign Relations, vol. iii. p. 267.
128. American State Papers, Foreign Relations, vol. iii. p. 443.

State, replied that with Fox "an official formal complaint was not likely to be resorted to, because friendly communications were invited and preferred. The want of such a document is no proof that the measure was approved by me, or no complaint made."[129] The general tenor of his home letters, however, was that of satisfaction; and it is natural to men dealing with questions of immediate difficulty to hail relief, without too close scrutiny into its ultimate consequences. It may be added that ministers abroad, in close contact with the difficulties and perplexities of the government to which they are accredited, recognize these more fully than do their superiors at home, and are more susceptible to the advantages of practical remedies over the maintenance of abstract principle.

The legitimacy of the blockade of May 16, 1806, was afterwards sharply contested by the United States. There was no difference between the two governments as to the general principle that a blockade, to be lawful, must be supported by the presence of an adequate force, making it dangerous for a vessel trying to enter or leave the port. "Great Britain," wrote Madison, "has already in a formal communication admitted the principle for which we contend." The difficulty turned on a point of definition, as to what situation, and what size, of a blockading division constituted adequacy. The United States authorities based themselves resolutely on the position that the blockaders must be close to the ports named for closure, and denied that a coast-line in its entirety could thus be shut off from commerce, without specifying the particular harbours before which ships would be stationed. Intent, as neutrals naturally are, upon narrowing belligerent rights, usually adverse to their own, they placed the strictest construction on the words "port" and "force." This is perhaps best shown by quoting the definition proposed by American negotiators to the British Government over a year later,—July 24, 1807. "In order to determine what characterizes a blockade, that denomination is given only to a *port*, where there is, by the disposition of

---

129. American State Papers, Foreign Relations, vol. iii. p. 446.

the Power which blockades it *with ships stationary*, an evident danger in entering."[130] Madison, in 1801, discussing vexations to Americans bound into the Mediterranean, by a Spanish alleged blockade of Gibraltar, had anticipated and rejected the British action of 1806.

> Like blockades might be proclaimed by any particular nation, enabled by its naval superiority to distribute its ships at the mouth of that or any similar sea, *or across channels or arms of the sea*, so as to make it dangerous for the commerce of other nations to pass to its destination. These monstrous consequences condemn the principle from which they flow.[131]

The blockade of May 16 offered a particularly apt illustration of the point at issue. From the entrance of the English Channel to the Straits of Dover, the whole of both shore-lines was belligerent. On one side all was British; on the other all French. Evidently a line of ships disposed from Ushant to the Lizard, the nearest point on the English coast, would constitute a very real danger to a vessel seeking to approach any French port on the Channel. Fifteen vessels would occupy such a line, with intervals of only six miles, and in combination with a much smaller body at the Straits of Dover would assuredly bring all the French coast between them within the limits of any definition of danger. That these particular dispositions were adopted does not appear; but that very much larger numbers were continually moving in the Channel, back and forth in every direction, is certain. As to the remainder of the coast declared under restriction, from the Straits to the Elbe,—about four hundred miles,—with the great entrances to Antwerp, Rotterdam, Amsterdam, the Ems, the Weser, and the Elbe, there can be no doubt that it was within the power of Great Britain to establish the blockade within the requirements of international law. Whether she did so was a question

---

130. American State Papers, Foreign Relations, vol. iii. p. 195. Author's italics.
131. Ibid., p. 371.

of fact, on which both sides were equally positive. The British to the last asserted that an adequate force had been assigned, "and actually maintained,"[132] while the blockade lasted.

The incident derived its historical significance chiefly from subsequent events. It does not appear at the first to have engaged the special attention of the United States Government, the general position of which, as to blockades, was already sufficiently defined. The particular instance was only one among several, and interest was then diverted to two other leading points,—impressment and the colonial trade. Peculiar importance began to attach to it only in the following November, when Napoleon issued his Berlin decree. Upon this ensued the exaggerated oppressions of neutral commerce by both antagonists; and the question arose as to the responsibility for beginning the series of measures, of which the Berlin and Milan Decrees on one side, and the British Orders in Council of 1807 and 1809 on the other, were the most conspicuous features. Napoleon contended that the whole sprang from the extravagant pretensions of Great Britain, particularly in the Order of May 16, which he, in common with the United States, characterized as illegal. The British Government affirmed that it was strictly within belligerent rights, and was executed by an adequate force; that consequently it gave no ground for the course of the French Emperor. American statesmen, while disclaiming with formal gravity any purpose to decide with which of the two wrong-doers the ill first began,[133] had no scruples about reiterating constantly that the Order of May 16 contravened international right; and in so far, although wholly within the limits of diplomatic propriety, they supported Napoleon's assertion. Thus it came to pass that the United States was more and more felt, not only in Europe, but by dissentients at home, to side with France; and as the universal contest grew more embittered, this feeling became emphasized.

While these discussions were in progress between Monroe

---

132. See, particularly, Foster to Monroe, July 3, 1811. American State Papers, Foreign Relations, vol. iii. p. 436.
133. Ibid., pp. 428, 439.

and Fox, the United States Government had taken a definite step to bring the dispute to an issue by commercial restriction. The remonstrances from the mercantile community, against the seizures under the new ruling as to direct trade, were too numerous, emphatic, and withal reasonable, to be disregarded. Congress therefore, before its adjournment on April 23, 1806, passed a law shutting the American market, after the following November 15, against certain articles of British manufacture, unless equitable arrangements between the two countries should previously be reached. This recourse was in line with the popular action of the period preceding the War of Independence, and foreshadowed the general policy upon which the Administration was soon to enter on a larger scale. The measure was initiated before news was received of Pitt's death, and the accession of a more friendly ministry; but, having been already recommended in committee, it was not thought expedient to recede in consequence of the change. At the same time, the Administration determined to constitute an extraordinary mission, for the purpose of "treating with the British Government concerning the maritime wrongs which have been committed, and the regulation of commercial navigation between the parties." For this object Mr. William Pinkney, of Maryland, was nominated as colleague to Monroe, and arrived in England on June 24.

The points to be adjusted by the new commissioners were numerous, but among them two were made pre-eminent,—the question of colonial trade, already explained, and that of impressment of seamen from American vessels. These were named by the Secretary of State as the motive of the recent Act prohibiting certain importations. The envoys were explicitly instructed that no stipulation requiring the repeal of that Act was to be made, unless an effectual remedy for these two evils was provided. The question of impressment, wrote Madison, "derives urgency from the licentiousness with which it is still pursued, and from the growing impatience of this country under it."[134] When Pinkney

---

134. The Instructions to Monroe and Pinkney are found in American State Papers, Foreign Relations, vol. iii. p. 120.

arrived, the matter of the colonial trade had already been settled indirectly by the Order of May 16, and it was soon to disappear from prominence, merged in the extreme measures of which that blockade was the precursor; but impressment remained an unhealed sore to the end.

To understand the real gravity of this dispute, it is essential to consider candidly the situation of both parties, and also the influence exerted upon either by long-standing tradition. The British Government did not advance a crude claim to impress American seamen. What it did assert, and was enforcing, was a right to exercise over individuals on board foreign merchantmen, upon the high seas, the authority which it possessed on board British ships there, and over all ships in British ports. The United States took the ground that no such jurisdiction existed, unless over persons engaged in the military service of an enemy; and that only when a vessel entered the ports or territorial waters of Great Britain were those on board subject to arrest by her officers. There, as in every state, they came under the law of the land.

The British argument in favour of this alleged right may be stated in the words of Canning, who became Foreign Secretary a year later. Writing to Monroe, September 23, 1807, he starts from the premise, then regarded by many even in America as sound, that allegiance by birth is inalienable,—not to be renounced at the will of the individual; consequently—

> .... when mariners, subjects of his Majesty, are employed in the private service of foreigners, they enter into engagements inconsistent with the duty of subjects. In such cases, the species of redress which the practice of all times has admitted and sanctioned is that of taking those subjects at sea out of the service of such foreign individuals, and recalling them to the discharge of that paramount duty, which they owe to their sovereign and to their country. That the exercise of this right involves some of the dearest interests of Great Britain, your Government is ready to acknowledge. . . . It is needless to repeat that these rights

existed in their fullest force for ages previous to the establishment of the United States of America as an independent government; and it would be difficult to contend that the recognition of that independence can have operated any change in this respect.[135]

Had this been merely a piece of clever argumentation, it would have crumbled rapidly under an appreciation of the American case; but it represented actually a conviction inherited by all the British people, and not that of Canning only. Whether the foundation of the alleged right was solidly laid in reason or not, it rested on alleged prescription, indorsed by a popular acceptance and suffrage which no ministry could afford to disregard, at a time when the manning of the Royal Navy was becoming a matter of notorious and increasing difficulty. If Americans saw with indignation that many of their fellow-citizens were by the practice forced from their own ships to serve in British vessels of war, it was equally well known, in America as in Great Britain, that in the merchant vessels of the United States were many British seamen, sorely needed by their country. Public opinion in the United States was by no means united in support of the position then taken by Jefferson and Madison, as well as by their predecessors in office, proper and matter-of-course as that seems to-day. Many held, and asserted even with vehemence, that the British right existed, and that an indisputable wrong was committed by giving the absentees shelter under the American flag. The claim advanced by the United States Government, and the only one possible to it under the circumstances, was that when outside of territorial limits a ship's flag and papers must be held to determine the nation, to which alone belonged jurisdiction over every person on board, unless demonstrably in the military service of a belligerent.

As a matter involving extensive practical consequences, this contention, like that concerning the colonial trade, had its origin from the entrance into the family of European nations of a new-comer, foreign to the European community of states and

---

135. American State Papers, Foreign Relations, vol. iii. pp. 200, 201.

their common traditions; indisposed, consequently, to accept by mere force of custom rules and practices unquestioned by them, but traversing its own interests. As Canning argued, the change of political relation, by which the colonies became independent, could not affect rights of Great Britain which did not derive from the colonial connection; but it did introduce an opposing right,—that of the American citizen to be free from British control when not in British territory. This the United States possessed in common with all foreign nations; but in her case it could not, as in theirs, be easily reconciled with the claim of Great Britain. When everyone whose native tongue was English was also by birth the subject of Great Britain, the visitation of a foreign neutral, in order to take from her any British seamen, involved no great difficulty of discrimination, nor—granting the theory of inalienable allegiance—any injustice to the person taken. It was quite different when a large maritime English-speaking population, quite comparable in numbers to that remaining British, had become independent. The exercise of the British right, if right it was, became liable to grievous wrong, not only to the individuals affected, but to the nation responsible for their protection; and the injury was greater, both in procedure and result, because the officials entrusted with the enforcement of the British claim were personally interested in the decisions they rendered. No one who understands the affection of a naval officer for an able seaman, especially if his ship be short-handed, will need to have explained how difficult it became for him to distinguish between an Englishman and an American, when much wanted. In short, there was on each side a practical grievance; but the character of the remedy to be applied involved a question of principle, the effect of which would be unequal between the disputants, increasing the burden of the one while it diminished that of the other, according as the one or the other solution was adopted.

Except for the fact that the British Government had at its disposal overwhelming physical force, its case would have shared that of all other prescriptive rights when they come into collision with present actualities, demanding their modification. It might be never so true that long-standing precedent made legal the impressment of British seamen from neutral vessels on the open sea; but it remained that in practice many American seamen were seized, and forced into involuntary servitude, the duration of which, under the customs of the British Navy, was terminable certainly only by desertion or death. The very difficulty of distinguishing between the natives of the two countries, "owing to similarity of language, habits, and manners,"[136] alleged in 1797 by the British Foreign Secretary, Lord Grenville, to Rufus King, the American Minister, did but emphasize the incompatibility of the British claim with the security of the American citizen. The Consul-General of Great Britain at New York during most of this stormy period, Thomas Barclay, a loyalist during the War of Independence, affirms from time to time, with evident sincerity of conviction, the wishes of the British Government and naval officers not to impress American seamen; but his published correspondence contains none the less several specific instances, in which he assures British admirals and captains that impressed men serving on board their ships are beyond doubt native Americans, and his editor remarks that "only a few of his many appeals on behalf of Americans unlawfully seized are here printed."[137] This, too, in the immediate neighbourhood of the United States, where evidence was most readily at hand. The condition was intolerable, and in principle it mattered nothing whether one man or many thus suffered. That the thing was possible, even for a single most humble and unknown native of the United States, condemned the system, and called imperiously for remedy. The only effectual remedy, however, was the abandonment of the practice altogether, whether or not the theoretic ground for such abandonment was that advanced by the United States. Long before 1806, experience had demonstrated, what had

---

136. American State Papers, Foreign Relations, vol. ii. p. 148.
137. Correspondence of Thomas Barclay, edited by George L. Rives, New York, 1894. For instances, see Index, Impressment.

been abundantly clear to foresight, that a naval lieutenant or captain could not safely be entrusted with a function so delicate as deciding the nationality of a likely English-speaking top man, whom, if British, he had the power to impress.

The United States did not refuse to recognize, distinctly if not fully, the embarrassment under which Great Britain laboured by losing the services of her seamen at a moment of such national exigency; and it was prepared to offer many concessions in municipal regulations, in order to exclude British subjects from American vessels. Various propositions were advanced looking to the return of deserters and to the prevention of enlistments; coupled always with a renunciation of the British claim to take persons from under the American flag. There had been much negotiation by individual ministers of the United States in the ordinary course of their duties; beginning as far back as 1787, when John Adams had to remonstrate vigorously with the Cabinet "against this practice, which has been too common, of impressing American citizens, and especially with the aggravating circumstances of going on board American vessels, which ought to be protected by the flag of their sovereign."[138] Again, in 1790, on hostilities threatening with Spain, a number of American seamen were impressed in British ports. The arrests, being within British waters, were not an infringement of American jurisdiction, and the only question then raised was that of proving nationality. Gouverneur Morris, who afterwards so violently advocated the British claim to impress their own subjects in American vessels on the seas,[139] was at this time in London on a special semi-official errand, committed to him by President Washington. There being then no American resident minister, he took upon himself to mention to the Foreign Secretary "the conduct of their pressgangs, who had taken many American seamen, and had entered American vessels with as little ceremony as those belonging to Britain;" adding, with a caustic humour characteristic of him, "I believe, my Lord, this is the only in-

---

138. Works of John Adams, vol. viii. p. 456.
139. Ante, p. 6.

stance in which we are not treated as aliens." He suggested certificates of citizenship, to be issued by the Admiralty Courts of the United States. This was approved by the Secretary and by Pitt; the latter, however, remarking that the plan was "very liable to abuse, notwithstanding every precaution."[140] Various expedients for attaching to the individual documentary evidence of birth were from time to time tried; but the heedless and inconsequent character and habits of the sailor of that day, and the facility with which the papers, once issued, could be transferred or bought, made any such resource futile. The United States was thus driven to the position enunciated in 1792 by Jefferson, then Secretary of State: "The simplest rule will be that the vessel being American shall be evidence that the seamen on board of her are such."[141] If this demand comprehended, as it apparently did, cases of arrest in British harbours, it was clearly extravagant, resembling the idea proceeding from the same source that the Gulf Stream should mark the neutral line of United States waters; but for the open sea it formulated the doctrine on which the country finally and firmly took its stand.

The history of the practice of impressment, and of the consequent negotiations, from the time of Jefferson's first proposition down to the mission of Monroe and Pinkney, had shown conclusively that no other basis of settlement than that of the flag vouching for the crew could adequately meet and remove the evil of which the United States complained; an evil which was not only an injury to the individuals affected, but a dishonour to the nation which should continue to submit. The subject early engaged the care of Rufus King, who became Minister to Great Britain in 1796. In 1797, Lord Grenville and he had a correspondence,[142] which served merely to develop the difficulties on both sides, and things drifted from bad to worse. Not only was there the oppression of the individual, but the safety of ships was endangered by the ruthless manner in which they were robbed

---

140. American State Papers, Foreign Relations, vol. i. pp. 123-124.
141. Jefferson's Works, Letter to T. Pinckney, Minister to Great Britain, June 11, 1792.
142. American State Papers, Foreign Relations, vol. ii. pp. 145-150.

Thomas Jefferson From the painting by Gilbert Stuart, in Bowdoin College, Brunswick, Me.

of their crews; an evil from which British merchant vessels often suffered.[143] On October 7, 1799, King again presented Grenville a paper,[144] summarizing forcibly both the abuses undergone by Americans, and the inconsistency of the British principle of inalienable allegiance with other British practices, which not only conferred citizenship upon aliens serving for a certain time in their merchant ships, but even attributed it compulsorily to seamen settled or married in the land.[145] No satisfactory action followed upon this remonstrance. In March, 1801, Grenville having resigned with Pitt, King brought the question before their successors, referring to the letter of October, 1799, as "a full explanation, requiring no further development on the present occasion."[146] At the same time, by authority from his Government, he made a definite proposal, "that neither party shall upon the high seas impress seamen out of the vessels of the other." The instructions for this action were given under the presidency of John Adams, John Marshall being then Secretary of State. On the high seas the vessels of the country were not under British jurisdiction for any purpose. The only concession of international law was that the ship itself could be arrested, if found by a belligerent cruiser under circumstances apparently in violation of belligerent rights, be brought within belligerent jurisdiction, and the facts there determined by due process of law. But in the practice of impressment the whole procedure, from arrest to trial and sentence, was transferred to the open sea; therefore to allow it extended thither a British jurisdiction, which possessed none of the guarantees for the sifting of evidence, the application of law, or the impartiality of the judge, which may be presumed in regular tribunals.

Yet, while holding clearly the absolute justice of the American contention, demonstrated both by the faulty character of the method and the outrageous injustice in results, let us not be blind to the actuality of the loss Great Britain was undergo-

---

143. See, for example, Naval Chronicle, vol. xxvi. pp. 215-221, 306-309.
144. Life and Correspondence of Rufus King, vol. iii. p. 115.
145. American State Papers, Foreign Relations, vol. ii. p. 150.
146. Ibid., p. 493.

ing, nor to her estimate of the compensation offered for the relinquishment of the practice. The New England States, which furnished a large proportion of the maritime population, affirmed continually by their constituted authorities that very few of their seamen were known to be impressed. Governor Strong of Massachusetts, in a message to the Legislature, said:

> The number of our native seamen impressed by British ships has been grossly exaggerated, and the number of British seamen employed by us has at all times been far greater than those of all nations who have been impressed from our vessels. If we are contending for the support of a claim to exempt British seamen from their allegiance to their own country, is it not time to inquire whether our claim is just?[147]

It seems singular now that the fewness of the citizens hopelessly consigned to indefinite involuntary servitude should have materially affected opinion as to the degree of the outrage; but, after making allowance for the spirit of faction then prevalent, it can be readily understood that such conditions, being believed by the British, must colour their judgment as to the real extent of the injustice by which they profited. At New York, in 1805, Consul-General Barclay,[148] who had then been resident for six years, in replying to a letter from the Mayor, said, "It is a fact, too notorious to have escaped your knowledge, that many of his Majesty's subjects are furnished with American protection, to which they have no title." This being brought to Madison's attention produced a complaint to the British Minister. In justifying his statements, Barclay wrote there were—

> .... innumerable instances where British subjects within a month after their arrival in these states obtain certificates of citizenship.... The documents I have already furnished you prove the indiscriminate use of those certificates.[149]

---

147. Niles' Register, vol. v. p. 343.
148. Correspondence, p. 210.
149. Correspondence, p. 219.

Representative Gaston of North Carolina, whose utterances on another aspect of the question have been before quoted,[150] said in this relation:

> In the battle, I think of the *President* and the *Little Belt*, a neighbour of mine, now an industrious farmer, noticed in the number of the slain one of his own name. He exclaimed, 'There goes one of my protections.' On being asked for an explanation, he remarked that in his wild days, when he followed the sea, it was an ordinary mode of procuring a little spending money to get a protection from a notary for a dollar, and sell it to the first foreigner whom it at all fitted for fifteen or twenty." But, while believing that the number of impressed Americans "had been exaggerated infinitely beyond the truth," Gaston added, with the clear perceptions of patriotism, "Be they more or less, the right to the protection of their country is sacred and must be regarded.[151]

The logic was unimpeachable which, to every argument based upon numbers, replied that the question was not of few or many, but of a system, under which American seamen—one or more—were continually liable to be seized by an irresponsible authority, without protection or hearing of law, and sent to the uttermost part of the earth, beyond power of legal redress, or of even making known their situation. Yet it can be understood that the British Government, painfully conscious of the deterioration of its fighting force by the absence of its subjects, and convinced of its right, concerning which no hesitation was ever by it expressed, should have resolved to maintain it, distrustful of offers to exclude British seamen from the American merchant service, the efficacy of which must have been more than doubtful to all familiar with shipping procedures in maritime ports. The protections issued to seamen as American citizens fell under the suspicion which in later days not infrequently attached

---

150. Ante, p. 7.
151. Niles' Register, vol. v. Supplement, p. 105.

to naturalization papers; and, if questioned by some of our own people, it is not to be wondered that they seemed more than doubtful to a contrary interest.

In presenting the proposition, "that neither party should impress from the ships of the other," King had characterized it as a temporary measure, "until more comprehensive and precise regulations can be devised to secure the respective rights of the two countries." Nevertheless, the United States would doubtless have been content to rest in this, duly carried out, and even to waive concession of the principle, should it be thus voided in practice. As King from the first foresaw,[152] acceptance by the British Cabinet would depend upon the new head of the Admiralty, Lord St. Vincent, a veteran admiral, whose reputation, and experience of over fifty years, would outweigh the opinions of his colleagues. In reply to a private letter from one of St. Vincent's political friends, sent at King's request, the admiral wrote:

> Mr. King is probably not aware of the abuses which are committed by American Consuls in France, Spain, and Portugal, from the generality of whom every Englishman, knowing him to be such, may be made an American for a dollar. I have known more than one American master carry off soldiers, in their regimentals, arms, and accoutrements, from the garrison at Gibraltar; and there cannot be a doubt but the American trade is navigated by a majority of British subjects; and a very considerable one too.

However inspired by prejudice, these words in their way echo Gaston's statements just quoted; while Madison in 1806 admitted that the number of British seamen in American merchant ships was "considerable, though probably less than supposed."

Entertaining these impressions, the concurrence of St. Vincent seemed doubtful; and in fact, through the period of nominal peace which soon ensued, and continued to May, 1803,

---

152. King to Thomas Erskine. Life of King, vol. iii. p. 401.

the matter dragged. When the renewal of the war was seen to be inevitable, King again urged a settlement, and the Foreign Secretary promised to sign any agreement which the admiral would approve. After conference, King thought he had gained this desired consent, for a term of five years, to the American proposition. He drew up articles embodying it, together with the necessary equivalents to be stipulated by the United States; but, before these could be submitted, he received a letter from St. Vincent, saying that he was of the opinion that the narrow seas should be expressly excepted from the operation of the clause, "as they had been immemorially considered to be within the dominions of Great Britain." Since this would give the consent of the United States to the extension of British jurisdiction far beyond the customary three miles from the shore, conceded by international law, King properly would not accept the solution, tempting as was the opportunity to secure immunity for Americans in other quarters from the renewed outrages that could be foreseen. He soon after returned to the United States, where his decision was of course approved; for though the Gulf Stream appeared to Jefferson the natural limit for the neutral jurisdiction of America, the claim of Great Britain to the narrow seas was evidently a grave encroachment upon the rights of others.

In later years Lord Castlereagh, in an interview with the American *chargé d'affaires*, Jonathan Russell, assured him that Mr. King had misapprehended St. Vincent's meaning; reading, from a mass of records then before him, a letter of the admiral to Sir William Scott, Judge of the High Court of Admiralty, "asking for counsel and advice, and confessing his own perplexity and total incompetency to discover any practical project for the safe discontinuance of the practice." "You see," proceeded Lord Castlereagh, "that the confidence of Mr. King on this point was entirely unfounded."[153]

Wherever the misunderstanding lay, matters had not advanced

---

153. Russell to the Secretary of State, Sept. 17, 1812. American State Papers, Foreign Relations, vol. iii. p. 593.

in the least towards a solution when Monroe reached England, in 1803, as King's successor. Up to that time, no tabular statement seems to have been prepared, showing the total number of seamen impressed from American vessels during the first war, 1793-1801; nor does the present writer think it material to ascertain, from the fragmentary data at hand, the exact extent of an injury to which the question of more or less was secondary. The official agent of the American Government, for the protection of seamen, upon quitting his post in London in 1802, wrote that he had transferred to his successor—

> A list of 597 seamen, where answers have been returned to me, stating that, having no documents to prove their citizenship, the Lords Commissioners of the Admiralty could not consent to their discharge.

Only seven cases then remained without replies, which shows at the least a decent attention to the formalities of intercourse; and King, in his letter of October 7, 1799, had acknowledged that the Secretary to the Admiralty had—

> .... given great attention to the numerous applications, and that a disposition has existed to comply with our demands, when the same could be done consistently with the maxims and practice adopted and adhered to by Great Britain.

The Admiralty, however, maintained that—

> .... the admission of the principle, that a man declaring himself to belong to a foreign state should, upon that assertion merely, and without direct or very strong circumstantial proof, be suffered to leave the service, would be productive of the most dangerous consequences to his Majesty's Navy.

The agent himself had written to the Secretary of the Admiralty:

> I freely confess that I believe many of them are British subjects; but I presume that all of them were impressed from

American vessels, and by far the greater proportion are American citizens, who, from various causes, have been deprived of their certificates, and who, from their peculiar situation, have been unable to obtain proofs from America.[154]

When Mr. Monroe arrived in England in 1803, after the conclusion of the Louisiana purchase from France, war had just re-begun. Instructions were sent him, in an elaborate series of articles framed by Madison, for negotiating a convention to regulate those matters of difference which experience had shown were sure to arise between the two countries in the progress of the hostilities. Among them, impressment was given the first place; but up to 1806, when Pinkney was sent as his associate, nothing had been effected, nor does urgency seem to have been felt. So long as in practice things ran smoothly, divergences of opinion were easily tolerable. Soon after the receipt of the instructions, in March, 1804,[155] the comparatively friendly administration of Addington gave way to that of Pitt; and upon this had followed Monroe's nine-months absence in Spain. Before departure, however, he had written, "The negotiation has not failed in its great objects,. . . . nor was there ever less cause of complaint furnished by impressment."[156] The outburst of seizure upon the plea of a constructively direct trade, already mentioned, had followed, and, with the retaliatory non-importation law of the United States, made the situation acute and menacing. Further cause for exasperation was indicated in a report from the Secretary of State, March 5, 1806, giving, in reply to a resolution of the House, a tabulated statement, by name, of 913 persons, who "appear to have been impressed from American vessels;" to which was added that "the aggregate number of impressments into the British service since the commencement of the present war in Europe (May, 1803) is found to be 2,273."[157]

---

154. American State Papers, Foreign Relations, vol. ii. pp. 427, 473.
155. Ibid., vol. iii. p. 90.
156. Ibid., p. 98.
157. American State Papers, Foreign Relations, vol. ii. pp. 776-798.

Confronted by this situation of wrongs endured, by commerce and by seamen, the mission of Monroe and Pinkney was to negotiate a comprehensive treaty of "amity, commerce, and navigation," the first attempted between the two countries since Jay's in 1794. When Pinkney landed, Fox was already in the grip of the sickness from which he died in the following September. This circumstance introduced an element of delay, aggravated by the inevitable hesitations of the new ministry, solicitous on the one hand to accommodate, but yet more anxious not to incense British opinion. The Prime Minister, in room of Mr. Fox, received the envoys on August 5, and, when the American demand was explained to him, defined at once the delicacy of the question of impressment.

> On the subject of the impressment of our seamen, he suggested doubts of the practicability of devising the means of discrimination between the seamen of the two countries, within (as we understood him) their respective jurisdictions; and he spoke of the importance to the safety of Great Britain, in the present state of the power of her enemy, of preserving in their utmost strength the right and capacity of Government to avail itself in war of the services of its seamen. These observations were connected with frequent professions of an earnest wish that some liberal and equitable plan should be adopted, for *reconciling the exercise* of this essential right with the just claims of the United States, and for removing from it all cause of complaint and irritation.[158]

In consequence of Mr. Fox's continued illness two negotiators, one of whom, Lord Holland, was a near relative of his, were appointed to confer with the American envoys, and to frame an agreement, if attainable. The first formal meeting was on August 27, the second on September 1.[159] As the satisfactory arrangement of the impressment difficulty was a *sine quâ non* to the ratification of any treaty, and to the repeal of the Non-Impor-

---

158. American State Papers, Foreign Relations, vol. iii. p. 131. Author's italics.
159. For the American report of these interviews, see Ibid., pp. 133-135.

tation Act, this American requirement was necessarily at once submitted. The reply was significant, particularly because made by men apparently chosen for their general attitude towards the United States, by a ministry certainly desirous to conciliate, and to retain the full British advantage from the United States market, if compatible with the preservation of an interest deemed greater still. "It was soon apparent that they felt the strongest repugnance to a formal renunciation, or the abandonment, of their claim to take from our vessels on the high seas such seamen as should appear to be their own subjects, and they pressed upon us with much zeal a provision" for documentary protection to individuals; "but that, subject to such protections, the ships of war of Great Britain should continue to visit and impress on the main ocean as heretofore."

In the preliminary discussions the British negotiators presented the aspect of the case as it appeared to them and to their public. They observed:

> . . . . that they supposed the object of our plan to be to prevent the impressment at sea of American seamen, and not to withdraw British seamen from the naval service of their country in times of great national peril, for the purpose of employing them ourselves; that the first of these purposes would be effectually accomplished by a system which should introduce and establish a clear and conclusive distinction between the seamen of the two countries, which on all occasions would be implicitly respected; that if they should consent to make our commercial navy a floating asylum for all the British seamen who, tempted by higher wages, should quit their service for ours, the effect of such a concession upon their maritime strength, on which Great Britain depended, not only for her prosperity but for her safety, might be fatal; that on the most alarming emergency they might be deprived, to an extent impossible to calculate, of their only means of security; that our vessels might become receptacles for deserters to any amount, and when once at sea might set at defiance

the just claims of the service to which such deserters belonged; that, even within the United States, it could not be expected that any plan for recovering British deserters could be efficacious; and that, moreover, the plan we proposed was inadequate in its range and object, inasmuch as it was merely prospective, confined wholly to deserters, and in no respect provided for the case of the vast body of British seamen *now* employed in our trade to every part of the world.

To these representations, which had a strong basis in fact and reason, if once the British principle was conceded, the American negotiators replied in detail as best they could. In such detail, the weight of argument and of probability appears to the writer to rest with the British case; but there is no adequate reply to the final American assertion, which sums up the whole controversy, "that impressment upon the high seas by those to whom that service is necessarily confided must under any conceivable guards be frequently abused;" such abuse being the imprisonment without trial of American citizens, as "a pressed man," for an indefinite period. Lord Cochrane, a British naval officer of rare distinction, stated in the House of Commons a few years later that "the duration of the term of service in his Majesty's Navy is absolutely without limitation."[160]

The American envoys were prevented by their instructions from conceding this point, and from signing a treaty without some satisfactory arrangement. Meantime, impressed by the conciliatoriness of the British representatives, and doubtless in measure by the evident seriousness of the difficulty experienced by the British Government, they wrote home advising that the date for the Non-Importation Act going into operation, now close at hand, should be postponed; and, in accordance with a recommendation from the President, the measure was suspended by Congress, with a provision for further prolongation in the discretion of the Executive. On September 13 Fox died, an event which introduced further delays, esteemed not unreason-

---

160. Cobbett's Parliamentary Debates, vol. xxvi. p. 1103.

able by Monroe and Pinkney. Their next letter home, however, November 11,[161] while reporting the resumption of the negotiation, announced also its failure by a deadlock on this principal subject of impressment:

> We have said everything that we could in support of our claim, that the flag should protect the crew, which we have contended was founded in unquestionable right.... This right was denied by the British commissioners, who asserted that of their Government to seize its subjects on board neutral vessels on the high seas, and also urged that the relinquishment of it at this time would go far to the overthrow of their naval power, on which the safety of the state essentially depended.

In support of the abstract right was quoted the report from a law officer of the Crown, which—

> .... justified the pretension by stating that the King had a right, by his prerogative, to require the services of all his seafaring subjects against the enemy, and to seize them by force wherever found, not being within the territorial limits of another Power; that as the high seas were extraterritorial, the merchant vessels of other Powers navigating on them were not admitted to possess such a jurisdiction as to protect British subjects from the exercise of the King's prerogative over them.

This was a final and absolute rejection of Madison's doctrine, that merchant vessels on the high seas were under the jurisdiction only of their own country. Asserted right was arrayed directly and unequivocally against asserted right. Negotiation on that subject was closed, and to diplomacy was left no further resort, save arms, or submission to continued injury and insult. The British commissioners did indeed submit a project,[162] in place of that of the United States, rejected by

---
161. American State Papers, Foreign Relations, vol. iii. pp. 137-140.
162. American State Papers, Foreign Relations, vol. iii. p. 140.

their Government. By this it was provided that thereafter the captain of a cruiser who should impress an American citizen should be liable to heavy penalties, to be enacted by law; but as the preamble to this proposition read, "Whereas it is not lawful for a belligerent to impress or carry off, from on board a neutral, seafaring persons *who are not the subjects of the belligerent,*" there was admitted implicitly the right to impress those who were such subjects, the precise point at issue. The Americans therefore pronounced it wholly inadmissible, and repeated that no project could be adopted "which did not allow our ships to protect their crews."

The provision made indispensable by the United States having thus failed of adoption, the question arose whether the negotiation should cease. The British expressed an earnest desire that it should not, and as a means thereto communicated the most positive assurances from their Government that—

> .... instructions have been given, and will be repeated and enforced, for the observance of the greatest caution in the impressing of British seamen; that the strictest care shall be taken to preserve the citizens of the United States from molestation or injury; and that prompt redress shall be afforded upon any representation of injury.[163]

To this assurance the American commissioners attached more value as a safeguard for the future than past experience warranted; but in London they were able to feel, more accurately than an official in Washington, the extent and complexity of the British problem, both in actual fact and in public feeling. They knew, too, the anxious wish of the President for an accommodation on other matters; so they decided to proceed with their discussions, having first explicitly stated that they were acting on their own judgment.[164] Consequently, whatever instrument might result from their joint labours would be liable to rejection at home, because of the failure of the impressment demand.

---

163. American State Papers, Foreign Relations, vol. iii. p. 140.
164. Ibid., p. 139.

The discussions thus renewed terminated in a treaty of amity, commerce, and navigation, signed by the four negotiators, December 31, 1806. Into the details of this instrument it is unnecessary to go, as it never became operative. Jefferson persisted in refusing approval to any formal convention which did not provide the required stipulation against impressment. He was dissatisfied also with particular details connected with the other arrangements. All these matters were set forth at great length in a letter[165] of May 20, 1807, from Mr. Madison to the American commissioners; in which they were instructed to reopen negotiations on the basis of the treaty submitted, endeavouring to effect the changes specified. The danger to Great Britain from American commercial restriction was fully expounded, as an argument to compel compliance with the demands; the whole concluding with the characteristic remark that, "as long as negotiation can be honourably protracted, it is a resource to be preferred, under existing circumstances, to the peremptory alternative of improper concessions or inevitable collisions." In other words, the United States Government did not mean to fight, and that was all Great Britain needed to know. That she would suffer from the closure of the American market was indisputable; but, being assured of transatlantic peace, there were other circumstances of high import, political as well as commercial, which rendered yielding more inexpedient to her than a commercial war.

At the end of March, 1807, within three months of the signature at London, the British Ministry fell, and the disciples of Pitt returned to power. Mr. Canning became Foreign Secretary. Circumstances were then changing rapidly on the continent of Europe, and by the time Madison's letter reached England a very serious event had modified also the relations of the United States to Great Britain. This was the attack upon the United States frigate *Chesapeake* by a British ship of war, upon the high seas, and the removal of four of her crew, claimed as deserters from the British Navy. Unofficial information of this

---

165. Ibid., pp. 166-173.

transaction reached England July 25, just one day after Monroe and Pinkney had addressed to Canning a letter communicating their instructions to reopen negotiations, and stating the changes deemed desirable in the treaty submitted. The intervention of the *Chesapeake* affair, to a contingent adjustment of which all other matters had been postponed, delayed to October 22 the reply of the British Minister.[166] In this, after a preamble of "distinct protest against a practice, altogether unusual in the political transactions of states, by which the American Government assumes to itself the privilege of revising and altering agreements concluded and signed on its behalf by its agents duly authorized for that purpose," Canning thus announced the decision of the Cabinet:

> The proposal of the President of the United States for proceeding to negotiate anew, upon the basis of a treaty already solemnly concluded and signed, is a proposal wholly inadmissible. And his Majesty has therefore no option, under the present circumstances of this transaction, but to acquiesce in the refusal of the President of the United States to ratify the treaty signed on December 31, 1806.

The settlement of the *Chesapeake* business having already been transferred to Washington, by the appointment of a special British envoy, this rejection of further consideration of the treaty closed all matters pending between the two governments, except those appertaining to the usual duties of a legation, and Monroe's mission ended. A fortnight later he sailed for the United States. His place as regularly accredited Minister to the British Court was taken by Pinkney, through whom were conducted the subsequent important discussions, which arose from the marked extension given immediately afterwards by France and Great Britain to their several policies for the forcible restriction of neutral trade.

Those who have followed the course of the successive events traced in this chapter, and marked their accelerating

---

166. American State Papers, Foreign Relations, vol. iii. p. 198.

momentum, will be prepared for the more extreme and startling occurrences which soon after ensued as a matter of inevitable development. They will be able also to understand how naturally the phrase, "Free Trade and Sailors' Rights," grew out of these various transactions, as the expression of the demands and grievances which finally drove the United States into hostilities; and will comprehend in what sense these terms were used, and what the wrongs against which they severally protested. "Free Trade" had no relation of opposition to a system of protection to home industries, an idea hardly as yet formulated to consciousness, except by a few advanced economists. It meant the trade of a nation carried on according to its own free will, relieved from fetters forcibly imposed by a foreign yoke, in which, under the circumstances of the time, the resurrection of colonial bondage was fairly to be discerned. "Sailors' Rights" expressed not only the right of the American seaman to personal liberty of action,—in theory not contested, but in practice continually violated by the British,—but the right of all seamen under the American flag to its protection in the voluntary engagements which they were then fulfilling. It voiced the sufferings of the individual; the personal side of an injury, the reverse of which was the disgrace of the nation responsible for his security.

It was afterwards charged against the administrations of Jefferson and Madison, under which these events ran their course to their culmination in war, that impressment was not a cause of the break between the two countries, but was adduced subsequently to swell the array of injuries, in which the later Orders in Council were the real determinative factor. The drift of this argument was, that the Repeal of the Orders, made almost simultaneously with the American Declaration of War, and known in the United States two months later, should have terminated hostilities. The British Government, in an elaborate vindication of its general course, published in January, 1813, stated that:

> .... in a manifesto, accompanying their declaration of hostilities, in addition to the former complaints against the

Orders in Council, a long list of grievances was brought forward; but none of them such as were ever before alleged by the American Government to be grounds for war.

In America itself similar allegations were made by the party in opposition. The Maryland House of Delegates, in January, 1814, adopted a memorial, in which it was said that:

> The claim of impressment, which has been so much exaggerated, but which was never deemed of itself a substantive cause of war, has been heretofore considered susceptible of satisfactory arrangement in the judgment of both the commissioners, who were selected by the President then in office to conduct the negotiation with the English ministry in the year 1806.[167]

The words of the commissioners in their official letters of November 11, 1806,[168] and April 22, 1807,[169] certainly sustain this statement as to their opinion, which was again deliberately affirmed by Monroe in a justificatory review of their course, addressed to Madison in February, 1808,[170] after his return. Gaston, speaking in the House in February, 1814, said: "Sir, the question of seamen was not a cause of this war. More than five years had passed over since an arrangement on this question, perfectly satisfactory to our ministers,(Monroe and Pinkney) had been made with Great Britain; but it pleased not the President, and was rejected. Yet, during the whole period that afterwards elapsed until the declaration of war, no second effort was made to adjust this cause of controversy."[171]

Gaston here is slightly in error as to fact, for the attack upon the *Chesapeake* was made by the Government the occasion for again demanding an abandonment of the practice of impressment from American merchant ships; but, accepting the statements otherwise, nothing more could be required of

---

167. Niles' Register, vol. v. p. 377.
168. American State Papers, Foreign Relations, vol. iii. p. 139.
169. Ibid., p. 161.
170. Ibid., p. 173.
171. Niles' Register, vol. v. Supplement, p. 102.

the Administration, so far as words went, than its insistence upon this relinquishment as a *sine quâ non* to any treaty. Its instructions to its ministers in 1806 had placed this demand first, not only in order, but in importance, coupling with it as indispensable only one other condition, the freedom of trade; the later and more extreme infringements of which were constituted by the Orders in Council of 1807. After protracted discussion, the American requirement as to impressment had been refused by Great Britain, deliberately, distinctly, and in the most positive manner; nor does it seem possible to concur with the opinion of our envoys that the stipulations offered by her representatives, while not sacrificing the British principle, did substantially and in practice secure the American demands. These could be satisfactorily covered only by the terms laid down by the Administration. Thereafter, any renewal of the subject must come from the other side; it was inconsistent with self-respect for the United States again to ask it, unless with arms in her hands. To make further advances in words would have been, not to negotiate, but to entreat. This, in substance, was the reply of the Government to its accusers at home, and it is irrefutable.

It is less easy—rather, it is impossible—to justify the Administration for refraining from adequate deeds, when the impotence of words had been fully and finally proved. In part, this was due to miscalculation, in itself difficult to pardon, from the somewhat sordid grounds and estimates of national feeling upon which it proceeded. The two successive presidents, and the party behind them, were satisfied that Great Britain, though standing avowedly and evidently upon grounds considered by her essential to national honour and national safety, could be compelled to yield by the menace of commercial embarrassment. That there was lacking in them the elevated instinct, which could recognize that they were in collision with something greater than a question of pecuniary profits, is in itself a condemnation; and their statesmanship was at fault in not appreciating that the enslaved conditions of the European continent had justly aroused in Great Britain an exaltation of spirit, which was prepared to undergo every extreme, in resistance to a like subjection, till exhaustion itself should cause her weapons to drop from her hands.

The resentment of the United States Government for the injuries done its people was righteous and proper. It was open to it to bear them under adequate protest, sympathizing with the evident embarrassments of the old cradle of the race; or, on the other hand, to do as she was doing, strain every nerve to compel the cessation of outrage. The Administration preferred to persist in its military and naval economies, putting forth but one-half of its power, by measures of mere commercial restriction. These impoverished its own people, and divided national sentiment, but proved incapable within reasonable time to reduce the resolution of the opponent. That that finally gave way when war was clearly imminent proves, not that commercial restriction alone was sufficient, but that coupled with military readiness it would have attained its end more surely, and sooner; consequently with less of national suffering, and no national ignominy.

Entire conviction of the justice and urgency of the American contentions, especially in the matter of impressment, and only to a less degree in that of the regulation of trade by foreign force, as impeaching national independence, is not enough to induce admiration for the course of American statesmanship at this time. The acuteness and technical accuracy of Madison's voluminous arguments make but more impressive the narrowness of outlook, which saw only the American point of view, and recognized only the force of legal precedent, at a time when the foundations of the civilized world were heaving. American interests doubtless were his sole concern; but what was practicable and necessary to support those interests depended upon a wide consideration and just appreciation of external conditions. That laws are silent amid the clash of arms, seems in his apprehension transformed to the conviction that at no time are they more noisy and compulsive. Upon this political obtuseness there fell a kind of poetical retribution, which gradually worked the Administration round to the position of substantially supporting Napoleon, when putting forth all his power to oppress the liberties of Spain, and of embarrassing Great Britain at the time when a people in insurrection against perfidy and outrage found in her their sole support. During these eventful five years, the history of which we are yet to trace, the bearing of successive British ministries towards the United States was usually uncompromising, often arrogant, sometimes insolent, hard even now to read with composure; but in the imminent danger of their country, during a period of complicated emergencies, they held, with cool heads, and with steady hands on the helm, a course taken in full understanding of world conditions, and with a substantially just forecast of the future. Among their presuppositions, in the period next to be treated, was that America might argue and threaten, but would not fight. There was here no miscalculation, for she did not fight till too late, and she fought wholly unprepared.

CHAPTER 4

From the Orders in Council to War, 1807-1812

When the treaty of December 31, 1806, was about to be signed, the British negotiators delivered to the Americans a paper, of the general character of which they had been forewarned, but which in precise terms then first came before them. Its origin was due to a pronouncement of the French Emperor, historically known as the Decree of Berlin, which was dated November 21, while the negotiations were in progress, but had become fully known only when they had reached a very advanced stage. The pretensions and policy set forth in the Decree were considered by the British Government to violate the rights of neutrals, with a specific and far-reaching purpose of thereby injuring Great Britain. It was claimed that acquiescence in such violations by the neutral, or submission to them, would be a concurrence in the hostile object of the enemy; in which case Great Britain might feel compelled to adopt measures retaliatory against France, through the same medium of neutral navigation. In such steps she might be fettered, should the present treaty take effect. In final ratification, therefore, the British Government would be guided by the action of the United States upon the Berlin Decree. Unless the Emperor abandoned his policy, or "the United States by its conduct or assurances will have given security to his Majesty that it will not submit to such innovations on the established system of maritime law, ... his Majesty will not consider himself bound by the present signature of his commissioners to ratify the treaty, or precluded from adopting such measures as may seem necessary for counteracting the designs of his enemy."[172] The American representatives transmitted this paper to Washington, with the simple observation that "we do not consider ourselves a party to it, or as having given it in any the slightest degree our sanction."[173]

The Berlin Decree was remarkable not only in scope and spirit, but in form. "It had excited in us apprehensions," wrote Madison to the United States minister in Paris, "which were repressed only by the inarticulate import of its articles, and the presumption that it would be executed in a sense not inconsistent with the respect due to the treaty between France and the United States." It bore, in fact, the impress of its author's mind, which, however replete with knowledge concerning conventional international law, defined in accordance with the momentary and often hasty impulses of his own will, and consequently often also with the obscurity attendant upon ill-digested ideas. The preamble recited various practices of Great Britain as subversive of international right; most of which were not so, but in accordance with long-standing usage and general prescription. The methods of blockade instituted by her were more exceptionable, and were given prominence, with evident reference to the Order of May 16, declaring the blockade of a long coast-line. It being evident, so ran the Emperor's reasoning, that the object of this abuse of blockade was to interrupt neutral commerce in favour of British, it followed that "whoever deals on the Continent in English merchandise favours that design, and becomes an accomplice." He therefore decreed, as a measure of just retaliation, "that the British Islands were thenceforward in a state of blockade; that all correspondence and commerce with them was prohibited; that trade in English merchandise was forbidden; and that all merchandise belonging to England, or" (even if neutral property) "proceeding from its manufactories and colonies, is lawful prize." No vessel coming directly from British dominions

---

172. American State Papers, Foreign Relations, vol. iii. p. 152.
173. Ibid., p. 147.

should be received in any port to which the Decree was applicable. The scope of its intended application was shown in the concluding command, that it should be communicated "to the Kings of Spain, of Naples, of Holland, of Etruria, and to our allies, whose subjects, like ours, are the victims of the injustice and barbarism of the English maritime laws."[174]

The phrasing of the edict was ambiguous, as Madison indicated. Notably, while neutral vessels having on board merchandise neutral in property, but British in origin, were to be seized when voluntarily entering a French port, it was not clear whether they were for the same reason to be arrested when found on the high seas; and there was equal failure to specify whether the proclaimed blockade authorized the capture of neutrals merely because bound to the British Isles, as was lawful if destined to a seaport effectively blockaded. Again, some of the proposed measures, such as refusal of admission to vessels or merchandise coming to French ports from British, were matters of purely local concern and municipal regulation; whereas the seizure of neutral property, because of English manufacture, was at least of doubtful right, if exercised within municipal limits, and certainly unlawful, if effected on the high seas. Whether such application was intended could not certainly be inferred from the text. The genius of the measure, as a whole, its inspiring motive and purpose, was revealed in the closing words of the preamble:

> This decree shall be considered as the fundamental law of the Empire, until England has acknowledged that the rights of war are the same an land and on sea; that it (war) cannot be extended to any private property whatever; nor to persons who are not military; and until the right of blockade be restrained to fortified places, actually invested by competent forces.

These words struck directly at measures of war resting upon long-standing usage, in which the strength of a maritime state such as Great Britain was vitally implicated.

---

174. American State Papers, Foreign Relations, vol. iii. p. 290.

The claim for private property possesses particular interest; for it involves a play upon words to the confusion of ideas, which from that time to this has vitiated the arguments upon which have been based a prominent feature of American policy. Private property at a standstill is one thing. It is the unproductive money in a stocking, hid in a closet. Property belonging to private individuals, but embarked in that process of transportation and exchange which we call commerce, is like money in circulation. It is the life-blood of national prosperity, upon which war depends; and as such is national in its employment, and only in ownership private. To stop such circulation is to sap national prosperity; and to sap prosperity, upon which war depends for its energy, is a measure as truly military as is killing the men whose arms maintain war in the field. Prohibition of commerce is enforced at will where an enemy's army holds a territory; if permitted, it is because it inures to the benefit of the conqueror, or at least from its restricted scope does not injure him. It will not be doubted that, should a prohibition on shore be disregarded, the offending property would be seized in punishment. The sea is the great scene of commerce. The property transported back and forth, circulating from state to state in exchanges, is one of the greatest factors in national wealth. The maritime nations have been, and are, the wealthy nations. To prohibit such commerce to an enemy is, and historically has been, a tremendous blow to his fighting power; never more conspicuously so than in the Napoleonic wars. But prohibition is a vain show, in war as it is in civil government, if not enforced by penalties; and the natural penalty against offending property is fine, extending even to confiscation in extreme cases. The seizure of enemy's merchant ships and goods, for violating the prohibition against their engaging in commerce, is what is commonly called the seizure of private property. Under the methods of the last two centuries, it has been in administration a process as regular, legally, as is libelling a ship for an action in damages; nor does it differ from it in principle. The point at issue really is not, "Is the property private?" but, "Is the method conducive to the purposes of war?" Property strictly private, on board ship, but not in process of commercial exchange, is for this reason never touched; and to do so is considered as disgraceful as a common theft.

Napoleon, as a ruler, was always poverty-stricken. For that reason he levied heavy contributions on conquered states, which it is needless to say were paid by private taxpayers; and for the same reason, by calling French ships and French goods "private property," he would compel for them the freedom of the sea, which the maritime preponderance of Great Britain denied them. He needed the revenue that commerce would bring in. So as to blockades. In denying the right to capture under a nominal blockade, unsupported by an effective force, he took the ground which the common-sense of nations had long before embodied in the common consent called international law. But he went farther. Blockade is very inconvenient to the blockaded, which was the role played by France. Along with the claim for "private property," he formulated the proposition that the right of blockade is restrained to fortified places; to which was afterwards added the corollary that the place must be invested by land as well as by sea. It is to be noticed that here also American policy showed a disposition to go astray, by denying the legitimacy of a purely commercial blockade; a tendency natural enough at that passing moment, when, as a weak nation, it was desired to restrict the rights of belligerents, but which in its results on the subsequent history of the country would have been ruinous. John Marshall, one of the greatest names in American jurisprudence, when Secretary of State in 1800, wrote to the minister in London:

> On principle it might well be questioned whether this rule (of blockade) can be applied to a place not completely invested, by land as well as by sea. If we examine the reasoning on which is founded the right to intercept and confiscate supplies designed for a blockaded town, it will be difficult to resist the conviction that its extension to towns invested by sea only is an unjustifiable encroach-

ment on the rights of neutrals. But it is not of this departure from principle (a departure which has received some sanction from practice) that we mean to complain.[175]

In 1810, the then Secretary of State enclosed to the American minister in London the letter from which this extract is taken, among other proofs of the positions maintained by the United States on the subject of blockade. The particular claim cited was not directly indorsed; but as its mention was unnecessary to the matter immediately in hand, we may safely regard its retention as indicative of the ideal of the Secretary, and of the President, Mr. Madison. In consequence, we find the minister, William Pinkney, in his letter of January 14, 1811, adducing Marshall's view to the British Foreign Secretary:

It is by no means clear that it may not fairly be contended, on principle and early usage, that a maritime blockade is incomplete, with regard to States at peace,[176] unless the place which it would affect is invested by land, as well as by sea. The United States, however, have called for the recognition of no such rule. They appear to have contented themselves, etc.[177]

The error into which both these eminent statesmen fell is military in character, and proceeds from the same source as the agitation in favour of exempting so-called private property from capture. Both spring from the failure to recognize a function of the sea, vital to the maintenance of war by states which depend upon maritime commerce. To forbid the free use of the seas to enemy's merchant ships and material of commerce, differs in no wise in principle from shutting his ports to neutral vessels, as well as to his own, by blockade. Both are aimed at the enemy's sources of supply, at his communications; and the penalty inflicted by the laws of war in both cases is the same,—forfeiture of the offending property. With clear recognition of this military principle involved, and of the importance of sustaining it by Great Britain, British high officials repeatedly declared that the

---

175. American State Papers, Foreign Relations, vol. ii. p. 488.
176. That is, as restrictive of neutral shipping.
177. American State Papers, Foreign Relations, vol. iii. p. 410.

Berlin Decree was to be regarded, not chiefly in its methods, but in its object, or principle, which was to deprive Great Britain of her principal weapon. This purpose stood avowed in the words, "this decree shall be considered the fundamental law of the Empire until England has acknowledged," etc. British statesmen correctly paraphrased this, "has renounced the established foundations, admitted by all civilized nations, of her maritime rights and interests, upon which depend the most valuable rights and interests of the nation."[178] The British authorities understood that, by relinquishing these rights, they would abandon in great measure the control of the sea, so far as useful to war. The United States have received their lesson in history. If the principle contended for by their representatives, Marshall and Pinkney, had been established as international law before 1861, there could have been no blockade of the Southern coast in the Civil War. The cotton of the Confederacy, innocent "private property," could have gone freely; the returns from it would have entered unimpeded; commerce, the source of national wealth, would have flourished in full vigour; supplies, except contraband, would have flowed unmolested; and all this at the price merely of killing some hundred thousands more men, with proportionate expenditure of money, in the effort to maintain the Union, which would probably have failed, to the immeasurable loss of both sections.

The British Government took some time to analyze the "inarticulate import" of the Berlin Decree. Hence, in the paper presented to Monroe and Pinkney, stress was laid upon the methods only, ignoring the object of compelling Great Britain to surrender her maritime rights. In the methods, however, instinct divined the true character of the plotted evil. There was to be formed, under military pressure, a vast political combination of states pledged to exclude British commerce from the markets of the Continent; a design which in execution received the name of the Continental System. The Decree being issued after the

---

178. Wellesley, Minister of Foreign Affairs, to Pinkney, Dec. 29, 1810; also, Feb. 11, 1811. American State Papers, Foreign Relations, vol. iii. pp. 409, 412. See also Sir Wm. Scott, in the Court of Admiralty, Ibid., p. 421.

battle of Jena, upon the eve of the evident complete subjugation of Prussia, following that of Austria the year before, there was room to fear that the predominance of Napoleon on the Continent would compel in Europe universal compliance with these measures of exclusion. It so proved, in fact, in the course of 1807, leading to a commercial warfare of extraordinary rigor, the effects of which upon Europe have been discussed by the author in a previous work.[179] Its influence upon the United States is now to be considered; for it was a prominent factor in the causes of the War of 1812.

Although in a military sense weak to debility, and politically not welded as yet into a nation, strong in a common spirit and accepted traditions, the United States was already in two respects a force to be considered. She possessed an extensive shipping, second in tonnage only to that of the British Islands, to which it was a dangerous rival in maintaining the commercial intercourse of Europe; while her population and purchasing power were so increased as to constitute her a very valuable market, manufacturing for which was chiefly in the hands of Great Britain. It became, therefore, an object with Napoleon, in prosecution of the design of the Berlin Decree, to draw the United States into co-operation with the European continental system, by shutting her ports to Great Britain; while the latter, confronted by this double danger, sought to impose upon neutral navigation—almost wholly American—such curtailment as should punish the Emperor and his tributaries for their measures of exclusion, and also neutralize the effect of these by forcing the British Islands into the chain of communication by which Europe in general was supplied. To retaliate the Berlin Decree upon the enemy, and by the same means to nourish the trade of Great Britain, was the avowed twofold object. The shipping of the United States found itself between hammer and anvil, crushed by these opposing policies. Napoleon banned it from continental harbours, if coming from England or freighted with English goods; Great

---

179. Influence of Sea Power upon the French Revolution and Empire, chaps. xvii., xviii.

Britain forbade it going to a continental port, unless it had first touched at one of hers; and both inflicted penalties of confiscation, when able to lay hands on a vessel which had violated their respective commands.

The lack of precision in the terms of the Berlin Decree exposed it from the first to much latitude of interpretation; and the Emperor remaining absent from France for eight months after its promulgation, preoccupied with an arduous warfare in Eastern Europe, the construction of the edict by the authorities in Paris made little alteration in existing conditions. Nevertheless, the impulse to retaliate prevailed; and the British ministry with which Monroe and Pinkney had negotiated, though comparatively liberal in political complexion, would not wait for more precise knowledge. The occasion was seized with a precipitancy which lent colour to Napoleon's assertion, that the leading aim was to favour their own trade by depressing that of others. This had already been acknowledged as the motive for interrupting American traffic in West India produce. Now again, one week only after stating to Monroe and Pinkney that they "could not believe that the enemy will ever seriously attempt to enforce such a system," and without waiting to ascertain whether neutral nations, the United States in particular, would, "contrary to all expectations, acquiesce in such usurpations,"[180] the Government on January 7, 1807, with no information as to the practical effect given to the Decree in operation, issued an Order in Council, which struck Americans directly and chiefly. Neutrals were forbidden to sail from one port to another, both of which were so far under the control of France or her allies that British vessels might not freely trade thereat. This was aimed immediately at trade along the coast of Europe, but it included, of course, the voyages from a hostile colony to a hostile European port already interdicted by British rulings, of which the new Order was simply an extension. It fell with particular severity on Americans, accustomed to go from port to port, not carrying on local coasting, but seeking markets

---

180. Declaration of the King's reservations, Dec. 31, 1806. American State Papers, vol. iii. p. 152.

for their outward cargoes, or making up a homeward lading. It is true that the Cabinet by which the Order was issued did not intend to forbid this particular procedure; but the wording naturally implied such prohibition, and was so construed by Madison,[181] who communicated his understanding to the British minister at Washington. Before this letter could reach London, the ministry changed, and the new Government refrained from correcting the misapprehension. For this it was taken to task in Parliament, by Lords Holland and Grenville.[182]

> Monroe had once written to the British Foreign Secretary that "it cannot well be conceived how it should be lawful to carry on commerce from one port to another of the parent country, and not from its colonies to the mother country."[183] This well meant argument, in favour of opening the colonial trade, gave to the new step of the British Cabinet a somewhat gratuitous endorsement of logical consistency. A consciousness of this may have underlain the remarkable terms in which this grievous restriction was imparted to the United States Government, as evincing the singular indulgence of Great Britain. Her minister in Washington, in conveying the Order to the State Department, wrote:

His Majesty, with that forbearance and moderation which have at all times distinguished his conduct, has determined for the present to confine himself to exercising his decided naval superiority in such a manner only as is authorized by the acknowledged principles of the laws of nations, and has issued an Order for preventing all commerce from port to port of his enemies; comprehending in this Order not only the ports of France, but those of other nations, as, either in alliance with France, or subject to her dominion, have, by measures of active offence or by the exclusion of British ships, taken part in the present war.[184]

---

181. American State Papers, Foreign Relations, vol. iii. p. 159.
182. Cobbett's Parliamentary Debates, vol. x. p. 1274.
183. Aug. 12, 1805. American State Papers, Foreign Relations, vol. iii. p. 104.
184. American State Papers, Foreign Relations, vol. iii. p. 158.

These words characterized the measure as strictly retaliatory. They implied that the extra-legal action of the enemy would warrant extra-legal action by Great Britain, but asserted expressly that the present step was sanctioned by existing law,—"in such a manner only as is authorized by the acknowledged principles of the law of nations." The prohibition of coasting trade could be brought under the law of nations only by invoking the Rule of 1756, forbidding neutrals to undertake for a state at war employment denied to them in peace. Of this, coasting was a precise instance; but to call the Rule an acknowledged principle of the law of nations was an assumption peculiarly calculated to irritate Madison, who had expended reams in refutation. He penned two careful replies, logical, incisive, and showing the profound knowledge of the subject which distinguished him; but in a time of political convulsion he contended in vain against men who wore swords and thought their country's existence imperilled.

The United States authorities argued by text and precedent. To the end they persisted in shutting their eyes to the important fact, recognized intuitively by Great Britain, that the Berlin Decree was no isolated measure, to be discussed on its separate merits, but an incident in an unprecedented political combination, already sufficiently defined in tendency, which overturned the traditional system of Europe. It destroyed the checks inherent in the balance of power, concentrating the whole in the hands of Napoleon, to whom there remained on the Continent only one valid counterweight, the Emperor of Russia, whom he soon after contrived to lead into his scheme of policy. The balance of power was thus reduced to the opposing scales of Great Britain and France, and for five years so remained. The Continental System, embracing all the rest of Europe, was arrayed against Great Britain, and might well look to destroy her, if it could command the support of the United States. Founded upon armed power, it proposed by continuous exertion of the same means to undermine the bases of British prosperity, and so to subvert the British Empire. The enterprise was distinctly military, and could be met only by measures of a similar character, to which existing international law was unequal. The corner-stone was the military power of Napoleon, which, by nullifying the independence of the continental states, compelled them to adopt the methods of the Berlin Decree contrary to their will, and contrary to the wishes, the interests, and the bare well-being of their populations. "You will see," wrote an observant American representative abroad, "that Napoleon stalks at a gigantic stride among the pygmy monarchs of Europe, and bends them to his policy. It is even an equal chance if Russia, after all her blustering, does not accede to his demands without striking a blow."[185] To meet the danger Great Britain opposed a maritime dominion, equally exclusive, equally founded on force, and exercised in equally arbitrary fashion over the populations of the sea.

At the end of March, 1807, the British Cabinet with which Monroe and Pinkney had negotiated went out of office. Their successors came in prepared for extreme action in consequence of the Berlin Decree; but their hand was for the moment stayed, because its enforcement remained in abeyance, owing to the Emperor's continued absence in the field. Towards the claims of the United States their attitude was likely to be uncompromising; and the Secretary for Foreign Affairs, Canning, to whom fell the expression of the Government's views and purposes, possessed an adroitness in fastening upon minor weaknesses in a case, and postponing to such the consideration of the important point at issue, which, coupled with a peremptoriness of tone often bordering on insolence, effected nothing towards conciliating a people believed to be both unready and unwilling to fight. The American envoys, at their first interview, in April, met him with the proposition of their Government to reopen negotiations on the basis of the treaty of December 31. Learning from them that the treaty would not be ratified without a satisfactory arrangement concerning impressment, Canning asked what relations would then obtain between the two nations. The reply was that the United States Government wished

---

185. Jonathan Russell to the Secretary of State, Nov. 15, 1811. U.S. State Department MSS.

them placed informally on the most friendly footing; that is, that an understanding should be reached as to practical action to be expected on either side, without concessions of principle.[186] As final instructions from Washington were yet to come, it was agreed that the matter should be postponed. When they arrived, on July 16, the envoys drew up a letter, submitting the various changes desired; but conveying also the fixed determination of the President—

> .... to decline any arrangement, formal or informal, which does not comprise a provision against impressments from American vessels on the high seas, and which would, notwithstanding, be a bar to legislative measures by Congress for controlling that species of aggression.[187]

This letter was dated July 24, but by the time it could be delivered news arrived which threw into the background all matters of negotiation and illustrated with what respect British naval officers regarded "the instructions, repeated and enforced, for the observance of the greatest caution in impressing British seamen."[188] It is probable, indeed, that the change of ministry, and the well-understood tone of the new-comers, had modified the influence of these restraining orders; and Canning evidently felt that such an inference was natural, for Monroe reported his noticeable desire "to satisfy me that no new orders had been issued by the present ministry to the commandant of the British squadron at Halifax," who was primarily responsible for the lamentable occurrence which here traversed the course of negotiation. It had been believed, and doubtless correctly, that some deserters from British ships of war had found their way into the naval service of the United States. In June, 1807, the American frigate *Chesapeake*, bearing the broad pendant of Commodore James Barron, had been fitting for sea in Hampton Roads. At this time two French ships of war were

---
186. American State Papers, Foreign Relations, vol. iii. pp. 154, 160.
187. Ibid., p. 166.
188. The British Commissioners to Monroe and Pinkney, Nov. 8, 1806. Ibid., p. 140.

lying off Annapolis, a hundred miles up Chesapeake Bay; and, to prevent their getting to sea, a small British squadron had been assembled at Lynnhaven Bay, just within Cape Henry, a dozen miles below the *Chesapeake*'s anchorage. They were thus, as Jefferson said, enjoying the hospitality of the United States. On June 22 the American frigate got under way for sea, and as she stood down, one of the British, the *Leopard* of fifty guns, also made sail, going out ahead of her. Shortly after noon the *Chesapeake* passed the Capes. When about ten miles outside, a little after three o'clock, the *Leopard* approached, and hailed that she had a despatch for Commodore Barron. This was brought on board by a lieutenant, and proved to be a letter from the captain of the *Leopard*, enclosing an order from Vice-Admiral Berkeley, in charge of the Halifax station, "requiring and directing the captains and commanders of his Majesty's vessels under my command, in case of meeting the American frigate, the *Chesapeake*, at sea, without the limits of the United States, to show her captain this order, and to require to search his ship for deserters from certain British ships," specified by name. Upon Barron's refusal, the *Leopard* fired into the *Chesapeake*, killed or wounded twenty-one men, and reduced her to submission. The order for search was then enforced. Four of the American crew, considered to be British deserters, were taken away. Of these, one was hanged; one died; and the other two, after prolonged disputation, were returned five years later to the deck of the *Chesapeake*, in formal reparation.

Word of this transaction reached the British Government before it did Monroe, who was still sole American minister for all matters except the special mission. Canning at once wrote him a letter of regret, and spontaneously promised "prompt and effectual reparation," if upon receipt of full information British officers should prove culpable. Four days later, July 29, Monroe and Canning met in pursuance of a previous appointment, the object of which had been to discuss complaints against the conduct of British ships of war on the coast of the United States. The *Chesapeake* business naturally now overshadowed all others.

Monroe maintained that, on principle, a ship of war could not be entered to search for deserters, or for any purpose, without violating the sovereignty of her nation. Canning was very guarded; no admission of principle could then be obtained from him; but he gave Monroe to understand that, in whatever light the action of the British officer should be viewed by his Government, the point whether the men seized were British subjects or American citizens would be of consideration, in the question of restoring them, now that they were in British hands. Monroe, in accordance with the position of his Government on the subject of impressment, replied that the determining consideration was not the nationality of the men, but of the ship, the flag of which had been insulted.

The conference ended with an understanding that Monroe would send in a note embodying his position and claims. This he did the same day;[189] but his statements were grounded upon newspaper accounts, as the British Government had not yet published Berkeley's official report. He would not await the positive information that must soon be given out, but applied strong language to acts not yet precisely ascertained; and he mingled with the *Chesapeake* affair other very real, but different and minor, subjects of complaint, seemingly with a view to cumulative effect. He thus made the mistake of encumbering with extraneous or needless details a subject which required separate, undivided, and lucid insistence; while Canning found an opportunity, particularly congenial to his temperament, to escape under a cloud of dignified words from the simple admission of wrong, and promise of reparation, which otherwise he would have had to face. He could assume a tone of haughty rebuke, where only that of apology should have been left open. His reply ran thus:

> I have the honour to acknowledge your official note of the 29th *ultimo*, which I have lost no time in laying before the King.
>
> As *the statement* of the transaction to which this note

---
189. American State Papers, Foreign Relations, vol. iii. p. 187.

refers is not brought forward either by the authority of the Government of the United States, *or with any precise knowledge of the facts on which it is founded*, it might have been sufficient for me to express to you his Majesty's readiness to take the whole of the circumstances of the case, *when fully disclosed*, into his consideration, and to make reparation for any *alleged injury* to the sovereignty of the United States, whenever it should be *clearly shown* that such injury has been *actually sustained*, and that such reparation is *really due*.

Of the existence of such a disposition on the part of the British Government, you, Sir, cannot be ignorant; I have already assured you of it, though in an unofficial form, by the letter which I addressed you on the first receipt of the intelligence of this unfortunate transaction; and I may, perhaps, be permitted to express my surprise, after such an assurance, at the tone of that representation which I have just had the honour to receive from you.

But the earnest desire of his Majesty to evince, in the most satisfactory manner, the principles of justice and moderation by which he is uniformly actuated, has not permitted him to hesitate in commanding me to assure you, that his Majesty neither does, nor has at any time maintained the pretension of a right to search ships of war, in the national service of any State, for deserters.

If, therefore, *the statement in your note should prove to be correct*, and to contain all the circumstances of the case, upon which the complaint is intended to be made, and it shall appear that the action of his Majesty's officers rested on no other grounds than the simple and unqualified assertion of the pretension above referred to, his Majesty has no difficulty in disavowing the act, and will have no difficulty in manifesting his displeasure at the conduct of his officers.

With respect to the other causes of complaint, (whatever they may be,) which are hinted at in your note, I perfectly agree with you, in the sentiment which you express, as to the propriety of not involving them in a question, which of itself is of sufficient importance to claim a separate and most serious consideration.

I have only to lament that the same sentiment did not induce you to abstain from alluding to these subjects, on an occasion which you were yourself of opinion was not favourable for pursuing the discussion of them.[190]

I have the honour to be, with great consideration, your most obedient, humble servant

George Canning

James Monroe, Esq. &c.

While the right of the occasion was wholly with the American nation, the honours of the discussion, the weight of the first broadside, rested so far with the British Secretary; the more so that Monroe, by his manner of adducing his "other causes of complaint," admitted their irrelevancy and yet characterized them irritatingly to his correspondent.

> I might state other examples of great indignity and outrage, many of which are of recent date, to which the United States have been exposed off their own coast, and even within several of their harbours, from the British squadron; but it is improper to mingle them with the present more serious causes of complaint.

This invited Canning's retort,—*You do mingle them, in the same sentence in which you admit the impropriety.* And why, he shrewdly insinuated, precipitate action ahead of knowledge, when the facts must soon be known? The unspoken reason is evident. Because a government, which by its own fault is weak, will try with big words to atone to the public opinion of its people for that which it cannot, or will not, effect in deeds. Bluster, whether measured or intemperate in terms, is bluster still, as long as it means only talk, not act.

Monroe comforted himself that, though Canning's note was "harsh," he had obtained the "concession of the point de-

---

190. American State Papers, Foreign Relations, vol. iii. p. 188. Author's italics.

sired."[191] he had in fact obtained less than would probably have resulted from a policy of which the premises were assured, and the demands rigorously limited to the particular offence. Canning's note set the key for the subsequent British correspondence, and dictated the methods by which he persistently evaded an amends spontaneously promised under the first emotions produced by an odious aggression. He continued to offer it; but under conditions impossible of acceptance, and as discreditable to the party at fault as they were humiliating to the one offended. In themselves, the first notes exchanged between Monroe and Canning are trivial, a revelation chiefly of individual characteristics. Their interest lies in the exemplification of the general course of the American administration, imposed by its years of temporizing, of money-getting, and of military parsimony. President Jefferson in America met the occasion precisely as did Monroe in London, with the same result of a sharp correspondence, abounding in strong language, but affording Canning further opportunity to confuse issues and escape from reparations, which, however just and wise, were distasteful. It was a Pyrrhic victory for the British minister, destroying the last chance of conciliating American acquiescence in a line of action forced upon Great Britain by Napoleon; but as a mere question of dialectics he had scored a success.

When the news of the *Chesapeake* outrage was received in Washington, Jefferson issued a proclamation, dated July 2, 1807, suited chiefly for home consumption, as the phrase goes. He began with a recitation of the various wrongs and irritations, undeniable and extreme, which his long-suffering Administration had endured from British cruisers, and to which Monroe alluded in his note to Canning. Upon this followed an account of the *Chesapeake* incident, thus inextricably entangled with other circumstances differing from it in essential feature. Then, taking occasion by a transaction which, however reprehensible, was wholly external to the territory of the United States,—un-

---

191. Monroe to Madison, Aug. 4, 1807. American State Papers, Foreign Relations, vol. iii. p. 186.

less construed to extend to the Gulf Stream, according to one of Jefferson's day-dreams,—action was based upon the necessity of providing for the internal peace of the nation and the safety of its citizens, and consequently of refusing admission to British ships of war, as inconsistent with these objects. Therefore:

> . . . . all armed vessels, bearing commissions under the Government of Great Britain, now within the harbours of the United States, are required immediately and without any delay to depart from the same; and entrance of all the said harbours and waters is interdicted to the said armed vessels, and to all others bearing commissions under the authority of the British Government.

Vessels carrying despatches were excepted.

This procedure had the appearance of energy which momentarily satisfies a public demand that something shall be done. It also afforded Canning the peg on which to hang a grievance, and dexterously to prolong discussion until the matter became stale in public interest. By the irrelevancy of the punishment to the crime, and by the intrusion of secondary matters into the complaint, the *Chesapeake* issue, essentially clear, sharp, and impressive, became hopelessly confused with other considerations. Upon the proclamation followed a despatch from Madison to Monroe, July 6, which opened with the just words, "This enormity is not a subject for discussion," and then proceeded to discuss at length. Demand was to be made, most properly, for a formal disavowal, and for the restoration of the seamen to the ship. This could have been formulated in six lines, and had it stood alone could scarcely have been refused; but to it was attached indissolubly an extraneous requirement. "As a security for the future, an entire abolition of impressment from vessels[192] under the flag of the United States, if not already arranged, is also to make an *indispensable part of the satisfaction.*"[193]

This made accommodation hopeless. Practically, it was an ul-

---

192. That is, all vessels, including merchantmen.
193. American State Papers, Foreign Relations, vol. iii. pp. 183-185. Author's italics.

timatum; for recent notorious discussion had demonstrated that this the British Government would not yield, and as it differed essentially from the point at issue in the *Chesapeake* affair, there was no reason to expect a change of attitude in consequence of that. Great as was the wrong to a merchant vessel, it has not the status of a ship of war, which carries even into foreign ports a territorial immunity resembling that of an ambassador, representing peculiarly the sovereignty of its nation. Further, the men taken from the *Chesapeake* were not seized as liable to impressment, but arrested as deserters; the case was distinct. Finally, Great Britain's power to maintain her position on impressment had certainly not waned under the *Chesapeake* humiliation, and was not likely to succumb to peremptory language from Madison. No such demand should have been advanced, in such connection, by a self-respecting government, unless prepared to fight instantly upon refusal. The despatch indeed contains cautions and expressions indicating a sense of treading on dangerous ground; an apprehension of exciting hostile action, though no thought of taking it. The exclusion of armed vessels was justified "by the vexations and dangers to our peace, experienced from these visits." The reason, if correct, was adequate as a matter of policy under normal conditions; but it became inconsistent with self-respect when the national flag was insulted in the attack on the *Chesapeake*. Entire composure, and forbearance from demonstrations bearing a trace of temper, alone comport with such a situation. To distinguish against British ships of war at such a moment, by refusing them only, and for the first time, admission into American harbours, was either a humiliating confession of impotence to maintain order within the national borders, or it justified Canning's contention that it was in retaliation for the *Leopard*'s action. His further plea, that it must therefore be taken into the account in determining the reparation due, was pettifogging, reducing a question of insult and amends to one of debit and credit bookkeeping; but the American claim that the step was necessary to internal quiet was puerile, and its precipitancy carried the appearance of petulance.

Monroe received Madison's despatch August 30, and on September 3 had an interview with Canning. In it he specified the redress indicated by Madison. With this was coupled an intimation that a special mission to the United States ought to be constituted, to impart to the act of reparation "a solemnity which the extraordinary nature of the aggression particularly required." This assertion of the extraordinary nature of the occasion separated the incident from the impressment grievance, with which Madison sought to join it; but what is more instructively noticeable is the contrast between this extreme formality, represented as requisite, and the wholly informal, and as it proved unreal, withdrawal by Napoleon of his Decrees, which the Administration of Madison at a later day maintained to be sufficient for the satisfaction of Great Britain.

In this interview[194] Canning made full use of the advantages given him by his adversaries' method of presentation and action.

> He said that by the President's proclamation, and the seizure and detention of some men who had landed on the coast to procure water, the Government seemed to have taken redress into its own hands.

To Monroe's statement that "the suppression of the practice of impressment from merchant vessels had been made indispensable by the late aggression, for reasons which were sufficiently known to him," he retorted that—

> .... the late aggression was an act different in all respects to the former practice; and ought not to be connected with it, as it showed a disposition to make a particular incident, in which Great Britain was in the wrong, instrumental to an accommodation in a case in which his Government held a different doctrine.

The remark went to the root of the matter. This was what the Administration was trying to do. As Madison afterwards put it to Rose, the President was desirous—

---

194. American State Papers, Foreign Relations, vol. iii. pp. 191-193.

. . . . of converting a particular incident into an occasion for removing another and more extensive source of danger to the harmony of the two countries.

This plausible rendering was not likely to recommend to a resolute nation such a method of obtaining surrender of a claimed right. The exclusion proclamation Monroe represented to be "a mere measure of police indispensable for the preservation of order within the United States." Canning declined to be shaken from his stand that it was an exhibition of partiality against Great Britain, the vessels of which alone were excluded, because of an outrage committed by one of them outside of American waters. The time at which the proclamation issued, and the incorporation in it of the *Chesapeake* incident, made this view at least colourable.

This interview also was followed by an exchange of notes. Monroe's of September 7, 1807, developed the American case and demand as already given. That of Canning, September 23, stated as follows the dilemma raised by the President's proclamation: either it was an act of partiality between England and France, the warships of the latter being still admitted, or it was an act of retaliation for the *Chesapeake* outrage, and so of the nature of redress, self-obtained, it is true, but to be taken into account in estimating the reparation which the British Government "acknowledged to have been originally due."[195] To the request for explanation Monroe replied lamely, with a statement which can scarcely be taken as other than admitting the punitive character of the proclamation. "There certainly existed no desire of giving a preference;" but—

> *Before, this aggression* it is well known that His Britannic Majesty's ships of war lay within the waters of the Chesapeake, and enjoyed all the advantages of the most favoured nation; it cannot therefore be doubted that my Government will be ready *to restore them to the same situation as soon as it can be done consistently with the honour and rights of the United States.*[196]

---

195. American State Papers, vol. iii. pp. 199, 200.
196. American State Papers, vol. iii. p. 202. Author's italics.

In closing his letter of September 23, Canning asked Monroe whether he could not, consistently with his instructions, separate the question of impressment from that of the *Chesapeake*. If not, as it was the fixed intention of his Government not to treat the two as connected, the negotiation would be transferred to Washington, and a special envoy sent.

> But in order to avoid the inconvenience which has arisen from the mixed nature of your instructions, he will not be empowered to entertain, as connected with this subject, any proposition respecting the search of merchant vessels.[197]

Monroe replied that his "instructions were explicit to consider the whole of this class of injuries as an entire subject."[198] To his inquiry as to the nature of the special mission, in particulars, Canning replied that it would be limited in the first instance to the question of the *Chesapeake*. Whether it would have any further scope, he could not say.[199]

Mr. George Henry Rose was nominated for this mission, and sailed from England in November. Before his departure, the British Government took a further step, which in view of the existing circumstances, and of all that had preceded, emphasized beyond the possibility of withdrawal the firmness of its decision not to surrender the claim to impress British subjects from foreign merchant vessels. On October 16, 1807, a Royal Proclamation was issued, recalling all seafaring persons who had entered foreign services, whether naval or merchant, directing them to withdraw at once from such service and return home, or else to ship on board any accessible British ship of war. Commanders of naval vessels were ordered to seize all such persons whenever found by them on board foreign merchantmen. In the case of British-born subjects, known to be serving on board foreign men-of-war,—which was the case of the *Chesapeake*,—the repetition of the outrage was implicitly forbidden, by prescribing the procedure to be observed. Requisition for the discharge of

---

197. Ibid., Foreign Relations, vol. iii. p. 201.
198. Ibid., p. 202.
199. Ibid., p. 203.

such persons was to be made on the foreign captain, and, in case of refusal, the particulars of the case were to be transmitted to the British minister to the nation concerned, or to the British home authorities; "in order that the necessary steps may be taken for obtaining redress. . . . for the injury done to us by the unwarranted detention of our natural-born subjects in the service of a foreign state." The proclamation closed by denying the efficacy of letters of naturalization to discharge native British from their allegiance of birth.

Rose's mission proved abortive. Like Monroe's, his instructions were positive to connect with his negotiation a matter which, if not so irrelevant as impressment, was at least of a character that a politic foreign minister might well have disregarded, in favour of the advantage to be gained by that most conciliatory of actions, a full and cordial apology. Rose was directed not to open his business until the President had withdrawn the proclamation excluding British ships of war. Having here no more option than Monroe as to impressment, the negotiation became iron-bound. The United States Government went to the utmost limit of concession to conclude the matter. Receding from its first attitude, it agreed to sever the question of impressment from that of the *Chesapeake*; but, with regard to the recalling of the President's proclamation, it demanded that Rose should show his cards, should state what was the nature and extent of the reparation he was empowered to offer, and whether it was conditioned or unconditioned. If this first outcome were such as to meet the just expectations of the Administration, revocation of the proclamation should bear the same date as the British act of reparation. Certainly, more could not be offered. The Government could not play a blind game, yielding point after point in reliance upon the unknown contents of Rose's budget. This, however, was what it was required to do, according to the British envoy's reading of his orders, and the matter terminated in a fruitless exchange of argumentation.[200] In April,

---

200. The principal part of the correspondence between Rose and Madison will be found in American State Papers, Foreign Relations, vol. iii. pp. 213-220. Rose's instructions from Canning were (continued opposite)

1808, Rose quitted the country, and redress for the *Chesapeake* injury remained in abeyance for three years longer. Interest in it had waned under more engrossing events which had already taken place, and it was relegated by both Governments to the background of diplomacy. Admiral Berkeley had been recalled, as a mark of his Majesty's disapproval. He arrived in England in the beginning of 1808, some six months after the outrage, accompanied by the *Leopard*. Her captain was not again given a ship; but before the end of the year the chief offender, the admiral, had been assigned to the important command at Lisbon. To Pinkney's observation upon this dissatisfying proceeding, Canning replied that it was impossible for the Admiralty to resist his claim to be employed (no other objection existing against him) after such a lapse of time since his return from Halifax, without bringing him to a court-martial.[201] In the final settlement, further punishment of Berkeley was persistently refused.

Although standing completely apart from the continuous stream of connected events which constituted contemporaneous history,—perhaps because of that very separateness,—the *Chesapeake* affair marks conspicuously the turning-point in the relations of the two countries. In point of time, its aptness as a sign-post is notable; for it occurred just at the moment when the British ministry, under the general exigencies of the situation, and the particular menace of the Tilsit compacts between Napoleon and the Czar, were meditating the new and extraordinary maritime system by which alone they might hope to counteract the Continental system that now threatened to become truly coextensive with Europe. But to the writer the significance of the *Chesapeake* business is more negative than positive; it suggests rather what might have been under different treatment by

---

first published by Mr. Henry Adams, History of the United States, vol. iv. pp. 178-182. They were of a character that completely justify the caution of the American Government in refusing to go further without knowing their contents, concerning which, indeed, Madison wrote that a glimpse had been obtained in the informal interviews, which showed their inadmissibility. Madison to Pinkney, Feb. 19, 1808, U.S. State Department MSS.
201. American State Papers, Foreign Relations, vol. iii. p. 300.

the Portland ministry. The danger to Great Britain was imminent and stupendous, and her measures of counteraction needed to correspond. These were confessedly illegal in the form they took, and were justified by their authors only on the ground of retaliation. Towards neutrals, among whom the United States were by far the chief, they were most oppressive. Yet for over four years not only did the American Government endure them, but its mercantile community conformed to the policy of Great Britain, found profit in so doing, and deprecated resort to war. At a later day Jefferson asserted bitterly that under British influence one fourth of the nation had compelled the other three fourths to abandon the embargo. Whether this be quite a fair statement may be doubted; but there was in it so much of truth as to suggest the possibility, if not of acquiescence in the Orders in Council, at least of such abstention from active resentment as would have been practically equivalent.

The acquiescence, if possible even the co-operation, of America was at this time momentous to Great Britain as well as to Napoleon. To complete his scheme for ruining his enemy, by closing against her commerce all the ports of Europe, the Emperor needed to deprive her also of access to the markets of the United States; while the grave loss to which Great Britain was exposed in the one quarter made it especially necessary to retain the large and increasing body of consumers across the Atlantic. In the United States there was a division of public opinion and feeling, which offered a fair chance of inclining national action in one direction or the other. Although the Treaty of Commerce and Navigation of December 31, 1806, had been rejected by the Administration, and disapproved by the stricter followers of Jefferson and Madison, it was regarded with favour in many quarters. Its negotiators had represented the two leading parties which divided the nation. Monroe was a republican, traditionally allied to Jefferson; Pinkney was a federalist. Although in it the principles of the United States had not been successfully asserted, as regarded either impressment or the transport of colonial produce, the terms of compromise had commanded their signatures, because they held that in effect the national objects were obtained; that impressment would practically cease, and the carrying trade, under the restrictions they had accepted, would not only nourish, but be as remunerative as before. Monroe, who had a large personal following in his state and party, maintained this view in strong and measured language after his return home; and it found supporters in both political camps, as well as upon the floor of the two houses of Congress. Then, and afterwards, it was made a reproach to the Administration that it had refused a working arrangement which was satisfactory in its substantial results and left the principles of the country untouched for future assertion. Whatever may be thought, from an American standpoint, of the justice or dignity of this position, it showed grave divergences of sentiment, from which it is the skill of an opposing diplomatist to draw profit. It is impossible to estimate the effect upon the subsequent course of America, if the British ministry, with a certain big-heartedness, had seized the opportunity of the *Chesapeake* affair; if they had disclaimed the act of their officers with frankness and cordiality, offering ungrudging regret, and reparation proportionate to the shame inflicted upon a community too weak in military power to avenge its wrongs. As it was, at a moment when the hostilities she had provoked would have been most embarrassing, Great Britain escaped only by the unreadiness of the American Government.

Left unatoned, the attack on the *Chesapeake* remained in American consciousness where Jefferson and Madison had sought to place it,—an example of the outrages of impressment. The incidental violence, which aroused attention and wrath, differed in nothing but circumstance from the procedure when an unresisting merchant vessel was deprived of men. In both cases there was the forcible exaction of a disputed claim. Canning, indeed, was at pains to explain that originally the British right extended to vessels of every kind; but—

> .... for nearly a century the Crown had forborne to instruct the commanders of its ships of war to search foreign ships of war for deserters. ... because to attack a national

ship of war is an act of hostility. The very essence of the charge against Admiral Berkeley, as you represent it, is the having taken upon himself to commit an act of hostility without the previous authority of his Government.

Under this construction, the incident only served to emphasize the fundamental opposition of principle, and to exasperate the war party in the United States. To deprive a foreign merchant vessel of men was not considered a hostile act; and the difference in the case of ships of war was only because the Crown chose so to construe. The argument was, that to retain seamen of British birth, when recalled by proclamation, was itself hostile, because every such seaman disobeying this call was a deserter. It was to be presumed that a foreign Power would not countenance their detention, and on this presumption no search of its commissioned ships was ordered. "But with respect to merchant vessels there is no such presumption."[202]

While the Chesapeake affair was still in its earlier stages of discussion, the passage of events in Europe was leading rapidly to the formulation of the extreme British measures of retaliation for the Berlin Decree. On June 14 Napoleon defeated the Russians at the battle of Friedland; and on June 22, the day the *Leopard* attacked the *Chesapeake*, an armistice was signed between the contending parties. Upon this followed the Conventions of Tilsit, July 8, 1807, by which the Czar undertook to support the Continental system, and to close his ports to Great Britain. The deadly purpose of the commercial warfare thus reinforced was apparent; and upon the Emperor's return to Paris, soon afterwards, the Berlin Decree received an execution more consonant to its wording than was the construction hitherto given it by French officials. In May, an American ship, the *Horizon*, bound from England to Peru, had been wrecked upon the coast of France. Her cargo consisted in part of goods of British origin. Up to that time, no decisions contrary to American neutral rights had been based upon the Decree by French courts; but final action in the case of the *Horizon* was not taken till some time after the

---

202. American State Papers, Foreign Relations, vol. iii. p. 200.

Emperor's return. Meanwhile, on August 9, General Armstrong, the American minister, had asked that Spain, which had formally adopted the Berlin Decree as governing its own course, should be informed of the rulings of the French authorities;

> .... for a letter from the *chargé des affaires* of the United States at Madrid shows that the fate of sundry American vessels, captured by Spanish cruisers, will depend, not on the construction which might be given to the Spanish decree by Spanish tribunals, but on the practice which shall have been established in France.[203]

This letter was referred in due course—August 21—to the Minister of Marine, and a reply promised when his answer should be received. Under Napoleon's eye, doubts not entertained in his absence seem to have occurred to the ministers concerned, and on September 24 Armstrong learned that the Emperor had been consulted, and had said that, as he had expressed no exceptions to the operation of his Decree, French armed vessels were authorized to seize goods of English origin on board neutral vessels. This decision, having the force of law, was communicated to the tribunals, and under it so much of the *Horizon*'s cargo as answered to this description was condemned. The rest was liberated.[204]

When this decision became known, it was evident that within the range of Napoleon's power there would henceforth be no refuge for British manufactures, or the produce of British colonies; that neutral ownership or jurisdiction would be no protection against force. Even the pity commonly extended to the shipwrecked failed, if his property had been bought in England. Recognition of the increased danger was shown in the doubling and trebling of insurance. The geographical sweep intended to be given to the edict was manifested by the action of state after state whither arms had extended Napoleon's influence; or, as Armstrong phrased it—

---

203. American State Papers, Foreign Relations, vol. iii. p. 243.
204. Ibid., pp. 244-245.

. . . . having settled the business of belligerents, with the exception of England, very much to his own liking, he was now on the point of settling that of neutrals in the same way.

In July, Denmark and Portugal, as yet at peace, had been notified that they must choose between France and England, and had been compelled to exclude English commerce. August 29, a French division entered Leghorn, belonging to the nominally independent Kingdom of Etruria, took possession of the harbour and forts, ordered the surrender of all British goods in the hands of the inhabitants, and laid a general embargo upon the shipping, among which were many Americans. In Lower Italy, the Papal States and Naples underwent the same restrictions. Prussia yielded under obvious constraint, and Austria acceded from motives of policy, distinguishable in form only from direct compulsion. Russia, as already said, had joined immediately after decisive defeat in the field. The co-operation of the United States, the second maritime nation in the world, was vital to the general plan. Could it be secured? Already, at an audience given to the diplomatic corps on August 2, the Danish minister had taken Armstrong aside and asked him whether any application had been made to him with regard to the projected *union of all commercial states against Great Britain*. Being answered in the negative, he said, "You are much favoured, but it will not last."[205] Armstrong characterized this incident as not important; but in truth the words italicized defined exactly the menacing scheme already matured in the Emperor's mind, for the execution of which, as events already showed, and continued to prove, he relied upon the force of arms. To this the United States was not accessible; but to coerce or cajole her by other means became a prominent feature of French policy, which was powerfully abetted by the tone of Great Britain speaking through Canning.

To appreciate duly the impending measures of the British ministry, attention should fasten upon the single decisive fact that this vast combination was not the free act of the parties

---
205. American State Papers, Foreign Relations, vol. iii. p. 243.

concerned, but a submission imposed by an external military power, which at the moment, and for five succeeding years, they were unable to resist. It is one thing to deny the right of any number of independent communities to join in a Customs Union; it is another to maintain the obligations upon third parties of such a convention, when extorted by external compulsion. Either action may be resisted, but means not permissible in the one case may be justified in the other. In the European situation the subjected states, by reason of their subjection, disappeared as factors in diplomatic consideration. There remained only their master Napoleon, with his momentary lieutenant the Czar, and opposed to them Great Britain. The French Minister of Foreign Affairs, Champagny, said to Armstrong—

> It is obvious that his Majesty *cannot permit* to his allies a commerce which he denies to himself. This would be at once to defeat his system and oppress his subjects.[206]

A few days later he wrote formally:

> His Majesty considered himself bound to *order* reprisals on American vessels *not only in his territory, but likewise in the countries which are under his influence,*—Holland, Spain, Italy, Naples.[207]

The Emperor by strength of arms oppressed to their grievous injury those who could not escape him; what should be the course of those whom he could not reach, to whom was left the choice between actual resistance and virtual co-operation? The two really independent states were Great Britain and the United States. In the universal convulsion of civilization, the case of the several nations recalls the law of Solon, that in civil tumults the man who took neither side should be disfranchised.

The United States chose neutrality, and expected that it would be permitted her. She chose to overlook the interposition of Napoleon, and to regard the exclusion laws, forced by

---

206. Armstrong to Smith, U.S. Secretary of State, Jan. 28, 1810. Ibid., p. 380. Author's italics.
207. American State Papers, vol. iii. p. 380. Author's italics.

him upon other states, as instances of municipal regulation, incontestable when freely exercised. Not only would she not go behind the superficial form, but on technical grounds of international law she denied the right of another to do so. Great Britain had no choice. She was compelled to resistance; the question was as to methods. Direct military action was impossible. The weapon used against her was commercial prohibition, which meant eventual ruin, unless adequately parried by her own action. From Europe no help was to be expected. If the United States also decided so far to support Napoleon as to prosecute her trade subject to his measures, accepting as legal regulations extorted by him from other European countries, the trade of Europe would be transferred from Great Britain to America, and the revenues of France would expand in every way, while those of Great Britain shrank,—a result militarily fatal. In this the British Government would not acquiesce. It chose instead war with the United States, under the forms of peace.

That the tendency of the course pursued by the United States was to destroy British commerce, and that this tendency was successfully counteracted by the means framed by the British Government,—the Orders in Council,—admits of little doubt. When the American policy had worked out to its logical conclusion, in open trade with France, and complete interdict of importation from Great Britain, Joel Barlow, American Minister to France in 1811-12, and an intimate of Jefferson and Madison, wrote thus to the French Minister of Foreign Affairs:

> In adopting the late arrangements with France the United States could not contemplate the deprivation of revenue. They really expected to draw from this country and from the rest of continental Europe the same species of manufactures, and to as great an amount as they were accustomed to do from England. They calculated with the more confidence on such a result as they saw how intimately it was combined with the great and essential interests of the Imperial Government. They perceived that *it*

would promote in an unexpected degree the Continental system, which the Emperor has so much at heart.... The Emperor now commands nearly all the ports of continental Europe. The whole interior of the Continent must be supplied with American products. These must pass through French territory, French commercial houses, canals, and wagons. They must pay (toll to France in various ways) and thus render these territories as tributary to France as if they were part of her own dominions.[208]

But Napoleon replied that his system, as it stood, had greatly crippled British commerce, and that if he should admit American shipping freely to the Continent, trade could not be carried on, because the English under the Orders in Council would take it all, going or coming.[209]

"The peril of the moment is truly supposed to be great beyond all former example," wrote Pinkney, now American minister in London, when communicating to his Government the further Orders in Council adopted by Great Britain, in response to the attempted "union of all the commercial states" against her. As defined by Canning to Pinkney,[210] "the principle upon which the whole of this measure has been framed is that of refusing to the enemy those advantages of commerce which he has forbidden to this country. The simplest method of enforcing this system of retaliation would have been to follow the example of the enemy, by prohibiting altogether all commercial intercourse between him and other states." America then would not be allowed to trade with the countries under his Decrees. It was considered, however, more indulgent to neutrals—to the second parties in commercial intercourse with the enemy—to allow this intercourse subject to duties in transit to be paid in Great Britain. This would raise the cost to the continental consumer and pay revenue to Great Britain.

The Orders in Council of November 11, 1807, therefore for-

---
208. Barlow to Bassano, Nov. 10, 1811. U.S. State Department MSS. Author's italics.
209. Barlow to Monroe, Dec. 19, 1811. U.S. State Department MSS.
210. Feb. 22, 1808. American State Papers, Foreign Relations, vol. iii. p. 206.

bade all entrance to ports of the countries which had embraced the Continental system. It was not pretended that they would be blockaded effectively.

> All ports from which the British flag is excluded shall from henceforth be subject to the same restrictions, in point of trade and navigation, with the exceptions hereinafter mentioned, *as if the same were actually blockaded* in the most strict and rigorous manner by his Majesty's naval forces.

The exception was merely that a vessel calling first at a British port would be allowed to proceed to one of those prohibited, after paying certain duties upon her cargo and obtaining a fresh clearance. This measure was instituted by the Executive, in pursuance of the custom of regulating trade with America by Orders in Council, prevalent since 1783; but it received legislative sanction by an Act of Parliament, March 28, 1808, which fixed the duties to be paid on the foreign goods thus passing through British custom-houses. Cotton, for instance, was to pay nine pence a pound, an amount intended to be prohibitory; tobacco, three halfpence. These were the two leading exports of United States domestic produce. In the United States this Act of Parliament was resented more violently, if possible, than the Order in Council itself. In the colonial period there had been less jealousy of the royal authority than of that of Parliament, and the feeling reappears in the discussion of the present measures. "This," said a Virginia senator,[211] "is the Act regulating our commerce, of which I complain. An export duty, which could not be laid in Charleston because forbidden by our Constitution, is laid in London, or in British ports." It was literally, and in no metaphorical sense, the reimposition of colonial regulation, to increase the revenues of Great Britain by reconstituting her the *entrepôt* of commerce between America and Europe. "The Orders in Council," wrote John Quincy Adams in a public letter, "if submitted to, would have degraded us to the condition of colonists."[212]

---

211. Giles, Annals of Congress, 1808-09, pp. 123-125.
212. N.Y. Evening Post, May 12, 1808.

This just appreciation preponderated over other feelings throughout the middle and southern states. Adams, a senator from Massachusetts, had separated himself in action and opinion from the mass of the people in New England, where, although the Orders were condemned, hatred of Napoleon and his methods overbore the sense of injury received from Great Britain. The indignation of the supporters of the Administration was intensified by the apparent purpose of the British Government to keep back information of the measure. Rose had sailed the day after its adoption, Monroe two days later, but neither brought any official intimation of its issuance, although that was announced in the papers of the day. Adams wrote:

> The Orders in Council were not merely without official authenticity. Rumours had been for several weeks in circulation, derived from English prints and from private correspondence, that such Orders were to issue,[213] and no inconsiderable pains were taken to discredit the facts. Suspicions were lulled by declarations equivalent as nearly as possible to positive denial, and these opiates were continued for weeks after the embargo was laid, until Mr. Erskine received orders to make official communication of the Orders themselves, in proper form, to our Government.[214]

This remissness, culpable as it certainly was in a matter of such importance, was freely attributed to the most sinister motives.

These Orders in Council were designedly concealed from Mr.

---

213. Jefferson, under date of Nov. 15, 1807, alludes to such a report. (Jefferson's Works, vol. v. p. 211.) Already, indeed, on Aug. 19, 1807, an Order in Council, addressed to vessels bearing the neutral flags of Mecklenburg, Oldenburg, Papenburg, or Kniphausen, had been issued, which, though brief, imposed precisely the same restrictions as the later celebrated ones here under discussion. (Annual Register, 1807, State Papers, p. 730; Naval Chronicle, vol. xviii. p. 151.) The fact is interesting, as indicative of the date of formulating a project, for the execution of which the "*Horizon*" decision probably afforded the occasion.

214. Erskine's communication was dated Feb. 23, 1808. (American State Papers, vol. iii. p. 209.) Pinkney, however, had forwarded a copy of the Orders on November 17. (Ibid., p. 203.) Canning's letter, of which Erskine's was a transcript, was dated Dec. 1, 1807. (British Foreign Office Archives.)

Rose, although they had long been deliberated upon, and almost matured, before he left London. They were the besom which was intended to sweep, and would have swept, our commerce from the ocean. Great Britain in the most insidious manner had issued orders for the entire destruction of our commerce.[215]

The wrath was becoming, but in this particular the inference was exaggerated. The Orders, modelled on the general plan of blockades, provided for the warning of a vessel which had sailed before receiving notification; and not till after a first notice by a British cruiser was she liable to capture. Mention of such cases occurs in the journals of the day.[216] Some captains persisted, and, if successful in reaching a port under Napoleon's control, found themselves arrested under a new Decree,—that of Milan,—for having submitted to a visit they could not resist. Such were sequestered, subject to the decision of the United States to take active measures against Great Britain.

Arrived at New York, March 23, (1808), ship *Eliza*, Captain Skiddy, 29 days from Bordeaux. All American vessels in France which had been boarded by British cruisers were under seizure. The opinion was, they would so remain till it was known whether the United States had adjusted its difficulties with Great Britain, in which case they would be immediately condemned. A letter from the Minister of

---

215. Senator Giles of Virginia. Annals of Congress, 1808-09, p. 218.
216. The following are instances: Philadelphia, February 23. The ship "Venus," King, hence to the Isle of France, has returned to port. January 17, Lat. 25° N., Long. 34° W., fell in with an English merchant fleet of thirty-six sail, under convoy of four ships of war. Was boarded by the sloop of war *Wanderer*, which endorsed on all her papers, forbidding to enter any port belonging to France or her allies, they all being declared in a state of blockade. Captain King therefore put back. (N.Y. Evening Post, Feb. 24, 1808.) Salem, Mass., February 23. Arrived bark *Active*, Richardson. Sailed hence for Malaga, December 12. January 2, Lat. 37° N., Long. 17° W., boarded by a British cruiser, and papers endorsed against entering any but a British port. The voyage being thus frustrated, Captain Richardson returned. Marblehead, February 29. Schooner *Minerva* returned, having been captured under the Orders in Council, released, and come home. Ship *George*, from Amsterdam, arrived at New York, March 6, via Yarmouth. Was taken by an English cruiser into Yarmouth and there cleared. (*Evening Post*, March 6.)

Marine was published that the Decree of Milan must be executed severely, strictly, and literally.[217]

Independent of a perpetual need to raise money, by methods more consonant to the Middle Ages than to the current period, Napoleon thus secured hostages for the action of the United States in its present dilemma.

The Orders in Council of November 11, having been announced in English papers of the 10th, 11th, and 12th, appeared in the Washington *National Intelligencer* of December 18.[218] The general facts were therefore known to the Executive and to the Legislature; and, though not officially adduced, could not but affect consideration, when the President, on December 18, 1807, sent a message to Congress recommending "an inhibition of the departure of our vessels from the ports of the United States." With his customary exaggerated expression of attendance upon instructions from Congress, he made no further definition of wishes which were completely understood by the party leaders. "The wisdom of Congress will also see the necessity of making every preparation for whatever events may grow out of the present crisis." Accompanying the message, as documents justificatory of the action to be taken, were four official papers. One was the formal communication to the French Council of Prizes of Napoleon's decision that goods of English origin were lawful prize on board neutral vessels; the second was the British proclamation directing the impressment of British seamen found on board neutral ships. These two were made public. Secrecy was imposed concerning the others, which were a letter of September 24, from Armstrong to the French Minister of Exterior Relations, and the reply, dated October 7. In this the minister, M. Champagny, affirmed the Emperor's decision, and added a sentence which, while susceptible of double meaning, certainly covertly suggested that the United States should join in supporting the Berlin Decree.

The decree of blockade has now been issued eleven months.

---

217. N.Y. Evening Post, March 24, 1808.
218. Letter of John Quincy Adams to Harrison Gray Otis.

The principal Powers of Europe, far from protesting against its provisions, have adopted them. They have perceived that its execution must be complete to render it more effectual, and it has seemed easy to reconcile these measures with the observance of treaties, especially at a time when the infractions by England of the rights of *all maritime* Powers render their interests common, and tend to *unite them in support of the same cause.*[219]

This doubtless might be construed as applicable only to the European Powers; but as a foremost contention of Madison and Armstrong had been that the Berlin Decree contravened the treaty between France and the United States, the sentence lent itself readily to the interpretation, placed upon it by the Federalists, that the United States was invited to enforce in her own waters the continental system of exclusion, and so to help bring England to reason.

This the United States immediately proceeded to do. Though the motive differed somewhat, the action was precisely that suggested. On the same day that Jefferson's message was received, the Senate passed an Embargo Bill. This was sent at once to the House, returned with amendments, amendments concurred in, and bill passed and approved December 22. This rapidity of action—Sunday intervened—shows a purpose already decided in general principle; while the enactment of three supplementary measures, before the adjournment of Congress in April, indicates a precipitancy incompatible with proper weighing of details, and an avoidance of discussion, commendable only on the ground that no otherwise than by the promptest interception could American ships or merchandise be successfully jailed in port. The bill provided for the instant stoppage of all vessels in the ports of the United States, whether cleared or not cleared, if bound to any foreign port. Exception was made only in favour of foreign ships, which of course could not be held. They might depart with cargo already on board, or in ballast. Vessels cleared coastwise were to be deterred from turning foreign by bonds exacted in double the value of ship and cargo. American export

---

219. American State Papers, Foreign Relations, vol. iii. p. 245. Author's italics.

and foreign navigation were thus completely stopped; and as the Non-Importation Act at last went into operation on December 14,[220] there was practical exclusion of all British vessels, for none could be expected to enter a port where she could neither land her cargo nor depart.

In communicating the embargo to Pinkney, for the information of the British Government,[221] Madison was careful to explain, as he had to the British minister at Washington, that it was a measure of precaution only; not to be considered as hostile in character. This was scarcely candid; coercion of Great Britain, to compel the withdrawal of her various maritime measures objectionable to the United States, was at least a silent partner in the scheme, as formulated to the consciousness of Jefferson and his followers.[222] The motive transpired, as such motives necessarily do; but, even had it not, the operation of the Act, under the conditions of the European war, was so plainly partial between the two belligerents, as to amount virtually to co-operation with Napoleon by the preponderance of injury done to Great Britain. It deprived her of cotton for raw material; of tobacco, which, imported in payment for British manufactures, formed a large element in her commerce with the Continent; of wheat

---

220. Correspondence of Thomas Barclay, p. 272.
221. American State Papers, Foreign Relations, vol. iii. p. 206.
222. "We expected, too, some effect from coercion of interest." (Jefferson to Armstrong, March 5, 1809. Works, vol. v. p. 433.) "The embargo is the last card we have to play short of war." (Jefferson to Madison, March 11, 1808. Ibid., p. 258.) "The coercive experiment we have made." (Monroe to John Taylor. Works, vol. v. p. 89.) "I place immense value on the experiment being fully made how far an Embargo may be an *effectual weapon* in future, as well as on this occasion." (Jefferson. Works, vol. v. p. 289.) "Bonaparte ought to be particularly satisfied with us, by whose unyielding adherence to principle England has been forced into the revocation of her Orders." (Jefferson to Madison, April 27, 1809. Works, vol. v. p. 442.) This revocation was not actual, but a mistake of the British minister at Washington. "I have always understood that there were two objects contemplated by the Embargo Laws. The first, precautionary; the second, coercive, operating upon the aggressive belligerents, by addressing strong appeals to the interests of both." (Giles of Virginia, in Senate, Nov. 24, 1808.) "The embargo is not designed to affect our own citizens, but to make an impression in Europe." (Williams of South Carolina, in House of Representatives, April 14, 1808.)

and flour, which to some extent contributed to the support of her people, though in a much less degree than many supposed. It closed to her the American market at the moment that Napoleon and Alexander were actively closing the European; and it shut off from the West Indies American supplies known to be of the greatest importance, and fondly, but mistakenly, believed to be indispensable.

All this was well enough, if national policy required. Great Britain then was scarcely in a position to object seriously to retaliation by a nation thinking itself injured; but to define such a measure as not hostile was an insult to her common-sense. It was certainly hostile in nature, it was believed to be hostile in motive, and it intensified feelings already none too friendly. In France, although included in the embargo, and although her action was one of the reasons alleged for its institution, Napoleon expressed approval. It was injurious to England, and added little to the pressure upon France exerted by the Orders in Council through the British control of the ocean. Senator Smith of Maryland, a large shipping merchant, bore testimony to this.

> It has been truly said by an eminent merchant of Salem, that not more than one vessel in eight that sailed for Europe within a short time before the embargo reached its destination. My own experience has taught me the truth of this; and as further proof I have in my hand a list of fifteen vessels which sailed for Europe between September 1 and December 23, 1807. Three arrived; two were captured by French and Spaniards; one was seized in Hamburg; and nine carried into England. But for the embargo, ships that would have sailed would have fared as ill, or worse. Not one in twenty would have arrived.

Granting the truth of this anticipation, Great Britain might have claimed that, so far as evident danger was concerned, her blockades over long coast-lines were effective.

The question speedily arose,—If the object of embargo be precaution only, to save our vessels from condemnation under the sweeping edicts of France and Great Britain, and seamen from impressment on American decks, why object to exporting native produce in foreign bottoms, and to commerce across the Canada frontier? If, by keeping our vessels at home, we are to lose the profits upon sixty million dollars' worth of colonial produce which they have heretofore been carrying, with advantage to the national revenue, why also forbid the export of the forty to fifty million dollars' worth of domestic produce which foreign ship-owners would gladly take and safely carry? for such foreigners would be chiefly British, and would sail under British convoy, subject to small proportionate risk.[223] Why, also, to save seamen from impressment, deprive them of their living, and force them in search of occupation to fly our ports to British, where lower wages and more exposure to the pressgang await them? On the ground of precaution, there was no reply to these questions; unless, perhaps, that with open export of domestic produce the popular suffering would be too unequally distributed, falling almost wholly on New England shipping industries. Logically, however, if the precaution were necessary, the suffering must be accepted; its incidence was a detail only. The embargo was distinctly a hostile measure; and more and more, as people talked, in and out of Congress, was admitted to be simply an alternative for open war.

As such it failed. It entailed most of the miseries of war, without any of its compensations. It could not arouse the popular enthusiasm which elevates, nor command the popular support that strengthens. Hated and despised, it bred elusion, sneaking and demoralizing, and so debased public sentiment with reference to national objects, and individual self-sacrifice to national ends, that the conduct of the many who now evaded it was reproduced, during the War of 1812, in dealings with the enemy which even now may make an American's head hang for shame. Born of the Jeffersonian horror of war, its evil communication corrupted morals among those whose standards were conventional only; for public opinion failed to

---

223. The writer, in a previous work (Sea Power in the French Revolution), believes himself to have shown that the losses by capture of British traders did not exceed two and one half per cent.

condemn breaches of embargo, and by a natural declension equally failed soon after to condemn aid to the enemy in an unpopular war. Was it wonderful that an Administration which bade the seamen and the ship-owners of the day to starve, that a foreign state might be injured, and at the same time refused to build national ships to protect them, fell into contempt? that men, so far as they might, simply refused to obey, and wholly departed from respect? Mr. Adams wrote:

> I have believed, and still do believe, that our internal resources are competent to establish and maintain a naval force, if not fully adequate to the protection and defence of our commerce, at least sufficient to induce a retreat from these hostilities, and to deter from the renewal of them by either of the harrying parties.[224]

In short, to compel peace, the first object of military preparation.

> I believed that a system to that effect might be formed, ultimately far more economical, and certainly more energetic than a three years' embargo. I did submit such a proposition to the Senate, and similar attempts had been made in the House of Representatives, but equally discountenanced.[224]

This was precisely the effect of Jefferson's teaching, which then dominated his party, and controlled both houses. At this critical moment he wrote:

> Believing, myself, that gunboats are the only water defence which can be useful to us, and protect us from the ruinous folly of a navy, I am pleased with everything which promises to improve them.[225]

Not thus was a nation to be united, nor foreign governments impressed. The panacea recommended was to abandon the sea;

---

224. Letter to Otis.
225. To Thomas Paine, concerning an improved gunboat devised by him. Sept. 6, 1807. (Jefferson's Works, vol. v. p. 189.)

to yield practical submission to the Orders in Council, which forbade American ships to visit the Continent, and to the Decrees of Napoleon, which forbade them entrance to any dominion of Great Britain. By a curious mental process this was actually believed to be resistance. The American nation was to take as its model the farmer who lives on his own produce, sternly independent of his neighbour; whose sons delved, and wife span, all that the family needed. This programme, half sentiment, half philosophy, and not at all practical, or practicable, was the groundwork of Jefferson's thought. To it co-operated a dislike approaching detestation for the carrying trade; the very opposite, certainly, of the other ideal. American shipping was then handling sixty million dollars' worth of foreign produce, and rolling up the wealth which for some reason follows the trader more largely than the agriculturist, who observed with ill-concealed envy. Jefferson wrote:

> I trust that the good sense of our country will see that its greatest prosperity depends on a due balance between agriculture, manufactures, and commerce, and not on this protuberant navigation, which has kept us in hot water from the commencement of our government. This drawback system enriches a few individuals, but lessens the stock of native productions, by withdrawing all the hands (seamen) thus employed. It is essentially necessary for us to have shipping and seamen enough to carry our surplus products to market, but beyond that I do not think we are bound to give it encouragement by drawbacks or other premiums.[226]

This meant that it was unjust to the rest of the community to allow the merchant to land his cargo, and send it abroad, without paying as much duty as if actually consumed in the country.

> This exuberant commerce brings us into collision with other Powers in every sea, and will force us into every war with European Powers.... It is now engaging us in war.[226]

---

226. Jefferson's Works, vol. v. pp. 417, 426.

Whether for merchant ships or navies the sea was odious to Jefferson's conception of things. As a convenient medium for sending to market surplus cotton and tobacco, it might be tolerated; but for that ample use of it which had made the greatness of Holland and England, he had only aversion. This prepossession characterized the whole body of men, who willingly stripped the seaman and his employers of all their living, after refusing to provide them with an armed protection to which the resources of the state were equal. Up to the outbreak of the war not a ship was added to the navy. With this feeling, Great Britain, whose very being was maritime, not unnaturally became the object of a dislike so profound as unconsciously to affect action. Napoleon decreed, and embargoed, and sequestered, with little effect upon national sentiment outside of New England. "Certainly all the difficulties and the troubles of the Government during our time proceeded from England," wrote Jefferson soon after quitting office,[227] to Dearborn, his Secretary of War. "At least all others were trifling in comparison." Yet not to speak of the Berlin Decree, by which ships were captured for the mere offence of sailing for England,[228] Bonaparte, by the Bayonne Decree, April 17, 1808, nearly a year before Jefferson left office, pronounced the confiscation of all American vessels entering ports under his control, on the

---

227. June 14, 1809. Works, vol. v. p. 455.
228. An American ship putting into England, leaky, reported that on Dec. 18, 1807, she had been boarded by a French privateer, which allowed her to proceed because bound to Holland. The French captain said he had captured four Americans, all sent into Passage, in Spain; and that his orders were to bring in all Americans bound to English ports. (N.Y. Evening Post, March 1, 1808.) This was under the Berlin Decree, as that of Milan issued only December 17. The Berlin Decree proclaimed the British Islands under blockade, but Napoleon for a time reserved decision as to the mere act of sailing for them being an infringement. Mr. James Stephen, in Parliament, stated that in 1807 several ships, not less than twenty-one, he thought, were taken for the mere fact of sailing between America and England; in consequence, insurance on American vessels rose 50 per cent, from 2½ to 3¾. (Parliamentary Debates, vol. xiii. p. xxxix. App.) In the Evening Post of March 3, 1808, will be found, quoted from a French journal, cases of four vessels carried into France, apparently only because bound to England.

ground that under the existing embargo they could not lawfully have left their own country; a matter which was none of his business. Within a year were condemned one hundred and thirty-four ships and cargoes, worth $10,000,000.[229]

That Jefferson consciously leaned to France from any regard to Napoleon is incredible; the character and procedures of the French Emperor were repugnant to his deepest convictions; but that there was a still stronger bias against the English form of government, and the pursuit of the sea for which England especially stood, is equally clear. Opposition to England was to him a kind of mission. His best wish for her had been that she might be republicanized by a successful French invasion.[230] He wrote to a political disciple:

> I came into office under circumstances calculated to generate peculiar acrimony. I found all the offices in the possession of a political sect, who wished to transform it ultimately into the shape of their darling model, the English government; and in the meantime to familiarize the public mind to the change, by administering it on English principles, and in English forms. The elective interposition of the people had blown all their designs, and they found themselves and their fortresses of power and profit put in a moment in the hand of other trustees.[231]

These words, written in the third of the fifteen embargo months, reveal an acrimony not wholly one-sided. It was perceived by the parties hardest hit by this essentially Jeffersonian scheme; by the people of New England and of Great Britain. In the old country it intensified bitterness. In the following summer, at a dinner given to representatives of the Spanish revolt

---

229. Henry Adams's History of the United States, vol. v. p. 242.
230. "Nothing can establish firmly the republican principles of our government but an establishment of them in England. France will be the apostle for this." (Jefferson's Works, vol. iv. p. 192.) "The subjugation of England would be a general calamity. Happily it is impossible. Should invasion end in her being only republicanized, I know not on what principles a true republican of our country could lament it." (Ibid., p. 217; Feb. 23, 1798.)
231. Jefferson to Richard M. Johnson, March 10, 1808. Works, vol. v. p. 257.

against Napoleon, the toast to the President of the United States was received with hisses,[232] "and the marks of disapprobation continued till a new subject drew off the attention of the company." The embargo was not so much a definite cause of complaint, for at worst it was merely a retaliatory measure like the Orders in Council. Enmity was recognized, alike in the council boards and in the social gatherings of the two peoples; the spirit that leads to war was aroused. Nor could this hostile demonstration proceed from sympathy with the Spanish insurgents; for, except so far as might be inferred from the previous general course of the American Administration, there was no reason to believe that they would regard unfavourably the Spanish struggle for liberty. Yet they soon did, and could not but do so.

It is a coincidence too singular to go unnoticed, that the first strong measure of the American Government against Great Britain—Embargo—was followed by Napoleon's reverses in Spain, which, by opening much of that country and of her colonies to trade, at once in large measure relieved Great Britain from the pressure of the Continental system and the embargo; while the second, the last resort of nations, War, was declared shortly before the great Russian catastrophe, which, by rapidly contracting the sphere of the Emperor's control, both widened the area of British commerce and deprived the United States of a diversion of British effort, upon which calculation had rightly been based. It was impossible for the American Government not to wish well to Napoleon, when for it so much depended upon his success; and to wish him well was of course to wish ill to his opponents, even if fighting for freedom.

Congress adjourned April 25, having completed embargo legislation, as far as could then be seen necessary. On May 2 occurred the rising in Madrid, consequent upon Napoleon's removal of the Spanish Royal Family; and on July 21 followed the surrender of Dupont's corps at Baylen. Already, on July 4, the British Government had stopped all hostilities against Spain, and withdrawn the blockade of all Spanish ports, except such as

---

232. London Times of August 6, quoted in N.Y. Evening Post of Oct. 10, 1808.

might still be in French control. On August 30, by the Convention of Cintra, Portugal was evacuated by the French, and from that time forward the Peninsula kingdoms, though scourged by war, were in alliance with Great Britain; their ports and those of their colonies open to her trade.

This of itself was a severe blow to the embargo, which for coercive success depended upon the co-operation of the Continental system. It was further thwarted and weakened by extensive popular repudiation in the United States. The political conviction of the expediency, or probable efficacy, of the measure was largely sectional; and it is no serious imputation upon the honesty of its supporters to say that they mustered most strongly where interests were least immediately affected. Tobacco and cotton suffered less in keeping than flour and salt fish; and the deterioration of these was by no means so instant as the stoppage of a ship's sailing or loading. The farmer ideal is realizable on a farm; but it was not so for the men whose sole occupation was transporting that which the agriculturist did not need to markets now closed by law. Wherever employment depended upon commerce, distress was immediate. The seamen, improvident by habit, first felt the blow. "I cannot conceive," said Representative (afterwards Justice) Story, "why gentlemen should wish to paralyze the strength of the nation by keeping back our naval force, and particularly now, when many of our native seamen (and I am sorry to say from my own knowledge I speak it) are starving in our ports."[233] The Commandant of the New York Navy Yard undertook to employ, for rations only, not wages, three hundred of those adrift in the streets; the corporation of the city undertaking to pay for the food issued.[234] They moved off, as they could get opportunity, towards the British Provinces; and thus many got into the British service, by enlistment or impressment. "Had your frigate arrived here instead of the *Chesapeake*, wrote the British Consul General at New York, as early as February 15, 1808, "I have no doubt two or three hundred able British

---

233. Annals of Congress, 1808-09, p. 1032.
234. Captains' Letters, U.S. Navy Department MSS. Jan. 11, 1808.

seamen would have entered on board her for his Majesty's service; and even now, was your station removed to this city, I feel confident, *provided the embargo continues*, you would more than complete your complement."[235]

Six months later, "Is it not notorious that not a seaport in the United States can produce seamen enough to man three merchant ships?"[236] In moving the estimates for one hundred and thirty thousand seamen a year later (February, 1809), the Secretary of the Admiralty observed that Parliament would learn with satisfaction that the number of seamen now serving in the navy covered, if it did not exceed, the number here voted.[237] It had not been so once. Sir William Parker, an active frigate captain during ten years of this period, wrote in 1805:

> I dread the discharge of our crew; for I do not think the miserable wretches with which the ships lately fitted out were manned are equal to fight their ships in the manner they are expected to do.[238]

The high wages, which the profits of the American merchant service enabled it to pay, outbade all competition by the British navy. "Dollars for shillings," as the expression ran. The embargo stopped all this, and equivalent conditions did not return before the war. The American Minister to France in 1811 wrote:

> We complain with justice of the English practice of pressing our seamen into their service. But the fact is, and there is no harm in saying it, there are at present more American seamen who seek that service than are forced into it."[239]

After the seamen followed the associated employments; those whose daily labour was expended in occupations connected with transportation, or who produced objects which men could not eat, or with which they could dispense. Before the end of

---

235. Thomas Barclay's Correspondence, p. 274. Author's italics.
236. N.Y. Evening Post, Sept. 1, 1808.
237. Cobbett's Parliamentary Debates, vol. xii. p. 326.
238. Life of Sir William Parker, vol. i. p. 304.
239. Barlow to Bassano, Nov. 10, 1811. U.S. State Department MSS.

the year testimony came from every quarter of the increase of suffering among the deserving poor; and not they only, but those somewhat above them as gainers of a comfortable living. They were for the most part helpless, except as helped by their richer neighbours. Work for them there was not, and they could not rebel. Not so with the seafarers, or the dwellers upon the frontiers. On the great scale, of course, a sure enforcement of the embargo was possible; the bulk of the shipping, especially the bigger, was corralled and idle. In the port of New York, February 17, 1808, lay 161 ships, 121 brigs, and 98 smaller sea-going vessels; in all 380 unoccupied, of which only 11 were foreign. In the much smaller port of Savannah, at this early period there were 50. In Philadelphia, a year later, 293, mostly of large tonnage for the period. A New York journal asked:

> What is that huge forest of dry trees that spreads itself before the town? You behold the masts of ships thrown out of employment by the embargo.[240]

> Our dismantled, ark-roofed vessels are indeed decaying in safety at our wharves, forming a suitable monument to the memory of our departed commerce. But where are your seamen? Gone, sir! Driven into foreign exile in search of subsistence."[241]

Yet not all; for illicit employment, for evading the Acts, enough remained to disconcert the Government, alike by their numbers and the boldness of their movements.

"This Embargo law," wrote Jefferson to Gallatin, August 11, 1808, "is certainly the most embarrassing we ever had to execute. I did not expect a crop of so sudden and rank growth of fraud, and open opposition by force, could have grown up within the United States."[242] Apostle of pure democracy as he was, he had forgotten to reckon with the people, and had mistaken the convictions of himself and a coterie for national

---

240. N.Y. Evening Post, Feb. 18, June 30, 1808; Feb. 24, 1809.
241. Senator White of Delaware. Annals of Congress, 1808-09, p. 52.
242. Works, vol. v. p. 336.

sentiment. From all parts of the country men began silently and covertly to undermine the working of the system. Passamaquoddy Bay on the borders of New Brunswick, and St. Mary's on the confines of Florida, remote from ordinary commerce, became suddenly crowded with vessels.[243] Coasters, not from recalcitrant New England only, but from the Chesapeake and Southern waters, found it impossible to reach their ports of destination. Furious gales of wind drove them from their course; spars smitten with decay went overboard; butts of planking started, causing dangerous leaks. Safety could be found only by bearing up for some friendly foreign port, in Nova Scotia or the West Indies, where cargoes of flour and fish had to be sold for needed repairs, to enable the homeward voyage to be made. Not infrequently the vessel's name had been washed off the stern by the violence of the waves, and the captain could remember neither it nor his own. The New York and Vermont frontiers became the scene of widespread illegal trade, the shameful effects of which upon the patriotism of the inhabitants were conspicuous in the following war. A gentleman returning from Canada in January, 1809, reported that he had counted seven hundred sleighs, going and returning between Montreal and Vermont.[244] This on one line only. A letter received in New York stated that, during the embargo year, 1808, thirty thousand barrels of potash had been brought into Quebec.[245] "While our gunboats and cutters are watching the harbours and sounds of the Atlantic," said a senator from his place, "a strange inversion of business ensues, and by a retrograde motion of all the interior machinery of the country, potash and lumber are launched upon the lakes, and Ontario and Champlain feel the bustle of illicit traffic. . . . Violators of the laws are making fortunes, while the conscientious observ-

---

243. "Trinidad, July 1, 1808. We have just received 15,000 barrels of flour from Passamaquoddy, and not a week passes but some drops in from Philadelphia, Norfolk, etc. Cargo of 1,000 barrels would not now command more than twelve dollars; a year ago, eighteen." (N.Y. Evening Post, July 25.)
244. N.Y. Evening Post, Jan. 17, 1809.
245. Ibid., February 6.

ers of them are suffering sad privations."[246] Not the conscientious only, but the unlucky. Unlike New York, North Carolina had not a friendly foreign boundary nigh to her naval stores.

Under these circumstances the blow glanced from the British dominions. At the first announcement of the embargo, prices of provisions and lumber rose heavily in the West Indies; but reaction set in, as the leaks in the dam became manifest and copious. The British Government fostered the rebellious evasions of American citizens by a proclamation, issued April 11, directing commanders of cruisers not to interrupt any neutral vessel laden with provisions or lumber, going to the West Indies; no matter to whom the property belonged, nor whether the vessel had any clearance, or papers of any kind. A principal method of eluding the embargo, Gallatin informed Jefferson, was by loading secretly and going off without clearing. "Evasions are chiefly effected by vessels going coastwise."[247] The two methods were not incompatible. Besides the sea-going vessels already mentioned as lying in New York alone, there were there over four hundred coasters. It was impossible to watch so many. The ridiculous gunboats, identified with this Administration, derisively nicknamed "Jeffs"[248] by the unbelieving, were called into service to arrest the evil; but neither their numbers nor their qualities fitted them to cope with the ubiquity and speed of their nimble opponents. "The larger part of our gunboats," wrote Commodore Shaw[249] from New Orleans, "are well known to be dull sailers." "For enforcing the embargo," said Secretary Gallatin, "gunboats are better calculated as a stationary force, and for the purpose of stopping vessels in certain places, than for pursuit."[250] A double bond was a mockery, when in West Indian ports the cargo was worth from four to eight times what it was at the place of loading. These were the palmier days of the embargo breakers; the ease and frequency with which they escaped soon

---

246. Mitchill of N.Y. Annals of Congress, 1808-09, pp. 86, 92.
247. Jefferson's Works, vol. v. pp. 298, 318.
248. N.Y. Evening Post, Aug. 31, 1808.
249. Feb. 17, 1812. Captains' Letters, U.S. Navy Department MSS.
250. American State Papers, Finance, vol. ii. p. 306.

brought prices down. Randolph, in the House, asserted that in the first four months of embargo one hundred thousand barrels of flour had been shipped from Baltimore alone; and the West India planters, besides opening new sources of supply, devoted part of their ground to raising food. They thus turned farmer, after the Jefferson ideal, supporting themselves off their own grounds; an economical error, for sugar was their better crop, but unavoidable in the circumstances. With all this, the difficulty in the way of exportation so cheapened articles in the United States as to maintain a considerable disproportion in prices there and abroad, which kept alive the spirit of speculation, and maintained the opportunity of large profits,[251] at the same time that it distressed the American grower.

Upon the whole, after making allowance for the boasts which succeeded the first fright in the West Indies, the indications seem to be that they escaped much better than had been expected, either by themselves or by the American Government. Just before adjourning, Congress had passed a supplementary measure, which, besides drawing restrictions tighter, authorized the President to license vessels to go abroad in ballast, in order to bring home property belonging to American citizens. These dispersed in various directions, and in very large numbers.[252] Many doubtless remained away; but those which returned brought constant confirmation of the numerous American shipping in the various ports of the West Indies, and the general abundance of American produce. A letter from Havana, September 12, said: "We have nearly one hundred American vessels in port. Three weeks ago there were but four or five. If the property, for which these vessels were ostensibly despatched, had been really here, why have they been so long delayed? The truth is, the property is not here. A host of people have been let loose, who could not possibly

---

251. With flour varying at short intervals from $30 to $18, and $12, a barrel, it is evident that speculation must be rife, and also that only general statements can be made as to conditions over any length of time.
252. Orchard Cook, of Massachusetts, said in the House of Representatives that 590 vessels sailed thus by permission. Annals of Congress, 1808-09, p. 1250.

have had any other motive than procuring freight and passengers from merchants of this country, or from the French, who are supposed to be going off with their property (in consequence of the Spanish outbreak). The vast number of evasions and smugglers which the embargo has created is surprising. For some days after the last influx of American vessels, the quays and custom-house were every morning covered with all kinds of provisions, which had been landed during the preceding night."[253]

To Quebec and Halifax the embargo was a positive boon, from the diversion upon them of smuggling enterprise, by the lakes and by land, or by coasters too small to make the direct voyage to the West Indies. In consequence of the embargo, these towns became an *entrepôt* of commerce, such as the Orders in Council were designed to make the British Islands. There was, of course, a return trade, through them, of British manufactures smuggled into the United States. These imports seem to have exceeded the exports by the same route. A New Bedford town meeting, in August, affirmed that gold was already at a premium, from the facility with which it was transported through the country, and across the frontier, in payment of purchases.[254] At the end of the summer one hundred and fifty vessels were despatched from Quebec with full cargoes, and it may be believed they had not arrived empty.

> From a Canada price current now before us, it will be seen that since the embargo was laid the single port of Quebec has done more foreign business than the whole United States. In less than eleven months there cleared thence three hundred and thirty-four vessels.[255]

An American merchant visiting Halifax wrote home:

> Our embargo is an excellent thing for this place. Every inhabitant of Nova Scotia is exceedingly desirous of its continuance, as it will be the making of their fortunes.[256]

---

253. N.Y. Evening Post, Oct. 3, 1808.
254. Ibid., Sept. 2, 1808.
255. N.Y. Evening Post, Feb. 28, 1809.
256. Ibid., Sept. 21, 1808.

Independent of the *entrepôt* profit, the British provinces themselves produced several of the articles which figured largely among the exports of the middle and eastern states; not to the extent imagined by Sheffield, sufficient to supply the West Indies, but, in the artificial scarcity caused by the embargo, the enhanced prices redounded directly to their advantage. Sir George Prevost, governor of Nova Scotia, summed up the experience of the year by saying that—

> .... the embargo has totally failed. New sources have been resorted to with success to supply deficiencies produced by so sudden an interruption of commerce, and the vast increase of export and import of this province proves that the embargo is a measure well adapted to promote the true interests of his Majesty's American colonies.[257]

Upon the British Islands themselves the injury was more appreciable and conspicuous. It was, moreover, in the direction expected by Jefferson and his supporters. The supply of cotton nearly ceased. Mr. Baring, March 6, 1809, said in the House of Commons that raw material had become so scarce and so high, that in many places it could not be procured.

> In Manchester during the greatest part of the past year, only nine cotton mills were in full employment; about thirty-one at half work, and forty-four without any at all.[258]

Flaxseed, essential to the Irish linen manufactures, and of which three fourths came from America, had risen from £2½ to £23 the quarter.[259] The exports for the year 1808 had fallen fifteen per cent; the imports the same amount, involving a total diminution in trade of £14,000,000. An increase of distress was manifested in the poor rates. In Manchester they had risen from £24,000 to £49,000. On the other hand, the harvest for the year, contrary to first anticipation, had been very good; and, in part compensation for intercourse with the United States,

---

257. Ibid., Dec. 8, 1808.
258. Cobbett's Parliamentary Debates, vol. xii. p. 1194.
259. Lord Grenville in House of Lords. Ibid., p. 780.

there was the opening of Spain, Portugal, and their extensive colonies, the effect of which was scarcely yet fully felt.

There was, besides, the relief of American competition in the carrying trade. This was a singularly noteworthy effect of the embargo; for this industry was particularly adverse to United States navigation, and particularly benefited by the locking up of American shipping. On April 28, 1808, there was not in Liverpool a vessel from Boston or New York.[260] The year before, four hundred and eighty-nine had entered, paying a tonnage duty of £36,960.[261] In Bristol at the same time there were only ten Americans. In consequence of the loss of so much tonnage, "those who have anything to do with vessels for freight or charter are absolutely insolent in their demands. For a ship of 330 tons from this to St. Petersburg and back £3,300 have been paid; £2,000 for a ship of 199 tons to Lisbon and back."[262] At the end of August, in Liverpool, the value of British shipping had increased rapidly, and vessels which had long been laid up found profitable employment at enormous freights.[263]

Thus, while the effect of the embargo doubtless was to raise prices of American goods in England, it stopped American competition with the British carrying trade, especially in West India produce. This occurred also at the time when the revolt of Spain opened to British navigation the colonies from which Americans hitherto had been the chief carriers. The same event had further relieved British shipping by the almost total destruction of French

---

260. N.Y. Evening Post, June 28, 1808.
261. Ibid., April 8.
262. Ibid., June 28.
263. Ibid., October 27. The same effect, though on a much smaller scale, was seen in France. Deprived, through the joint operation of the embargo and the Orders in Council, of colonial produce brought by Americans, a number of vessels were fitted out, and armed as letters of *marque*, to carry on this trade. These adventures were very successful, though they by no means filled the void caused by the absence of American carriers. See Evening Post of Dec. 29, 1808, and March 22 and 28, 1809. One of these, acting on her commission as a letter of *marque*, captured an American brig, returning from India, which was carried into Cayenne and there condemned under the Milan Decree. Ibid., Dec. 6, 1808.

privateering, thenceforth banished from its former ports of support in the Caribbean. From all these causes, the appreciation quoted from a London letter of September 5 seems probably accurate.

> The continuance of the embargo is not as yet felt in any degree adequate to make a deep impression on the public mind.... Except with those directly interested (merchants in the American trade), the dispute with the United States seems almost forgotten, or remembered only to draw forth ironical gratitude, that the kind embargo leaves the golden harvest to be reaped by British enterprise alone.[264]

Upon the whole, through silent popular resistance, and the concurrence of the Spanish revolution, the United States by cutting its own throat underwent more distress than it inflicted upon the enemy. Besides the widespread individual suffering,[265] already mentioned, the national revenue, dependent almost wholly on customs, shrank with the imports. Despite the relief afforded by cargoes bound home when the embargo passed, and the permits issued to bring in American property abroad, the income from this source sank from over $16,000,000 to $8,400,000.[266] Gallatin wrote in a public report:

> However dissimilar in some respects it is not believed that in their effect upon national wealth and public revenue war and embargo would be materially different. In case of war, some part of that revenue will remain; but if embargo and suspension of commerce continue, that which arises from commerce will entirely disappear."[267]

---

264. N.Y. Evening Post, Nov. 23, 1808.
265. For some instances see: Annals of Congress, 1808-09, p. 428; N.Y. Evening Post, Feb. 5, 8, 12; May 13; Aug. 26; Sept. 27, 1808. Gallatin, in a report dated Dec. 10, 1808, said, "At no time has there been so much specie, so much redundant unemployed capital in the country;" scarcely a token of prosperity in so new a country. (American State Papers, Finance, vol. ii. p. 309.)
266. American State Papers, Finance, vol. ii. pp. 307, 373, 442. The second figure is an average of the two years, 1808, 1809, within which fell the fifteen months of embargo.
267. Ibid., p. 309 (Dec. 10, 1808).

Jefferson nevertheless clung to the system, even to the end of his life, with a conviction that defied demonstration. The fundamental error of conception, of course, was in considering embargo an efficient alternative for war. The difference between the two measures, regarded coercively, was that embargo inflicted upon his own people all the loss that war could, yet spared the opponent that which war might do to him. For the United States, war would have meant, and when it came did mean, embargo, and little more. To Great Britain it would have meant all that the American embargo could do, plus the additional effort, expense, and actual loss, attendant upon the increased exposure of her maritime commerce, and its protection against active and numerous foes, singularly well fitted for annoyance by their qualities and situation. War and embargo, combined, with Napoleon in the plenitude of his power, as he was in 1808, would sorely have tried the enemy; even when it came, amid the Emperor's falling fortunes, the strain was severe. But Jefferson's lack of appreciation for maritime matters, his dislike to the navy, and the weakness to which he had systematically reduced it, prevented his realizing the advantages of war over embargo, as a measure of coercion. To this contributed also his conviction of the exposure of Canada to offensive operations, which was just, though fatally vitiated by an unfounded confidence in untrained troops, or militia summoned from their farms. Neither was there among his advisers any to correct his views; rather they had imbibed their own from him, and their utterances in debate betray radical misapprehension of military considerations.

Among the incidents attendant upon the embargo was the continuance abroad of a number of American vessels, which were there at the passage of the Act. They remained, willing exiles, to share the constant employment and large freights which the sudden withdrawal of their compatriots had opened to British navigation. They were doubtless joined by many of those which received permission to sail in quest of American property. One flagrant instance of such abuse of privilege turned up at Leghorn, with a load of tropical produce;[268] and the comments above quoted from an Havana letter doubtless depended upon that current acquaintance with facts which men in the midst of affairs pick up. It was against this class of traders specifically that Napoleon launched the Bayonne Decree, April 17, 1808. Being abroad contrary to the law of the United States, he argued, was a clear indication that they were not American, but British in disguise. This they were not; but they were carrying on trade under the Orders in Council, and often under British convoy.[269] The fact was noteworthy, as bearing upon the contention of the United States Government soon after, that the Non-Intercourse Law was adequate security for the action of American merchant vessels; a grotesque absurdity, in view of the embargo experiences. That it

---

268. "The schooner *John Clayton*, from La Guayra, with two hundred thousand pounds of coffee, has been seized at Leghorn, and it was expected would be condemned under the Bayonne Decree. The 'John' sailed from Baltimore for La Guayra, by permission, under the fourth supplementary Embargo Act. By some means or other she found her way to Leghorn, where it was vainly hoped she might safely dispose of her cargo." (N.Y. Evening Post, Dec. 20, 1808.) "The frigate '*Chesapeake*,' Captain Decatur, cruising in support of the embargo, captured off Block Island the brig 'Mount Vernon' and the ship 'John' loaded with provisions. Of these the former, at least, is expressly stated to have cleared 'in ballast,' by permission." (Ibid., Aug. 15, 1808.)

269. Two or three quotations are sufficient to illustrate a condition notorious at the time. "Jamaica. Nine Americans came with the June fleet, (from England) with full cargoes. At first it was thought these vessels would not be allowed to take cargoes, (because contrary to Navigation Act); but a little reflection taught the Government better. Rum is the surplus crop of Jamaica, and to keep on hand that which they do not want is too much our way (*i.e.* embargo). The British admiral granted these vessels convoy without hesitation, which saved them from five to seven and one half percent in insurance." (N.Y. Evening Post, Aug. 2, 1808.) "Gibraltar. A large number of American vessels are in these seas, sailing under license from Great Britain, to and from ports of Spain, without interruption. Our informant sailed in company with eight or ten, laden with wine and fruit for England." (Ibid., June 30.) Senator Hillhouse, of Connecticut: "Many of our vessels which were out when the embargo was laid have remained out. They have been navigating under the American flag, and have been constantly employed, at vast profit." (Annals of Congress, 1808, p. 172.)

is not consonant with national self-esteem to accept foreign assistance to carry out national laws is undeniable; but it is a step further to expect another nation to accept, as assured, the efficiency of an authority notoriously and continually violated by its own subjects.

Under the general conditions named, the year 1808 wore on to its close. Both the British Orders in Council and the Decrees of the French Emperor continued in force and received execution;[270] but so far as the United States was concerned their effect was much limited, the embargo retaining at home the greater part of the nation's shipping. The vessels which had remained abroad, and still more those which escaped by violation of the law, or abuse of the permission to sail unloaded to bring back American property, for the most part purchased immunity by acquiescence in the British Orders. They accepted British licenses, and British convoy also, where expedient. It was stated in Congress that, of those which went to sea under permission, comparatively few were interrupted by British cruisers.[271] Na-

270. "At Gibraltar, between January 1 and April 15, eight vessels were sent in for breach of the Orders, of which seven were condemned." (N.Y. Evening Post, May 25, 1808.) "Baltimore, Sept. 30. 1808. Arrived brig. *Sophia* from Rotterdam, July 28, *via* Harwich, England. Boarded by British brig 'Phosphorus', and ordered to England. After arrival, cargo (of gin) gauged, and a duty exacted of eight pence sterling per gallon. Allowed to proceed, with a license, after paying duty. In company with the 'Sophia', and sent in with her, were three vessels bound for New York, with similar cargoes." (Ibid., Oct. 3.) "American ship 'Othello,' from New York for Nantes, with assorted cargo. Ship, with thirty hogsheads of sugar condemned on ground of violating blockade;" *i.e.* Orders in Council. (*Naval Chronicle*, vol. xx. p. 62.) Besides the *Othello* there are two other cases, turning on the Orders, by compliance or evasion. From France came numerous letters announcing condemnations of vessels, because boarded by British cruisers. (*N.Y. Evening Post*, Sept. 10, Oct. 5, Oct. 27, Dec. 6, Dec. 10, 1808; March 17, 1809.) Proceedings were sometimes even more peremptory. More than one American vessel, though neutral, was burned or sunk at sea, as amenable under Napoleon's decrees. (Ibid., Nov. 3 and Nov. 5, Dec. 10, 1808.) See also affidavits in the case of the "Brutus", burned, and of the "Bristol Packet", scuttled. (Ibid., April 5 and April 7, 1808.)
271. Hillhouse in the Senate (Annals of Congress, 1808, p. 172), and Cook, of Massachusetts, in the House. "Of about five hundred and ninety which sailed, only eight or ten have been captured." (Ibid., 1808-09, p. 1250.) Yet many went to Guadaloupe and other (continued o n next page)

poleon's condemnations went on apace, and in the matter of loss,—waiving questions of principle,—were at this moment a more serious grievance than the British Orders. Nor could it be said that the grounds upon which he based his action were less arbitrary or unjust. The Orders in Council condemned a vessel for sailing for an enemy's port, because constructively blockaded—a matter as to which at least choice was free; the Milan Decree condemned because visited by a British cruiser, to avoid which a merchant ship was powerless. The American brig *Vengeance* sailed from Norfolk before the embargo was laid, for Bilboa, then a port in alliance with France. On the passage the British frigate *Iris* boarded her, and indorsed on her papers that, in accordance with the orders of November 11, she must not proceed. That night the *Vengeance* gave the cruiser the slip, and pursued her course. She was captured off Bilboa by a French vessel, sent in as a prize, and condemned because of the frigate's visit.[272] This case is notable because of the pure application of a single principle, not obscured by other incidental circumstances, as often happens. The brig *George*, equally bound to Bilboa, after visitation by a British vessel had been to Falmouth, and there received a British license to go to her destination. She was condemned for three offenses: the visit, the entrance to Falmouth, and the license.[272] These cases were far from isolated, and quite as flagrant as anything done by Great Britain; but, while not overlooked, nor unresented, by the supporters of the embargo, there was not evident in the debates of Congress any such depth of feeling as was aroused by the British measures. As was said by Mr. Bayard, an Opposition Senator, "It may be from the habit of enduring, but we do not feel an aggression from France with the same quickness and sensibility that we do from England."[273]

---

forbidden French islands. At Saint Pierre, Martinique, in the middle of September, were nearly ninety American vessels. "Flour, which had been up to fifty dollars per barrel, fell to thirty dollars, in consequence of the number of arrivals from America." (N.Y. Evening Post, Sept. 20, 1808.) This shows how the permission to sail "in ballast" was abused.
272. N.Y. Evening Post, Sept. 7, 1808.
273. Annals of Congress, 1808-09, p. 406.

Throughout the year 1808, the embargo was maintained by the Administration with as much vigour as was possible to the nature of the administrator, profoundly interested in the success of a favourite measure. Congress had supplemented the brief original Act by a prohibition of all intercourse with foreign territories by land, as well as by sea. This was levelled at the Florida and Canada frontiers. Authority had been given also for the absolute detention of all vessels bound coastwise, if with cargoes exciting suspicion of intention to evade the laws. Part of the small navy was sent to cruise off the coast, and the gunboats were distributed among the maritime districts, to intercept and to enforce submission. Steps were taken to build vessels on Lakes Ontario and Champlain; for, in the undeveloped condition of the road systems, these sheets of water were principal means of transportation, after snow left the ground. To the embargo the Navy owed the brig *Oneida*, the most formidable vessel on Ontario when war came. All this restrictive service was of course extremely unpopular with the inhabitants; or at least with that active, assertive element, which is foremost in pushing local advantages, and directs popular sentiment. Nor did feeling in all cases refrain from action. April 19, the President had to issue a proclamation against combinations to defy the law in the country about Champlain. The collector at Passamaquoddy wrote that, with upwards of a hundred vessels in port, he was powerless; and the mob threatened to burn his house.[274] A Kennebec paper doubted whether civil society could hang together much longer. There were few places in the region where it was safe for civil officers to execute the laws.[274] Troops and revenue vessels were despatched to the chief centres of disturbance; but, while occasional rencounters occurred, attended at times with bloodshed, and some captures of smuggled goods were effected, the weak arm of the Government was practically powerless against universal connivance in the disaffected districts. Smuggling still continued to a large extent, and was very profitable; while the determination of the smugglers assumed the character commonly styled desperate.

---

274. N.Y. Evening Post, May 4 and 13, 1808.

Such conditions, with a falling revenue, and an Opposition strong in sectional support, confronted the supporters of the Administration when Congress again met in November. Confident that embargo was an efficient coercive weapon, if relentlessly wielded, the President wished more searching enactments, and power for more extensive and vigorous enforcement. This Congress proceeded to grant. Additional revenue cutters were authorized; and after long debate was passed an Act for the Enforcement of the Embargo, approved January 9, 1809.[275] The details of this law were derived from a letter[276] addressed to a Committee of Congress by Gallatin, the Secretary of the Treasury, upon whom the administration of the embargo system chiefly fell. The two principal difficulties so far encountered were the evasions of vessels bound coastwise, and departure without clearance. "The infractions thus practised threaten to prostrate the law and the Government itself." Even to take cargo on board should not be permitted, without authorization from the collector of the district. "The great number of vessels now laden and in a state of readiness to depart shows the necessity of this provision."

It was therefore enacted that no vessel, coasting or registered, should load, without first having obtained permission from the custom-house, and given bond, in six times the value of the cargo, that she would not depart without a clearance, nor after clearing go to any foreign port, or transfer her lading to any other vessel. The loading was to be under the inspection of revenue officers. Ships already loaded, when notice of the Act was received, must unload or give bonds. Further to insure compliance, vessels bound coastwise must, within two months after sailing, deposit with the collector at the port of clearance a certificate from the collector at the port of destination, that they had arrived there. If going to New Orleans from the Atlantic coast, four months were allowed for this formality. Failing this, proof of total loss at sea would alone relieve the bond. "Neither capture, distress, nor

---

275. For the text of the Act see Annals of Congress, 1808-09, pp. 1798-1803.
276. Ibid., p. 233.

any other accident, shall be pleaded or given in evidence." Collectors were empowered to take into custody specie and goods, whether on vessels or land vehicles, when there was reason to believe them intended for exportation; and authority was given to employ the army and navy, and the militia, for carrying out this and the other embargo legislation. A further provision of thirty armed vessels, to stop trade, was made by this Congress; which otherwise, like its predecessors and successors, was perfectly faithful to the party tradition not to protect trade, or seek peace, by providing a navy.

All this was sitting on the safety valve. However unflattering to national self-esteem it might be to see national legislation universally disregarded, the leakage of steam by evasion had made the tension bearable. The Act also opened to a number of subaltern executive officers, of uncertain discretion, an opportunity for arbitrary and capricious action, to which the people of the United States were unaccustomed. Already a justice of a circuit court had decided in opposition to instructions issued by the President himself. The new legislation was followed by an explosion of popular wrath and street demonstrations. These were most marked in the Eastern states, where the opposition party and the shipping interest were strongest. Feeling was the more bitter, because the revolt of Spain, and the deliverance of Portugal, had exempted those nations and their extensive colonies from the operation of the British Orders in Council, had paralyzed in many of their ports the edicts of Napoleon, and so had extended widely the field safe for neutral commerce. It was evident also that, while the peninsula everywhere was the scene of war, it could not feed itself; nor could supplies for the population, or for the British armies there, come from England, often narrowly pressed herself for grain. Cadiz was open on August 26; all neutrals admitted, and the British blockade raised. Through that portal and Lisbon might flow a golden tide for American farmers and shipmen. The town meetings of New England again displayed the power for prompt political agitation which so impressed the imagination of Jefferson. The

Governor of Connecticut refused, on constitutional grounds, to comply with the President's request to detail officers of militia, to whom collectors could apply when needing assistance to enforce the laws. The attitude of the Eastern people generally was that of mutiny; and it became evident that it could only be repressed by violence, and with danger to the Union.

Congress was not prepared to run this risk. On February 8, less than a month after the Enforcement Act became law, its principal supporter in the Senate[277] introduced a resolution for the partial repeal of the Embargo Act. "This is not of my choice," he said, "nor is the step one by which I could wish that my responsibility should be tested. It is the offspring of conciliation, and of great concession on my part. On one point we are agreed,—resistance to foreign aggressions. The points of difficulty to be adjusted,—and compromised,—relate to the extent of that resistance and the mode of its application. In my judgment, if public sentiment could be brought to support them, wisdom would dictate the combined measures of embargo, non-intercourse, and war. Sir, when the love of peace degenerates into fear of war, it becomes of all passions the most despicable." It was not the first time the word "War" had been spoken, but the occasion made it doubly significant and ominous; for it was the requiem of the measure upon which the dominant party had staked all to avoid war, and the elections had already declared that power should remain in the same hands for at least two years to come. Within four weeks Madison was to succeed his leader, Jefferson; with a Congressional majority, reduced indeed, but still adequate.

The debate over the new measure, known as the Non-Intercourse Act, was prolonged and heated, abounding in recriminations, ranging over the whole gamut of foreign injuries and domestic misdoings, whether by Government policy or rebellious action; but clearer and clearer the demand for war was heard, through and above the din. An emotional follower of the Administration said:

---

277. Giles of Virginia. Annals of Congress, 1808-09, pp. 353-381.

When the late intelligence from the north-east reached us it bore a character most distressful to every man who valued the integrity of the Government. Choosing not to enforce the law with the bayonet, I thought proper to acknowledge to the House that I was ready to abandon the embargo. . . . The excitement in the East renders it necessary that we should enforce it by the bayonet, or repeal. I will repeal, and could weep over it more than over a lost child.

There was, he said, nothing now but war.[278] "The very men who now set your laws at defiance," cried another, "will be against you if you go to war;" but he added, "I will never let go the embargo, unless on the very same day on which we let it go, we draw the sword."[279]

Josiah Quincy, an extremist on the other side, gave a definition of the position of Massachusetts, which from his ability, and his known previous course on national questions, is particularly valuable. In the light of the past, and of what was then future, it may be considered to embody the most accurate summary of the views prevailing in New England, from the time of the Chesapeake affair to the war. He wished—

> . . . . a negotiation to be opened, unshackled with the impedimenta which now exist. As long as they remained, people in the part of the country whence he came would not deem an unsuccessful attempt at negotiation cause for war. If they were removed, and an earnest attempt at negotiation made, unimpeded by these restrictions, and should not meet with success, they would join heartily in a war. They would not, however, go to war to contest the right of Great Britain to search American vessels for British seamen; for it was the general opinion with them that, if American seamen were encouraged, there would be no need for the employment of foreign seamen.[280]

---

278. Williams of South Carolina. Annals of Congress, 1808-09, p. 1236.
279. Nelson of Maryland. Annals of Congress, 1808-09, p. 1258.
280. Annals of Congress, 1808-09, pp. 1438-1439.

Quincy therefore condemned the retaliatory temper of the Administration, as shown in the Chesapeake incident by the proclamation excluding British ships of war, and in the embargo as a reply to the Orders in Council. The oppression of American trade, culminating in the Orders, was a just cause of war; but war was not expedient before a further attempt at negotiation, favoured by a withdrawal of all retaliatory acts. He was willing to concede the exercise of British authority on board American merchantmen on the high seas.

In the main these were the coincident opinions of Monroe, although a Virginian and identified with the opposite party. At this time he wrote to Jefferson privately, urging a special mission, for which he offered his services.

> Our affairs are evidently at a pause, and the next step to be taken, without an unexpected change, seems likely to be the commencement of war with both France and Great Britain, unless some expedient consistent with the honour of the Government and Country is adopted to prevent it.

To Jefferson's rejection of the proposition he replied:

> I have not the hope you seem still to entertain that our differences with either Power will be accommodated under existing arrangements. The embargo was not likely to accomplish the desired effect, if it did not produce it under the first impression.... Without evidence of firm and strong union at home, nothing favourable to us can be expected abroad, and from the symptoms in the Eastern states there is much cause to fear that tranquillity cannot be secured at present by adherence only to the measures which have heretofore been pursued.[281]

Monroe had already[282] expressed the opinion—not to Jefferson, who had refused to ratify, but to a common intimate—that had the treaty of December 31, 1806, signed by himself

---
281. Monroe to Jefferson, Jan. 18 and Feb. 2, 1809. Monroe's Works, vol. v. pp. 91, 93-95.
282. To John Taylor, January 9. Ibid., p. 89.

and Pinkney, been accepted by the Administration, none of the subsequent troubles with France and Great Britain would have ensued; that not till the failure of accommodation with Great Britain became known abroad was there placed upon the Berlin Decree that stricter interpretation which elicited the Orders in Council, whence in due sequence the embargo, the Eastern commotions, and the present alarming outlook. In principle, Quincy and Monroe differed on the impressment question, but in practical adjustment there was no serious divergence. In other points they stood substantially together.

Under the combined influences indicated by the expressions quoted, Congress receded rapidly from the extreme measures of domestic regulation embodied in the various Embargo Acts and culminating in that of January 9. The substitute adopted was pronouncedly of the character of foreign policy, and assumed distinctly and unequivocally the hostile form of retaliation upon the two countries under the decrees of which American commerce was suffering. It foreshadowed the general line of action followed by the approaching new Administration, with whose views and purposes it doubtless coincided. Passed in the House on February 27, 1809, it was to go into effect May 20, after which date the ports of the United States were forbidden to the ships of war of both France and Great Britain, except in cases of distress, or of vessels bearing despatches. Merchant vessels of the two countries were similarly excluded, with a provision for seizure, if entering. Importation from any part of the dominions of those states was prohibited, as also that of any merchandise therein produced. Under these conditions, and with these exceptions, the embargo was to stand repealed from March 15 following; but American and other merchant vessels, sailing after the Act went into operation, were to be under bonds not to proceed to any port of Great Britain or France, nor during absence to engage in any trade, direct or indirect, with such port. From the general character of these interdictions, stopping both navigation and commerce between the United States and the countries proscribed, this measure was commonly called the Non-Intercourse Act. Its stormy passage through the House was marked by a number of amendments and proposed substitutes, noticeable principally as indicative of the growth of warlike temper among Southern members. There were embodied with the bill the administrative and police clauses necessary for its enforcement. Finally, as a weapon of negotiation in the hands of the Government, there was a provision, corresponding to one in the original Embargo Act, that in case either France or Great Britain should so modify its measures as to cease to violate the neutral commerce of the United States, the President was authorized to proclaim the fact, after which trade with that country might be renewed. In this shape the bill was returned to the Senate, which concurred February 28. Next day it became law, by the President's signature.

The Enforcement Act and the Non-Intercourse Act, taken together and in their rapid sequence, symbolize the death struggle between Jefferson's ideal of peaceful commercial restriction, unmitigated and protracted, in the power of which he had absolute faith, and the views of those to whom it was simply a means of diplomatic pressure, temporary, and antecedent to war. Napoleon himself was not more ruthless than Jefferson in his desired application of commercial prohibition. Not so his party, in its entirety. The leading provisions of the Non-Intercourse Act, by partially opening the door and so facilitating abundant evasion, traversed Jefferson's plan. It was antecedently notorious that their effect, as regarded Great Britain, would be to renew trade with her by means of intermediary ports. Yet that they were features in the policy of the men about to become prominent under the coming Administration was known to Canning some time before the resolution was introduced by Giles; before the Enforcement Act even could reach England. Though hastened by the outburst in New England, the policy of the Non-Intercourse Act was conceived before the collapse of Jefferson's own measure was seen to be imminent.

On January 18 and 22 Canning, in informal conversations with Pinkney, had expressed his satisfaction at proceedings in

Congress, recently become known, looking to the exclusion of French ships equally with British, and to the extension of non-importation legislation to France as well as Great Britain.[283] He thought that such measures might open the way to a withdrawal of the Orders in Council, by enabling the British Government to entertain the overture, made by Pinkney August 23, under instructions, that the President would suspend the embargo, if the British Government would repeal its orders. This he conceived could not be done, consistently with self-respect, so long as there was inequality of treatment. In these anticipations he was encouraged by representations concerning the attitude of Madison and some intended members of his Cabinet, made to him by Erskine, the British Minister in Washington, who throughout seems to have cherished an ardent desire to reconcile differences which interfered with his just appreciation even of written words,—much more of spoken.

In the interview of the 22nd Pinkney confined himself to saying everything "which I thought consistent with candour and discretion to confirm him in his dispositions." He suggested that the whole matter ought to be settled at Washington, and "that it would be well (in case a special mission did not meet their approbation) that the necessary powers should be sent to Mr. Erskine."[284] He added, "I offered my intervention for the purpose of guarding them against deficiencies in these powers."[285] The remark is noteworthy, for it shows Pinkney's sense that Erskine's mere letter of credence as Minister Resident, not supplemented by full powers for the special transaction, was inadequate to a binding settlement of such important matters. In the sequel the American Administration did not demand of Erskine the production either of special powers or of the text of his instructions; a routine formality which would have forestalled the mortifying error into which it was betrayed by precipitancy, and which became the occasion of a breach with Erskine's successor.

---

283. Pinkney, in connection with these, speaks of the "expected" Act of Congress. American State Papers, Foreign Relations, vol. iii. p. 299.
284. American State Papers, Foreign Relations, vol. iii. p. 299.
285. This sentence was omitted in the papers when submitted to Congress.

The day after his interview with Pinkney, Canning sent Erskine instructions,[286] the starting-point of which was that the Orders in Council must be maintained, unless their object could be otherwise accomplished. Assuming, as an indispensable preliminary to any negotiation, that equality of treatment between British and French ships and merchandise would have been established, he said he understood further from Erskine's reports of conversations that the leading men in the new Administration would be prepared to agree to three conditions:

1. That, contemporaneously with the withdrawal of the Orders of January 7 and November 11, there would be a removal of the restrictions upon British ships and merchandise, leaving in force those against French.

2. The claim, to carry on with enemies' colonies a trade not permitted in peace, would be abandoned for this war.

3. Great Britain should be at liberty to secure the operation of the Non-Intercourse measures, still in effect against France, by the action of the British Navy, which should be authorized to capture American vessels seeking to enter ports forbidden them by the Non-Intercourse Act. Canning justly remarked that otherwise Non-Intercourse would be nugatory; there would be nothing to prevent Americans from clearing for England or Spain and going to Holland or France. This was perfectly true. Not only had a year's experience of the embargo so demonstrated, but a twelvemonth later[287] Gallatin had to admit that—

> . . . . the summary of destinations of these exports, being grounded on clearances, cannot be relied on under existing circumstances. Thus, all the vessels actually destined for the dominions of Great Britain, which left the United States between April 19 and June 10, 1809, cleared for other ports; principally, it is believed, for Sweden.

Nevertheless, the proposition that a foreign state should enforce national laws, because the United States herself could not,

---
286. State Papers, p. 300.
287. February 7, 1810. American State Papers, Commerce and Navigation, vol. i. p. 812.

was saved from being an insult only by the belief, extracted by Canning from Erskine's report of conversations, that Madison, or his associates, had committed themselves to such an arrangement. He added that Pinkney "recently (but for the first time)" had expressed an opinion to the same effect.

The British Government would consent to withdraw the Orders in Council on the conditions cited; and for the purpose of obtaining a distinct and official recognition of them, Canning authorized Erskine to read his letter *in extenso* to the American Government. Had this been done, as the three concessions were a *sine quâ non*, the misunderstanding on which the despatch was based would have been at once exposed; and while its assumptions and tone could scarcely have failed to give offence, there would have been saved the successive emotions of satisfaction and disappointment which swept over the United States, leaving bitterness worse than before. Instead of communicating Canning's letter, Erskine, after ascertaining that the conditions would not be accepted, sent in a paraphrase of his own, dated April 18,[288] in which he made no mention of the three stipulations, but announced that, in consequence of the impartial attitude resulting from the Non-Intercourse Act, his Majesty would send a special envoy to conclude a treaty on all points of the relations between the two countries, and meanwhile would be willing to withdraw the Orders of January 7 and November 11, so far as affecting the United States, in the persuasion that the President would issue the proclamation restoring intercourse. This advance was welcomed, the assurance of revocation given, and the next day Erskine wrote that he was "authorized to declare that the Orders will have been withdrawn as respects the United States on the 10th day of June next." The same day, by apparent preconcertment, in accordance with Canning's requirement that the two acts should be coincident, Madison issued his proclamation, announcing the fact of the future withdrawal, and that trade between the United States and Great Britain might be renewed on June 10.

---

288. The correspondence between Erskine and the Secretary of State on this occasion is in American State Papers, Foreign Relations, vol. iii. pp. 295-297.

Erskine's proceeding was disavowed instantly by the British Government, and himself recalled. A series of unpleasant explanations followed between him and the members of the American Government,[289] astonished by the interpretation placed upon their words, as shown in Canning's despatch. Canning also had to admit that he had strained Erskine's words, in reaching his conclusions as to the willingness of Madison and his advisers to allow the enforcement of the Non-Intercourse Act by British cruisers;[290] while Pinkney entirely disclaimed intending any such opinion as Canning imagined him to have expressed.[291] The British Secretary was further irritated by the tone of the American replies to Erskine's notes; but he "forbore to trouble"[292] Pinkney with any comment upon them. That would be made through Erskine's successor; an unhappy decision, as it proved. No explanation of the disavowal was given; but the instructions sent were read to Pinkney by Canning, and a letter followed saying that Erskine's action had been in direct contradiction to them. Things thus returned to the momentarily interrupted condition of American Non-Intercourse and British Orders in Council; the British Government issuing a temporary order for the protection of American vessels which might have started for the ports of Holland in reliance upon Erskine's assurances. From America there had been numerous clearances for England; and it may be believed that there would have been many more if the transient nature of the opportunity had been foreseen. August 9, Madison issued another proclamation, annulling the former.

While Erskine was conducting his side negotiation, the British Government had largely modified the scope of the restrictions laid upon neutral trade. In consequence of the various events which had altered its relations with European states and their dependencies, the Orders of November, 1807, were revoked; and for them was substituted a new one, dated April

---

289. American State Papers, Foreign Relations, vol. iii. pp. 304-308.
290. Ibid., p. 303.
291. Ibid.
292. Ibid., p. 301.

26, 1809,[293] similar in principle but much curtailed in extent. Only the coasts of France itself, of Holland to its boundary, the River Ems, and those of Italy falling under Napoleon's own dominion, from Orbitello to Pesaro, were thenceforth to be subject to "the same restrictions as if actually blockaded." Further, no permission was given, as in the former Orders, to communicate with the forbidden ports by first entering one of Great Britain, paying a transit duty, and obtaining a permit to proceed. In terms, prohibition was now unqualified; and although it was known that licenses for intercourse with interdicted harbours were freely issued, the overt offence of prescribing British channels to neutral navigation was avoided. Within the area of restriction, "No trade save through England" was thus converted, in form, to no trade at all. This narrowing of the constructive blockade system, combined with the relaxations effected by the Non-Intercourse Act, and with the food requirements of the Spanish peninsula, did much to revive American commerce; which, however, did not again before the war regain the fair proportions of the years preceding the embargo. The discrepancy was most marked in the re-exportation of foreign tropical produce, sugar and coffee, a trade dependent wholly upon war conditions, and affecting chiefly the shipping interest engaged in carrying it. For this falling off there were several causes. After 1809 the Continental system was more than ever remorselessly enforced, and it was to the Continent almost wholly that Americans had carried these articles. The Spanish colonies were now open to British as well as American customers; and the last of the French West Indies having passed into British possession, trade with them was denied to foreigners by the Navigation Act. In 1807 the value of the colonial produce re-exported from the United States was $59,643,558; in 1811, $16,022,790. The exports of domestic productions in the same years were: 1807, $48,699,592; in 1811, $45,294,043. In connection with these figures, as significant of political conditions, it is interesting to note that of the latter sum $18,266,466 went

---

293. American State Papers, Foreign Relations, vol. iii. p. 241.

to Spain and Portugal, chiefly to supply demands created by war. So with tropical produce; out of the total of $16,022,790, $5,772,572 went to the Peninsula, and an equal amount to the Baltic, that having become the centre of accumulation, from which subsequent distribution was made to the Continent in elusion of the Continental System. The increasing poverty of the Continent, also, under Napoleon's merciless suppression of foreign commerce, greatly lessened the purchasing power of the inhabitants. The great colonial trade had wasted under the combined action of British Orders and French Decrees, supplemented by changes in political relations. The remote extremities of the Baltic lands and the Spanish peninsula now alone sustained its drooping life.

Coincident with Erskine's recall had been the appointment of his successor, Mr. Francis J. Jackson, who took with him not only the usual credentials, but also full powers for concluding a treaty or convention.[294] He departed for his post under the impulse of the emotions and comments excited by the manner and terms in which Erskine's advances had been met, with which Canning had forborne to trouble Pinkney. Upon his arrival in Washington, disappointment was expressed that he had no authority to give any explanations of the reasons why his Government had disavowed arrangements, entered into by Erskine, concerning not only the withdrawal of the Orders in Council,—as touching the United States,—but also the reparation for the Chesapeake business. This Erskine had offered and concluded, coincidently with the revocation of the Orders, though not in connection with it; but in both instances his action was disapproved by his Government. After two verbal conferences, held within a week of Jackson's arrival, the Secretary of State, Mr. Robert Smith, notified him on October 9 that it was thought expedient, for the present occasion, that further communication on this matter should be in writing. There followed an exchange of letters, which in such circumstances passed necessarily under the eyes of President Madison, who for the eight preceding years had held Smith's present office.

---

294. American State Papers, Foreign Relations, vol. iii. p. 318.

This correspondence[295] presents an interesting exhibition of diplomatic fencing; but beyond the discussion, pro and con, of the matters in original and continuous dispute between the two countries, the issue turned upon the question whether the United States had received the explanation due to it,—in right and courtesy,—of the reasons for disavowing Erskine's agreements. Smith maintained it had not. Jackson rejoined that sufficient explanation had been given by the terms of Canning's letter of May 27 to Pinkney, announcing that Erskine had been recalled because he had acted in direct contradiction to his instructions; an allegation sustained by reading to the American minister the instructions themselves. In advancing this argument, Jackson stated also that Canning's three conditions had been made known by Erskine to the American Government, which, in declining to admit them, had suggested substitutes finally accepted by Erskine; so that the United States understood that the arrangement was reached on another basis than that laid down by Canning. This assertion he drew from the expressions of Erskine in a letter to Canning, after the disavowal. Smith replied that Erskine, while not showing the despatch, had stated the three stipulations; that they had been rejected; and that the subsequent arrangement had been understood to be with a minister fully competent to recede from his first demand and to accept other conditions. Distinctly he affirmed, that the United States Government did not know, at any time during the discussion preceding the agreement, that Erskine's powers were limited by the conditions in the text of his instructions, afterwards published. That he had no others, "is now for the first time made known to this Government," by Jackson's declaration.

Jackson had come prepared to maintain, not only the British contention, but the note set by Canning for British diplomatic correspondence. He was conscious too of opposing material force to argument, and had but recently been amid the scenes at Copenhagen, which had illustrated Nelson's maxim that a fleet of ships of the line were the best negotiators in Europe. The

---

295. American State Papers, Foreign Relations, vol. iii. pp. 308-319.

JAMES MADISON FROM THE PAINTING BY GILBERT STUART, IN BOWDOIN COLLEGE, BRUNSWICK, ME.

position has its advantages, but also its dangers, when the field of warfare is that of words, not deeds; and in Madison, who superintended the American case, he was unequally matched with an adversary whose natural dialectical ability had been tempered and sharpened in many campaigns. There is noticeable, too, on the American side, a laboured effort at acuteness of discrimination, an adroitness to exaggerate shades of difference practically imperceptible, and an aptitude to give and take offence, not so evident under the preceding Administration. These suggest irresistibly the absence, over Madison the President, of a moderating hand, which had been held over Madison the Secretary of State. It may be due also to the fact that both the President and his Cabinet were somewhat less indisposed to war than his predecessor had been.

In his answer to Smith Jackson reiterated, what Smith had admitted, that Erskine had made known the three conditions. He added, "No stronger illustration of the deviation from them which occurred can be given than by a reference to the terms of the agreement." As an incidental comment, supporting the contention that Erskine's departure from his sole authority was so decisive as to be a sufficient explanation for the disavowal of his procedure, the words were admissible; so much so as to invite the suspicion that the opponent, who had complained of the want of such explanation, felt the touch of the foil, and somewhat lost temper. Whatever impression of an insinuation the phrase may have conveyed should have been wholly removed by the further expression, in close sequence, "You are already acquainted with the instruction given; and *I have had*[296] the honour of informing you it was the only one." Smith's knowledge that Erskine's powers were limited to the one document is here attributed explicitly to Jackson. The Secretary (or President) saw fit not to recognize this, but took occasion to administer a severe rebuke, which doubtless the general tone of Jackson's letter tended to provoke.

> I abstain, sir, from making any particular animadversions on several irrelevant and improper allusions in your letter. . . .

---

296. Author's italics.

But it would be improper to conclude the few observations to which I purposely limit myself, without adverting to your repetition of a language implying a knowledge, on the part of this Government, that the instructions of your predecessor did not authorize the arrangement formed by him. After the explicit and peremptory asseveration that this Government had no such knowledge, and that with such a knowledge no such arrangement would have been entered into, the view which you have again presented of the subject makes it my duty to apprise you that such insinuations are inadmissible in the intercourse of a foreign minister with a Government that understands what it owes to itself.

Whatever may be thought of the construction placed upon Jackson's words by his opponent, this thrust should have made him look to his footing; but arrogance and temper carried the day, and laid him open to the fatal return which he received. By drawing attention to the qualifying phrase, he could have shown that he had been misunderstood, but he practically accepted the interpretation; for, instead of repelling it, he replied:

> In my correspondence with you I have carefully avoided drawing conclusions that did not necessarily follow from the premises advanced by me, and least of all should I think of uttering an insinuation where I was unable to substantiate a fact. To facts, such as I have become acquainted with them, I have scrupulously adhered, and in so doing I must continue, whenever the good faith of his Majesty's Government is called in question, etc.

To this outburst the reply was:

> You have used language which cannot but be understood as reiterating, and even aggravating, the same gross insinuation. It only remains, in order to preclude opportunities which are thus abused, to inform you that no further communications will be received from you, and that the necessity for this determination will, without delay, be made known to your Government.

Jackson thereupon quitted Washington for New York, leaving a *chargé d'affaires* for transacting current business.

Before leaving the city, however, Jackson, through the channel of the *chargé*, made a statement to the Secretary of State. In this he alleged that the facts which he considered it his duty to state, and to the assertion of which, as facts, exception was taken, and his dismissal attributed, were two. One was, that the three conditions had been submitted by Mr. Erskine to the Secretary of State. This the Secretary had admitted.

> The other, namely: that that instruction is the only one, in which the conditions were prescribed to Mr. Erskine, for the conclusion of an arrangement on the matter to which it related, is known to Mr. Jackson by the instructions which he has himself received.

This he had said in his second letter; if somewhat obscurely, still not so much so but that careful reading, and indisposition to take offence, could have detected his meaning, and afforded him the opportunity to be as explicit as in this final paper. If Madison, who is understood to have given special supervision to this correspondence,[297] meant the severe rebuke conveyed by his reply as a feint, to lead the British minister incautiously to expose himself to a punishment which his general bearing and that of his Government deserved, he assuredly succeeded; yet it may be questioned who really came best out of the encounter. Jackson had blundered in words; the American Administration had needlessly intensified international bitterness.

Prepossession in reading, and proneness to angry misconception, must be inferred in the conduct of the American side of this discussion; for another notable and even graver instance occurs in the despatch[298] communicating Jackson's dismissal to Pinkney, beyond whose notice it probably was not allowed to go. Canning, in his third rejected condition, had written:

---

297. See Madison's Works, vol. ii. p. 499.
298. American State Papers, Foreign Relations, vol. iii. 319-322.

Great Britain, for the purpose of securing *the operation of the embargo*, and of the *bonâ fide* intention of America to prevent her citizens from trading with France, and the Powers adopting and acting under the French decrees, is to be considered as being at liberty to capture all such American vessels as shall be found attempting to trade with the ports of such Powers;[299] and he explained that, unless such permission was granted, "the raising of the embargo nominally as to Great Britain, would raise it, in fact, with respect to all the world," owing to the evident inability of the United States to enforce its orders beyond its own ports.

In the passage quoted, both the explanatory comment and the syntax show that the object of this proposed concession was to secure *the operation*, the effectual working, of the *bonâ fide* intention expressly conceded to the American Government. The repetition of the preposition "of," before *bonâ fide*, secures this meaning beyond peradventure. Nevertheless Smith, in laboured arraignment of the whole British course, wrote to Pinkney as follows:

> In urging this concession, Mr. Canning has taken a ground forbidden by those principles of decorum which regulate and mark the proceedings of Governments towards each other. In his despatch the condition is stated to be for the purpose of *securing the bonâ fide intention* of America, to prevent her citizens from trading with France and certain other Powers; in other words to secure a pledge to that effect against the *malâ fide* intention of the United States. And this despatch too was authorized to be communicated *in extenso* to the Government, of which such language was used.[300]

---

299. The italics in this quotation (American State Papers, vol. iii. p. 300) are introduced by the author, to draw attention to the words decisive to be noted.

300. The italics are Smith's. They serve exactly, however, to illustrate just wherein consists the perverseness of omission (the words "operation of"), and the misstatement of this remarkable passage.

Being addressed only to Pinkney, a man altogether too careful and shrewd not to detect the mistake, no occasion arose for this grave misstatement doing harm, or receiving correction. But, conjoined with the failure to note that Jackson in his second letter had attributed to his own communication the American Government's knowledge that Erskine had no alternative instructions, the conclusion is irresistible that the President acted, perhaps unconsciously, under impulses foreign to the deliberate care which should precede and accompany so momentous an act as the refusal to communicate with an accredited foreign minister. It will be remembered that this action was taken on grounds avowedly independent of the reasonableness or justice of the British demands. It rested purely on the conduct of the minister himself.

This incident powerfully furthered the alienation of the two nations, for the British Government not only refused to disapprove Jackson's conduct, but for nearly two years neglected to send a successor, thus establishing strained diplomatic relations. Before finally leaving this unlucky business, it is due to a complete appreciation to mention that, in its very outset, at the beginning of Erskine's well-meant but blundering attempt, the United States Government had overpassed the limits of diplomatic civility. Canning was a master of insolence; he could go to the utmost verge of insult and innuendo, without absolutely crossing the line which separates them from formal observance of propriety; but it cannot be said that the American correspondence in this instance was equally adroit. In replying to Erskine's formal offer of reparation for the Chesapeake affair, certain points essential to safeguarding the position of the United States were carefully and properly pointed out; then the reparation, as tended, was accepted. There the matter might have dropped; acceptance is acceptance; or, if necessary, failure of full satisfaction on the part of the United States might have been candidly stated, as due to itself. But the Secretary[301] proceeded to words—and mere words—reflecting on the British Sovereign and Government.

---

301. Secretary Smith subsequently stated that this sentence was added by express interposition of the President. (Smith's Address to the American people.)

I have it in express charge from the President to state, that, while he forbears to insist upon the further punishment of the offending officer, he is not the less sensible of the justice and utility of such an example, nor the less persuaded that it would best comport with what is due from his Britannic Majesty to his own honour.

To the writer nothing quite as bad as this occurs in Jackson's letters, objectionable as they were in tone. With the opinion he agrees; the further employment of Berkeley was indecent, nor was he a man for whom it could be claimed that he was indispensable; but it is one thing to hold an opinion, and another to utter it to the person concerned. Had Madison meant war, he might have spoken as he did, and fought; but to accept, and then to speak words barren of everything but useless insult, is intolerable. Jackson very probably believed that the American Government was lying when it said it did not know the facts as to Erskine's instructions.[302] It would be quite in character that he should; but he did not say so. There was put into his mouth a construction of his words which he heedlessly accepted.

Jackson's dismissal was notified to the British Government through Pinkney, on January 2, 1810.[303] Some time before, a disagreement within the British Cabinet had led to a duel between Castlereagh and Canning, in which the latter was severely wounded. He did not return to the Foreign Office, but was succeeded by the Marquis Wellesley, brother of the future Duke of Wellington. After presenting the view of the correspondence taken by his Government, Pinkney seems to betray a slight uneasiness as to the accuracy of the interpretation placed on Jackson's words.

---

302. Canning in his instructions to Jackson (No. 1, July 1, 1809, Foreign Office MSS.) wrote: "The United States cannot have believed that such an arrangement as Mr. Erskine consented to accept was conformable to his instructions. *If* Mr. Erskine availed himself of the liberty allowed to him of communicating those instructions in the affair of the Orders in Council, they must have *known* that it was not so." My italics.
303. American State Papers, Foreign Relations, vol. iii. p. 352

I willingly leave your Lordship to judge whether Mr. Jackson's correspondence will bear any other construction than that it in fact received; and whether, supposing it to have been erroneously construed, his letter of the 4th of November should not have corrected the mistake, instead of confirming and establishing it.

Wellesley, with a certain indolent nonchalance, characteristic of his correspondence with Pinkney, delayed to answer for two months, and then gave a reply as indifferent in manner as it was brief in terms. Jackson had written:

> There appears to have prevailed, throughout the whole of this transaction (Erskine's), a fundamental mistake, which would suggest that his Majesty had proposed to propitiate the Government of the United States, to consent to the renewal of commercial intercourse;. . . . as if, in any arrangement, his Majesty would condescend to barter objects of national policy and dignity for permission to trade with another country.

The phrase was Canning's, and summarized precisely the jealous attitude towards its own prestige characteristic of the British policy of the day. It also defined exactly the theory upon which the foreign policy of the United States had been directed for eight years by the party still in power. Madison and Jefferson had both placed just this construction upon Erskine's tender.

> The British Cabinet must have changed its course under a full conviction that an adjustment with this country had become essential.[304]

> Gallatin had a conversation with Turreau at his residence near Baltimore. He professes to be confident that his Government will consider England broken down, by the examples she has given in repealing her Orders.[305]

---

304. Writings of James Madison. Published by Order of Congress, 1865. Vol. ii. p. 439.
305. Ibid., p. 440. Turreau was the French minister.

By our unyielding adherence to principle Great Britain has been forced into revocation.[306]

Canning and his associates intuitively divined this inference, which after all was obvious enough. The feeling increased their discontent with Erskine, who had placed his country in the false light of receding under commercial pressure from America, and probably enough prepossessed them with the conviction that the American Government could not but have realized that Erskine was acting beyond his powers.

Wellesley, after his manner,—which was not Canning's,—asserted equally the superiority of the British Government to concession for the sake of such advantage. His Majesty regretted the Jackson episode, the more so that no opportunity had been given for him to interpose, which "was the usual course in such cases." Mr. Jackson had written positive assurances that it was not his purpose to give offence; to which the reply was apt, that in such matters it is not enough to intend, but to succeed in avoiding offence.[307]

> His Majesty has not marked, with any expression of his displeasure, the conduct of Mr. Jackson, who does not appear, on this occasion, to have committed any intentional offence against the Government of the United States.

A *chargé* would be appointed to carry on the ordinary intercourse, but no intention was expressed of sending another minister. Persistence in this neglect soon became a further ground of bad feeling.

By its own limitations the Non-Intercourse Act was to expire at the end of the approaching spring session of the new Congress, but it was renewed by that body to the end of the winter session. During the recess the Jackson episode occurred, and was the first subject to engage attention on reassembling, November

---

306. Works of Jefferson, vol. v. pp. 442-445.
307. "When Lord Wellesley's answer speaks of the offence imputed to Jackson, it does not say he gave no such cause of offence, but simply relied on his repeated asseverations that he did not mean to offend." Pinkney to Madison, Aug. 13, 1810. Wheaton's Life of Pinkney, p. 446.

27, 1809. After prolonged discussion in the lower house,[308] a joint resolution was passed approving the action of the Executive, and pledging to him the support of the nation. Despite a lucid exposition by Josiah Quincy, that the offence particularly attributed to the British minister was disproved by a reasonable attention to the construction of his sentences, the majority persisted in sustaining the party chief. That disposed of, the question of commercial restriction was again taken up.

It was conceded on all sides that Non-Intercourse had failed, and precisely in the manner predicted. On the south, Amelia Island,—at the mouth of the St. Mary's River, just outside the Florida boundary,—and on the north Halifax, and Canada in general, had become ports of deposit for American products, whence they were conveyed in British ships to Great Britain and her dependencies, to which the Act forbade American vessels to go. The effect was to give the carrying of American products to British shipping, in precise conformity with the astute provisions of the Navigation Acts. British markets were reached by a broken voyage, the long leg of which, from Amelia and Halifax to Europe and elsewhere, was taken by British navigation. It was stated that there were at a given moment one hundred British vessels at Amelia,[309] the shores of which were encumbered with American goods awaiting such transportation. The freight from the American ports to Amelia averaged a cent a pound, from Amelia to England eight cents;[310] the latter amount going to British pockets, the former to Americans who were debarred from full transatlantic freight by the prohibitions of the Non-Intercourse Act. The absence of competition necessarily raised the prices obtainable by the British shipper, and this, together with the additional cost of transhipment and delays, attendant upon a broken voyage, fell upon the American agriculturist, whose goods commanded just so much less at their place of origin. The measure was even ingeniously *malaprop*, considered from the point of view of its

---

308. Annals of Congress, 1809-10.
309. Ibid., January 8, 1810, pp. 1164, 1234.
310. Ibid., p. 1234.

purpose towards Great Britain, whether retaliatory or coercive. Upon France its effect was trivial, in any aspect. There was no French navigation, and the Orders in Council left little chance for American vessels to reach French ports.

All agreed that the Non-Intercourse Act must go; the difficulty was to find a substitute which should not confessedly abandon the whole system of commercial restrictions, idealized by the party in power, but from which it was being driven foot by foot. A first measure proposed was to institute a Navigation Act, borrowed in broad outline from that of Great Britain, but in operation applied only to that nation and France, in retaliation for their injurious edicts.[311] Open intercourse with the whole world should be restored; but British and French merchant ships, as well as vessels of war, should be excluded from American harbours. British and French products could be imported only in vessels owned wholly by American citizens; and after April 15, 1810, could be introduced only by direct voyage from the place of origin. This was designed to prevent the continuance of trade by way of Amelia or Halifax. It was pointed out in debate, however, that French shipping practically did not exist, and that in the days of open trade, before the embargo, only about eight thousand tons of British shipping yearly entered American ports, whereas from three hundred thousand to four hundred thousand American tons visited Great Britain.[312] Should she, by a strict retaliation, resent this clumsy attempt at injuring her, the weight of the blow would fall on Americans. American ships would be excluded from British ports; the carrying trade to Amelia and Halifax would be resumed, to the detriment of American vessels by a competition which otherwise would not exist, and British manufactures would be introduced by smuggling, to the grievous loss of the revenue, as had been notoriously and abundantly the case under the Non-Intercourse Act. In truth, a purely commercial war with Great Britain was as injurious as a military war, and more hopeless.

---

311. Annals of Congress, 1809-10, pp. 754, 755.
312. Ibid., pp. 606, 607.

The bill consequently failed in the Senate, though passed by the House. In its stead was adopted an Act which repealed that of Non-Intercourse, but prescribed that in case either Great Britain or France, before March 3, 1811, should so revoke or modify its edicts as that they should cease to violate the neutral commerce of the United States, the President should declare the fact by proclamation; and if the other nation should not, within three months from the date of such proclamation, in like manner so modify or revoke its edicts, there should revive against it those sections of the Non-Intercourse Act which excluded its vessels from American ports, and forbade to American vessels importation from its ports, or of its goods from any part of the world whatsoever. The determination of the fact of revocation by either state was left to the sole judgment of the President, by whose approval the Act became law May 1, 1810.[313]

As Great Britain and France, by the Orders in Council and the Berlin and Milan Decrees, were then engaged in a commercial warfare, in which the object of each was to exhaust its rival, the effect of this Act was to tender the co-operation of the United States to whichever of them should embrace the offer. In terms, it was strictly impartial between the two. In fact, forasmuch as France could not prevent American intercourse with Great Britain, whereas Great Britain, in furtherance of her purposes, could and did prevent American trade with France, the latter had much more to gain; and particularly, if she should so word her revocation as to save her face, by not appearing the first to recede,—to show weakening,—as Great Britain had been made for the moment to seem by Erskine's arrangement. Should this ingenious diplomacy prove satisfactory to the President, yet fail so to convince Great Britain as to draw from her the recall of the Orders in Council, the United States, by the simple operation of the law itself, would become a party to the Emperor's Continental system, in its specific aim of reducing his opponent's strength.

---

313. Annals of Congress, 1810, p. 2582.

At this very moment Napoleon was putting into effect against the United States one of those perverse and shameless interpretations of international relations, or actions, by which he not infrequently contrived to fill his pockets. The Non-Intercourse Act, passed March 3, 1809, had decreed forfeiture of any French or British ship, or goods, which should enter American waters after May 20, of the same year. The measure was duly communicated to the French Government, and no remonstrance had been made against a municipal regulation, which gave ample antecedent warning. There the matter rested until March 23, 1810, when the Emperor, on the ground of the Act, imposing these confiscations and forbidding American vessels to visit France, signed a retroactive decree that all vessels under the flag of the United States, which, since May 20, 1809, had entered ports of his empire, colonies, or of the countries occupied by his arms, should be seized and sold. Commissioners were sent to Holland to enforce there this edict, known as the Decree of Rambouillet, which was not actually published till May 14.[314] It took effect upon vessels which, during a twelvemonth previous, unwarned, had gone to France, or the other countries indicated. Immediately before it was signed, the American minister, Armstrong, had written to Champagny, Duke of Cadore, the French Minister of Foreign Affairs, "Your Excellency knows that there are not less than one hundred American ships within his Majesty's possession, or that of his allies;" and he added that, from several sources of information, he felt warranted in believing that not a single French vessel had violated the Non-Intercourse law, and therefore none could have been seized.[315]

The law of May 1 was duly communicated to the two states concerned, by the United States ministers there resident. Great Britain was informed that not only the Orders in Council, but the blockade of May, 1806,[316] were included among the edicts

---

314. For Armstrong's letter and the text of the Decree, see American State Papers, Foreign Relations, vol. iii. p. 384.
315. Armstrong to Champagny, March 10, 1810. American State Papers, Foreign Relations, vol. iii. p. 382.
316. American State Papers, Foreign Relations, vol. iii. p. 362.

affecting American commerce, the repeal of which was expected, as injurious to that commerce. France was told that this demand would be made upon her rival;[317] but that it was also the purpose of the President not to give the law effect favourable to herself, by publishing a proclamation, if the late seizures of the property of citizens of the United States had been followed by absolute confiscation, and restoration were finally refused.[318] This referred not to the Rambouillet Decree, as yet unknown in America, but to the previous seizures upon various pretexts, mentioned above by Armstrong. Ultimately this purpose was not adhered to; but the Emperor was attentive to the President's intimation that "by putting in force, agreeably to the terms of this statute, the non-intercourse against Great Britain, the very species of resistance would be made which France has constantly been representing as most efficacious."[319] Thus, the co-operation of America to the Continental System was no longer asked, but offered.

The Emperor did not wait even for information by the usual official channels. By some unexplained delay, Armstrong's first knowledge was through a copy of the Gazette of the United States containing the Act, which he at once transmitted to Champagny, who replied August 5, 1810.[320] His Majesty wished that the acts of the United States Government could be more promptly communicated; not till very lately had he heard of the Non-Intercourse,—a statement which Armstrong promptly denied, referring Champagny to the archives of his own department.[321] In view of the Act of May 1, the Emperor's decision was announced in a paragraph of the same letter, in the following words:

> In this new state of things I am authorized to declare to you, Sir, that the Decrees of Berlin and Milan are revoked, and that after the first of November they will cease to have effect; it being understood that, in consequence of this dec-

---

317. Ibid., p. 385.
318. Ibid.
319. The Secretary of State to Armstrong, June 5, 1810. American State Papers, Foreign Relations, vol. iii. p. 385.
320. American State Papers, Foreign Relations, vol. iii. p. 386.
321. Ibid., p. 387

laration, the English shall revoke their Orders in Council, and renounce the new principles of blockade, which they have wished to establish; or that the United States, conformably to the Act which you have just communicated, shall cause their rights to be respected by the English.

Definition is proverbially difficult; and over this superficially simple definition of circumstances and conditions, under which the Decrees of Berlin and Milan stood revoked, arose a discussion concerning construction and meaning which resembled the wrangling of scholars over a corrupt text in an obscure classical author. Clear-headed men became hopelessly involved, as they wrestled with each others' interpretations; and the most got no farther than sticking to their first opinions, probably reached in the majority of cases by sheer prepossession. The American ministers to France and Great Britain both accepted the words as a distinct, indisputable, revocation; and Madison followed suit. These hasty conclusions are not very surprising; for there was personal triumph, dear to diplomatists as to other men, in seeing the repeal of the Decrees, or of the Orders, result from their efforts. It has been seen how much this factor entered into the feelings of Madison and Jefferson in the Erskine business, and to Armstrong the present turn was especially grateful, as he was about quitting his mission after several years buffeting against wind and tide. His sun seemed after all about to set in glory. He wrote to Pinkney, "I have the honour to inform you that his Majesty, the Emperor and King, has been pleased to revoke his Decrees of Berlin and Milan."[322] Pinkney, to whom the recall of the British Orders offered the like laurels, was equally emphatic in his communication to Wellesley; adding, "I take for granted that the revocation of the British Orders in Council of January and November, 1807, April, 1809, and all other orders dependent upon, or analogous, or in execution of them, will follow of course."[323] The British Government demurred to the interpretation; but

---

322. American State Papers, Foreign Relations, vol. iii. p. 364.
323. Ibid., p. 365.

Madison accepted it, and on November 2 proclaimed it as a fact. In consequence, by the terms of the Act, non-intercourse would revive against Great Britain on February 2, 1811.

When Congress met, distrust on one side and assertion on the other gave rise to prolonged and acute discussion. Napoleon had surprised people so often, that no wonder need be felt at those who thought his words might bear a double meaning. The late President, who did not lack sagacity, had once written to his successor:

> Bonaparte's policy is so crooked that it eludes conjecture. I fear his first object now is to dry up the sources of British prosperity, by excluding her manufactures from the Continent. He may fear that opening the ports of Europe to our vessels will open them to an inundation of British wares.[324]

This was exactly Bonaparte's dilemma, and suggested the point of view from which his every action ought to be scrutinized. Then there was the recent deception with Erskine, which, if it increased the doubts of some concerning the soundness of Madison's judgment, made it the more incumbent on others to show that on this occasion at least he had not been precipitate. Certainly, as regards the competency of the foreign official in either case, there was no comparison. A simple Minister Resident should produce particular powers or definite instructions, to guarantee his authority for concluding so important a modification of national policy as was accepted from Erskine; but by common usage the Minister of Foreign Affairs, at a national capital, is understood to speak for the Chief Executive. The statement of Champagny, at Paris, that he was "authorized" to make a specific declaration, could be accepted as the voice of Napoleon himself. The only question was, what did the voice signify?

In truth, explicit as Champagny's words sound, Napoleon's memoranda,[325] on which they were based, show a deliberate

---

324. Jefferson to Madison, April 27, 1809. Works, vol. v. p. 442.
325. Correspondance de Napoléon. Napoleon to Champagny, July 31, and August 2, 1810, vol. xx. p. 644, and vol. xxi. p. 1.

purpose to avoid a formal revocation, for reasons analogous to those suggested by Jefferson. Throughout he used *rapporter* instead of *révoquer*. In the particular connection, the words are nearly synonymous; yet to the latter attaches a natural fitness and emphasis, the avoidance of which betrays the bias, perhaps unconscious, towards seeking escape from self-committal on the matter in hand. His phrases are more definite. July 31 he wrote:

> After much reflection upon American affairs, I have decided that to withdraw (*rapporter*) my decrees of Berlin and Milan would conduce to nothing (*n'aurait aucun effet*); that it is better you should address a note to Mr. Armstrong, in which you will acquaint him that you have placed before me the details contained in the American gazette,.... . and since he assures us it may be regarded as official, he may depend (*compter*) that my decrees of Berlin and Milan will not receive execution (*n'auront aucun effet*) dating from November 1; and that he should consider them as withdrawn (*rapportés*) in consequence of the Act of the American Congress; provided, etc....
> This seems to me more suitable than a decree, which would cause disturbance and would not fulfil my aim. This method seems to me more conformable to my dignity and to the serious character of the business.

The Decrees, as touching the United States alone, were to be quietly withdrawn from action, but not formally revoked. They were to be dormant, yet potential. As convenience might dictate, it would be open to say that they were revoked (in effect), or not revoked (in form). The one might, and did, satisfy the United States; the other might not, and did not, content Great Britain, against whom exclusion from the continent remained in force. The two English-speaking peoples were set by the ears. August 2 the Emperor made a draft of the note to be sent to Armstrong. This Champagny copied almost verbatim in the declaration quoted; substituting, however, *révoquer* for *rapporter*.

It would be intolerable to attempt to drag readers through the mazes of analysis, and of comparison with other papers, by which the parties to the discussion, ignorant of the above memoranda, sought to establish their respective views. One thing, however, should have been patent to all,—that, with a man so subtle and adroit as Napoleon, any step in apparent reversal of a decided and cherished policy should have been complete and unequivocal, both in form and in terms. The Berlin Decree was put forth with the utmost formality with which majesty and power could invest it; the asserted revocation, if apparently explicit, was simply a paragraph in ordinary diplomatic correspondence, stating that revocation had taken place. If so, where was it? An act which undoes another, particularly if an injury, must correspond fully in form to that which it claims to undo. A private insult may receive private apology; but no private expression can atone for public insult or public wrong. In the appreciation of Mr. Madison, in 1807, so grave an outrage as that of the Chesapeake called for a special envoy, to give adequate dignity to the proffered reparation. Yet his followers now would have form to be indifferent to substantial effect. Champagny's letter, it is true, was published in the official paper; but, besides being in form merely a diplomatic letter, it bore the signature of Champagny, whereas the decree bore that of Napoleon. The Decree of Rambouillet, then less than six months old, was clothed with the like sanction. Even Pinkney, usually so clear-headed, and in utterance incisive, suffered himself here to be misled. Does England find inadequate the "manner" of the French Revocation? he asked. "It is precisely that in which the orders of its own Government, establishing, modifying, or removing blockades, are usually proclaimed." But the Decree of Berlin was no mere proclamation of a blockade. It had been proclaimed, in the Emperor's own name, a fundamental law of the Empire, until England had abandoned certain lines of action. This was policy against policy, to which the blockade was incidental as a method. English blockades were announced and withdrawn under identical forms of circular letter; but when an Order in Council, as that of November, 1807, was modified, as in April,

1809, it was done by an Order in Council, not by a diplomatic letter. In short, Champagny's utterance was the declaration of a fact; but where was the fact itself?

Great Britain therefore refused to recognize the letter as a revocation, and could not be persuaded that it was by the opinion of the American authorities. Nor was the form alone inadequate; the terms were ambiguous, and lent themselves to a construction which would deprive her of all benefit from the alleged revocation. She had to look to her own battle, which reached its utmost intensity in this year 1810. Except the helpless Spanish and Portuguese insurgents, she had not an open friend in Europe; while Napoleon, freed from all opponents by the overthrow of Austria in 1809, had organized against Great Britain and her feeble allies the most gigantic display of force made in the peninsula since his own personal departure thence, nearly two years before. The United States had plain sailing; so far as the letter went, the Decrees were revoked, conditional on her executing the law of May 1. But Great Britain must renounce the "new" principles of blockade. What were these principles, pronounced new by the Decree? They were, that unfortified ports, commercial harbours, might be blockaded, as the United States a half century later strangled the Southern Confederacy. Such blockades were lawful then and long before. To yield this position would be to abandon rights upon which depended the political value of Great Britain's maritime supremacy; yet unless she did so the Berlin Decree remained in force against her. The Decree was universal in application, not limited to the United States commerce, towards which Champagny's letter undertook to relax it; and British commerce would remain excluded from neutral continental ports unless Great Britain not only withdrew the Orders in Council, but relinquished prescriptive rights upon which, in war, depended her position in the world.

In declining to repeal, Great Britain referred to her past record in proof of consistency. In the first communication of the Orders in Council, February 23, 1808,[326] Erskine had written:

---

326. American State Papers, Foreign Relations, vol. iii. p. 209. Author's italics.

I am commanded by his Majesty especially to represent to the Government of the United States the earnest desire of his Majesty to see the commerce *of the world* restored once more to that freedom which is necessary for its prosperity, and his readiness to abandon the system which has been forced upon him, *whenever the enemy shall retract the principles* which have rendered it necessary.

The British envoy in these sentences reproduced *verbatim* the instructions he had received,[327] and the words italicized bar expressly the subsequent contention of the United States, that revocation by one party as to one nation, irrespective of the rest *of the world*, and that in practice only, not in principle, entitled the nation so favoured to revocation by the other party. They exclude therefore, by all the formality of written words at a momentous instant, the singular assertion of the American Government, in 1811, that Great Britain had pledged herself to proceed *pari passu*[328] with France in the revocation of their respective acts. As far as can be ascertained, the origin of this confident assumption is to be found in letters of February 18 and 19, 1808,[329] from Madison, then Secretary of State, to Armstrong and Pinkney. In these he says that Erskine, in communicating the Orders,[330] expressed his Majesty's regrets, and "assurances that his Majesty would readily follow the example, in case the Berlin Decree should be rescinded, or would proceed *pari passu* with France in relaxing the rigor of their measures." By whichever of the colloquists the expression was used, the contrast between this report of an interview and the official letter quoted sufficiently shows the snare latent in conversations, and the superior necessity of relying upon written communications, to which informal talk only smoothes the way. On the very day of Madison's writing to Armstrong, February 18, the Advocate

---

327. Canning to Erskine, Dec. 1, 1807, transmitting the Orders in Council of November 11. British Foreign Office MSS.
328. Monroe to Foster, Oct. 1, 1811. American State Papers, Foreign Relations, vol. iii. p. 445. See also, more particularly, ibid., pp. 440, 441.
329. U.S. State Department MSS., and State Papers, vol. iii. p. 250.
330. That is, verbally, before his formal letter of February 23.

General, who may be presumed to have understood the purposes of the Government, was repudiating such a construction in the House of Commons.

> Even let it be granted that there had been a public assurance to America that she alone was to be excepted from the influence of the Berlin Decree, would that have been a sufficient ground for us not to look further to our own interest? What! Because France chooses to exempt America from her injurious decrees, are we to consent to their continuance?[331]

Where such a contradiction exists, to assert a pledge from a Government, and that two years after Erskine's singular performance of 1809, which led to his recall, is a curious example of the capacity of the American Administration, under Madison's guidance, for putting words into an opponent's mouth. In the present juncture, Wellesley replied[332] to Pinkney's claim for the revocation of the Orders in Council by quoting, and repeating, the assurance of Erskine's letter of February 23, 1808, given above.

Yet, unless the Orders in Council were repealed, Napoleon's concessions would not go far to relieve the United States. The vessels he would admit would be but the gleanings, after British cruisers had reaped the ocean field. Pinkney, therefore, had to

---

331. Cobbett's Parliamentary Debates, vol. x. p. 669. A search through the correspondence of Canning and Erskine, as well as through the debates of Parliament upon the Orders in Council, January-April, 1808, reveals nothing confirmatory of the *pari passu* claim, put forth in Madison's letters quoted, and afterwards used by Monroe in his arguments with Foster. But in Canning's instructions to Jackson, July 1, 1809 (No. 3), appears a sentence which may throw some light on the apparent misunderstanding. "As to the willingness or ability of neutral nations to resist the Decrees of France, his Majesty has always professed. . . . *a disposition to relax or modify his measures of retaliation and self-defence in proportion as those of neutral, nations* should come in aid of them and take their place." This would be action *pari passu* with a neutral; and if the same were expressed to Erskine, it is far from incredible, in view of his remarkable action of 1809, that he may have extended it verbally without authority to cover an act of France. My italics.
332. Wellesley to Pinkney, Aug. 31, 1810. American State Papers, Foreign Relations, vol. iii. p. 366.

be importunate in presenting the demands of his Government. Wellesley persisted in his method of procrastination. At last, on December 4, he wrote briefly to say that after careful inquiry he could find no authentic intelligence of the repeal, nor of the restoration of the commerce of neutral nations to its previous conditions. He invited, however, a fresh statement from Pinkney, who then, in a letter dated December 10,[333] argued the case at length, under the three heads of the manner, or form, the terms, and the practical effect of the alleged repeal. Having completed the argument, he took incidental occasion to present the views of the United States concerning the whole system of the Orders in Council; animadverting severely, and emphasizing with liberal italics. The Orders went far beyond any intelligible standard of *retaliation*; but it soon appeared that neutrals might be permitted to traffic, if they would submit with a dependence *truly colonial* to carry on their trade through British ports, to pay such duties as the British Government might impose, and such charges as British agents might make. The modification of April 26, 1809, was one of appearance only. True, neutrals were no longer compelled to enter British ports; their prohibition from interdicted ports was nominally absolute; but it was known that by coming to Great Britain they could obtain a license to enter them, so that the effect was the same; and by forged papers this license system was so extended "that the commerce of *England* could advantageously find its way to those ports."[334]

Wellesley delayed reply till December 29.[335] He regretted the intrusion of these closing remarks, which might tend to interfere with a conciliatory spirit, but without further comment on them addressed himself to the main question. His Government did not find the "notification" of the repeal of the French Decrees such as would justify it in recalling the Orders in Council. The United States having demanded the formal revocation of the blockade of May, 1806, as well as of the Orders in Council, he—

---

333. American State Papers, Foreign Relations, vol. iii. p. 376.
334. The American flag was used in this way to cover British shipping. For instances see American State Papers, Foreign Relations, vol. iii. p. 342.
335. American State Papers, Foreign Relations, vol. iii. p. 408.

.... must conclude, combining your requisition with that of the French Minister, that America demands the revocation of that order of blockade, as a practical instance of our renunciation of those principles of blockade which are condemned by the French Government.

This inference seems overstrained; but certainly much greater substantial concession was required of Great Britain than of France. Wellesley intimated that this concert of action was partial—not neutral—between the two belligerents.

I trust that the justice of the American Government will not consider that France, by the repeal of her obnoxious decrees, *under such a condition*,[336] has placed the question in that state which can warrant America in enforcing the Non-Intercourse Act against Great Britain, and not against France.

He reminded Pinkney of the situation in which the commerce of neutral nations had been placed by many recent acts of the French Government; and said that its system of violence and injustice required some precautions of defence on the part of Great Britain. In conclusion, his Majesty stood ready to repeal, when the French Decrees should be repealed without conditions injurious to the maritime rights and honour of the United Kingdom.

Unhappily for Pinkney's argument on the actuality of Napoleon's repeal, on the very day of his own writing, December 10, the American *chargé*[337] in Paris, Jonathan Russell, was sending Champagny a remonstrance[338] upon the seizure of an American vessel at Bordeaux, under the decrees of Berlin and Milan, on December 1,—a month after their asserted repeal. That the Director of Customs at a principal seaport should understand them to be in force, nearly four months after the publication of Champagny's letter in the *Moniteur*, would cer-

---

336. Author's italics.
337. Armstrong had sailed for the United States two months before.
338. American State Papers, Foreign Relations, vol. iii. p. 391.

tainly seem to imply some defect in customary form;[339] and the ensuing measures of the Government would indicate also something misleading in the terms. Russell told Champagny that, since November 1, the alleged day of repeal, this was the first case to which the Berlin and Milan Decrees could apply; and lo! to it they were applied. Yet, "to execute the Act of Congress against the English requires the previous revocation of the decrees." It was, indeed, ingeniously argued in Congress, by an able advocate of the Administration, that all the law required was the revocation in terms of the Decrees; their subsequent enforcement in act was immaterial.[340] Such a solution, however, would scarcely content the American people. The French Government now took a step which clearly showed that the Decrees were still in force, technically, however honest its purpose to hold to the revocation, if the United States complied with the conditions. Instructions to the Council of Prizes,[341] from the proper minister, directed that the vessel, and any others falling under the same category of entry after November 1, should "remain suspended" until after February 2, the period at which the United States should have fulfilled its obligation. Then they should be restored.

The general trend of argument, pro and con, with the subsequent events, probably shook the confidence of the Administration, and of its supporters in Congress, in the certainty of the revocation, which the President had authenticated by his proclamation. Were the fact unimpeachable, the law was clear; non-intercourse with Great Britain would go into effect February 2, without further action. But the doubts started were so

---

339. Russell on November 17 wrote that he had reason to believe that the revocation of the Decrees had not been notified to the ministers charged with the execution of them. On December 4 he said that, as the ordinary practice in seizing a vessel was to hold her sequestered till the papers were examined in Paris, this might explain why the local Custom-House was not notified of the repeal. Russell to the Secretary of State, U.S. State Department MSS.
340. Langdon Cheves of South Carolina. Annals of Congress, 1810-11, pp. 885-887.
341. American State Papers, Foreign Relations, vol. iii. p. 393.

plausible that it was certain any condemnation or enforcement under the law would be carried up to the highest court, to test whether the fact of revocation, upon which the operativeness of the statute turned, was legally established. Even should the court decline to review the act of the Executive, and accept the proclamation as sufficient evidence for its own decision, such feeble endorsement would be mortifying. A supplementary Act was therefore framed, doing away with the original, and then reviving it, as a new measure, against Great Britain alone. In presenting this, the member charged with its introduction said:

> The Committee thought proper that in this case the legislature should step forward and decide; that it was not consistent with the responsibility they owed the community to turn over to judicial tribunals the decision of the question, whether the Non-Intercourse was in force or not.[342]

The matter was thus taken from the purview of the courts, and decided by a party vote. After an exhausting discussion, this bill passed at 4 a.m., February 28, 1811. It was approved by the President, March 2.

For the settlement of American litigation this course was adequate; not so for the vindication of international procedure. The United States at this time had abundant justification for war with both France and Great Britain, and it was within the righteous decision of her own policy whether she should declare against either or both; but it is a serious impeachment of a Government's capacity and manfulness when, with such questions as Impressment, the Orders in Council, Napoleon's Decrees, and his arbitrary sequestrations, war comes not from a bold grappling with difficulties, but from a series of huckstering attempts to buy off one antagonist or the other, with the result of being fairly overreached. The outcome, summarily stated, had been that a finesse of the French Government had attached the United States to Napoleon's Continental System. She was henceforth, in effect, allied with the leading feature of French policy hostile to Great

---

342. Annals of Congress, 1810-11, p. 990.

Britain. It was perfectly competent and proper for her so to attach herself, if she saw fit. The Orders in Council were a national wrong to her, justifying retaliation and war; still more so was Impressment. But it is humiliating to see one's country finally committed to such a step through being outwitted in a paltry bargain, and the justification of her course rested, not upon a firm assertion of right, but upon the refusal of another nation to accept a manifestly unequal proposition. The course of Great Britain was high-handed, unjust, and not always straightforward; but it was candour itself alongside of Napoleon's.

There remained but one step to complete the formal breach; and that, if the writer's analysis has been correct, resulted as directly as did the final Non-Intercourse Act from action erroneously taken by Mr. Madison's Administration. Jackson's place, vacated in November, 1809, by the refusal to communicate further with him, remained still unfilled. This delay was thought deliberate by the United States Government, which on May 22 wrote to Pinkney that it seemed to manifest indifference to the character of the diplomatic intercourse between the two countries, arising from dissatisfaction at the step necessarily taken with regard to Mr. Jackson. Should this inference from Wellesley's inaction prove correct, Pinkney was directed to return to the United States, leaving the office with a *chargé d'affaires*, for whom a blank appointment was sent. He was, however, to exercise his own judgment as to the time and manner. In consequence of his interview with Wellesley, and in reply to a formal note of inquiry, he received a private letter, July 22, 1810, saying it was difficult to enter upon the subject in an official form, but that it was the Secretary's intention immediately to recommend a successor to Jackson. Still the matter dragged, and at the end of the year no appointment had been made.

In other ways, too, there was unexplained delay. In April Pinkney had received powers to resume the frustrated negotiations committed first to him and Monroe. Wellesley had welcomed the advance, and had accepted an order of discussion which gave priority to satisfaction for the Chesapeake affair.

After that an arrangement for the revocation of the Orders in Council should be attempted. On June 13 Pinkney wrote home that a verbal agreement conformable to his instructions had been reached concerning the *Chesapeake*, and that he was daily expecting a written overture embodying the terms. August 14 this had not been received,—to his great surprise, for Wellesley's manner had shown every disposition to accommodate. Upon this situation supervened Cadore's declaration of the revocation of the French Decrees, Pinkney's acceptance of the fact as indisputable, and his urgency to obtain from the British Government a corresponding measure in the repeal of the Orders. Through all ran the same procrastination, issuing in entire inaction.

Pinkney's correspondence shows a man diplomatically self-controlled and patient, though keenly sensible to the indignity of unwarrantable delays. The rough speaking of his mind concerning the Orders in Council, in his letter of December 10, suggests no loss of temper, but a deliberate letting himself go. There appeared to him now no necessity for further endurance. To Wellesley's rejoinder of December 29 he sent an answer on January 14, 1811, "written," he said, "under the pressure of indisposition, and the influence of more indignation than could well be suppressed."[343] The questions at issue were again trenchantly discussed, but therewith he brought to an end his functions as minister of the United States. Under the same date, but by separate letter, he wrote that as no steps had been taken to replace Jackson by an envoy of equal rank, his instructions imposed on him the duty of informing his lordship that the Government of the United States could not continue to be represented in England by a minister plenipotentiary. Owing to the insanity of the King, and the delays incident to the institution of a regency, his audience of leave was delayed to February 28; and it is a noticeable coincidence that the day of this formal diplomatic act was also that upon which the Non-Intercourse Bill against Great Britain passed the House

---

343. Pinkney to the Secretary of State, Jan. 17, 1811. American State Papers, Foreign Relations, vol. iii. p. 408.

of Representatives. In the course of the spring Pinkney embarked in the frigate "*Essex*" for the United States. He had no successor until after the War of 1812, and the Non-Intercourse Act remained in vigour to the day of hostilities.

On February 15, a month after Pinkney's notification of his intended departure, Wellesley wrote him that the Prince Regent, whose authority as such dated only from February 5, had appointed Mr. Augustus J. Foster minister at Washington. The delay had been caused in the first instance, "as I stated to you repeatedly," by the wish to make an appointment satisfactory to the United States, and afterwards by the state of his Majesty's Government; the regal function having been in abeyance until the King's incapacity was remedied by the institution of the Regent. Wellesley suggested the possibility of Pinkney reconsidering his decision, the ground for which was thus removed; but the minister demurred. He replied that he inferred, from Wellesley's letter, that the British Government by this appointment signified its intention of conceding the demands of the United States; that the Orders in Council and blockade of May, 1806, would be annulled; without this a beneficial effect was not to be expected. Wellesley replied that no change of system was intended unless France revoked her Decrees. The effect of this correspondence, therefore, was simply to place Pinkney's departure upon the same ground as the new Non-Intercourse Act against Great Britain.

Mr. Augustus John Foster was still a very young man, just thirty-one. He had but recently returned from the position of minister to Sweden, the duties of which he had discharged[344] during a year very critical for the fortunes of that country, and in the event for Napoleon and Europe. Upon his new mission Wellesley gave him a long letter of instructions,[345] in which he dealt elaborately with the whole course of events

---

344. Foster had succeeded as *chargé d'affaires* in May, 1809, by the departure of Merry, formerly minister to the United States. He was afterwards appointed minister; but in June, 1810, under pressure from Bonaparte, Sweden requested him to leave the country.
345. Pearce, Life and Correspondence of the Marquis Wellesley, vol. iii. p. 193.

connected with the Orders in Council and Bonaparte's Decree, especially as connected with America. In this occurs a concise and lucid summary of the British policy, which is worth quoting.

> From this view of the origin of the Orders in Council, you will perceive that the object of our system was not to crush the trade of the continent, but to counteract an attempt to crush British trade; that we have endeavoured to permit the continent to receive as large a portion of commerce as might be practicable through Great Britain, and that all our subsequent regulations, and every modification of the system, by new orders, or modes of granting or withholding licenses, have been calculated for *the purpose of encouraging the trade of neutrals through Great Britain*,[346] whenever such encouragement might appear advantageous to the general interests of commerce and consistent with the public safety of the nation,—the preservation of which is the primary object of all national councils, and the paramount duty of the Executive power.

In brief, the plea was that Bonaparte by armed constraint had forced the continent into a league to destroy Great Britain through her trade; that there was cause to fear these measures would succeed, if not counteracted; that retaliation by similar measures was therefore demanded by the safety of the state; and that the method adopted was retaliation, so modified as to produce the least possible evil to others concerned. It was admitted and deplored that prohibition of direct trade with the ports of the league injuriously affected the United States. That this was illegal, judged by the law of nations, was also admitted; but it was justified by the natural right of retaliation. Wellesley scouted the view, pertinaciously urged by the American Government, that the exclusion of British commerce from neutral continental ports by the Continental System was a mere municipal regulation, which the United States could not resist. Municipal regulation was merely the cloak, beneath

---
346. Author's italics.

which France concealed her military coercion of states helpless against her policy.

> The pretext of municipal right, under which the violence of the enemy is now exercised against neutral commerce in every part of the continent, will not be admitted by Great Britain; nor can we ever deem the repeal of the French Decrees to be effectual, until neutral commerce shall be restored to the conditions in which it stood, previously to the commencement of the French system of commercial warfare, as promulgated in the Decrees.

Foster's mission was to urge these arguments, and to induce the repeal of the Non-Intercourse law against Great Britain, as partial between the two belligerents; who, if offenders against accepted law, were in that offenders equally. The United States was urged not thus to join Napoleon's league against Great Britain, from which indeed, if so supported, the direst distress must arise. It is needless to pursue the correspondence which ensued with Monroe, now Secretary of State. By Madison's proclamation, and the passage of the Non-Intercourse Act of March 2, 1811, the American Government was irretrievably committed to the contention that France had so revoked her Decrees as to constitute an obligation upon Great Britain and upon the United States. To admit mistake, even to one's self, in so important a step, probably passes diplomatic candour, and especially after the blunder in Erskine's case. Yet, even admitting the adequacy of Champagny's letter, the Decrees were not revoked; seizures were still made under them. In November, 1811, Monroe had to write to Barlow, now American minister to France:

> It is not sufficient that it should appear that the French Decrees are repealed, in the *final decision* of a cause brought *before a French tribunal.* An active prohibitory policy should be adopted *to prevent seizures* on the principle."[347]

---

347. American State Papers, Foreign Relations, vol. iii. p. 514. Author's italics.

This was in the midst of his correspondence with Foster. The two disputants threshed over and over again the particulars of the controversy, but nothing new was adduced by either.[348] Conditions were hopeless, and war assured, even when Foster arrived in Washington, in June, 1811.

One thing, however, was finally settled. In behalf of his Government, in reparation for the *Chesapeake* affair, Foster repeated the previous disavowal of Berkeley's action, and his consequent recall; and offered to restore to the ship herself the survivors of the men taken from her. Pecuniary provision for those who had suffered in the action, or for their families, was also tendered. The propositions were accepted, while denying the adequacy of Berkeley's removal from one command to another. The men were brought to Boston harbour, and there formally given up to the *Chesapeake*.

Tardy and insufficient as was this atonement, it was further delayed, at the very moment of tendering, by an incident which may be said to have derived directly from the original injury. In June, 1810, a squadron of frigates and sloops had been constituted under Commodore John Rodgers, to patrol the coast from the Capes of the Chesapeake northward to the eastern limit of the United States. Its orders, generally, were to defend from molestation by a foreign armed ship all vessels of the United States within the marine league, seaward, to which neutral jurisdiction was conceded by international law. Force was to be used, if necessary, and, if the offender were a privateer, or piratical, she was to be sent in. So weak and unready was the nominal naval force of the United States, that piracy near her very shores was apprehended; and concern was expressed in Congress regarding vessels from Santo Domingo, thus converted into a kind of local Barbary power. To these general instructions the Secretary of the Navy attached a special reminder. Recalling the Chesapeake affair, as a merely exaggerated instance of the contumely everywhere heaped upon the American flag by both belligerents, he wrote:

---

348. Ibid., p. 435.

What has been perpetrated may be again attempted. It is therefore our duty to be prepared and determined at every hazard to vindicate the injured honour of our navy, and revive the drooping spirit of the nation. It is expected that, while you conduct the force under your command consistently with the principles of a strict and upright neutrality, you are to maintain and support at every risk and cost the dignity of our flag; and that, offering yourself no unjust aggression, you are to submit to none, not even a menace or threat from a force not materially your superior.

Under such reminiscences and such words, the ships' guns were like to go off of themselves. It requires small imagination to picture the feelings of naval officers in the years after the *Chesapeake*'s dishonour. In transmitting the orders to his captains, Rodgers added:

> Every man, woman, and child, in our country, will be active in consigning our names to disgrace, and even the very vessels composing our little navy to the ravages of the worms, or the detestable transmigration to merchantmen, should we not fulfil their expectations. I should consider the firing of a shot by a vessel of war, of either nation, and particularly England, at one of our public vessels, whilst the colours of her nation are flying on board of her, as a menace of the grossest order, and in amount an insult which it would be disgraceful not to resent by the return of two shot at least; while should the shot strike, it ought to be considered an act of hostility meriting chastisement to the utmost extent of all your force.[349]

The Secretary indorsed approval upon the copy of this order forwarded to him. Rodgers' apprehension for the fate of the navy reflected accurately the hostile views of leaders in the dominant political party. Demoralized by the gunboat system, and disorganized and browbeaten by the loud-mouthed disfavour of representative Congressmen, the extinction of the service was

---

349. Rodgers to Secretary of the Navy, Aug. 4, 1810. Captains' Letters.

not unnaturally expected. Bainbridge, a captain of standing and merit, applied at this time for a furlough to make a commercial voyage to China, owing to straitened means.

> I have hitherto refused such offers, on the presumption that my country would require my services. That presumption is removed, and even doubts entertained of the permanency of our naval establishment.[350]

The following year, 1811, Rodgers' squadron and orders were continued. The British admirals of adjacent stations, acting doubtless under orders from home, enjoined great caution upon their ships of war in approaching the American coast.[351] While set not to relax the Orders in Council, the ministry did not wish war by gratuitous offence. Cruising, however, continued, though charged with possibilities of explosion. Under these circumstances Rodgers' ship, the *President* frigate, and a British sloop of war, the *Little Belt*, sighted each other on May 16, 1811, fifty miles east of Cape Henry. Independent of the general disposition of ships of war in troublous times to overhaul and ascertain the business of any doubtful sail, Rodgers' orders prescribed the capture of vessels of certain character, even outside the three-mile limit; and, the *Little Belt* making sail from him, he pursued. About 8 p.m., it being then full dark, the character and force of the chase were still uncertain, and the vessels within range. The two accounts of what followed differ diametrically; but the British official version[352] is less exhaustive in matter and manner

---

350. Bainbridge to the Secretary of the Navy, May 3, 1810. Captains' Letters. The case was not singular.
351. Orders of Admiral Sawyer to the Captain of the "*Little Belt.*" American State Papers, Foreign Relations, vol. iii. p. 475.
352. American State Papers, vol. iii. p. 473. In the absence of the British admiral, the senior officer at Halifax assembled a board of captains which collected what his letter styles the depositions of the *Little Belt*'s officers. Depositions would imply that the witnesses were sworn, but it is not so said in the report of the Board, where they simply "state." In the case of honourable gentlemen history may give equal credit in either case; but the indication would be that inquiry was less particular. The Board reports no question by itself; the "statements" are in the first person, apparently in reply to the request "tell all you know," and are uninterrupted by comment.

than the American, which rests upon the sworn testimony of numerous competent witnesses before a formal Court of Inquiry.[353] By this it was found proved that the *Little Belt* fired the first gun, which by Rodgers' statement cut away a backstay and went into the mainmast. The batteries of both ships opened, and an engagement followed, lasting twelve or fifteen minutes, during which the *Little Belt*, hopelessly inferior in force, was badly cut up, losing nine killed and twenty-three wounded. Deplorable as was this result, and whatever unreconciled doubts may be entertained by others than Americans as to the blame, there can be no question that the affair was an accident, unpremeditated. It was clearly in evidence that Rodgers had cautioned his officers against any firing prior to orders. There was nothing of the deliberate purpose characterizing the Chesapeake affair; yet Mr. Foster, with the chariness which from first to last marked the British handling of that business, withheld the reparation authorized by his instructions until he had received a copy of the proceedings of the court.

On July 24, 1811, the President summoned Congress to meet November 4, a month before the usual time, in consequence of the state of foreign affairs. His message spoke of ominous indications; of the inflexible hostility evidenced by Great Britain in trampling upon rights which no independent nation can relinquish; and recommended legislation for increasing the military force. As regarded the navy, his words were indefinite and vague, beyond suggesting the expediency of purchasing materials for ship-building. The debates and action of Congress reflected the tone of the Executive. War was anticipated as a matter of course, and mentioned freely in speeches. That the regular army should be enlarged, and dispositions made for more effective use of the militia, was granted; the only dispute being about the amount of development. In this the legislature exceeded the President's wishes, which were understood, though not expressed in the message. Previ-

---

353. The proceedings of this court are printed in American State Papers, Foreign Relations, vol. iii. pp. 477-497.

ous Congresses had authorized an army of ten thousand, of which not more than five thousand were then in the ranks. It was voted to complete this; to add twenty-five thousand more regulars, and to provide for fifty thousand volunteers. Doubts, based upon past experience, and which proved well founded, were expressed as to the possibility of raising so many regular troops, pledged for five years to submit to the restrictions of military life. It was urged that, in the economical conditions of the country, the class did not exist from which such a force could be recruited.

This consideration did not apply to the navy. Seamen could be had abundantly from the merchant shipping, the activities of which must necessarily be much curtailed by war with a great naval power. Nevertheless, the dominance of Jefferson, though in this particular already shaken, remained upon the mass of his party. The new Secretary of the Navy was from South Carolina, not reckoned among the commercial states; but, however influenced, he ventured to intimate doubts as to the gunboat system. Of one thing there was no doubt. On a gunboat a gun cost twelve thousand dollars a year; the same on a frigate cost but four thousand.[354] In the House of Representatives, the strongest support to the development of the navy as a permanent force came from the Secretary's state, backed by Henry Clay from Kentucky, and by the commercial states; the leading representative of which, Josiah Quincy, expressed, however, a certain diffidence, because in the embittered politics of the day the mere fact of Federalist support tended rather to damage the cause.

So much of the President's message as related to the navy—three lines, wholly non-committal—was referred to a special committee. The report[355] was made by Langdon Cheves of South Carolina, whose clear and cogent exposition of the capabilities of the country and the possibility of providing a force efficient against Great Britain, under her existing embarrassments, was

---

354. Annals of Congress, 1811-12, p. 890.
355. Dec. 17, 1811. American State Papers, Naval Affairs, vol. i. p. 247.

supported powerfully and perspicuously by William Lowndes of the same state. The text for their remarks was supplied by a sentence in the committee's report:

> The important engine of national strength and national security, which is formed by a naval force, has hitherto been treated with a neglect highly impolitic, or supported by a spirit so languid, as, while it has preserved the existence of the establishment, has had the effect of loading it with the imputations of wasteful expense, and comparative inefficiency.... Such a course is impolitic under any circumstances.

This was the condemnation of the party's past. Clay found his delight in dealing with some of the oratory, which on the present occasion still sustained—and for the moment successfully sustained—the prepossessions of Jefferson. Carthage, Rome, Venice, Genoa, were republics with free institutions and great navies; Carthage, Rome, Venice, and Genoa had lost their liberties, and their national existence. Clearly navies, besides being very costly, were fatal to constitutional freedom. Not in reply to such *non sequitur*, but quickened by an insight which was to receive earlier vindication than he could have anticipated, Quincy prophesied that, amid the diverse and contrary interests of the several states, which the lack of a common object of affection left still imperfectly unified in sentiment, a glorious navy, identified with the whole country because of its external action, yet local to no part, would supply a common centre for the enthusiasm not yet inspired by the central government, too closely associated for years back with a particular school of extreme political thought, narrowly territorial and clannish in its origin and manifestation. Within a twelvemonth, the *Constitution*, most happily apt of all names ever given to a ship, became the embodiment of this verified prediction.

The report of the committee was modest in its scope.

To the defence of your ports and harbours, and the protection of your coasting trade, should be confined the present objects and operations of any navy which the United States can, or ought, to have.

To this office it was estimated that twelve ships of the line and twenty frigates would suffice. Cheves and Lowndes were satisfied that such a fleet was within the resources of the country; and to insure the fifteen thousand seamen necessary to man it, they would be willing to limit the number of privateers,—a most wholesome and necessary provision. By a careful historical examination of Great Britain's past and present exigencies, it was shown that such a force would most probably keep clear the approaches to all American ports, the most critical zone for shipping, whether inward or outward bound; because, to counteract it, the enemy would have to employ numbers so largely superior that they could not be spared from her European conflict. The argument was sound; but unhappily Cheves, Lowndes, Clay, and Quincy did not represent the spirit of the men who for ten years had ruled the country and evolved the gunboat system. These, in their day of power, not yet fully past, had neither maintained the fleet nor accumulated material, and there was no seasoned timber to build with. The Administration which expired in 1801 had left timber for six 74-gun ships, of which now remained only enough for four. The rest had been wasted in gunboats, or otherwise. The committee therefore limited its recommendations to building the frigates, for which it was believed materials could be procured.

Even in this reduced form it proved impossible to overcome the opposition to a navy as economically expensive and politically dangerous. The question was amply debated; but as, on the one hand, little doubt was felt about the rapid conquest of Canada by militia and volunteers, so, on the other, the same disposition to trust to extemporized irregular forces encouraged reliance simply upon privateering. Private enterprise in such a cause undoubtedly has from time to time attained marked results; but in general effect the method is a wasteful expenditure of national resources, and, historically, saps the strength of the regular navy. In the manning of inefficient privateers—and the majority were inefficient and ineffective—were thrown away resources of seamen which, in an adequate naval force, organized and directed as it would have been by the admirable officers of that period, could have accomplished vastly more in the annoyance of British trade,—the one offensive naval undertaking left open to the nation. Even with the assistance of the Federalists the provision for the frigates could not be carried, though the majority was narrow—62 to 59. The same fate befell the proposition to provide a dockyard. All that could be had was an appropriation of six hundred thousand dollars, distributed over three successive years, for buying timber. These votes were taken January 27, 1812, in full expectation of war, and only five months before it was declared.

Early in April, Congress, in secret session, passed an Act of Embargo for ninety days, which became law on the fourth by the President's signature. The motive was twofold: to retain at home the ships and seamen of the nation, in anticipation of war, to keep them from falling into the hands of the enemy; and also to prevent the carriage of supplies indispensably necessary to the British armies in Spain. Both objects were defeated by the action of Quincy, in conjunction with Senator Lloyd of Massachusetts and Representative Emott of New York. Learning that the President intended to recommend the embargo, these gentlemen, as stated by Quincy on the floor of the House, despatched at once to Philadelphia, New York, and Boston, expresses which left Washington March 31, the day before Madison's letter was dated. Four or five days' respite was thus secured, and the whole mercantile community set zealously to work to counteract the effects of the measure. *Niles' Register*, published in Baltimore, said:

> Drays were working night and day, from Tuesday night, March 31, and continued their toil till Sunday morning, incessantly. In this hurly-burly to palsy the arm of the Government all parties united. On Sunday perhaps not twenty seamen, able to do duty, could be found in all Baltimore.

A New York paper is quoted as saying:

The property could not have been moved off with greater expedition had the city been enveloped in flames.

From that port forty-eight vessels cleared; from Baltimore thirty-one; Philadelphia and Alexandria in like proportions. It was estimated that not less than two hundred thousand barrels of flour, besides grain in other shapes, and provisions of all kinds, to a total value of fifteen million dollars, were rushed out of the country in those five days, when labour-saving appliances were nearly unknown.[356]

Jonathan Russell, who was now *chargé d'affaires* at London, having been transferred from Paris upon the arrival of Armstrong's successor, Joel Barlow, wrote home:

The great shipments of provisions, which were hurried from America in expectation of the embargo, have given the Peninsula a supply for about two months; and at the expiration of that period the harvest in that region will furnish a stock for about three months more.... The avidity discovered by our countrymen to escape from the embargo, and the disregard of its policy, have encouraged this Government to hope that supplies will still continue to be received from the United States. The ship *Lady Madison*, which left Liverpool in March, has returned thither with a cargo taken in off Sandy Hook without entering an American port. There are several vessels now about leaving this country with the intention not only of procuring a cargo in the same way, but of getting rid, illicitly, of one they carry out.[357]

It was, indeed, a conspicuous instance of mercantile avidity, wholly disregardful of patriotic considerations, such as is to be found in all times and in all countries; strictly analogous to the constant smuggling between France and Great Britain at this

---

356. Niles' Register, vol. ii. pp. 101-104.
357. Russell to Monroe, May 30, 1812. U.S. State Department MSS.

very time. Its significance in the present case, however, is as marking the widespread lack of a national patriotism, as distinct from purely local advantage and personal interests, which unhappily characterized Americans at this period. Of this Great Britain stood ready to avail herself, by extending to the United States the system of licenses, by which, combined with the Orders in Council, she was combating with a large degree of success Napoleon's Continental System. She hoped, and the sequel showed not unreasonably, that even during open hostilities she could in the same manner thwart the United States in its efforts to keep its own produce from her markets. Less than a fortnight after the American Declaration of War was received, Russell, who had not yet left England, wrote to the Secretary of State that the Board of Trade had given notice that licenses would be granted for American vessels to carry provisions from the United States to Cadiz and Lisbon, for the term of eight months; and that a policy had been issued at Lloyds to a New York firm, insuring flour from that port to the peninsula, warranted free from British capture, and from capture or detention by the Government of the United States.[358]

The British armies were thus nourished and dependent, both in Spain and in Canada. The supplying of the latter scarcely fell short of treason, and decisively affected the maintenance of the war in that quarter. It is difficult to demonstrate a moral distinction between what was done there, disregardful of national success, in shameful support of the enemy, and the supplying of the peninsula; but an intuitive sympathy extends to the latter a tolerance which the motives of the individual agents probably do not deserve, and for which calm reason cannot give a perfectly satisfactory account. But it was the misfortune of American policy, as shaped by the Administration, that it was committed to support Napoleon in his iniquitous attack upon the liberties of Spain; that it saw in his success the probable fulfilment of its designs upon the Floridas;[359] and that

---

358. Russell to Monroe, August 15 and 21, 1812. U.S. State Department MSS.
359. See Jefferson's Works, vol. v. pp. 335, 337, 338, 339, 419, 442-445.

its chosen ground for proceeding against Great Britain, rather than France, was her refusal to conform her action to a statement of the Emperor's, the illusory and deceptive character of which became continually more apparent.

To declare war because of the Orders in Council was a simple, straightforward, and wholly justifiable course; but the flying months made more and more evident, to the Government and its agents abroad, that it was vain to expect revocation on the ground of Napoleon's recall of his edicts, for they were not recalled. Having entered upon this course, however, it seemed impossible to recede, or to acknowledge a mistake, the pinch of which was nevertheless felt. Writing to Russell, whose service in Paris, from October, 1810, to October, 1811, and transfer thence to London, made him unusually familiar, on both sides of the Channel, with the controversy over Champagny's letter of August 5, 1810, Madison speaks—

> .... of the delicacy of our situation, having in view, on the one hand, the importance of obtaining from the French Government confirmation of the repeal of the Decrees, and on the other that of not weakening the ground on which the British repeal was urged.[360]

That is, it would be awkward to have the British ministry find out that we were pressing France for a confirmation of that very revocation which we were confidently asserting to them to be indisputable, and to require in good faith the withdrawal of their Orders. Respecting action taken under the so-called repeal, Russell had written on March 15, 1811, over three months after it was said to take effect:

> By forbearing to condemn, or to acquit, distinctly and loyally, (the vessels seized since November 1), this Government encourages us to persevere in our non-importation against England, and England to persist in her orders against us. This state of things appears calculated to produce mutual complaint and irritation, and cannot prob-

---

360. Madison to Russell, Nov. 15, 1811. U.S. State Department MSS.

ably be long continued without leading to a more serious contest,. . . . which is perhaps an essential object of this country's policy."[361]

July 15, he expressed regret to the Duke of Bassano, the French Minister of Foreign Affairs, that the proceedings concerning captured American vessels—

> . . . . had been so partial, and confined to cases which from their peculiar circumstances proved nothing conclusively in relation to the revocation of the French Edicts.[362]

Russell might have found some light as to the causes of these delays, could he have seen a note addressed by the Emperor to the Administration of Commerce, April 29. In this, renewing the reasoning of the Bayonne Decree, he argued that every American vessel which touched at an English port was liable to confiscation in the United States; consequently, could be seized by an American cruiser on the open sea; therefore, was equally open to seizure there by a French cruiser—the demand advanced by Canning[363] which gave such just offence; and if by a French cruiser at sea, likewise in a French port by the French Government. She was in fact no longer American, not even a denationalized American, but an English vessel. Under this supposition, Napoleon luminously inferred:

> It could be said: The Decrees of Berlin and Milan are recalled as to the United States, but, as every ship which has stopped in England, or is destined thither, is a ship unacknowledged (*sans aveu*), which American laws punish and confiscate, she may be confiscated in France.

The Emperor concluded that should this theory not be capable of substantiation, the matter might for the present be left obscure.[364] On September 13 the ships in question had not been liberated.

---

361. Russell to Robert Smith, March 15, 1811. U.S. State Department MSS.
362. Russell to the Secretary of State, July 15, 1811. Ibid.
363. Ante, p. 217.
364. *Note dictée en conseil d'Administration du Commerce*, April 29, 1811. *Correspondance de Napoléon*, vol. xxii. p. 144.

Coincidently with his note to Bassano, Russell wrote to Monroe:

> It is my conviction that the great object of their policy is to entangle us in a war with England. They therefore abstain from doing any act which would furnish clear and unequivocal testimony of the revocation of their decrees, lest it should induce the extinction of the British Orders, and thereby appease our irritation against their enemy. Hence, of all the captured vessels since November 1, the three which were liberated were precisely those which had not violated the Decrees.[365]

Yet, such were the exigencies of the debate with England, those three cases were transmitted by him at the same time to the American *chargé* in London as evidence of the revocation.[366] To the French Minister he wrote again, August 8:

> After the declarations of M. de Champagny and yourself, I cannot permit myself to doubt the revocation;.... but I may be allowed to lament that no fact has yet come to my knowledge of a character unequivocally and incontrovertibly to confirm that revocation.... That none of the captured vessels have been condemned, instead of proving the extinction of the edicts, appears rather to be evidence, at best, of a commutation of the penalty from prompt confiscation to perpetual detention.[367]

The matter was further complicated by an announcement of Napoleon to the Chamber of Commerce, in April of the same year, that the Berlin and Milan Decrees were the fundamental law of the Empire concerning neutral commerce, and that American ships would be repelled from French ports, unless the United States conformed to those decrees, by excluding British ships and merchandise.[368] Under such conditions, argument

---
365. Russell to Monroe, July 13, 1811. U.S. State Department MSS.
366. Russell to J.S. Smith, July 14, 1811. American State Papers, Foreign Relations, vol. iii. p. 447.
367. Russell to Bassano, Aug. 8, 1811. U.S. State Department MSS.
368. Russell to Robert Smith, April, 1811. Ibid.

with a sceptical British ministry was attended with difficulties. The position to which the Government had become reduced, by endeavouring to play off France and Great Britain against each other, in order to avoid a war with either, was as perplexing as humiliating. "Great anxiety,"[369] to which little sympathy can be extended, was felt in Washington as to the evidence for the actuality of the repeals.

The situation was finally cleared up by a clever move of the British Cabinet, forcing Napoleon's hand at a moment when the Orders in Council could with difficulty be maintained longer against popular discontent. On March 10, 1812, the French Minister of Foreign Affairs, in a report to the Senate, reiterated the demands of the Decrees, and asserted again that, until those demands were conceded by England, the Decrees must be enforced against Powers which permitted their flags to be denationalized. The position thus reaffirmed was emphasized by a requirement for a large increase of the army for this object.

> It is necessary that all the disposable forces of France be available for sending everywhere where the English flag, and other flags, denationalized or convoyed by English ships of war, may seek to enter.[370]

No exceptions in favour of the United States being stated, the British ministry construed the omission as conclusive proof of the unqualified continuance of the Decrees;[371] and the occasion was taken to issue an Order in Council, defining the Government's position, both in the past and for the future. Quoting the French minister's Report, as removing all doubts of Napoleon's persistence in the maintenance of a system, "as inconsistent with neutral rights and independence as it was hostile to the maritime rights and commercial interests of Great Britain," the Prince Regent declared that—

---

369. Monroe to Russell, June 8, 1811. Ibid.
370. Reports of the Ministers of Foreign Relations and of War, March 10, 1812. Moniteur, March 16.
371. Russell to Monroe, April 19, 1812. U.S. State Department MSS.

. . . . if at any time thereafter the Berlin and Milan Decrees should be absolutely and unconditionally repealed, by some authentic act of the French Government, publicly promulgated, then the Orders in Council of January, 1807, and April, 1809, shall without any further order be, and the same are hereby declared from thenceforth to be, wholly and absolutely revoked.[372]

No exception could be taken to the phrasing or form of this Order. The wording was precise and explicit; the time fixed was definite,—the date of the French Repeal; the manner of revocation was the same as that of promulgation, an Order in Council observant of all usual formalities.

In substance, this well-timed State Paper challenged Champagny's letter of August 5, 1810, and the American Non-Importation Act based upon it. Both these asserted the revocation of the French Decrees. The British Cabinet, seizing a happy opportunity, asked of the world the production of the revocation, or else the justification of its own course. The demand went far to silence the growing discontents at home, and to embarrass the American Government in the grounds upon which it had chosen to base its action. It was well calculated also to disconcert the Emperor, for, unless he did something more definite, dissension would increase in the United States, where, as Barlow wrote:

> It is well known to the world, for our public documents are full of it, that great doubts exist, even among our best informed merchants, and in the halls of Congress itself, whether the Berlin and Milan Decrees are to this day repealed, or even modified, in regard to the United States.

The sentence is taken from a letter[373] which he addressed to the French Minister of Foreign Affairs, May 1, 1812, when he

---

372. The copy of this Order in Council which the author is here using is in the Naval Chronicle, vol. xxvii. p. 466.

373. This letter, which is given in a very mutilated form in the American State Papers, Foreign Relations, vol. iii. p. 602, has been published in full by the Bureau of Historical Research, Carnegie Institution, Washington. Report on the Diplomatic Archives of the Department of State, 1904, p. 64.

had received the recent British Order. He pointed out how astutely this step was calculated to undo the effect of Champagny's letter, and to weaken the American Administration at the critical moment when it was known to be preparing for war. He urged that the French Government should now make and publish an authentic Act, declaring the Berlin and Milan Decrees, as relative to the United States, to have ceased in November, 1810.

> Such an act is absolutely necessary to the American Government; and, though solicited as an accommodation, it may be demanded as a right. If it was the duty of France to cease to apply those Decrees to the United States, it is equally her duty to promulgate it to the world in as formal a manner as we have promulgated our law for the exclusion of British merchandise. She ought to declare and publish the non-application of these Decrees in the same forms in which she enacted the Decrees. The President has instructed me to propose and press this object.

At last the demand was made which should have been enforced eighteen months before. After sending the letter, Barlow had "a pretty sharp conversation" with Bassano, in which he perceived a singular reluctance to answer his letter. At last the Duke placed before him a Decree, drawn up in due and customary form, dated a year before,—April 28, 1811,—declaring that "the Decrees of Berlin and Milan are definitively, and to date from the first day of November last, 1810, considered as not having existed in regard to American vessels."[374] This Decree, Bassano said, had been communicated to Russell, and also sent to Serrurier, the French minister at Washington, with orders to convey it to the American Government. Both Russell and Serrurier denied ever having received the paper.[375]

Barlow made no comment upon the strange manner in which

---

374. American State Papers, Foreign Relations, vol. iii. p. 603.
375. Barlow's interview with Bassano, and the letters exchanged, will be found in American State Papers, Foreign Relations, vol. iii. p. 602-603. Russell's denial is on p. 614. Serrurier's is mentioned in a Report made to the House by Monroe, Secretary of State, ibid., p. 609.

this document was produced to him, and confined himself to inquiring if it had been published. The reply could only be, *No*; a singular admission with regard to a formal paper a year old, and of such importance to all concerned. He then asked that a copy might be sent him. Upon receipt, he at once hastened it to Russell in London, by the sloop of war *Wasp*, then lying in a French port. He wrote:

> You will doubtless render an essential service to both Great Britain and the United States by communicating it without loss of time to the Foreign Secretary. If by this the cause of war should be removed, there is an obvious reason for keeping the secret, if possible, so long as that the *Wasp* may not bring the news to this country in any other manner but in your despatch. This Government, as you must long have perceived, wishes not to see that effect produced; and I should not probably have obtained the letter and documents from the Minister, if the Prince Regent's Declaration had not convinced this Government that the war was now become inevitable.[376]

Russell transmitted the Decree to the British Foreign Secretary May 20, 1812. The Government was at the moment in confusion, through the assassination, May 11, of Mr. Perceval, the Prime Minister; who, though not esteemed of the first order of statesmanship by his contemporaries and colleagues, had been found in recent negotiations the only available man about whom a cabinet could unite. A period of suspense followed, in which the difficulty of forming a new government, owing to personal antagonisms, was complicated by radical differences as to public policy, especially in the cardinal point of pursuing or relinquishing the war in the peninsula. Not till near the middle of June was an arrangement reached. The same ministry, substantially, remained in power, with Lord Liverpool as premier; Castlereagh continuing as Foreign Secretary. This retained in

---

376. Barlow to Russell, May 10, 1812. U.S. State Department MSS.

office the party identified with the Orders in Council, and favouring armed support to the Spanish revolt.

The delay in settling the government afforded an excuse for postponing action upon the newly discovered French Decree. It permitted also time for reflection. Just before Perceval's death, Russell had noted a firm determination to maintain the Orders in Council, conditioned only by the late Declaration of April 21; but at the same time there was evident apprehension of the consequences of war with the United States.[377] This, he carefully explained, was due to no apprehension of American military power. Even Lord Grenville, one of the chief leaders of the Opposition, was satisfied that the United States could not conquer Canada.

> We are, indeed, most miserably underrated in Europe.... It is not believed here, notwithstanding the spirited report of the Committee on Foreign Relations, that we shall resort to any definitive measures. We have indeed a reputation in Europe for saying so much and doing so little that we shall not be believed in earnest until we act in a manner not to be mistaken.... I am persuaded this Government has presumed much on our weakness and divisions, and that it continues to believe that we have not energy and union enough to make effective war. Nor is this confined to the ministry, but extends to the leaders of the Opposition.
>
> Mr. Perceval is well known to calculate with confidence that even in case of war we shall be obliged to resort to a license trade for a supply of British manufactures.... He considers us incapable even of bearing the privations of a state of hostility with England, and much more incapable of becoming a formidable enemy.

On March 3 Perceval in a debate in the House had indicated the most positive intentions of maintaining the Orders, and asserted that, in consequence of Napoleon's Decrees, Great Britain was no longer restrained by the law of nations in the extent or form of retaliation to which she may resort upon the enemy.

---

377. Russell to Monroe, May 9, 1812. Ibid.

I cannot perceive the slightest indication of apprehension of a rupture with the United States, or any measure of preparation to meet such an event. Such is the conviction of our total inability to make war that the five or six thousand troops now in Canada are considered to be amply sufficient to protect that province against our mightiest efforts.[378]

A revolution of sentiment was to be noted even in the minds of former advocates. Castlereagh, at a levee on March 12, said to Russell that the movements in the United States appeared to him to be nothing but party evolutions.

There was, however, another side to the question which occasioned more concern to the British ministry. "It is the increasing want of our intercourse," wrote Russell May 9, "rather than the apprehension of our arms which leads to a conciliatory spirit" which he had recently noticed.

> They will endeavour to avoid the calamity of war with the United States by every means which can save their pride and their consistency. The scarcity of bread in this country, the distress of the manufacturing towns, and the absolute dependency of the allied troops in the Peninsula on our supplies, form a check on their conduct which they can scarcely have the hardihood to disregard.[379]

Two days after these words were written, the murder of Perceval added political anarchy to the embarrassments of the Government. The crisis then impending was indeed momentous. War between France and Russia was certain. Upon its outcome depended the fall of the Continental System, or its prevalence over all Europe in an extent and with a rigor never yet reached. "Some of the Powers of Europe," said the Emperor, "have not fulfilled their promise with respect to the Continental System. I must force them to it." In carrying this message to the Senate, the Minister of Foreign Affairs said: "In whatever

---

378. The passages cited above are from Russell's correspondence with the State Department, under the dates of January 10, February 3 and 19, March 4 and 20, 1812. U.S. State Department MSS.

379. Russell to Monroe, May 9, 1812. U.S. State Department MSS.

port of Europe a British ship can enter there must be a French garrison to prevent it;"[380] an interesting commentary upon the neutral regulations to which the United States professed that neither she nor Great Britain had any claim to object, because municipal. Great Britain had already touched ruin too nearly to think lightly of the conditions. By her Orders in Council she had so retorted Napoleon's Decrees as to induce him, in order still further to enforce them, into the Peninsular War, and now into that with Russia. To uphold the latter, her busy negotiators, profiting by his high-handedness, had obtained for the Czar peace with Sweden and Turkey. More completely to sustain him, it was essential to support in fullest effect the powerful diversion which retained three hundred thousand French troops in Spain. To do this, the assistance of American food supplies was imperative.

If peace with the United States could be maintained, the triumph of British diplomacy would be unqualified. The announcement of the alleged Decree of April 28, 1811, came therefore most opportunely to save their pride and self-consistency. On June 23 Castlereagh transmitted to Russell an Order in Council published that day, revoking as to the United States the celebrated Orders of January 7, 1807, and April 26, 1809. His letter ran:

> I am to request you that you will acquaint your Government that the Prince Regent's ministers have taken *the earliest opportunity, after the resumption of the Government*, to advise his Royal Highness to the adoption of a measure grounded upon the document communicated by you to this office on the 20th ....[381]

That is upon the Decree of April 28. No one affected to believe that this had been framed at the date it bore.

There was something so very much like fraud on the

---

380. Barlow to Monroe, March 15, 1812. Ibid. Published by Bureau of Historical Research, Carnegie Institution, 1904, p. 63.
381. American State Papers, Foreign Relations, vol. iii. p. 433. Author's italics.

face of it, that in several conversations which I have since had with Lord Castlereagh, particularly at a dinner at the Lord Mayor's, when I was placed next his lordship, I have taken care not to commit the honour of my Government by attempting its vindication. When his lordship called it a strange proceeding, a new specimen of French diplomacy, a trick unworthy of a civilized government, I have merely replied that the motives or good faith of the Government which issued it, or the real time when it was issued, were of little importance as to the effect which it ought to have here; that it was sufficient that it contained a most precise and formal declaration that the Berlin and Milan Decrees were revoked, in relation to America, from November 1, 1810.[382]

This was true; but the contention of the British Government had been that the system of the Decrees was one whole; that its effect upon America could not be dissociated from that upon continental neutral states, where it was enforced under the guise of municipal regulations; and that it must be revoked as a whole, in order to impose the repeal of the Orders in Council. This position had been reaffirmed in the recent Order of April 21. Opinion will therefore differ as to the ministry's success in escaping, under the cover of the new Decree, from the dilemma in which they were placed by the irresistible agitation against the Orders in Council spreading through the nation, and the necessity of avoiding war with the United States, if possible, because of the affairs of the Peninsula. They made the best of it by alleging, as it were, the spirit of the Order of April 21; the disposition "to take such measures as may tend to re-establish the intercourse between neutral and belligerent nations upon its accustomed principles." For this reason, while avowing explicitly that the tenor of the Decree did not meet the requirements of the late Order, the Orders in Council were revoked from August 1 next following; and vessels captured after May 20, the date of Russell's communicat-

---

382. Russell to Monroe, June 30, 1812. U.S. State Department MSS.

ing the Decree, would be released. The ministry thus receded gracefully under compulsion; and for their own people at least saved their face.

Superficially the British diplomatic triumph for the moment seemed complete. They had withdrawn their head from the noose just as it began to tighten; and they had done so not on any ground of stringent requirement, but with expressions of desire to go even farther than their just claims, in order to promote conciliation. Russell naturally felt a moment of bitter discomfiture.

> In yielding, the ministers appear to have been extremely perplexed in seeking for a subterfuge for their credit. All their feelings and all their prejudices revolted at the idea of publicly bending to the Opposition, or truckling to the United States, and they were compelled to seize on the French Decree of April 28, 1811, as the only means of saving themselves from the degradation of acknowledging that they were vanquished. Without this decree they would have been obliged to yield, and I almost regret that it existed to furnish a salvo, miserable as it is, for their pride. Our victory, however, is still complete, and I trust that those who have refused to support our Government in the contest will at least be willing to allow it the honours of a triumph.[383]

Russell wrote under the mistaken impression that the repeal of the Orders had come in time to save war; in which event the yielding of the British ministry, identified as it was with the Orders in Council, might be construed as a triumph for the system of peaceable coercion, by commercial restrictions, which formed the whole policy of Jefferson and Madison. The triumph claimed by him must be qualified, however, by the reflection that it was obtained at the expense of becoming the dupe of a French deception, on its face so obvious as to deprive mistake of the excuse of plausibility. The eagerness of the Government,

---

383. Russell to Monroe, June 30, 1812. U.S. State Department MSS.

and of its representatives abroad, for a diplomatic triumph, had precipitated them into a step for which, on the grounds taken, no justification existed; and they had since then been dragged at the wheels of Napoleon's chariot, in a constant dust of mystification, until he had finally achieved the end of his scheming and landed them in a war for which they were utterly unprepared, and which it had been the chief object of commercial reprisals to avoid. Thus considered, the triumph was barren.

On June 1, 1812, President Madison sent to Congress a message,[384] reciting the long list of international wrongs endured at the hands of Great Britain, and recommending to the deliberations of Congress the question of peace or war. On June 4 the House of Representatives, by a vote of seventy-nine yeas to forty-nine nays, declared that a state of war existed between the United States and Great Britain. The bill then went to the Senate, where it was discussed, amended, and passed on June 17, by nineteen *yeas* to thirteen *nays*. The next day the House concurred in the Senate's amendments, and the bill thus passed received the President's signature immediately. The war thus began, formally, on June 18, 1812, five days before the repeal of the British Orders in Council.

While the Declaration of War was still under debate, the Secretary of War, Eustis, on June 8 reported to the Senate that of the ten thousand men authorized as a peace establishment, there were in service six thousand seven hundred and forty-four. He was unable to state what number had been enlisted of the twenty-five thousand regulars provided by the legislation of the current session; a singular exhibition of the efficiency of the Department. He had no hesitation, however, in expressing an unofficial opinion that there were five thousand of these recruits. It is scarce necessary to surmise what the condition of the army was likely to be, with James Wilkinson as the senior general officer of consecutive service, and with Dearborn, a man of sixty, and in civil life ever since the War of Independence, as the first major-general appointed under the new legislation. The

---

384. American State Papers, Foreign Relations, vol. iii. p. 405.

navy had a noble and competent body of officers, in the prime of life, a large proportion of whom had seen instructive service in the Barbary conflict; but, as has been seen, Congress had no faith in a navy, and refused it any increase. In this distrust the Administration shared.

Mr. Monroe, indeed, probably through his residence abroad, had attained a juster view of the influence of a navy on foreign relations. He has already been quoted in this connection,[385] but in a letter to a friend, two years before 1812, he developed his opinions with some precision.

> I gave my opinion that our naval force ought to be increased. In advising this, I urged that the naval force of the United States ought not to be regulated by reference to the navies of the Great Powers, but to the strength of the squadrons which they usually stationed in time of war on our coasts, at the mouths of great rivers, and in our harbours. I thought that such a force, incorporated permanently with our system, would give weight at all times to our negotiations, and by means thereof prevent wars and save money.[386]

Monroe at this time was not in the Administration. Such a policy was diametrically opposed to that of Jefferson, Madison, and Gallatin; and when war came, ships had not been provided. Under the circumstances the disposition of the Government was to put the ships they had under a glass case. Monroe wrote to Jefferson—

> At the commencement of the war I was decidedly of your opinion, that the best disposition which could be made of our little navy would be to keep it in a body in a safe port, from which it might sally, only on some important occasion, to render essential service. Its safety, in itself, appeared an important object; as, while safe, it formed a check on the enemy in all operations along our coast, and

---

385. Ante, p. 106.
386. To John Taylor, Sept. 10, 1810. Works of James Monroe, vol. vi. p. 128.

increased proportionately his expense, in the force to be kept up, as well to annoy our commerce as to protect his own. The reasoning against this, in which all naval officers have agreed, is that, if stationed together in a port,—New York, for example,—the British would immediately block up this, by a force rather superior, and then harass our coast and commerce, without restraint, and with any force, however small. In that case a single frigate might, by cruising along the coast, and menacing continually different parts, keep in motion great bodies of militia; that, while our frigates are at sea, the expectation that they may be met together will compel the British to keep in a body, whenever they institute a blockade or cruise, a force equal at least to our own whole force; that they, (the American vessels) being the best sailors, hazard little by cruising separately, or together occasionally, as they might bring on an action, or avoid one, as they saw fit; that in that measure they would annoy the enemy's commerce wherever they went, excite alarm in the West Indies and elsewhere, and even give protection to our own trade by drawing the enemy's squadron from our own coast. . . . The reasoning in favour of each plan is so nearly equal that it is hard to say which is best.[387]

It is to be hoped that the sequel will show which was best, although little can be hoped when means, military and naval, have been allowed to waste as they had under the essentially unmilitary Administrations since 1801.

On November 25, 1811, seven months before the war began, the Secretary of the Treasury, Gallatin, communicated to the Senate a report on the State of the Finances,[388] in which he showed that since 1801, by economies which totally crippled the war power of the nation, the public debt had been diminished from $80,000,000 to $34,000,000,—a saving of $46,000,000, which lessened the annual interest on the debt by $2,000,000. A

---

387. Monroe to Jefferson, Monroe's Works, vol. v. p. 268.
388. Annals of Congress, 1811-12, p. 2046.

good financial showing, doubtless; but, had there been on hand the troops and the ships, which the saved money represented, the War of 1812 might have had an issue more satisfactory to national retrospect. Gallatin also showed, in this paper, that by the restrictive system, enforced against Great Britain in consequence of the Administration's decision that Napoleon's revocation of his Decrees was real, the revenue had dropped from $12,000,000 to $6,000,000; leaving the nation with a probable deficiency of $2,000,000, on the estimate of a year of peace for 1812.

CHAPTER 5

The Theatre of Operations

War being now immediately at hand, it is advisable, for the better appreciation of the course of events, the more accurate estimate of their historical and military value, to consider the relative conditions of the two opponents, the probable seats of warlike operations, and the methods which it was open to either to pursue.

Invasion of the British Islands, or of any transmarine possession of Great Britain—save Canada—was denied to the United States by the immeasurable inferiority of her navy. To cross the sea in force was impossible, even for short distances. For this reason, land operations were limited to the North American Continent. This fact, conjoined with the strong traditional desire, received from the old French wars and cherished in the War of Independence, to incorporate the Canadian colonies with the Union, determined an aggressive policy by the United States on the northern frontier. This was indeed the only distinctively offensive operation available to her upon the land; consequently it was imposed by reasons of both political and military expediency. On the other hand, the sea was open to American armed ships, though under certain very obvious restrictions; that is to say, subject to the primary difficulty of evading blockades of the coast, and of escaping subsequent capture by the very great number of British cruisers, which watched all seas where British commerce went and came, and most of the ports whence hostile ships might issue to prey upon it. The principal trammel which now rests upon the movements of vessels destined to cripple an

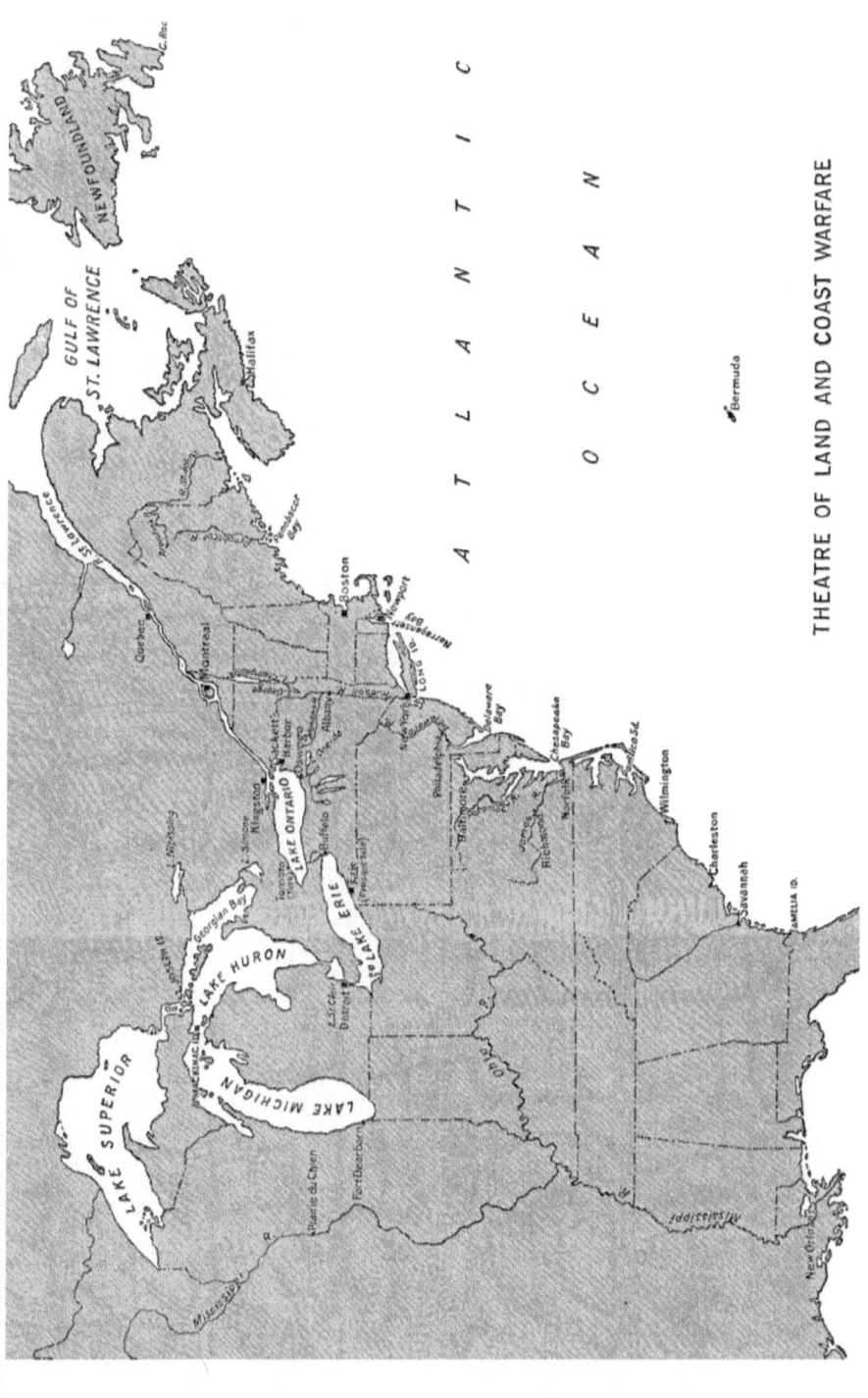

THEATRE OF LAND AND COAST WARFARE

enemy's commerce—the necessity to renew the motive power, coal, at frequent brief intervals—did not then exist. The wind, upon which motion depended, might at particular moments favour one of two antagonists relatively to the other; but in the long run it was substantially the same for all. In this respect all were on an equal footing; and the supply, if fickle at times, was practically inexhaustible. Barring accidents, vessels were able to keep the sea as long as their provisions and water lasted. This period may be reckoned as generally three months, while by watchful administration it might at times be protracted to six.

It is desirable to explain here what was, and is, the particular specific utility of operations directed toward the destruction of an enemy's commerce; what its bearing upon the issues of war; and how, also, it affects the relative interests of antagonists, unequally paired in the matter of sea power. Without attempting to determine precisely the relative importance of internal and external commerce, which varies with each country, and admitting that the length of transportation entails a distinct element of increased cost upon the articles transported, it is nevertheless safe to say that, to nations having free access to the sea, the export and import trade is a very large factor in national prosperity and comfort. At the very least, it increases by so much the aggregate of commercial transactions, while the ease and copiousness of water carriage go far to compensate for the increase of distance. Furthermore, the public revenue of maritime states is largely derived from duties on imports. Hence arises, therefore, a large source of wealth, of money; and money—ready money or substantial credit—is proverbially the sinews of war, as the War of 1812 was amply to demonstrate. Inconvertible assets, as business men know, are a very inefficacious form of wealth in tight times; and war is always a tight time for a country, a time in which its positive wealth, in the shape of every kind of produce, is of little use, unless by freedom of exchange it can be converted into cash for governmental expenses. To this sea-commerce greatly contributes, and the extreme embarrassment under which the United States as a nation laboured in 1814 was mainly due to commercial exclusion from the sea. To attack the commerce of the enemy is therefore to cripple him, in the measure of success achieved, in the particular factor which is vital to the maintenance of war. Moreover, in the complicated conditions of mercantile activity no one branch can be seriously injured without involving others.

This may be called the financial and political effect of "commerce destroying," as the modern phrase runs. In military effect, it is strictly analogous to the impairing of an enemy's communications, of the line of supplies connecting an army with its base of operations, upon the maintenance of which the life of the army depends. Money, credit, is the life of war; lessen it, and vigour flags; destroy it, and resistance dies. No resource then remains except to "make war support war;" that is, to make the vanquished pay the bills for the maintenance of the army which has crushed him, or which is proceeding to crush whatever opposition is left alive. This, by the extraction of private money, and of supplies for the use of his troops, from the country in which he was fighting, was the method of Napoleon, than whom no man held more delicate views concerning the gross impropriety of capturing private property at sea, whither his power did not extend. Yet this, in effect, is simply another method of forcing the enemy to surrender a large part of his means, so weakening him, while transferring it to the victor for the better propagation of hostilities. The exaction of a pecuniary indemnity from the worsted party at the conclusion of a war, as is frequently done, differs from the seizure of property in transit afloat only in method, and as peace differs from war. In either case, money or money's worth is exacted; but when peace supervenes, the method of collection is left to the Government of the country, in pursuance of its powers of taxation, to distribute the burden among the people; whereas in war, the primary object being immediate injury to the enemy's fighting power, it is not only legitimate in principle, but particularly effective, to seek the disorganization of his financial system by a crushing attack upon one of its important factors, because effort thus is concentrated on a readily accessible, fundamental element of his general prosperity. That the loss falls directly on individuals, or a class, instead of upon the whole community, is but an incident of war, just as some men are killed and others not. Indirectly, but none the less surely, the whole community, and, what is more important, the organized government, are crippled; offensive powers impaired.

But while this is the absolute tendency of war against commerce, common to all cases, the relative value varies greatly with the countries having recourse to it. It is a species of hostilities easily extemporized by a great maritime nation; it therefore favours one whose policy is not to maintain a large naval establishment. It opens a field for a sea militia force, requiring little antecedent military training. Again, it is a logical military reply to commercial blockade, which is the most systematic, regularized, and extensive form of commerce-destruction known to war. Commercial blockade is not to be confounded with the military measure of confining a body of hostile ships of war to their harbour, by stationing before it a competent force. It is directed against merchant vessels, and is not a military operation in the narrowest sense, in that it does not necessarily involve fighting, nor propose the capture of the blockaded harbour. It is not usually directed against military ports, unless these happen to be also centres of commerce. Its object, which was the paramount function of the United States Navy during the Civil War, dealing probably the most decisive blow inflicted upon the Confederacy, is the destruction of commerce by closing the ports of egress and ingress. Incidental to that, all ships, neutrals included, attempting to enter or depart, after public notification through customary channels, are captured and confiscated as remorselessly as could be done by the most greedy privateer. Thus constituted, the operation receives far wider scope than commerce-destruction on the high seas; for this is confined to merchantmen of belligerents, while commercial blockade, by universal consent, subjects to capture neutrals who attempt to infringe it, because, by attempting to defeat the efforts of one belligerent, they make themselves parties to the war.

In fact, commercial blockade, though most effective as a military measure in broad results, is so distinctly commerce-destructive in essence, that those who censure the one form must logically proceed to denounce the other. This, as has been seen,[389] Napoleon did; alleging in his Berlin Decree, in 1806, that war cannot be extended to any private property whatever, and that the right of blockade is restricted to *fortified* places, actually invested by competent forces. This he had the face to assert, at the very moment when he was compelling every vanquished state to extract, from the private means of its subjects, coin running up to hundreds of millions to replenish his military chest for further extension of hostilities. Had this dictum been accepted international law in 1861, the United States could not have closed the ports of the Confederacy, the commerce of which would have proceeded unmolested; and hostile measures being consequently directed against men's persons instead of their trade, victory, if accomplished at all, would have cost three lives for every two actually lost. It is apparent, immediately on statement, that against commerce-destruction by blockade, the recourse of the weaker maritime belligerent is commerce-destruction by cruisers on the high sea. Granting equal efficiency in the use of either measure, it is further plain that the latter is intrinsically far less efficacious. To cut off access to a city is much more certainly accomplished by holding the gates than by scouring the country in search of persons seeking to enter. Still, one can but do what one can. In 1861 to 1865, the Southern Confederacy, unable to shake off the death grip fastened on its throat, attempted counteraction by means of the *Alabama*, *Sumter*, and their less famous consorts, with what disastrous influence upon the navigation—the shipping—of the Union it is needless to insist. But while the shipping of the opposite belligerent was in this way not only crippled, but indirectly was swept from the seas, the Confederate cruisers, not being able to establish a blockade, could not prevent neutral vessels from carrying on the commerce of the Union. This consequently suffered no serious interruption; whereas the

---

389. Ante, p. 144.

produce of the South, its inconvertible wealth—cotton chiefly—was practically useless to sustain the financial system and credit of the people. So, in 1812 and the two years following, the United States flooded the seas with privateers, producing an effect upon British commerce which, though inconclusive singly, doubtless co-operated powerfully with other motives to dispose the enemy to liberal terms of peace. It was the reply, and the only possible reply, to the commercial blockade, the grinding efficacy of which it will be a principal object of these pages to depict. The issue to us has been accurately characterized by Mr. Henry Adams, in the single word "Exhaustion."[390]

Both parties to the War of 1812 being conspicuously maritime in disposition and occupation, while separated by three thousand miles of ocean, the sea and its navigable approaches became necessarily the most extensive scene of operations. There being between them great inequality of organized naval strength and of pecuniary resources, they inevitably resorted, according to their respective force, to one or the other form of maritime hostilities against commerce which have been indicated. To this procedure combats on the high seas were merely incidental. Tradition, professional pride, and the combative spirit inherent in both peoples, compelled fighting when armed vessels of nearly equal strength met; but such contests, though wholly laudable from the naval standpoint, which under ordinary circumstances cannot afford to encourage retreat from an equal foe, were indecisive of general results, however meritorious in particular execution. They had no effect upon the issue, except so far as they inspired moral enthusiasm and confidence. Still more, in the sequel they have had a distinctly injurious effect upon national opinion in the United States. In the brilliant exhibition of enterprise, professional skill, and usual success, by its naval officers and seamen, the country has forgotten the precedent neglect of several administrations to constitute the navy as strong in proportion to the means of the country as it was excellent through the spirit and acquirements of its officers. Sight also has been

---

390. Adams, History of the United States, vol. viii. chap. viii.

lost of the actual conditions of repression, confinement, and isolation, enforced upon the maritime frontier during the greater part of the war, with the misery and mortification thence ensuing. It has been widely inferred that the maritime conditions in general were highly flattering to national pride, and that a future emergency could be confronted with the same supposed facility, and as little preparation, as the odds of 1812 are believed to have been encountered and overcome. This mental impression, this picture, is false throughout, alike in its grouping of incidents, in its disregard of proportion, and in its ignoring of facts. The truth of this assertion will appear in due course of this narrative, and it will be seen that, although relieved by many brilliant incidents, indicative of the real spirit and capacity of the nation, the record upon the whole is one of gloom, disaster, and governmental incompetence, resulting from lack of national preparation, due to the obstinate and blind prepossessions of the Government, and, in part, of the people.

This was so even upon the water, despite the great names—for great they were in measure of their opportunities—of Decatur, Hull, Perry, Macdonough, Morris, and a dozen others. On shore things were far worse; for while upon the water the country had as leaders men still in the young prime of life, who were both seamen and officers,—none of those just named were then over forty,—the army at the beginning had only elderly men, who, if they ever had been soldiers in any truer sense than young fighting men,—soldiers by training and understanding,—had long since disacquired whatever knowledge and habit of the profession they had gained in the War of Independence, then more than thirty years past. "As far as American movements are concerned," said one of Wellington's trusted officers, sent to report upon the subject of Canadian defence, "the campaign of 1812 is almost beneath criticism."[391] Instructed American opinion must sorrowfully admit the truth of the comment. That of 1813 was not much better, although some younger men—Brown, Scott, Gaines, Macomb, Ripley—were beginning to show their met-

---

391. Sir J. Carmichael Smyth, Précis of Wars in Canada, p. 116.

tle, and there had by then been placed at the head of the War Department a secretary who at least possessed a reasoned understanding of the principles of warfare. With every material military advantage, save the vital one of adequate preparation, it was found too late to prepare when war was already at hand; and after the old inefficients had been given a chance to demonstrate their incapacity, it was too late to utilize the young men.

Jefferson, with curious insanity of optimism, had once written—

> We begin to broach the idea that we consider the whole Gulf Stream as of our waters, within which hostilities and cruising are to be frowned on for the present, and prohibited as soon as either consent or force will permit.[392]

While at the same time, under an unbroken succession of maritime humiliations, he of purpose neglected all naval preparation save that of two hundred gunboats, which could not venture out of sight of land without putting their guns in the hold. With like blindness to the conditions to which his administration had reduced the nation, he now wrote: "The acquisition of Canada this year 1812, as far as the neighbourhood of Quebec, will be a mere matter of marching."[393] This would scarcely have been a misappreciation, had his care for the army and that of his successor given the country in 1812 an effective force of fifteen thousand regulars. Great Britain had but forty-five hundred in all Canada,[394] from Quebec to St. Joseph's, near Mackinac; and the American resources in militia were to hers as ten to one. But Jefferson and Madison, with their Secretary of the Treasury, had reduced the national debt between 1801 and 1812 from $80,000,000 to $45,000,000, concerning which a Virginia Sen-

---

392. To Monroe, May 4, 1806. Jefferson's Writings, Collected and Edited by P.L. Ford, vol. viii. p. 450.
393. Ibid., vol. vi. p. 75.
394. Kingsford's History of Canada, vol. viii. p. 183. The author is indebted to Major General Sir F. Maurice, and Major G. Le M. Gretton, of the British Army, for extracts from the official records, from which it appears that, excluding provincial corps, not to be accounted regulars, the British troops in Canada numbered in January, 1812, 3,952; in July, 5,004.

ator remarked: "This difference has never been felt by society. It has produced no effect upon the common intercourse among men. For my part, I should never have known of the reduction but for the annual Treasury Report."[395] Something was learned about it, however, in the first year of the war, and the interest upon the savings was received at Detroit, on the Niagara frontier, in the Chesapeake and the Delaware.

The War of 1812 was very unpopular in certain sections of the United States and with certain parts of the community. By these, particular fault was found with the invasion of Canada.

> You have declared war, it was said, for two principal alleged reasons: one, the general policy of the British Government, formulated in the successive Orders in Council, to the unjustifiable injury and violation of American commerce; the other, the impressment of seamen from American merchant ships. What have Canada and the Canadians to do with either? If war you must, carry on your war upon the ocean, the scene of your avowed wrongs, and the seat of your adversary's prosperity, and do not embroil these innocent regions and people in the common ruin which, without adequate cause, you are bringing upon your own countrymen, and upon the only nation that now upholds the freedom of mankind against that oppressor of our race, that incarnation of all despotism—Napoleon.

So, not without some alloy of self-interest, the question presented itself to New England, and so New England presented it to the Government and the Southern part of the Union; partly as a matter of honest conviction, partly as an incident of the factiousness inherent in all political opposition, which makes a point wherever it can.

Logically, there may at first appear some reason in these arguments. We are bound to believe so, for we cannot entirely impeach the candour of our ancestors, who doubtless advanced them with some degree of conviction. The answer, of course, is,

---

395. Giles, Annals of Congress, 1811-12, p. 51.

that when two nations go to war, all the citizens of one become internationally the enemies of the other. This is the accepted principle of International Law, a residuum of the concentrated wisdom of many generations of international legists. When war takes the place of peace, it annihilates all natural and conventional rights, all treaties and compacts, except those which appertain to the state of war itself. The warfare of modern civilization assures many rights to an enemy, by custom, by precedent, by compact; many treaties bear express stipulations that, should war arise between the parties, such and such methods of warfare are barred; but all these are merely guaranteed exceptions to the general rule that every individual of each nation is the enemy of those of the opposing belligerent.

Canada and the Canadians, being British subjects, became therefore, however involuntarily, the enemies of the United States, when the latter decided that the injuries received from Great Britain compelled recourse to the sword. Moreover, war, once determined, must be waged on the principles of war; and whatever greed of annexation may have entered into the motives of the Administration of the day, there can be no question that politically and militarily, as a war measure, the invasion of Canada was not only justifiable but imperative. "In case of war," wrote the United States Secretary of State, Monroe, a very few days[396] before the declaration, "it might be necessary to invade Canada; not as an object of the war, but as a means to bring it to a satisfactory conclusion." War now is never waged for the sake of mere fighting, simply to see who is the better at killing people. The warfare of civilized nations is for the purpose of accomplishing an object, obtaining a concession of alleged right from an enemy who has proved implacable to argument. He is to be made to yield to force what he has refused to reason; and to do that, hold is laid upon what is his, either by taking actual possession, or by preventing his utilizing what he still may retain. An attachment is issued, so to say, or an injunction laid, according to circumstances; as men in law do to enforce payment of a

---

396. June 13, 1812. Works of James Monroe, vol. v. p. 207.

debt, or abatement of an injury. If, in the attempt to do this, the other nation resists, as it probably will, then fighting ensues; but that fighting is only an incident of war. War, in substance, though not perhaps in form, began when the one nation resorted to force, quite irrespective of the resistance of the other.

Canada, conquered by the United States, would therefore have been a piece of British property attached; either in compensation for claims, or as an asset in the bargaining which precedes a treaty of peace. Its retention even, as a permanent possession, would have been justified by the law of war, if the military situation supported that course. This is a political consideration; militarily, the reasons were even stronger. To Americans the War of 1812 has worn the appearance of a maritime contest. This is both natural and just; for, as a matter of fact, not only were the maritime operations more pleasing to retrospect, but they also were as a whole, and on both sides, far more efficient, far more virile, than those on land. Under the relative conditions of the parties, however, it ought to have been a land war, because of the vastly superior advantages on shore possessed by the party declaring war; and such it would have been, doubtless, but for the amazing incompetency of most of the army leaders on both sides, after the fall of the British general, Brock, almost at the opening of hostilities. This incompetency, on the part of the United States, is directly attributable to the policy of Jefferson and Madison; for had proper attention and development been given to the army between 1801 and 1812, it could scarcely have failed that some indication of men's fitness or unfitness would have preceded and obviated the lamentable experience of the first two years, when every opportunity was favourable, only to be thrown away from lack of leadership. That even the defects of preparation, extreme and culpable as these were, could have been overcome, is evidenced by the history of the Lakes. The Governor General, Prevost, reported to the home government in July and August, 1812, that the British still had the naval superiority on Erie and Ontario;[397] but this condition was re-

---
397. Prevost to Liverpool, July 15, 1812. Canadian Archives, Q. 118.

versed by the energy and capacity of the American commanders, Chauncey, Perry, and Macdonough, utilizing the undeniable superiority in available resources—mechanics and transportation—which their territory had over the Canadian, not for naval warfare only, but for land as well.

The general considerations that have been advanced are sufficient to indicate what should have been the general plan of the war on the part of the United States. Every war must be aggressive, or, to use the technical term, offensive, in military character; for unless you injure the enemy, if you confine yourself, as some of the grumblers of that day would have it, to simple defence against his efforts, obviously he has no inducement to yield your contention. Incidentally, however, vital interests must be defended, otherwise the power of offence falls with them. Every war, therefore, has both a defensive and an offensive side, and in an effective plan of campaign each must receive due attention. Now, in 1812, so far as general natural conditions went, the United States was relatively weak on the sea frontier, and strong on the side of Canada. The seaboard might, indeed, in the preceding ten years, have been given a development of force, by the creation of an adequate navy, which would have prevented war, by the obvious danger to British interests involved in hostilities. But this had not been done; and Jefferson, by his gunboat policy, building some two hundred of those vessels, worthless unless under cover of the land, proclaimed by act as by voice his adherence to a bare defensive. The sea frontier, therefore, became mainly a line of defence, the utility of which primarily was, or should have been, to maintain communication with the outside world; to support commerce, which in turn should sustain the financial potency that determines the issues of war.

The truth of this observation is shown by one single fact, which will receive recurrent mention from time to time in the narrative. Owing partly to the necessities of the British Government, and partly as a matter of favour extended to the New England States, on account of their antagonism to the war, the commercial blockade of the coast was for a long time—until

April 25, 1814—limited to the part between Narragansett Bay and the boundary of Florida, then a Spanish colony. During this period, which Madison angrily called one of "invidious discrimination between different parts of the United States," New England was left open to neutral commerce, which the British, to supply their own wants, further encouraged by a system of licenses, exempting from capture the vessels engaged, even though American. Owing largely to this, though partly to the local development of manufactures caused by the previous policy of restriction upon foreign trade, which had diverted New England from maritime commerce to manufactures, that section became the distributing centre of the Union. In consequence, the remainder of the country was practically drained of specie, which set to the northward and eastward, the surplusage above strictly local needs finding its way to Canada, to ease the very severe necessities of the British military authorities there; for Great Britain, maintaining her own armies in the Spanish peninsula, and supporting in part the alliance against Napoleon on the Continent, could spare no coin to Canada. It could not go far south, because the coasting trade was destroyed by the enemy's fleets, and the South could not send forward its produce by land to obtain money in return. The deposits in Massachusetts banks increased from $2,671,619, in 1810, to $8,875,589, in 1814; while in the same years the specie held was respectively $1,561,034 and $6,393,718.[398]

It was a day of small things, relatively to present gigantic commercial enterprises; but an accumulation of cash in one quarter, coinciding with penury in another, proves defect in circulation consequent upon embarrassed communications. That flour in Boston sold for $12.00 the barrel, while at Baltimore and Richmond it stood at $6.50 and $4.50, tells the same tale of congestion and deficiency, due to interruption of water communication; the whole proving that, under the conditions of 1812, as the United States Government had allowed them to become, through failure to foster a navy by which alone coast defence in the true

---

398. *Niles' Register*, vol. vii. p. 195.

sense can be effected, the coast frontier was essentially the weak point. There Great Britain could put forth her enormous naval strength with the most sensible and widespread injury to American national power, as represented in the financial stability which constitutes the sinews of war. Men enough could be had; there were one hundred thousand registered seamen belonging to the country; but in the preceding ten years the frigate force had decreased from thirteen of that nominal rate to nine, while the only additions to the service, except gunboats, were two sloops of war, two brigs, and four schooners. The construction of ships of the line, for six of which provision had been made under the administration which expired in 1801, was abandoned immediately by its successor. There was no navy for defence.

Small vessels, under which denomination most frigates should be included, have their appropriate uses in a naval establishment, but in themselves are inadequate to the defence of a coast-line, in the true sense of the word "defence." It is one of the first elements of intelligent warfare that true defence consists in imposing upon the enemy a wholesome fear of yourself. "The best protection against the enemy's fire," said Farragut, "is a rapid fire from our own guns." "No scheme of defence," said Napoleon, "can be considered efficient that does not provide the means of attacking the enemy at an opportue moment. In the defence of a river, for instance," he continues, "you must not only be able to withstand its passage by the enemy, but must keep in your own hands means of crossing, so as to attack him, when occasion either offers, or can be contrived." In short, you must command either a bridge or a ford, and have a disposable force ready to utilize it by attack. The fact of such preparation fetters every movement of the enemy.

At its very outbreak the War of 1812 gave an illustration of the working of this principle. Tiny as was the United States Navy, the opening of hostilities found it concentrated in a body of several frigates, with one or two sloops of war, which put to sea together. The energies of Great Britain being then concentrated upon the navy of Napoleon, her available force at Halifax and Bermuda was small, and the frigates, of which it was almost wholly composed, were compelled to keep together; for, if they attempted to scatter, in order to watch several commercial ports, they were exposed to capture singly by this relatively numerous body of American cruisers. The narrow escape of the frigate *Constitution* from the British squadron at this moment, on her way from the Chesapeake to New York, which port she was unable to gain, exemplifies precisely the risk of dispersion that the British frigates did not dare to face while their enemy was believed to be at hand in concentrated force. They being compelled thus to remain together, the ports were left open; and the American merchant ships, of which a great number were then abroad, returned with comparative impunity, though certainly not entirely without losses.

This actual experience illustrates exactly the principle of coast defence by the power having relatively the weaker navy. It cannot, indeed, drive away a body numerically much stronger; but, if itself respectable in force, it can compel the enemy to keep united. Thereby is minimized the injury caused to a coast-line by the dispersion of the enemy's force along it in security, such as was subsequently acquired by the British in 1813-14, and by the United States Navy during the Civil War. The enemy's fears defend the coast, and protect the nation, by securing the principal benefit of the coast-line—coastwise and maritime trade, and the revenue thence proceeding. In order, however, to maintain this imposing attitude, the defending state must hold ready a concentrated force, of such size that the enemy cannot safely divide his own—a force, for instance, such as that estimated by Gouverneur Morris, twenty years before 1812.[399] The defendant fleet, further, must be able to put to sea at a moment inconvenient to the enemy; must have the bridge or ford Napoleon required for his army. Such the United States had in her seaports, which with moderate protection could keep an enemy at a distance, and from which escape was possible under conditions exceedingly dangerous for the detached hostile divisions; but although possessing

---

399. Ante, p. 71.

these bridge heads leading to the scene of ocean war, no force to issue from them existed. In those eleven precious years during which Great Britain by American official returns had captured 917 American ships,[400] a large proportion of them in defiance of International Law, as was claimed, and had impressed from American vessels 6,257 seamen,[401] asserted to be mostly American citizens, the United States had built two sloops of 18 guns, and two brigs of 16; and out of twelve frigates had permitted three to rot at their moorings. To build ships of the line had not even been attempted. Consequently, except when weather drove them off, puny divisions of British ships gripped each commercial port by the throat with perfect safety; and those weather occasions, which constitute the opportunity of the defendant sea power, could not be improved by military action.

Such in general was the condition of the sea frontier, thrown inevitably upon the defensive. With the passing comment that, had it been defended as suggested, Great Britain would never have forced the war, let us now consider conditions on the Canadian line, where circumstances eminently favoured the offensive by the United States; for this war should not be regarded simply as a land war or a naval war, nor yet as a war of offence and again one of defence, but as being continuously and at all times both offensive and defensive, both land and sea, in reciprocal influence.

Disregarding as militarily unimportant the artificial boundary dividing Canada from New York, Vermont, and the eastern parts of the Union, the frontier separating the land positions of the two belligerents was the Great Lakes and the river St. Lawrence. This presented certain characteristic and unusual features. That it was a water line was a condition not uncommon; but it was exceptionally marked by those broad expanses which constitute inland seas of great size and depth, navigable by vessels of the

---

400. American State Papers, Foreign Relations, vol. iii. p. 584.
401. *Niles' Register*, vol. ii. p. 119. "Official Returns in the Department of State" are alleged as authority for the statement. Monroe to Foster, May 30, 1812, mentions "a list in this office of several thousand American seamen who have been impressed into the British service." American State Papers, Foreign Relations, vol. iii. p. 454.

largest sea-going dimensions. This water system, being continuous and in continual progress, is best conceived by applying to the whole, from Lake Superior to the ocean, the name of the great river, the St. Lawrence, which on the one hand unites it to the sea, and on the other divides the inner waters from the outer by a barrier of rapids, impassable to ships that otherwise could navigate freely both lakes and ocean.

The importance of the lakes to military operations must always be great, but it was much enhanced in 1812 by the undeveloped condition of land communications. With the roads in the state they then were, the movement of men, and still more of supplies, was vastly more rapid by water than by land. Except in winter, when iron-bound snow covered the ground, the routes of Upper Canada were well-nigh impassable; in spring and in autumn rains, wholly so to heavy vehicles. The mail from Montreal to York,—now Toronto,—three hundred miles, took a month in transit.[402] In October, 1814, when the war was virtually over, the British General at Niagara lamented to the Commander-in-Chief that, owing to the refusal of the navy to carry troops, an important detachment was left "to struggle through the dreadful roads from Kingston to York."[403] "Should reinforcements and provisions not arrive, the naval commander would," in his opinion, "have much to answer for."[404] The Commander-in-Chief himself wrote: "The command of the lakes enables the enemy to perform in two days what it takes the troops from Kingston sixteen to twenty days of severe marching. Their men arrive fresh; ours fatigued, and with exhausted equipment. The distance from Kingston to the Niagara frontier exceeds two hundred and fifty miles, and part of the way is impracticable for supplies."[405] On the United States side, road conditions were similar but much less disadvantageous. The water route by On-

---

402. Kingsford's History of Canada, vol. viii. p. 111.
403. Drummond to Prevost, Oct. 20, 1814. Report on Canadian Archives, 1896, Upper Canada, p. 9.
404. Ibid., Oct. 15.
405. Prevost to Bathurst, Aug. 14, 1814. Report on Canadian Archives, 1896, Lower Canada, p. 36.

tario was greatly preferred as a means of transportation, and in parts and at certain seasons was indispensable. Stores for Sackett's Harbour, for instance, had in early summer to be brought to Oswego, and thence coasted along to their destination, in security or in peril, according to the momentary predominance of one party or the other on the lake. In like manner, it was more convenient to move between the Niagara frontier and the east end of the lake by water; but in case of necessity, men could march. An English traveller in 1818 says:

> I accomplished the journey from Albany to Buffalo in October in six days with ease and comfort, whereas in May it took ten of great difficulty and distress.[406]

In the farther West the American armies, though much impeded, advanced securely through Ohio and Indiana to the shores of Lake Erie, and there maintained themselves in supplies sent over-country; whereas the British at the western end of the lake, opposite Detroit, depended wholly upon the water, although no hostile force threatened the land line between them and Ontario. The battle of Lake Erie, so disastrous to their cause, was forced upon them purely by failure of food, owing to the appearance of Perry's squadron.

From Lake Superior to the head of the first rapid of the St. Lawrence, therefore, the control of the water was the decisive factor in the general military situation. Both on the upper lakes, where water communication from Sault Sainte Marie to Niagara was unbroken, and on Ontario, separated from the others by the falls of Niagara, the British had at the outset a slight superiority, but not beyond the power of the United States to overtake and outpass. Throughout the rapids, to Montreal, military conditions resembled those which confront a general charged with the passage of any great river. If undertaken at all, such an enterprise requires the deceiving of the opponent as to the place and time when the attempt will be made, the careful provision of means and disposition of men for instant execution, and fi-

---

406. Travels, J.M. Duncan, vol. ii. p. 27.

nally the prompt and decisive seizure of opportunity, to transfer and secure on the opposite shore a small body, capable of maintaining itself until the bulk of the army can cross to its support. Nothing of the sort was attempted here, or needed to be undertaken in this war. Naval superiority determined the ability to cross above the rapids, and there was no occasion to consider the question of crossing between them. Immediately below the last lay Montreal, accessible to sea-going vessels from the ocean. To that point, therefore, the sea power of Great Britain reached, and there it ended.

The United States Government was conscious of its great potential superiority over Canada, in men and in available resources. So evident, indeed, was the disparity, that the prevalent feeling was not one of reasonable self-reliance, but of vainglorious self-confidence; of dependence upon mere bulk and weight to crush an opponent, quite irrespective of preparation or skill, and disregardful of the factor of military efficiency. Jefferson's words have already been quoted. Calhoun, then a youthful member of Congress, and a foremost advocate of the war, said in March, 1812: "So far from being unprepared, Sir, I believe that in four weeks from the time a declaration of war is heard, on our frontier, the whole of Upper Canada"—halfway down the St. Lawrence—"and a part of Lower Canada will be in our power." This tone was general in Congress; Henry Clay spoke to the same effect. Granting due preparation, such might indeed readily have been the result of a well-designed, active, offensive campaign. Little hope of any other result was held by the British local officials, and what little they had was based upon the known want of military efficiency in the United States. Brock, by far the ablest among them, in February declared his "full conviction that unless Detroit and Michilimackinac be both in our possession at the commencement of hostilities, not only Amherstburg"—on the Detroit River, a little below Detroit—"but most probably the whole country, must be evacuated as far as Kingston."[407] This place is at the foot of Ontario, close to the

---

407. Life of Sir Isaac Brock, p. 127.

entrance to the St. Lawrence. Having a good and defensible harbour, it had been selected for the naval station of the lake. If successful in holding it, there would be a base of operations for attempting recovery of the water, and ultimately of the upper country. Failing there, of course the British must fall back upon the sea, touch with which they would regain at Montreal, resting there upon the navy of their nation; just as Wellington, by the same dependence, had maintained himself at Lisbon unshaken by the whole power of Napoleon.

There was, however, no certainty that the Lisbon of Canada would be found at Montreal. Though secure on the water side, there were there no lines of Torres Vedras; and it was well within the fears of the governors of Canada that under energetic attack their forces would not be able to make a stand short of Quebec, against the overwhelming numbers which might be brought against them. In December, 1807, Governor General Craig, a soldier of tried experience and reputation, had written:

> Defective as it is, Quebec is the only post that can be considered tenable for a moment. If the Americans should turn their attention to Lower Canada, which is most probable, I have no hopes that the forces here can accomplish more than to check them for a short time. They will eventually be compelled to take refuge in Quebec, and operations must terminate in a siege.[408]

Consequent upon this report of a most competent officer, much had been done to strengthen the works; but pressed by the drain of the Peninsular War, heaviest in the years 1809 to 1812, when France elsewhere was at peace, little in the way of troops had been sent. As late as November 16, 1812, the Secretary for War, in London, notified Governor General Prevost that as yet he could give no hopes of reinforcements.[409] Napoleon had begun his retreat from Moscow three weeks before, but the full effects of the impending disaster were not yet forecast. Another three weeks, and the Secretary wrote that

---

408. Report on Canadian Archives, 1893, Lower Canada, p. 1.
409. Ibid., p. 75.

a moderate detachment would be sent to Bermuda, to await there the opening of the St. Lawrence in the spring.[410] But already the United States had lost Mackinac and Detroit, and Canada had gained time to breathe.

Brock's remark, expanded as has here been done, defines the decisive military points upon the long frontier from Lake Superior to Montreal. Mackinac, Detroit, Kingston, Montreal—these four places, together with adequate development of naval strength on the lakes—constituted the essential elements of the military situation at the opening of hostilities. Why? Mackinac and Detroit because, being situated upon extremely narrow parts of the vital chain of water communication, their possession controlled decisively all transit. Held in force, they commanded the one great and feasible access to the north-western country. Upon them turned, therefore, the movement of what was then its chief industry, the fur trade; but more important still, the tenure of those points so affected the interests of the Indians of that region as to throw them necessarily on the side of the party in possession. It is difficult for us to realize how heavily this consideration weighed at that day with both nations, but especially with the British; because, besides being locally the weaker, they knew that under existing conditions in Europe—Napoleon still in the height of his power, never yet vanquished, and about to undertake the invasion of Russia—they had nothing to hope from the mother country. Yet the leaders, largely professional soldiers, faced the situation with soldierly instinct. "If we could destroy the American posts at Detroit and Michilimackinac," wrote Lieutenant-Governor Gore of Upper Canada, to Craig, in 1808, "many Indians would declare for us;" and he agrees with Craig that, "if not for us, they will surely be against us."[411]

It was Gore's successor, Brock, that wrested from the Americans at once the two places named, with the effect upon the Indians which had been anticipated. The dependence of these upon this water-line communication was greatly increased by

---

410. Ibid.
411. Report on Canadian Archives, 1893, Lower Canada, p. 3.

various punitive expeditions by the United States troops in the Northwest, under General Harrison, in the autumn and winter of 1812-13. To secure further the safety of the whites in the outer settlements, the villages and corn of the hostile natives were laid waste for a considerable surrounding distance.[412] They were thus forced to remove, and to seek shelter in the Northwest. This increase of population in that quarter, relatively to a store of food never too abundant, made it the more urgent for them to remain friends of those with whom it rested to permit the water traffic, by which supplies could come forward and the exchange of commodities go on. The fall of Michilimackinac, therefore, determined their side, to which the existing British naval command of the upper lakes also contributed; and these causes were alleged by Hull in justification of his surrender at Detroit, which completed and secured the enemy's grip throughout the northwestern frontier. This accession of strength to the British was not without very serious drawbacks. Shortly before the battle of Lake Erie the British commissaries were feeding fourteen thousand Indians—men, women, and children. What proportion of these were warriors it is hard to say, and harder still how many could be counted on to take the field when wanted; but it is probable that the exhaustion of supplies due to this cause more than compensated for any service received from them in war. When Barclay sailed to fight Perry, there remained in store but one day's flour, and the crews of his ships had been for some days on half allowance of many articles.

The opinion of competent soldiers on the spot, such as Craig and Brock, in full possession of all the contemporary facts, may be accepted explicitly as confirming the inferences which in any event might have been drawn from the natural features of the situation. Upon Mackinac and Detroit depended the control and quiet of the north-western country, because they commanded vital points on its line of communication. Upon Kingston and Montreal, by their position and intrinsic advantages, rested the communication of all Canada, along and above the St.

---

412. Brackenridge, War of 1812, pp. 57, 63, 65, 66.

Lawrence, with the sea power of Great Britain, whence alone could be drawn the constant support without which ultimate defeat should have been inevitable. Naval power, sustained upon the Great Lakes, controlled the great line of communication between the East and West, and also conferred upon the party possessing it the strategic advantage of interior lines; that is, of shorter distances, both in length and time, to move from point to point of the lake shores, close to which lay the scenes of operations. It followed that Detroit and Michilimackinac, being at the beginning in the possession of the United States, should have been fortified, garrisoned, provisioned, in readiness for siege, and placed in close communication with home, as soon as war was seen to be imminent, which it was in December, 1811, at latest. Having in that quarter everything to lose, and comparatively little to gain, the country was thrown on the defensive. On the east the possession of Montreal or Kingston would cut off all Canada above from support by the sea, which would be equivalent to insuring its fall. "I shall continue to exert myself to the utmost to overcome every difficulty," wrote Brock, who gave such emphatic proof of energetic and sagacious exertion in his subsequent course. "Should, however, the communication between Montreal and Kingston be cut off, the fate of the troops in this part of the province will be decided."[413] "The Montreal frontier," said the officer selected by the Duke of Wellington to report on the defences of Canada, "is the most important, and at present 1826 confessedly most vulnerable and accessible part of Canada."[414] There, then, was the direction for offensive operations by the United States; preferably against Montreal, for, if successful, a much larger region would be isolated and reduced. Montreal gone, Kingston could receive no help from without; and, even if capable of temporary resistance, its surrender would be but a question of time. Coincidently with this military advance, naval development for the control of the lakes should have proceeded, as a discreet precaution; although, after the fall

---

413. Life of Brock, p. 193.
414. Smyth, Précis of the Wars in Canada, p. 167.

of Kingston and Montreal, there could have been little use of an inland navy, for the British local resources would then have been inadequate to maintain an opposing force.

Considered apart from the question of military readiness, in which the United States was so lamentably deficient, the natural advantages in her possession for the invasion of Canada were very great. The Hudson River, Lake George, and Lake Champlain furnished a line of water communication, for men and supplies, from the very heart of the resources of the country, centring about New York. This was not indeed continuous; but it was consecutive, and well developed. Almost the whole of it lay within United States territory; and when the boundary line on Champlain was reached, Montreal was but forty miles distant. Towards Kingston, also, there was a similar line, by way of the Mohawk River and Lake Oneida to Oswego, whence a short voyage on Ontario reached the American naval station at Sackett's Harbour, thirty miles from Kingston. As had been pointed out six months before the war began, by General Armstrong, who became the United States Secretary of War in January, 1813, when the most favourable conditions for initiative had already been lost, these two lines were identical as far as Albany.

> This should be the place of rendezvous; because, besides other recommendations, it is here that all the roads leading from the central portion of the United States to the Canadas diverge—a circumstance which, while it keeps up your enemy's doubts as to your real point of attack, cannot fail to keep his means of defence in a state of division.[415]

The perplexity of an army, thus uncertain upon which extreme of a line one hundred and fifty miles long a blow will fall, is most distressing; and trebly so when, as in this case, the means of communication from end to end are both scanty and slow. "The conquest of Lower Canada," Sir James Craig had written, "must still be effected by way of Lake Champlain;" but while this

---

415. Armstrong to Eustis, Jan. 2, 1812. Armstrong's Notices of the War of 1812, vol. i, p. 238.

was true, and dictated to the officer charged with the defence the necessity of keeping the greater part of his force in that quarter, it would be impossible wholly to neglect the exposure of the upper section. This requirement was reflected in the disposition of the British forces when war began; two thirds being below Montreal, chiefly at Quebec, the remainder dispersed through Upper Canada. To add to these advantages of the United States, trivial as was the naval force of either party on Champlain, the preponderance at this moment, and throughout the first year, was in her hands. She was also better situated to enlarge her squadrons on all the lakes, because nearer the heart of her power.

Circumstances thus had determined that, in general plan, the seaboard represented the defensive scene of campaign for the United States, while the land frontier should be that of offensive action. It will be seen, with particular reference to the latter, that the character of the front of operations prescribed the offensive in great and concentrated force toward the St. Lawrence, with preparations and demonstrations framed to keep the enemy doubtful to the last possible moment as to where the blow should fall; while on the western frontier, from Michilimackinac to Niagara, the defensive should have been maintained, qualifying this term, however, by the already quoted maxim of Napoleon, that no offensive disposition is complete which does not keep in view, and provide for, offensive action, if opportunity offer. Such readiness, if it leads to no more, at least compels the opponent to retain near by a degree of force that weakens by so much his resistance in the other quarter, against which the real offensive campaign is directed.

Similarly, the seaboard, defensive in general relation to the national plan as a whole, must have its own particular sphere of offensive action, without which its defensive function is enfeebled, if not paralyzed. Having failed to create before the war a competent navy, capable of seizing opportunity, when offered, to act against hostile divisions throughout the world, it was not possible afterwards to retrieve this mistake. Under the circumstances existing in 1812, the previous decade having been allowed by the country to pass in absolute naval indifference, offensive measures were necessarily confined to the injury of the enemy's commerce. Had a proper force existed, abundant opportunity for more military action was sure to occur. The characteristics of parts of the American coast prevented close blockade, especially in winter; and the same violent winds which forced an enemy's ships off, facilitated egress under circumstances favouring evasion. Escape to the illimitable ocean then depended at worst upon speed. This was the case at Boston, which Commodore Bainbridge before the war predicted could not be effectually blockaded; also at Narragansett, recommended for the same reason by Commodore John Rodgers; and in measure at New York, though there the more difficult and shoaler bar involved danger and delay to the passage of heavy frigates. In this respect the British encountered conditions contrary to those they had know before the French Atlantic ports, where the wind which drove the blockaders off prevented the blockaded from leaving. Once out and away, a squadron of respectable force would be at liberty to seek and strike one of the minor divisions of the enemy, imposing caution as to how he dispersed his ships in face of such a chance. To the south, both the Delaware and Chesapeake could be sealed almost hermetically by a navy so superior as was that of Great Britain; for the sheltered anchorage within enabled a fleet to lie with perfect safety across the path of all vessels attempting to go out or in. South of this again, Wilmington, Charleston, and Savannah, though useful commercial harbours, had not the facilities, natural or acquired, for sustaining a military navy. They were not maritime centres; the commerce of the South, even of Baltimore with its famous schooners, being in peace carried on chiefly by shipping which belonged elsewhere—New England or foreign. The necessities of a number of armed ships could not there be supplied; and furthermore, the comparatively moderate weather made the coast at once more easy and less dangerous for an enemy to approach. These ports, therefore, were entered only occasionally, and then by the smaller American cruisers.

For these reasons the northern portion of the coast, with its rugged shores and tempestuous weather, was the base of such offensive operations as the diminutive numbers of the United States Navy permitted. To it the national ships sought to return, for they could enter with greater security, and had better prospects of getting out again when they wished. In the Delaware, the Chesapeake, and on the Southern coast, the efforts of the United States were limited to action strictly, and even narrowly, defensive in scope. Occasionally, a very small enemy's cruiser might be attacked; but for the most part people were content merely to resist aggression, if attempted. The harrying of the Chesapeake, and to a less extent of the Delaware, are familiar stories; the total destruction of the coasting trade and the consequent widespread distress are less known, or less remembered. What is not at all appreciated is the deterrent effect upon the perfect liberty enjoyed by the enemy to do as they pleased, which would have been exercised by a respectable fighting navy; by a force in the Northern ports, equal to the offensive, and ready for it, at the time that Great Britain was so grievously preoccupied by the numerous fleet which Napoleon had succeeded in equipping, from Antwerp round to Venice. Of course, after his abdication in 1814, and the release of the British navy and army, there was nothing for the country to do, in the then military strength of the two nations, save to make peace on the best terms attainable. Having allowed to pass away, unresented and unimproved, years of insult, injury, and opportunity, during which the gigantic power of Napoleon would have been a substantial, if inert, support to its own efforts at redress, it was the mishap of the United States Government to take up arms at the very moment when the great burden which her enemy had been bearing for years was about to fall from his shoulders forever.

CHAPTER 6

Early Cruises and Engagements

War was declared on June 18. On the 21st there was lying in the lower harbour of New York a division of five United States vessels under the command of Commodore John Rodgers. It consisted of three frigates, the *President* and *United States*, rated of 44 guns, the *Congress* of 38, the ship-rigged sloop of war *Hornet* of 18, and the brig *Argus* of 16. This division, as it stood, was composed of two squadrons; that of Rodgers himself, and that of Commodore Stephen Decatur, the latter having assigned to him immediately the *United States*, the *Congress*, and the *Argus*. There belonged also to Rodgers' particular squadron the *Essex*, a frigate rated at 32 guns. Captain David Porter, one of the most distinguished names in American naval annals, commanded her then, and until her capture by a much superior force, nearly two years later; but at this moment she was undergoing repairs, a circumstance which prevented her from accompanying the other vessels, and materially affected her subsequent history.

It may be mentioned, as an indication of naval policy, that although Rodgers and Decatur each had more than one vessel under his control, neither was given the further privilege and distinction, frequent in such cases, of having a captain to command the particular ship on which he himself sailed. This, when done, introduces a very substantial change in the position of the officer affected. He is removed from being only first among several equals, and is advanced to a superiority of grade, in which he stands alone, with consequent enhancement of authority.

Rodgers was captain of the *President* as well as commodore of the small body of vessels assigned to him; Decatur held the same relation to the frigate *United States*, and to her consorts. Though apparently trivial, the circumstance is not insignificant; for it indicates clearly that, so far as the Navy Department then had any mind, it had not yet made it up as to whether it would send out its vessels as single cruisers, or combine them into divisions, for the one operation open to the United States Navy, namely, the destruction of the enemy's commerce. With divisions permanently constituted as such, propriety and effective action would have required the additional dignity for the officer in general charge, and they themselves doubtless would have asked for it; but for ships temporarily associated, and liable at any moment to be scattered, not only was the simple seniority of naval rank sufficient, but more would have been inexpedient. The commodores, now such only by courtesy and temporary circumstance, would suffer no derogation if deprived of ships other than their own; whereas the more extensive function, similarly curtailed, would become a mere empty show, a humiliation which no office, civil or military, can undergo without harm.

This indecision of the Department reflected the varying opinions of the higher officers of the service, which in turn but reproduced different schools of thought throughout all navies. Historically, as a military operation, for the injury of an enemy's commerce and the protection of one's own, it may be considered fairly demonstrated that vessels grouped do more effective work than the same number scattered. This is, of course, but to repeat the general military teaching of operations of all kinds. It is not the keeping of the several vessels side by side that constitutes the virtue of this disposition; it is the placing them under a single head, thereby insuring co-operation, however widely dispersed by their common chief under the emergency of successive moments. Like a fan that opens and shuts, vessels thus organically bound together possess the power of wide sweep, which insures exertion over a great field of ocean, and at the same time that of mutual support, because dependent upon and controlled from a common centre. Such is concentration, reasonably understood; not huddled together like a drove of cattle, but distributed with a regard to a common purpose, and linked together by the effectual energy of a single will.

There is, however, in the human mind an inveterate tendency to dispersion of effort, due apparently to the wish to do at once as many things as may be; a disposition also to take as many chances as possible in an apparent lottery, with the more hope that some one of them will come up successful. Not an aggregate big result, and one only, whether hit or miss, but a division of resources and powers which shall insure possible compensation in one direction for what is not gained, or may even be lost, in another. The Navy Department, when hostilities were imminent, addressed inquiries to several prominent officers as to the best means of employing the very small total force available. The question involved the direction of effort, as well as the method; but as regards the former of these, the general routes followed by British commerce, and the modes of protecting it, were so far understood as to leave not much room for differences of opinion.

Rodgers may have been unconsciously swayed by the natural bias of an officer whose seniority would insure him a division, if the single-cruiser policy did not prevail. Of the replies given, however, his certainly was the one most consonant with sound military views.[416] Send a small squadron, of two or three frigates and a sloop, to cruise on the coast of the British Islands, and send the light cruisers to the West Indies; for, though he did not express it, in the gentle breezes and smooth seas of the tropics small cruisers have a much better chance to avoid capture by big ships than in the heavy gales of the North Atlantic. This much may be termed the distinctly offensive part of Rodgers' project. For the defensive, employ the remainder of the frigates, singly or in squadron, to guard our own seaboard; either directly, by remaining off the coast, or by taking position in the track of the trade between Great Britain and the St. Lawrence. Irrespective

---

416. Captains' Letters, June 3, 1812. Navy Department MSS.

of direct captures there made, this course would contribute to protect the access to home ports, by drawing away the enemy's ships of war to cover their own threatened commerce. Alike in the size of his foreign squadron, and in the touch of uncertainty as to our own coasts, "singly or in squadron," Rodgers reflected the embarrassment of a man whose means are utterly inadequate to the work he wishes to do. One does not need to be a soldier or a seaman to comprehend the difficulty of making ends meet when there is not enough to go round.

Decatur and Bainbridge, whose written opinions are preserved, held views greatly modified from those of Rodgers, or even distinctly opposed to them. Decatur wrote:

> The plan which appears to me best calculated for our little navy to annoy the trade of Great Britain would be to send them out distant from our own coast, singly, or not more than two frigates in company, without specific instructions; relying upon the enterprise of their officers. Two frigates cruising together would not be so easily traced by an enemy as a greater number; their movements would be infinitely more rapid; they would be sufficiently strong in most instances to attack a convoy, and the probability is they would not meet with a superior cruising force. If, however, they should meet a superior, and cannot avoid it, we would not have to regret the whole of our marine crushed at one blow.[417]

Bainbridge is yet more absolute.

> I am anxious to see us all dispersed about various seas. If we are kept together in squadron, or lying in port, the whole are scarcely of more advantage than one ship. I wish all our public vessels here (Boston) were dispersed in various ports, for I apprehend it will draw speedily a numerous force of the enemy to blockade or attack.[418]

At the moment of writing this, Rodgers' squadron was in

---
417. Ibid., June 8, 1812.
418. Captains' Letters, Sept. 2, 1812. Navy Department MSS.

Boston, having returned from a cruise, and the *Constitution* also, immediately after her engagement with the *Guerrière*.

It will be observed that, in spirit even more than in letter, Rodgers' leading conception is that of co-operation, combined action. First, he would have a Department general plan, embracing in a comprehensive scheme the entire navy and the ocean at large, in the British seas, West Indies, and North Atlantic; each contributing, by its particular action and impression, to forward the work of the others, and so of the whole. Secondly, he intimates, not obscurely, though cautiously, in each separate field the concerted action of several ships is better than their disconnected efforts. Decatur and Bainbridge, on the contrary, implicitly, and indeed explicitly, favour individual movement. They would reject even combination by the Department—"no specific instructions, rely upon the enterprise of the officers." Nor will they have a local supervision or control in any particular; two frigates at the most are to act together, singly even is preferable, and they shall roam the seas at will.

There can be little doubt as to which scheme is sounder in general principle. All military experience concurs in the general rule of co-operative action; and this means concentration, under the liberal definition before given—unity of purpose and subordination to a central control. General rules, however, must be intelligently applied to particular circumstances; and it will be found by considering the special circumstances of British commerce, under the war conditions of 1812, that Rodgers' plan was particularly suited to injure it. It is doubtless true that if merchant vessels were so dispersed over the globe, that rarely more than one would be visible at a time, one ship of war could take that one as well as a half-dozen could. But this was not the condition. British merchant ships were not permitted so to act. They were compelled to gather at certain centres, and thence, when enough had assembled, were despatched in large convoys, guarded by ships of war, in force proportioned to that disposable at the moment by the local admiral, and to the anticipated danger. Consequently, while isolated merchant ships were to be met, they were but the crumbs that fell from the table, except in the near vicinity of the British Islands themselves.

Such were the conditions while Great Britain had been at war with France alone; but the declaration of the United States led at once to increased stringency. All licenses to cross the Atlantic without convoy were at once revoked, and every colonial and naval commander lay under heavy responsibility to enforce the law of convoy. Insurance was forfeited by breach of its requirements; and in case of parting convoy, capture would at least hazard, if not invalidate, the policy. Under all this compulsion, concentrated merchant fleets and heavy guards became as far as possible the rule of action. With such conditions it was at once more difficult for a single ship of war to find, and when found to deal effectually with, a body of vessels which on the one hand was large, and yet occupied but a small space relatively to the great expanse of ocean over which the pursuer might roam fruitlessly, missing continually the one moving spot he sought. For such a purpose a well-handled squadron, scattering within signal-distance from each other, or to meet at a rendezvous, was more likely to find, and, having found, could by concerted action best overcome the guard and destroy the fleet.

On June 22, 1812, the Navy Department issued orders for Rodgers,[419] which are interesting as showing its ideas of operations. The two squadrons then assembled under him were to go to sea, and there separate. He himself, with the frigates *President, Essex,* and *John Adams,* sloop *Hornet,* and the small brig *Nautilus,* was to go to the Capes of the Chesapeake, and thence cruise eastwardly, off and on. Decatur's two frigates, with the *Argus,* would cruise southwardly from New York. It was expected that the two would meet from time to time; and, should combined action be advisable, Rodgers had authority to unite them under his broad pendant for that purpose. The object of this movement was to protect the commerce of the country, which at this time was expected to be returning in great numbers from the Spanish peninsula; whither had been hurried every avail-

---

419. Navy Department MSS.

able ship, and every barrel of flour in store, as soon as the news of the approaching embargo of April 4 became public. "The great bulk of our returning commerce," wrote the secretary, "will make for the ports between the Chesapeake and our eastern extremities; and, in the protection to be afforded, such ports claim particular attention."

The obvious comment on this disposition is that protection to the incoming ships would be most completely afforded, not by the local presence of either of these squadrons, but by the absence of the enemy. This absence was best insured by beating him, if met; and in the then size of the British Halifax fleet it was possible that a detachment sent from it might be successfully engaged by the joint division, though not by either squadron singly. The other adequate alternative was to force the enemy to keep concentrated, and so to cover as small a part as might be of the homeward path of the scattered American trade. This also was best effected by uniting our own ships. Without exaggerating the danger to the American squadrons, needlessly exposed in detail by the Department's plan, the object in view would have been attained as surely, and at less risk, by keeping all the vessels together, even though they were retained between Boston Bay and the Capes of the Chesapeake for the local defence of commerce. In short, as was to be expected from the antecedents of the Government, the scheme was purely and narrowly defensive; there was not in it a trace of any comprehension of the principle that offence is the surest defence. The opening words of its letter defined the full measure of its understanding. "It has been judged expedient so to employ our public armed vessels, as to afford to our returning commerce all possible protection." It may be added, that to station on the very spot where the merchant vessels were flocking in return, divisions inferior to that which could be concentrated against them, was very bad strategy; drawing the enemy by a double motive to the place whence his absence was particularly desirable.

The better way was to influence British naval action by a distinct offensive step; by a movement of the combined divisions sufficiently obvious to inspire caution, but yet too vague to admit of precision of direction or definite pursuit. In accordance with the general ideas formulated in his letter, before quoted, Rodgers had already fixed upon a plan, which, if successful, would inflict a startling blow to British commerce and prestige, and at the same time would compel the enemy to concentrate, thus diminishing his menace to American shipping. It was known to him that a large convoy had sailed from Jamaica for England about May 20. The invariable course of such bodies was first to the north-northeast, parallel in a general sense to the Gulf Stream and American coast, until they had cleared the northeast trades and the belt of light and variable winds above them. Upon approaching forty degrees north latitude, they met in full force the rude west winds, as the Spanish navigators styled them, and before them bore away to the English Channel. That a month after their starting Rodgers should still have hoped to overtake them, gives a lively impression of the lumbering slowness of trade movement under convoy; but he counted also upon the far swifter joint speed of his few and well-found ships. To the effective fulfilment of his double object, defensive and offensive, however, he required more ships than his own squadron, and he held his course dependent upon Decatur joining him.[420]

On June 21 Decatur did join, and later in the same day arrived a Department order of June 18 with the Declaration of War. Within an hour the division of five ships was under way for sea. In consequence of this instant movement Rodgers did not receive the subsequent order of the Department, June 22, the purport of which has been explained and discussed. Standing off south-easterly from Sandy Hook, at 3 a.m. of June 23 was spoken an American brig, which four days before had seen the convoy steering east in latitude 36°, longitude 67°, or about three hundred miles from where the squadron then was. Canvas was crowded in pursuit, but three hours later was sighted in the northeast a large sail heading toward the squadron. The course of all the vessels was changed for her; but she, proving to be

---

420. Captains' Letters, J. Rodgers, Sept. 1, 1812. Navy Department MSS.

The Chase of the *Belvidera* From a drawing by Carlton T. Chapman

British,—the *Belvidera*, rated 32, and smaller than any one of the American frigates,—speedily turned and took flight. Pursuit was continued all that day and until half an hour before midnight, the *President* leading as the fastest ship; but the British vessel, fighting for her life, and with the friendly port of Halifax under her lee, could resort to measures impossible to one whose plan of distant cruising required complete equipment, and full stores of provisions and water. Boats and spare spars and anchors were thrown overboard, and fourteen tons of drinking water pumped out. Thus lightened, after being within range of the *President*'s guns for a couple of hours, the *Belvidera* drew gradually away, and succeeded in escaping, having received and inflicted considerable damage. In explanation of such a result between two antagonists of very unequal size, it must be remembered that a chasing ship of those days could not fire straight ahead; while in turning her side to bring the guns to bear, as the *President* several times did, she lost ground. The chased ship, on the other hand, from the form of the stern, could use four guns without deviating from her course.

After some little delay in repairing, the squadron resumed pursuit of the convoy. On June 29, and again on July 9, vessels were spoken which reported encountering it; the latter the evening before. Traces of its course also were thought to be found in quantities of cocoanut shell and orange peel, passed on one occasion; but, though the chase was continued to within twenty hours' sail of the English Channel, the convoy itself was never seen. To this disappointing result atmospheric conditions very largely contributed. From June 29, on the western edge of the Great Banks, until July 13, when the pursuit was abandoned, the weather was so thick that "at least six days out of seven" nothing was visible over five miles away, and for long periods the vessels could not even see one another at a distance of two hundred yards. The same surrounding lasted to the neighbourhood of Madeira, for which the course was next shaped. After passing that island on June 21 return was made toward the United States by way of the Azores, which were sighted, and thence again to the Banks of Newfoundland and Cape Sable, reaching Boston August 31, after an absence of seventy days.

Although Rodgers's plan had completely failed in what may properly be called its purpose of offence, and he could report the capture of "only seven merchant vessels, and those not valuable," he congratulated himself with justice upon success on the defensive side.[421] The full effect was produced, which he had anticipated from the mere fact of a strong American division being at large, but seen so near its own shores that nothing certain could be inferred as to its movements or intentions. The *Belvidera*, having lost sight of it at midnight, could, upon her arrival in Halifax, give only the general information that it was at sea; and Captain Byron, who commanded her, thought with reason that the *President*'s action warranted the conclusion that the anticipated hostilities had been begun. He therefore seized and brought in two or three American merchantmen; but the British admiral, Sawyer, thinking there might possibly be some mistake, like that of the meeting between the *President* and *Little Belt* a year before, directed their release.

A very few days later, definite intelligence of the declaration of war by the United States was received at Halifax. At that period, the American seas from the equator to Labrador were for administrative purposes divided by the British Admiralty into four commands: two in the West Indies, centring respectively at Jamaica and Barbados; one at Newfoundland; while the fourth, with its two chief naval bases of Halifax and Bermuda, lay over against the United States, and embraced the Atlantic coast-line in its field of operations. Admiral Sawyer now promptly despatched a squadron, consisting of one small ship of the line and three frigates, the *Shannon*, 38, *Belvidera*, 36, and *Æolus*, 32, which sailed July 5. Four days later, off Nantucket, it was joined by the *Guerrière*, 38, and July 14 arrived off Sandy Hook. There Captain Broke, of the *Shannon*, who by seniority of rank commanded the whole force, "received the

---

421. Letter of Sept. 1, 1812. Navy Department MSS.

first intelligence of Rodgers' squadron having put to sea."[422] As an American division of some character had been known to be out since the *Belvidera* met it, and as Rodgers on this particular day was within two days' sail of the English Channel, the entire ignorance of the enemy as to his whereabouts could not be more emphatically stated. The components of the British force were such that no two of them could justifiably venture to encounter his united command. Consequently, to remain together was imposed as a military necessity, and it so continued for some weeks. In fact, the first separation, that of the *Guerrière*, though apparently necessary and safe, was followed immediately by a disaster.

Rodgers was therefore justified in his claim concerning his cruise.

> It is truly unpleasant to be obliged to make a communication thus barren of benefit to our country. The only consolation I, individually, feel on the occasion is derived from knowing that our being at sea obliged the enemy to concentrate a considerable portion of his most active force, and thereby prevented his capturing an incalculable amount of American property that would otherwise have fallen a sacrifice.

On another occasion he wrote:

> My calculations were, even if I did not succeed in destroying the convoy, that leaving the coast as we did would tend to distract the enemy, oblige him to concentrate a considerable portion of his active navy, and at the same time prevent his single cruisers from lying before any of our principal ports, from their not knowing to which, or at what moment, we might return.[423]

This was not only a perfectly sound military conception, gaining additional credit from the contrasted views of Decatur and Bainbridge, but it was applied successfully at the most

---
422. James, Naval History (edition 1824), vol. v. p. 283.
423. Captains' Letters, Sept. 14, 1812. Navy Department MSS.

critical moment of all wars, namely, when commerce is flocking home for safety, and under conditions particularly hazardous to the United States, owing to the unusually large number of vessels then out. "We have been so completely occupied in looking out for Commodore Rodgers' squadron," wrote an officer of the *Guerrière*, "that we have taken very few prizes."[424] President Madison in his annual message[425] said:

> Our trade, with little exception, has reached our ports, having been much favoured in it by the course pursued by a squadron of our frigates under the command of Commodore Rodgers.

Nor was it only the offensive action of the enemy against the United States' ports and commerce that was thus hampered. Unwonted defensive measures were forced upon him. Uncertainty as to Rodgers' position and intentions led Captain Broke, on July 29, to join a homeward-bound Jamaica fleet, under convoy of the frigate *Thalia*, some two or three hundred miles to the southward and eastward of Halifax, and to accompany it with his division five hundred miles on its voyage. The place of this meeting shows that it was pre-arranged, and its distance from the American coast, five hundred miles away from New York, together with the length of the journey through which the additional guard was thought necessary, emphasize the effect of Rodgers' unknown situation upon the enemy's movements. The protection of their own trade carried this British division a thousand miles away from the coast it was to threaten. It is in such study of reciprocal action between enemies that the lessons of war are learned, and its principles established, in a manner to which the study of combats between single ships, however brilliant, affords no equivalent. The convoy that Broke thus accompanied has been curiously confused with the one of which Rodgers believed himself in pursuit;[426] and the British naval historian James chuckles obviously over the blunder of the Yankee

---
424. Naval Chronicle (British), vol. xxviii. p. 426.
425. Nov. 4, 1812.
426. Naval Chronicle, vol. xxviii. p. 159; James, vol. v. p. 274.

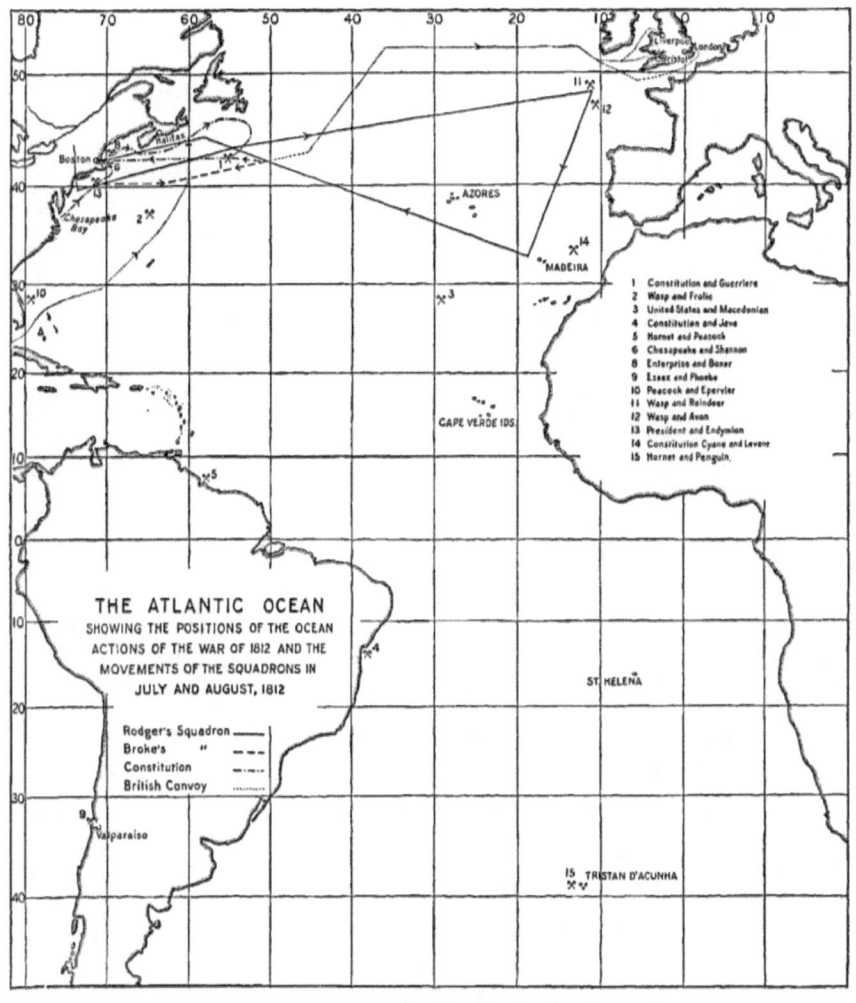

THE ATLANTIC OCEAN, SHOWING THE POSITIONS OF THE OCEAN
ACTIONS OF THE WAR OF 1812 AND THE MOVEMENTS OF THE
SQUADRONS IN JULY AND AUGUST, 1812

commodore, who returned to Boston "just six days after the *Thalia*, having brought home her charge in safety, had anchored in the Downs." Rodgers may have been wholly misinformed as to there being any Jamaica convoy on the way when he started; but as on July 29 he had passed Madeira on his way home, it is obvious that the convoy which Broke then joined south of Halifax could not be the one the American squadron believed itself to be pursuing across the Atlantic a month earlier.

Broke accompanied the merchant ships to the limits of the Halifax station. Then, on August 6, receiving intelligence of Rodgers having been seen on their homeward path, he directed the ship of the line, *Africa*, to go with them as far as 45° W., and for them thence to follow latitude 52° N., instead of the usual more southerly route.[427] After completing this duty the *Africa* was to return to Halifax, whither the *Guerrière*, which needed repairs, was ordered at once. The remainder of the squadron returned off New York, where it was again reported on September 10. The movement of the convoy, and the *Guerrière*'s need of refit, were linked events that brought about the first single-ship action of the war; to account for which fully the antecedent movements of her opponent must also be traced. At the time Rodgers sailed, the United States frigate *Constitution*, 44, was lying at Annapolis, enlisting a crew. Fearing to be blockaded in Chesapeake Bay, a position almost hopeless, her captain, Hull, hurried to sea on July 12. July 17, the ship being then off Egg Harbour, New Jersey, some ten or fifteen miles from shore, bound to New York, Broke's vessels, which had then arrived from Halifax for the first time in the war, were sighted from the masthead, to the northward and inshore of the *Constitution*. Captain Hull at first believed that this might be the squadron of Rodgers, of whose actual movements he had no knowledge, waiting for him to join in order to carry out commands of the Department. Two hours later, another sail was discovered to the northeast, off shore. The perils of an isolated ship, in the presence of a superior force of

---

427. Sir J.B. Warren to Admiralty, Aug 24, 1812. Canadian Archives MSS. M. 389. 1, p. 147.

possible enemies, imposed caution, so Hull steered warily toward the single unknown. Attempting to exchange signals, he soon found that he neither could understand nor be understood. To persist on his course might surround him with foes, and accordingly, about 11 p.m., the ship was headed to the southeast and so continued during the night.

The next morning left no doubt as to the character of the strangers, among whom was the *Guerrière*; and there ensued a chase which, lasting from daylight of July 18th to near noon of the 20th, has become historical in the United States Navy, from the attendant difficulties and the imminent peril of the favourite ship endangered. Much of the pursuit being in calm, and on soundings, resort was had to towing by boats, and to dragging the ship ahead by means of light anchors dropped on the bottom. In a contest of this kind, the ability of a squadron to concentrate numbers on one or two ships, which can first approach and cripple the enemy, thus holding him till their consorts come up, gives an evident advantage over the single opponent. On the other hand, the towing boats of the pursuer, being toward the stern guns of the pursued, are the first objects on either side to come under fire, and are vulnerable to a much greater degree than the ships themselves. Under such conditions, accurate appreciation of advantages, and unremitting use of small opportunities, are apt to prove decisive. It was by such diligent and skilful exertion that the *Constitution* effected her escape from a position which for a time seemed desperate; but it should not escape attention that thus early in the war, before Great Britain had been able to re-enforce her American fleet, one of our frigates was unable to enter our principal seaport. "Finding the ship so far to the southward and eastward," reported Hull, "and the enemy's squadron stationed off New York, which would make it impossible to get in there, I determined to make for Boston, to receive your further orders."

On July 28 he writes from Boston that there were as yet no British cruisers in the Bay, nor off the New England coast; that great numbers of merchant vessels were daily arriving from

THE FORECASTLE OF THE *CONSTITUTION* DURING THE CHASE
FROM A DRAWING BY HENRY REUTERDAHL

Europe; and that he was warning them off the southern ports, advising that they should enter Boston. He reasoned that the enemy would now disperse, and probably send two frigates off the port. In this he under-estimated the deterrent effect of Rodgers' invisible command, but the apprehension hastened his own departure, and on August 2 he sailed again with the first fair wind. Running along the Maine coast to the Bay of Fundy, he thence went off Halifax; and meeting nothing there, in a three or four days' stay, moved to the Gulf of St. Lawrence, to intercept the trade of Canada and Nova Scotia. Here in the neighbourhood of Cape Race some important captures were made, and on August 15 an American brig retaken, which gave information that Broke's squadron was not far away. This was probably a fairly correct report, as its returning course should have carried it near by a very few days before. Hull therefore determined to go to the southward, passing close to Bermuda, to cruise on the southern coast of the United States. In pursuance of this decision the *Constitution* had run some three hundred miles, when at 2 p.m. of August 19, being then nearly midway of the route over which Broke three weeks before had accompanied the convoy, a sail was sighted to the eastward, standing west. This proved to be the *Guerrière*, on her return to Halifax, whither she was moving very leisurely, having traversed only two hundred miles in twelve days.

As the *Constitution*, standing south-southwest for her destination, was crossing the *Guerrière*'s bows, her course was changed, in order to learn the character of the stranger. By half-past three she was recognized to be a large frigate, under easy sail on the starboard tack; which, the wind being north-westerly, gives her heading from west-southwest to southwest. The *Constitution* was to windward. At 3.45 the *Guerrière*, without changing her course, backed her main topsail, the effect of which was to lessen her forward movement, leaving just way enough to keep command with her helm (G 1). To be thus nearly motionless assured the steadiest platform for aiming the guns, during the period most critical for the *Constitution*, when, to get near, she must

CAPTAIN ISAAC HULL
FROM THE ENGRAVING BY D. EDWIN,
AFTER A PAINTING BY GILBERT STUART.

steer nearly head on, toward her opponent. The disadvantage of this approach is that the enemy's shot, if they hit, pass from end to end of the ship, a distance, in those days, nearly fourfold that of from side to side; and besides, the line from bow to stern was that on which the guns and the men who work them were ranged. The risks of grave injury were therefore greatly increased by exposure to this, which by soldiers is called enfilading, but at sea a raking fire; and to avoid such mischance was one of the principal concerns of a captain in a naval duel.

Seeing his enemy thus challenge him to come on, Hull, who had been carrying sail in order to close, now reduced his canvas to topsails, and put two reefs into them, bringing by the wind for that object (C 1). All other usual preparations were made at the same time; the *Constitution* during them lying side to wind, out of gunshot, practically motionless, like her antagonist. When all was ready, the ship kept away again, heading toward the starboard quarter of the British vessel; that is, she was on her right-hand side, steering toward her stern (C 2). As this, if continued, would permit her to pass close under the stern, and rake, Captain Dacres waited until he thought her within gunshot, when he fired the guns on the right-hand side of the vessel—the starboard broadside—and immediately wore ship; that is, turned the *Guerrière* round, making a half circle, and bringing her other side toward the *Constitution,* to fire the other, or port, battery (G 2). It will be seen that, as both ships were moving in the same general direction, away from the wind, the American coming straight on, while the British retired by a succession of semicircles, each time this manoeuvre was repeated the ships would be nearer together. This was what both captains purposed, but neither proposed to be raked in the operation. Hence, although the *Constitution* did not wear, she "yawed" several times; that is, turned her head from side to side, so that a shot striking would not have full raking effect, but angling across the decks would do proportionately less damage. Such methods were common to all actions between single ships.

These proceedings had lasted about three quarters of an hour, when Dacres, considering he now could safely afford to let his enemy close, settled his ship on a course nearly before the wind, having it a little on her left side (G 3). The American frigate was thus behind her, receiving the shot of her stern guns, to which the bow fire of those days could make little effective reply. To relieve this disadvantage, by shortening its duration, a big additional sail—the main topgallant sail—was set upon the *Constitution,* which, gathering fresh speed, drew up on the left-hand side of the *Guerrière,* within pistol-shot, at 6 p.m., when the battle proper fairly began (3). For the moment manoeuvring ceased, and a square set-to at the guns followed, the ships running side by side. In twenty minutes the *Guerrière*'s mizzen-mast[428] was shot away, falling overboard on the starboard side; while at nearly the same moment, so Hull reported, her main-yard went in the slings.[429] This double accident reduced her speed; but in addition the mast with all its hamper, dragging in the water on one side, both slowed the vessel and acted as a rudder to turn her head to starboard,—from the *Constitution.* The sail-power of the latter being unimpaired would have quickly carried her so far ahead that her guns would no longer bear, if she continued the same course. Hull, therefore, as soon as he saw the spars of his antagonist go overboard, put the helm to port, in order to "oblige him to do the same, or suffer himself to be raked by our getting across his bows."[430] The fall of the *Guerrière*'s mast effected what was desired by Hull, who continues: "On our helm being put to port the ship came to, and gave us an opportunity of pouring in upon his larboard bow several broadsides." The disabled state of the British frigate, and the promptness of the American captain, thus enabled the latter to take a raking position upon the port (larboard) bow of the enemy; that is, ahead, but on the left side (4).

The *Constitution* ranged on very slowly across the *Guer-*

---

428. Of the three masts of a "ship," the mizzen-mast is the one nearest the stern.
429. The middle, where the yard is hung.
430. Hull's report, Aug. 28, 1812. Captains' Letters, Navy Department MSS.

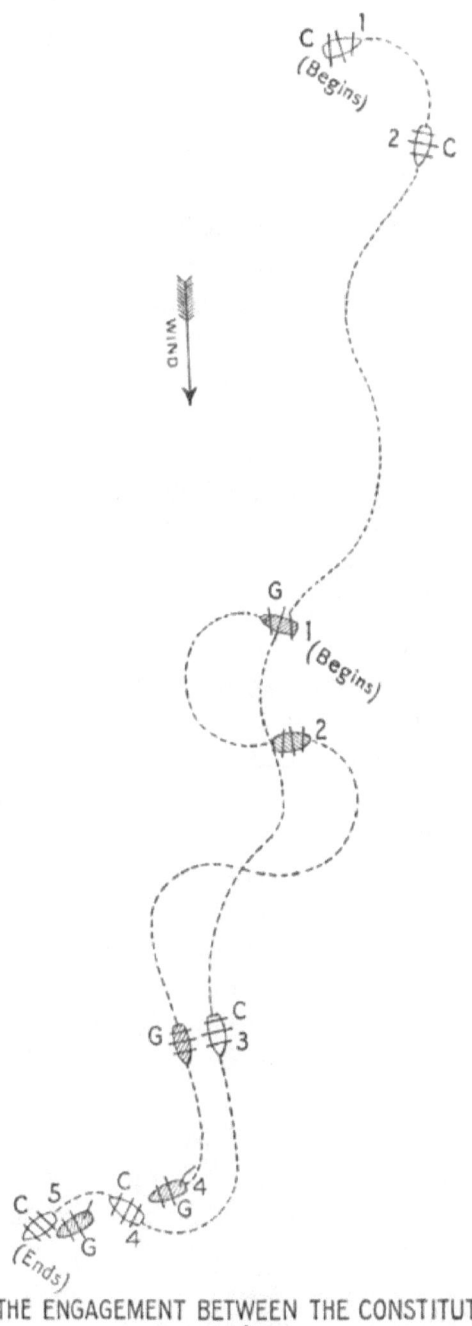

PLAN OF THE ENGAGEMENT BETWEEN THE CONSTITUTION AND GUERRIÈRE

rière's bows, from left to right; her sails shaking in the wind, because the yards could not be braced, the braces having been shot away. From this commanding position she gave two raking broadsides, to which her opponent could reply only feebly from a few forward guns; then, the vessels being close together, and the British forging slowly ahead, threatening to cross the American's stern, the helm of the latter was put up. As the *Constitution* turned away, the bowsprit of the *Guerrière* lunged over her quarter-deck, and became entangled by her port mizzen-rigging; the result being that the two fell into the same line, the *Guerrière* astern and fastened to her antagonist as described. (5) In her crippled condition for manoeuvring, it was possible that the British captain might seek to retrieve the fortunes of the day by boarding, for which the present situation seemed to offer some opportunity; and from the reports of the respective officers it is clear that the same thought occurred to both parties, prompting in each the movement to repel boarders rather than to board. A number of men clustered on either side at the point of contact, and here, by musketry fire, occurred some of the severest losses. The first lieutenant and sailing-master of the *Constitution* fell wounded, and the senior officer of marines dead, shot through the head. All these were especially concerned where boarding was at issue. This period was brief; for at 6.30 the fore and main-masts of the British frigate gave way together, carrying with them all the head booms, and she lay a helpless hulk in the trough of a heavy sea, rolling the muzzles of her guns under. A sturdy attempt to get her under control with the spritsail[431] was made; but this resource, a bare possibility to a dismasted ship in a fleet action, with friends around, was only the assertion of a sound never-give-up tradition, against hopeless odds, in a naval duel with a full-sparred antagonist. The *Constitution* hauled off for half an hour to repair damages, and upon returning received the *Guerrière*'s surrender. It was

---

431. The spritsail was set on a yard which in ships of that day crossed the bowsprit at its outer end, much as other yards crossed the three upright lower masts. Under some circumstances ships would forge slowly ahead under its impulse. It was a survival from days which knew not jibs.

then dark, and the night was passed in transferring the prisoners. When day broke, the prize was found so shattered that it would be impossible to bring her into port. She was consequently set on fire at 3 p.m., and soon after blew up.

In this fight the American frigate was much superior in force to her antagonist. The customary, and upon the whole justest, mode of estimating relative power, was by aggregate weight of shot discharged in one broadside; and when, as in this case, the range is so close that every gun comes into play, it is perhaps a useless refinement to insist on qualifying considerations. The broadside of the *Constitution* weighed 736 pounds, that of the *Guerrière* 570. The difference therefore in favour of the American vessel was thirty per cent, and the disparity in numbers of the crews was even greater. It is not possible, therefore, to insist upon any singular credit, in the mere fact that under such odds victory falls to the heavier vessel. What can be said, after a careful comparison of the several reports, is that the American ship was fought warily and boldly, that her gunnery was excellent, that the instant advantage taken of the enemy's mizzen-mast falling showed high seamanlike qualities, both in promptness and accuracy of execution; in short, that, considering the capacity of the American captain as evidenced by his action, and the odds in his favour, nothing could be more misplaced than Captain Dacres' vaunt before the Court:

> I am so well aware that the success of my opponent was owing to fortune, that it is my earnest wish to be once more opposed to the *Constitution*, with the same officers and crew under my command, in a frigate of similar force to the *Guerrière*.[432]

In view of the difference of broadside weight, this amounts to saying that the capacity and courage of the captain and ship's company of the *Guerrière*, being over thirty per cent greater than those of the *Constitution*, would more than compensate for the latter's bare thirty per cent superiority of force. It may safely

---

432. Dacres' Defence before the Court Martial. Naval Chronicle, vol. xxviii. p. 422.

The burning of the *Guerrière* From a drawing by Henry Reuterdahl

be said that one will look in vain through the accounts of the transaction for any ground for such assumption. A ready acquiescence in this opinion was elicited, indeed, from two witnesses, the master and a master's mate, based upon a supposed superiority of fire, which the latter estimated to be in point of rapidity as four broadsides to every three of the *Constitution*.[433] But rapidity is not the only element of superiority; and Dacres' satisfaction on this score, repeatedly expressed, might have been tempered by one of the facts he alleged in defence of his surrender—that "on the larboard side of the *Guerrière* there were about thirty shot which had taken effect about five sheets of copper down,"—far below the water-line.

Captain Hull with the *Constitution* reached Boston August 30, just four weeks after his departure; and the following day Commodore Rodgers with his squadron entered the harbour. It was a meeting between disappointment and exultation; for so profound was the impression prevailing in the United States, and not least in New England, concerning the irreversible superiority of Great Britain on the sea, that no word less strong than "exultation" can do justice to the feeling aroused by Hull's victory. Sight was lost of the disparity of force, and the pride of the country fixed, not upon those points which the attentive seaman can recognize as giving warrant for confidence, but upon the supposed demonstration of superiority in equal combat.

Consolation was needed; for since Rodgers' sailing much had occurred to dishearten and little to encourage. The nation had cherished few expectations from its tiny, navy; but concerning its arms on land the advocates of war had entertained the unreasoning confidence of those who expect to reap without taking the trouble to sow. In the first year of President Jefferson's administration, 1801, the "peace establishment" of the regular army, in pursuance of the policy of the President and party in power, was reduced to three thousand men. In 1808, under the excitement of the outrage upon the *Chesapeake* and of the Or-

---

433. *Guerrière* Court Martial. MS. British Records Office.

ders in Council, an "additional military force" was authorized, raising the total to ten thousand. The latter measure seems for some time to have been considered temporary in character; for in a return to Congress in January, 1810, the numbers actually in service are reported separately, as 2,765 and 4,189; total, 6,954, exclusive of staff officers.

General Scott, who was one of the captains appointed under the Act of 1808, has recorded that the condition of both soldiers and officers was in great part most inefficient.[434] Speaking of the later commissions, he said, "Such were the results of Mr. Jefferson's low estimate of, or rather contempt for, the military character, the consequence of the old hostility between him and the principal officers who achieved our independence."[435] In January, 1812, when war had in effect been determined upon in the party councils, a bill was passed raising the army to thirty-five thousand; but in the economical and social condition of the period the service was under a popular disfavour, to which the attitude of recent administrations doubtless contributed greatly, and recruiting went on very slowly. There was substantially no military tradition in the country. Thirty years of peace had seen the disappearance of the officers whom the War of Independence had left in their prime; and the Government fell into that most facile of mistakes, the choice of old men, because when youths they had worn an epaulette, without regarding the experience they had had under it, or since it was laid aside.

Among the men thus selected were Henry Dearborn, for senior major general, to command the northern division of the country, from Niagara to Boston Bay and New York; and William Hull, a brigadier, for the north-western frontier, centring round Detroit. The latter, who was uncle to Captain Hull of the *Constitution,* seems to have been chosen because already civil Governor of Michigan Territory. President Madison thus reversed the practice of Great Britain, which commonly was to

---

434. Memoirs of Gen. Winfield Scott, vol. i p. 31.
435. Ibid., p. 35.

choose a military man for civil governor of exposed provinces. Hull accepted with reluctance, and under pressure. He set out for his new duties, expecting that he would receive in his distant and perilous charge that measure of support which results from active operations at some other point of the enemy's line, presumably at Niagara. In this he was disappointed. Dearborn was now sixty-one, Hull fifty-nine. Both had served with credit during the War of Independence, but in subordinate positions; and Dearborn had been Secretary of War throughout Jefferson's two terms.

Opposed to these was the Lieutenant Governor of Upper Canada, Isaac Brock, a major-general in the British army. A soldier from boyhood, he had commanded a regiment in active campaign at twenty-eight. He was now forty-two, and for the last ten years had served in North America; first with his regiment, and later as a general officer in command of the troops. In October, 1811, he was appointed to the civil government of the province. He was thoroughly familiar with the political and military conditions surrounding him, and his mind had long been actively engaged in considering probable contingencies, in case war, threatening since 1807, should become actual. In formulated purpose and resolve, he was perfectly prepared for immediate action, as is shown by his letters, foreshadowing his course, to his superior, Sir George Prevost, Governor General of Canada. He predicted that the pressure of the Indians upon the western frontier of the United States would compel that country to keep there a considerable force, the presence of which would naturally tend to more than mere defensive measures. With the numerical inferiority of the British, the co-operation of the Indians was essential. To preserve Upper Canada, therefore, Michilimackinac and Detroit must be reduced. Otherwise the savages could not be convinced that Great Britain would not sacrifice them at a peace, as they believed her to have done in 1794, by Jay's Treaty. In this he agreed with Hull, who faced the situation far more efficiently than his superiors, and at the same moment was writing officially:

The British cannot hold Upper Canada without the assistance of the Indians, and that they cannot obtain if we have an adequate force at Detroit.[436]

Brock deemed it vital that Amherstburg, nearly opposite Detroit, should be held in force; both to resist the first hostile attack, and as a base whence to proceed to offensive operations. He apprehended, and correctly, as the event proved, that Niagara would be chosen by the Americans as the line for their main body to penetrate with a view to conquest. This was his defensive frontier; the western, the offensive wing of his campaign. These leading ideas dictated his preparations, imperfect from paucity of means, but sufficient to meet the limping, flaccid measures of the United States authorities.

To this well-considered view the War Department of the United States opposed no ordered plan of any kind, no mind prepared with even the common precautions of every-day life. This unreadiness, plainly manifested by its actions, was the more culpable because the unfortunate Hull, in his letter of March 6, 1812, just quoted, a month before his unwilling acceptance of his general's commission, had laid clearly before it the leading features of the military and political situation, recognized by him during his four years of office as Governor of the Territory. In this cogent paper, amid numerous illuminative details, he laid unmistakable emphasis on the decisive influence of Detroit upon the whole Northwest, especially in determining the attitude of the Indians. He dwelt also upon the critical weakness of the communications on which the tenure of it depended, and upon the necessity of naval superiority to secure them. This expression of his opinion was in the hands of the Government over three months before the declaration of war. As early as January, however, Secretary Eustis had been warned by Armstrong, who subsequently succeeded him in the War Department, that Detroit, otherwise advantageous in position, "would be positively bad, unless your naval means have an ascendency on Lake Erie."[437]

---

436. Hull to the War Department, March 6, 1812. Report of Hull's Trial, taken by Lieut. Col. Forbes, 42nd U.S. Infantry. Hull's Defence, p. 31.
437. Armstrong's Notices of the War of 1812, vol. i. p. 237.

Unfortunately for himself and for the country, Hull, upon visiting the capital in the spring, did not adhere firmly to his views as to the necessity for a lake navy. After the capitulation, President Madison wrote to his friend, John Nicholas:

> The failure of our calculations with respect to the expedition under Hull needs no comment. The worst of it was that we were misled by a reliance, authorized by himself, on its (the expedition) securing to us the command of the lakes.[438]

General Peter B. Porter, of the New York militia, a member also of the House of Representatives, who served well on the Niagara frontier, and was in no wise implicated by Hull's surrender, testified before the Court Martial, "I was twice at the President's with General Hull, when the subject of a navy was talked over. At first it was agreed to have one; but afterwards it was agreed to abandon it, doubtless as inexpedient."[439] The indications from Hull's earlier correspondence are that for the time he was influenced by the war spirit, and developed a hopefulness of achievement which affected his former and better judgment.

On May 25, three weeks before the declaration of war, Hull took command of the militia assembled at Dayton, Ohio. On June 10, he was at Urbana, where a regiment of regular infantry joined. June 30, he reached the Maumee River, and thence reported that his force was over two thousand, rank and file.[440] He had not yet received official intelligence of war having been actually declared, but all indications, including his own mission itself, pointed to it as imminent. Nevertheless, he here loaded a schooner with military stores, and sent her down the river for Detroit, knowing that, twenty miles before reaching there, she must pass near the British Fort Malden, on the Detroit River covering Amherstburg; and this while the British had local naval superiority. In taking this risk, the very imprudence of which

---

438. The Writings of Madison (ed. 1865), vol. ii. p. 563. See also his letter to Dearborn, Oct. 7, 1812. Ibid., p. 547.
439. Hull's Trial, p. 127. Porter was a witness for the defence.
440. Hull's Trial, Appendix, p. 4.

testifies the importance of water transportation to Detroit, Hull directed his aids to forward his baggage by the same conveyance; and with it, contrary to his intention, were despatched also his official papers. The vessel, being promptly seized by the boats of the British armed brig *Hunter*, was taken into Malden, whence Colonel St. George, commanding the district, sent the captured correspondence to Brock. "Till I received these letters," remarked the latter, "I had no idea General Hull was advancing with so large a force."[441]

When Brock thus wrote, July 20, he was at Fort George, on the shore of Ontario, near Niagara River, watching the frontier where he expected the main attack. He had already struck his first blow. Immediately upon being assured of the declaration of war, on June 28, he had despatched a letter to St. Joseph's, directing all preparations to be made for proceeding against Mackinac; the final determination as to offensive or defensive action being very properly left to the officer there in command. The latter, thus aware of his superior's wishes, started July 16, with some six hundred men,—of whom four hundred were Indians,—under convoy of the armed brig *Caledonia*, belonging to the Northwestern Fur Company. The next day he appeared before the American post, where the existence of war was yet unknown. The garrison numbered fifty-seven, including three officers; being about one third the force reported necessary for the peace establishment by Mr. Jefferson's Secretary of War, in 1801. The place was immediately surrendered. Under all the conditions stated there is an entertaining ingenuousness in the reference made to this disaster by President Madison:

> We have but just learned that the important post of Michilimackinac has fallen into the hands of the enemy, but from what cause remains to be known.[442]

Brock received this news at Toronto, July 29; but not till August 3 did it reach Hull, by the arrival of the paroled prisoners.

---

441. Life of Brock, p. 192.
442. Writings of James Madison (Lippincott, 1865), vol. ii. p. 543.

He was then on the Canada side, at Sandwich, opposite Detroit; having crossed with from fourteen to sixteen hundred men on July 12. This step was taken on the strength of a discretionary order from the Secretary of War, that if—

> .... the force under your command be equal to the enterprise, consistent with the safety of your own post, you will take possession of Malden, and extend your conquests as circumstances may justify.

It must be added, however, in justice to the Administration, that the same letter, received July 9, three days before the crossing, contained the warning, "It is also proper to inform you that an adequate force cannot soon be relied on for the reduction of the enemy's posts below you."[443] This bears on the question of Hull's expectation of support by diversion on the Niagara frontier, and shows that he had fair notice on that score. That over-confidence still possessed him seems apparent from a letter to the secretary dated July 7, in which he said:

> In your letter of June 18, you direct me to adopt measures for the security of the country, and to await further orders. I regret that I have not larger latitude.[444]

Now he received it, and his invasion of Canada was the result. It is vain to deny his liberty of action, under such instructions, but it is equally vain to deny the responsibility of a superior who thus authorizes action, and not obscurely intimates a wish, under general military conditions perfectly well known, such as existed with reference to Hull's communications. Hull's attempt to justify his movement on the ground of pressure from subordinates, moral effect upon his troops, is admissible only if his decision were consistently followed by the one course that gave a chance of success. As a military enterprise the attempt was hopeless, unless by a rapid advance upon Malden he could carry the works by instant storm. In that event the enemy's army and navy, los-

---

443. Eustis to Hull, June 24, 1812. From MS. copy in the Records of the War Department. This letter was acknowledged by Hull, July 9.
444. Hull's Trial, Appendix, p. 9.

ing their local base of operations, would have to seek one new and distant, one hundred and fifty miles to the eastward, at Long Point; whence attempts against the American positions could be only by water, with transportation inadequate to carrying large bodies of men. The American general thus might feel secure against attacks on his communications with Ohio, the critical condition of which constituted the great danger of the situation, whether at Detroit or Sandwich. Hull himself, ten days after crossing, wrote:

> It is in the power of this army to take Malden by storm, but it would be attended, in my opinion, with too great a sacrifice under the present circumstances.[445]

Instead of prompt action, two days were allowed to pass. Then, July 14, a council of war decided that immediate attack was inexpedient, and delay advisable. This conclusion, if correct, condemned the invasion, and should have been reached before it was attempted. The military situation was this: Hull's line of supplies and re-enforcements was reasonably secure from hostile interference between southern Ohio and the Maumee; at which river proper fortification would permit the establishment of an advanced depot. Thence to Detroit was seventy-two miles, through much of which the road passed near the lake shore. It was consequently liable to attack from the water, so long as that was controlled by the enemy; while by its greater distance from the centre of American population in the West, it was also more exposed to Indian hostilities than the portion behind the Maumee. Under these circumstances, Detroit itself was in danger of an interruption of supplies and re-enforcements, amounting possibly to isolation. It was open to the enemy to land in its rear, secure of his own communications by water, and with a fair chance, in case of failure, to retire by the way he came; for retreat could be made safely in very small vessels or boats, so long as Malden was held in force.

The reduction of Malden might therefore secure Detroit,

---

445. Hull to Eustis, July 22, 1812. Hull's Trial, Appendix, p. 10.

by depriving the enemy of a base suitable for using his lake power against its communications. Unless this was accomplished, any advance beyond Detroit with the force then at hand merely weakened that place, by just the amount of men and means expended, and was increasingly hazardous when it entailed crossing water. A sudden blow may snatch safety under such conditions; but to attempt the slow and graduated movements of a siege, with uncertain communications supporting it, is to court disaster. The holding of Detroit being imperative, efforts external to it should have been chiefly exerted on its rear, and upon its front only to prevent the easy passage of the enemy. In short, when Detroit was reached, barring the chance of a *coup de main* upon Malden, Hull's position needed to be made more solid, not more extensive. As it was, the army remained at Sandwich, making abortive movements toward the river Canard, which covered the approach to Malden, and pushing small foraging parties up the valley of the Thames. The greatest industry was used, Hull reported, in making preparations to besiege, but it was not till August 7, nearly four weeks after crossing, that the siege guns were ready; and then the artillery officers reported that it would be extremely difficult, if not impossible, to take them to Malden by land, and by water still more so, because the ship of war *Queen Charlotte*, carrying eighteen 24-pounders, lay off the mouth of the Canard, commanding the stream.

The first impression produced by the advance into Canada had been propitious to Hull. He himself in his defence admitted that the enemy's force had diminished, great part of their militia had left them, and many of their Indians.[446] This information of the American camp corresponded with the facts. Lieut. Colonel St. George, commanding Fort Malden, reported the demoralized condition of his militia. Three days after Hull crossed he had left but four hundred and seventy-one, in such a state as to be absolutely inefficient.[447] Colonel Procter, who

---

446. Hull's Trial, Defence, p. 45.
447. Canadian Archives MSS. C. 676, p. 177.

soon afterwards relieved him, could on July 18 muster only two hundred and seventy Indians by the utmost exertion, and by the 26th these had rather decreased.[448] Professing to see no immediate danger, he still asked for five hundred more regulars. At no time before Hull re-crossed did he have two hundred and fifty.[449] Under Hull's delay these favourable conditions disappeared. British re-enforcements, small but veteran, arrived; the local militia recovered; and the Indians, with the facile changefulness of savages, passed from an outwardly friendly bearing over to what began to seem the winning side. Colonel Procter then initiated the policy of threatening Hull's communications from the lake side. A body of Indians sent across by him on August 4 defeated an American detachment marching to protect a convoy from the Maumee. This incident, coming upon accumulating adverse indications, and coinciding with the bad news received from Mackinac, aroused Hull to the essential danger of his situation. August 8 he re-crossed to Detroit. August 9 another vigorous effort was made by the enemy to destroy a detachment sent out to establish communications with the rear. Although the British were defeated, the Americans were unable to proceed, and returned to the town without supplies. In the first of these affairs some more of Hull's correspondence was captured, which revealed his apprehensions, and the general moral condition of his command, to an opponent capable of appreciating their military significance.

Brock had remained near Niagara, detained partly by the political necessity of meeting the provincial legislature, partly to watch over what he considered the more exposed portion of his military charge; for a disaster to it, being nearer the source of British power, would have upon the fortunes of the West an effect even more vital than a reverse there would exert upon the East. Being soon satisfied that the preparations of the United States threatened no immediate action, and finding that Hull's troops were foraging to a considerable distance east of Sandwich,

---

448. Ibid., p. 242.
449. Hull's Trial. Evidence of Lieutenant Gooding, p. 101, and of Sergeant Forbush, p. 147 (prisoners in Malden).

along the Thames, he had decided to send against them a small body of local troops with a number of Indians, while he himself gathered some militia and went direct by water to Malden. To his dismay, the Indians declined to assist, alleging their intention to remain neutral; upon which the militia also refused, saying they were afraid to leave their homes unguarded, till it was certain which side the savages would take. On July 25 Brock wrote that his plans were thus ruined; but July 29 it became known that Mackinac had fallen, and on that day the militia about York (Toronto), where he then was, volunteered for service in any part of the province. August 8 he embarked with three hundred of them, and a few regulars, at Long Point, on the north shore of Lake Erie; whence he coasted to Malden, arriving on the 13th.

Meanwhile batteries had been erected opposite Detroit, which opened on the evening of August 15, the fort replying; but slight harm was done on either side. Next day Brock crossed the greater part of his force, landing three miles below Detroit. His little column of assault consisted of 330 regulars, 400 militia, and 600 Indians, the latter in the woods covering the left flank.[450] The effective Americans present were by that morning's report 1,060;[451] while their field artillery, additional to that mounted in the works, was much superior to that of the enemy, was advantageously posted, and loaded with grape. Moreover, they had the fort, on which to retire.

Brock's movements were audacious. Some said nothing could be more desperate; "but I answer, that the state of Upper Canada admitted of nothing but desperate remedies."[452] The British general had served under Nelson at Copenhagen, and quoted him here. He knew also, through the captured correspondence, that his opponent was a prey to a desperation very different in temper from his own, and had lost the confidence of his men. He had hoped, by the threatening position assumed between the town and its home base, to force Hull to come out and attack;

---

450. Life of Brock, p. 250.
451. Letter of Colonel Cass to U.S. Secretary of War, Sept. 10, 1812. Hull's Trial, Appendix, p. 27.
452. Life of Brock, p. 267.

but learning now that the garrison was weakened by a detachment of three hundred and fifty, despatched two days before under Colonel McArthur to open intercourse with the Maumee by a circuitous road, avoiding the lake shore, he decided to assault at once. When the British column had approached within a mile, Hull withdrew within the works all his force, including the artillery, and immediately afterward capitulated. The detachment under McArthur, with another from the state of Ohio on its way to join the army, were embraced in the terms; Brock estimating the whole number surrendered at not less than twenty-five hundred. A more important capture, under the conditions, was an American brig, the "Adams," not yet armed, but capable of use as a ship of war, for which purpose she had already been transferred from the War Department to the Navy.

In his defence before the Court Martial, which in March, 1814, tried him for his conduct of the campaign, Hull addressed himself to three particulars, which he considered to be the principal features in the voluminous charges and specifications drawn against him. These were, "the delay at Sandwich, the retreat from Canada, and the surrender at Detroit."[453] Concerning these, as a matter of military criticism, it may be said with much certainty that if conditions imposed the delay at Sandwich, they condemned the advance to it, and would have warranted an earlier retreat. The capitulation he justified on the ground that resistance could not change the result, though it might protract the issue. Because ultimate surrender could not be averted, he characterized life lost in postponing it as blood shed uselessly. The conclusion does not follow from the premise; nor could any military code accept the maxim that a position is to be yielded as soon as it appears that it cannot be held indefinitely. Delay, so long as sustained, not only keeps open the chapter of accidents for the particular post, but supports related operations throughout the remainder of the field of war. Tenacious endurance, if it effected no more, would at least have held Brock away from Niagara, whither he hastened within a week after

---

453. Hull's Trial. Defence, p. 20.

the capitulation, taking with him a force which now could be well spared from the westward. No one military charge can be considered as disconnected; therefore no commander has a right to abandon defence while it is possible to maintain it, unless he also knows that it cannot affect results elsewhere; and this practically can never be certain. The burden of anxieties, of dangers and difficulties, actual and possible, weighing upon Brock, were full as great as those upon Hull, for on his shoulders rested both Niagara and Malden. His own resolution and promptitude triumphed because of the combined inefficiency of Hull and Dearborn. He scarcely could have avoided disaster at one end or the other of the line, had either opponent been thoroughly competent.

There was yet another reason which weighed forcibly with Hull, and probably put all purely military considerations out of court. This was the dread of Indian outrage and massacre. The general trend of the testimony, and Hull's own defence, go to show a mind overpowered by the agony of this imagination. After receiving word of the desertion of two companies, he said, "I now became impatient to put the place under the protection of the British; I knew that there were thousands of savages around us." These thousands were not at hand. Not till after September 1 did as many as a hundred arrive from the north—from Mackinac.[454] In short, unless what Cass styled the philanthropic reason can be accepted,—and in the opinion of the present writer it cannot,—Hull wrote the condemnation of his action in his own defence.

> I shall now state what force the enemy brought, or might bring, against me. I say, gentlemen, *might bring*, because it was that consideration which induced the surrender, and not the force which was actually landed on the American shore on the morning of the 16th. It is possible I might have met and repelled that force; and if I had no further to look than the event of a contest at that time, I should have

---

454. Hull's Trial. Testimony of Captain Eastman, p. 100, and of Dalliby, Ordnance Officer, p. 84.

trusted to the issue of a battle.... The force brought against me I am very confident was not less than one thousand whites, and as many savage warriors.[455]

The reproach of this mortifying incident cannot be lifted from off Hull's memory; but for this very reason, in weighing the circumstances, it is far less than justice to forget his years, verging on old age, his long dissociation from military life, his personal courage frequently shown during the War of Independence, nor the fact that, though a soldier on occasion, he probably never had the opportunity to form correct soldierly standards. To the credit account should also be carried the timely and really capable presentation of the conditions of the field of operations already quoted, submitted by him to the Government, which should not have needed such demonstration. The mortification of the country fastened on his name; but had the measures urged by him been taken, had his expedition received due support by energetic operations elsewhere, events need not have reached the crisis to which he proved unequal. The true authors of the national disaster and its accompanying humiliation are to be sought in the national administrations and legislatures of the preceding ten or twelve years, upon whom rests the responsibility for the miserably unprepared condition in which the country was plunged into war. Madison, too tardily repentant, wrote:

> The command of the Lakes by a superior force on the water ought to have been a fundamental part in the national policy from the moment the peace (of 1783) took place. What is now doing for the command proves what may be done.[456]

---

455. Ibid. Hull's Defence, pp. 59-60.
456. Madison to Dearborn, Oct. 7, 1812. Writings, vol. ii, p. 547.

Chapter 7

Operations on the Northern Frontier

By August 25, nine days after the capitulation of Detroit, Brock was again writing from Fort George, by Niagara. About the time of his departure for Malden, Prevost had received from Foster, late British minister to Washington, and now in Nova Scotia, letters foreshadowing the repeal of the Orders in Council. In consequence he had sent his adjutant-general, Colonel Baynes, to Dearborn to negotiate a suspension of hostilities. Like all intelligent flags of truce, Baynes kept his eyes wide open to indications in the enemy's lines. The militia, he reported, were not uniformed; they were distinguished from other people of the country only by a cockade. The regulars were mostly recruits.

The war was unpopular, the great majority impatient to return to their homes; a condition Brock observed also in the Canadians. They avowed a fixed determination not to pass the frontier. Recruiting for the regular service went on very slowly, though pay and bounty were liberal. Dearborn appeared over sixty, strong and healthy, but did not seem to possess the energy of mind or activity of body requisite to his post.

In short, from the actual state of the American forces assembled on Lake Champlain, Baynes did not think there was any intention of invasion. From its total want of discipline and order, the militia could not be considered formidable when opposed to well-disciplined British regulars.[457] Of this prog-

---
457. Baynes to Prevost. Canadian Archives, C. 377, pp. 27-37.

nostic the war was to furnish sufficient saddening proof. The militia contained excellent material for soldiers, but soldiers they were not.

Dearborn declined to enter into a formal armistice, as beyond his powers; but he consented to a cessation of hostilities pending a reference to Washington, agreeing to direct all commanders of posts within his district to abstain from offensive operations till further orders. This suspension of arms included the Niagara line, from action upon which Hull had expected to receive support. In his defence Hull claimed that this arrangement, in which his army was not included, had freed a number of troops to proceed against him; but the comparison of dates shows that every man present at Detroit in the British force had gone forward before the agreement could be known. The letter engaging to remain on the defensive only was signed by Dearborn at Greenbush, near Albany, August 8. The same day Brock was three hundred and fifty miles to the westward, embarking at Long Point for Malden; and among his papers occurs the statement that the strong American force on the Niagara frontier compelled him to take to Detroit only one half of the militia that volunteered.[458] His military judgment and vigour, unaided, had enabled him to abandon one line, and that the most important, concentrate all available men at another point, effect there a decisive success, and return betimes to his natural centre of operations. He owed nothing to outside military diplomacy. On the contrary, he deeply deplored the measure which now tied his hands at a moment when the Americans, though restrained from fighting, were not prevented from bringing up re-enforcements to the positions confronting him.

Dearborn's action was not approved by the Administration, and the armistice was ended September 4, by notification. Meantime, to strengthen the British Niagara frontier, all the men and

---

458. Life of Brock, p. 258. Brock first heard of the suspension August 23, at Fort Erie, on his return toward Niagara. Life, p. 274. See also a letter from Brock to the American General Van Rensselaer, in the Defence of General Dearborn, by H.A.S. Dearborn, p. 8.

ordnance that could now be spared from Amherstburg had been brought back by Brock to Fort Erie, which was on the lake of that name, at the upper end of the Niagara River. Although still far from secure, owing to the much greater local material resources of the United States, and the preoccupation of Great Britain with the Peninsular War, which prevented her succouring Canada, Brock's general position was immensely improved since the beginning of hostilities. His successes in the West, besides rallying the Indians by thousands to his support, had for the time so assured that frontier as to enable him to concentrate his efforts on the East; while the existing British naval superiority on both lakes, Erie and Ontario, covered his flanks, and facilitated transportation—communications—from Kingston to Niagara, and thence to Malden, Detroit, Mackinac, and the Great West. To illustrate the sweep of this influence, it may be mentioned here—for there will be no occasion to repeat—that an expedition from Mackinac at a later period captured the isolated United States post at Prairie du Chien, on the Mississippi, on the western border of what is now the state of Wisconsin. Already, at the most critical period, the use of the water had enabled Brock, by simultaneous movements, to send cannon from Fort George by way of Fort Erie to Fort Malden; while at the same time replacing those thus despatched by others brought from Toronto and Kingston. In short, control of the lakes conferred upon him the recognized advantage of a central position—the Niagara peninsula—having rapid communication by interior lines with the flanks, or extremities; to Malden and Detroit in one direction, to Toronto and Kingston in the other.

It was just here, also, that the first mischance befell him; and it cannot but be a subject of professional pride to a naval officer to trace the prompt and sustained action of his professional ancestors, who reversed conditions, not merely by a single brilliant blow, upon which popular reminiscence fastens, but by efficient initiative and sustained sagacious exertion through a long period of time. On September 3, Captain Isaac Chauncey had been ordered from the New York navy yard to command on Lakes Erie and Ontario. Upon the latter there was already serving Lieutenant Melancthon T. Woolsey, in command of a respectable vessel, the brig *Oneida*, of eighteen 24-pounder carronades. On Erie there was as yet no naval organization nor vessel. Chauncey consequently, on September 7, ordered thither Lieutenant Jesse D. Elliott to select a site for equipping vessels, and to contract for two to be built of three hundred tons each. Elliott, who arrived at Buffalo on the 14th, was still engaged in this preliminary work, and was fitting some purchased schooners behind Squaw Island, three miles below, when, on October 8, there arrived from Malden, and anchored off Fort Erie, two British armed brigs, the *Detroit*—lately the American *Adams*, surrendered with Hull—and the *Caledonia*, which co-operated so decisively in the fall of Mackinac. The same day he learned the near approach of a body of ninety seamen, despatched by Chauncey from New York on September 22.[459] He sent to hasten them, and they arrived at noon. The afternoon was spent in preparations, weapons having to be obtained from the army, which also supplied a contingent of fifty soldiers.

The seamen needed refreshment, having come on foot five hundred miles, but Elliott would not trifle with opportunity. At 1 a.m. of October 9 he shoved off with a hundred men in two boats, and at 3 was alongside the brigs. From Buffalo to Fort Erie is about two miles; but this distance was materially increased by the strong downward current toward the falls, and by the necessity of pulling far up stream in order to approach the vessels from ahead, which lessened the chance of premature discovery, and materially shortened the interval between being seen and getting alongside. The enemy, taken by surprise, were quickly overpowered, and in ten minutes both prizes were under sail for the American shore. The *Caledonia* was beached at Black Rock, where was Elliott's temporary navy yard, just above Squaw Island; but the wind did not enable the *Detroit*, in which he himself was, to stem the downward drift of the river. After being swept some time, she had to

---

459. Chauncey to the Secretary of the Navy, Sept. 26, 1812. Captains' Letters, Navy Department MSS.

anchor under the fire of batteries at four hundred yards range, to which reply was made till the powder on board was expended. Then, the berth proving too hot, the cable was cut, sail again made, and the brig run ashore on Squaw Island within range of both British and American guns. Here Elliott abandoned her, she having already several large shot through her hull, with rigging and sails cut to pieces, and she was boarded in turn by a body of the enemy. Under the conditions, however, neither side could remain to get her off, and she was finally set on fire by the Americans.[460] Besides the vessel herself, her cargo of ordnance was lost to the British. American seamen afterward recovered from the wreck by night four 12-pounders, and a quantity of shot, which were used with effect.

The conduct of this affair was of a character frequent in the naval annals of that day. Elliott's quick discernment of the opportunity to reverse the naval conditions which constituted so much of the British advantage, and the promptness of his action, are qualities more noticeable than the mere courage displayed. "A strong inducement," he wrote, "was that with these two vessels, and those I have purchased, I should be able to meet the remainder of the British force on the Upper Lakes." The mishap of the *Detroit* partly disappointed this expectation, and the British aggregate remained still superior; but the units lost their perfect freedom of movement, the facility of transportation was greatly diminished, and the American success held in it the germ of future development to the superiority which Perry achieved a year later. None realized the extent of the calamity more keenly than Brock. He wrote to the Governor General:

> This event is particularly unfortunate and may reduce us to incalculable distress. The enemy is making every exertion to gain a naval superiority on both lakes; which, if they accomplish, I do not see how we can retain the country. More vessels are fitting for war on the other side of Squaw Island, which I should have attempted to destroy

---

460. Elliott's report of this affair will be found in the Captains' Letters, Navy Department MSS., forwarded by Chauncey Oct. 16, 1812.

but for your Excellency's repeated instructions to forbear. Now such a force is collected for their protection as will render every operation against them very hazardous.[461]

To his subordinate, Procter, at Detroit, he exposed the other side of the calamity.[462]

This will reduce us to great distress. You will have the goodness to state the expedients you possess to enable us to replace, as far as possible, the heavy loss we have sustained in the *Detroit*.... A quantity of provisions was ready to be shipped; but as I am sending you the flank companies of the Newfoundland Regiment by the *Lady Prevost*, she cannot take the provisions.

Trivial details these may seem; but in war, as in other matters, trivialities sometimes decide great issues, as the touching of a button may blow up a reef. The battle of Lake Erie, as before said, was precipitated by need of food.

Brock did not survive to witness the consequences which he apprehended, and which, had he lived, he possibly might have done something to avert. The increasing strength he had observed gathering about Elliott's collection of purchased vessels corresponded to a gradual accumulation of American land force along the Niagara line; the divisions of which above and below the Falls were under two commanders, between whom co-operation was doubtful. General Van Rensselaer of the New York militia, who had the lower division, determined upon an effort to seize the heights of Queenston, at the head of navigation from Lake Ontario. The attempt was made on October 13, before daybreak. Brock, whose headquarters were at Fort George, was quickly on the ground; so quickly, that he narrowly escaped capture by the advance guard of Americans as they reached the summit. Collecting a few men, he endeavoured to regain the position before the enemy could establish himself in force, and in the charge was instantly killed at the head of his troops.

---

461. Life of Brock, p. 315.
462. Ibid., p. 316.

In historical value, the death of Brock was the one notable incident of the day, which otherwise was unproductive of results beyond an additional mortification to the United States. The Americans gradually accumulated on the height to the number of some six hundred, and, had they been properly re-enforced, could probably have held their ground, affording an opening for further advance. It was found impossible to induce the raw, unseasoned men on the other side to cross to their support, and after many fruitless appeals the American general was compelled to witness the shameful sight of a gallant division driven down the cliffs to the river, and there obliged to surrender, because their comrades refused to go betimes to their relief.

Van Rensselaer retired from service, and was succeeded by General Smyth, who now held command of the whole line, thirty miles, from Buffalo to Fort Niagara, opposite Fort George, where the river enters Lake Ontario. A crossing in force, in the upper part of the river, opposite Black Rock, was planned by him for November 28. In preparation for it an attack was to be made shortly before daylight by two advance parties, proceeding separately. One was to carry the batteries and spike the guns near the point selected for landing; the other, to destroy a bridge five miles below, by which re-enforcements might arrive to the enemy.

To the first of these was attached a party of seventy seamen, who carried out their instructions, spiking and dismounting the guns. The fighting was unusually severe, eight out of the twelve naval officers concerned being wounded, two mortally, and half of the seamen either killed or wounded. Although the bridge was not destroyed, favourable conditions for the crossing of the main body had been established; but, upon viewing the numbers at his disposal, Smyth called a council of war, and after advising with it decided not to proceed. This was certainly a case of useless bloodshed. General Porter of the New York militia, who served with distinguished gallantry on the Niagara frontier to the end of the war, was present in this business, and criticised Smyth's conduct so severely as to cause a duel between them. "If bravery be a virtue," wrote Porter, "if the gratitude of a country be due to those who gallantly and desperately assert its rights, the government will make ample and honourable provision for the heirs of the brave tars who fell on this occasion, as well as for those that survive."[463] Another abortive movement toward crossing was made a few days later, and with it land operations on the Niagara frontier ended for the year 1812. Smyth was soon afterward dropped from the rolls of the army.

In the eastern part of Dearborn's military division, where he commanded in person, toward Albany and Champlain, less was attempted than at Detroit or Niagara. To accomplish less would be impossible; but as nothing was seriously undertaken, nothing also disastrously failed. The Commander-in-Chief gave sufficient disproof of military capacity by gravely proposing to "operate with effect at the same moment against Niagara, Kingston, and Montreal."[464] Such divergence of effort and dissemination of means, scanty at the best, upon points one hundred and fifty to two hundred miles apart, contravened all sound principle; to remedy which no compensating vigour was discoverable in his conduct. In all these quarters, as at Detroit, the enemy were perceptibly stronger in the autumn than when the war began; and the feebleness of American action had destroyed the principal basis upon which expectation of success had rested—the disaffection of the inhabitants of Canada and their readiness to side with the invaders. That this disposition existed to a formidable extent was well known. It constituted a large element in the anxieties of the British generals, especially of Brock; for in his district there were more American settlers than in Lower Canada.[465] On the Niagara peninsula, especially, climatic conditions, favourable to farming, had induced a large immigration. But local disloyalty is a poor reed for an assailant to rest upon, and to sustain it in vigorous action commonly requires the presence of a force which will render its assistance

---

463. Porter's Address to the Public. Niles' Register, vol. iii. p. 284.
464. See Eustis's Letter to Dearborn, Aug. 15, 1812. Hall's Memoirs of the North-western Campaign, p. 87.
465. Life of Brock, pp. 106, 130, 181.

needless. Whatever inclination to rebel there might have been was effectually quelled by the energy of Brock, the weakness of Hull, and the impotence of Dearborn and his subordinates.

In the general situation the one change favourable to the United States was in a quarter the importance of which the Administration had been slow to recognize, and probably scarcely appreciated even now. The anticipated military laurels had vanished like a dream, and the disinclination of the American people to military life in general, and to this war in particular, had shown itself in enlistments for the army, which, the President wrote, "fall short of the most moderate calculation." The attempt to supplement "regulars" by "volunteers," who, unlike the militia, should be under the General Government instead of that of the States—a favourite resource always with the Legislature of the United States—was "extremely unproductive;" while the militia in service were not under obligation to leave their state, and might, if they chose, abandon their fellow-countrymen outside its limits to slaughter and capture, as they did at Niagara, without incurring military punishment. The governors of the New England States, being opposed to the war, refused to go a step beyond protecting their own territory from hostilities, which they declared were forced upon them by the Administration rather than by the British. For this attitude there was a semblance of excuse in the utter military inefficiency to which the policy of Jefferson and Madison had reduced the national government. It was powerless to give the several states the protection to which it was pledged by the Constitution. The citizens of New York had to fortify and defend their own harbour. The reproaches of New England on this score were seconded somewhat later by the outcries of Maryland; and if Virginia was silent under suffering, it was not because she lacked cause for complaint. It is to be remembered that in the matter of military and naval unpreparedness the great culprits were Virginians. South of Virginia the nature of the shore line minimized the local harrying, from which the northern part of the community suffered. Nevertheless, there also the coasting trade was nearly destroyed, and even the internal navigation seriously harassed.

Only on the Great Lakes had the case of the United States improved, when winter put an end to most operations on the northern frontier. As in the Civil War a half century later, so in 1812, the power of the water over the issues of the land not only was not comprehended by the average official, but was incomprehensible to him. Armstrong in January, and Hull in March, had insisted upon a condition that should have been obvious; but not till September 3, when Hull's disaster had driven home Hull's reasoning, did Captain Chauncey receive orders "to assume command of the naval force on lakes Erie and Ontario, and to use every exertion to obtain control of them this fall." All preparations had still to be made, and were thrown, most wisely, on the man who was to do the work. He was "to use all the means which he might judge essential to accomplish the wishes of the government."[466] It is only just to give these quotations, which indicate how entirely everything to be done was left to the energy and discretion of the officer in charge, who had to plan and build up, almost from the foundation, the naval force on both lakes. Champlain, apparently by an oversight, was not included in his charge. Near the end of the war he was directed to convene a court-martial on some occurrences there, and then replied that it had never been placed under his command.[467]

Chauncey, who was just turned forty, entered on his duties with a will. Having been for four years in charge of the navy yard at New York, he was intimately acquainted with the resources of the principal depot from which he must draw his supplies. On September 26, after three weeks of busy collecting and shipping, he started for his station by the very occasional steamboat of those days, which required from eighteen to twenty hours for the trip to Albany. On the eve of departure, he wrote the Government that he had despatched—

---

466. Chauncey to Secretary, Sept. 26, 1812. Captains' Letters, Navy Department MSS.
467. Chauncey to Secretary, Feb. 24, 1815. Ibid.

.... one hundred and forty ship-carpenters, seven hundred seamen and marines, more than one hundred pieces of cannon, the greater part of large calibre, with muskets, shot, carriages, etc. The carriages have nearly all been made, and the shot cast, in that time. Nay, I may say that nearly every article that has been sent forward has been made.[468]

The words convey forcibly the lack of preparation which characterized the general state of the country; and they suggest also the difference in energy and efficiency between a man of forty, in continuous practice of his profession, and generals of sixty, whose knowledge of their business derived over a disuse of more than thirty years, and from experience limited to positions necessarily very subordinate. From the meagreness of steamer traffic, all this provision of men and material had to go by sail vessel to Albany; and Chauncey wrote that his personal delay in New York was no injury, but a benefit, for as it was he should arrive well before the needed equipment.

On October 6 he reached Sackett's Harbour, "in company with his Excellency the Governor of New York, through the worst roads I ever saw, especially near this place, in consequence of which I have ordered the stores intended for this place to Oswego, from which place they will come by water." Elliott had reported from Buffalo that "the roads are good, except for thirteen miles, which is intolerably bad; so bad that ordnance cannot be brought in wagons; it must come when snow is on the ground, and then in sleds." All expectation of contesting Lake Erie was therefore abandoned for that year, and effort concentrated on Ontario. There the misfortune of the American position was that the only harbour on their side of the lake, Sackett's, close to the entrance of the St. Lawrence, was remote from the highways of United States internal traffic. The roads described by Chauncey cut it off from communications by land, except in winter and the height of summer; while the historic water route by the Mohawk River, Lake Oneida, and the outlet of the latter

---

468. The details of Chauncey's actions are appended to his letter of Sept. 26, 1812.

through the Oswego River, debouched upon Ontario at a point utterly insecure against weather or hostilities. It was necessary, therefore, to accept Sackett's Harbour as the only possible navy yard and station, under the disadvantage that the maintenance of it—and through it, of the naval command of Ontario—depended upon this water transport of forty miles of open lake from the Oswego River. The danger, when superiority of force lapsed, as at times it did, was lessened by the existence of several creeks or small rivers, within which coasting craft could take refuge and find protection from attack under the muskets of the soldiery. Sackett's Harbour itself, though of small area, was a safe port, and under proper precautions defensible; but in neither point of view was it comparable with Kingston.

While in New York, Chauncey's preparations had not been limited to what could be done there. By communication with Elliott and Woolsey, he had informed himself well as to conditions, and had initiated the purchase and equipment of lake craft, chiefly schooners of from forty to eighty tons, which were fitted to carry one or two heavy guns; the weight of battery being determined partly by their capacity to bear it, and partly by the guns on hand. Elliott's report concerning Lake Erie led to his being diverted, at his own suggestion, to the mouth of the Genesee and to Oswego, to equip four schooners lying there; for arming which cannon before destined to Buffalo were likewise turned aside to those points. When Chauncey reached Sackett's, he found there also five schooners belonging mainly to the St. Lawrence trade, which had been bought under his directions by Woolsey. There was thus already a very fair beginning of a naval force; the only remaining apprehension being that, "from the badness of the roads and the lowness of the water in the Mohawk, the guns and stores will not arrive in time for us to do anything decisive against the enemy this fall."[469] Should they arrive soon enough, he hoped to seek the British in their own waters by November. Besides these extemporized expedients, two ships of twenty-four guns

---

469. Chauncey to Secretary of the Navy, Oct. 8, 12, 21, 1812. Captains' Letters.

were under construction at Sackett's, and two brigs of twenty, with three gunboats, were ordered on Lake Erie—all to be ready for service in the spring, their batteries to be sent on when the snow made it feasible.

After some disappointing detention, the waters of the inlet and outlet of Lake *Oneida* rose sufficiently to enable guns to reach Oswego, whence they were safely conveyed to Sackett's. On November 2 the report of a hostile cruiser in the neighbourhood, and fears of her interfering with parts of the armaments still in transit, led Chauncey to go out with the *Oneida*, the only vessel yet ready, to cut off the return of the stranger to Kingston. On this occasion he saw three of the enemy's squadron, which, though superior in force, took no notice of him. This slackness to improve an evident opportunity may reasonably be ascribed to the fact that as yet the British vessels on the lakes were not in charge of officers of the Royal Navy, but of a force purely provincial and irregular. Returning to Sackett's, Chauncey again sailed, on the evening of November 6, with the *Oneida* and six armed schooners. On the 8th he fell in with a single British vessel, the *Royal George*, of twenty-one guns, which retreated that night into Kingston. The Americans followed some distance into the harbour on the 9th, and engaged both the ship and the works; but the breeze blowing straight in, and becoming heavy, made it imprudent longer to expose the squadron to the loss of spars, under the fire of shore guns, when retreat had to be effected against the wind. Beating out, a British armed schooner was sighted coming in from the westward; but after some exchange of shots, she also, though closely pressed, escaped by her better local knowledge, and gained the protection of the port. The squadron returned to Sackett's, taking with it two lake vessels as prizes, and having destroyed a third—all three possible resources for the enemy.[470]

Nothing decisive resulted from this outing, but it fairly opened the campaign for the control of the lakes, and served to temper

---

470. Chauncey to Secretary, October 27, November 4, 6, 13. Captains' Letters. Those for November 6 and 13 can be found in Niles, vol. iii, pp. 205, 206.

officers and men for the kind of task before them. It gave also some experience as to the strength of the works at Kingston, which exceeded Chauncey's anticipations, and seems afterward to have exerted influence upon his views of the situation; but at present he announced his intention, if supported by a military force, to attack the enemy's vessels at their anchorage. Although several shot had been seen to strike, Chauncey himself entertained no doubt that all their damages could readily be repaired, and that they would put out again, if only to join their force to that already in Toronto. Still, on November 13, he reported his certainty that he controlled the water, an assurance renewed on the 17th; adding that he had taken on board military stores, with which he would sail on the first fair wind for Niagara River, and that he was prepared to effect transportation to any part of the lake, regardless of the enemy, but not of the weather. The last reservation was timely, for, sailing two days later, the vessels were driven back, one schooner being dismasted. As navigation on Erie opened usually much later than that upon Ontario, there was reasonable certainty that stores could reach the upper lake before they were needed in the spring, and the attempt was postponed till then. Meantime, however, four of the schooners were kept cruising off Kingston, to prevent intercourse between it and the other ports.[471]

On December 1 Chauncey wrote that it was no longer safe to navigate the lake, and that he would soon lay up the vessels. He ascertained subsequently that the recent action of the squadron had compelled troops for Toronto to march by land, from Kingston, and had prevented the transport of needed supplies to Fort George, thus justifying his conviction of control established over the water communications. A few days before he had had the satisfaction of announcing the launch, on November 26, of the *Madison*, a new ship of the corvette type, of 590 tons, one third larger than the ocean cruisers *Wasp* and *Hornet*, of the same class, and with proportionately heavy armament; she carrying twenty-four 32-pounder carronades, and they sixteen to

---

471. Chauncey to Secretary, November 17. Captains' Letters.

eighteen of the like weight. "She was built," added Chauncey, "in the short time of forty-five days; and nine weeks ago the timber that she is composed of was growing in the forest."[472] It seems scarcely necessary to point the moral, which he naturally did not draw for the edification of his superiors in the Administration, that a like energy displayed on Lake Erie, when war was contemplated, would have placed Hull's enterprise on the same level of security that was obtained for his successor by Perry's victory a year later, and at much less cost.

With the laying up of the fleet on the lakes operations on the northern frontier closed, except in the far West, where General Harrison succeeded to the command after Hull's capitulation. The loss of Detroit had thrown the American front of operations back upon the Maumee; nor would that, perhaps, have been tenable, had conditions in Upper Canada permitted Brock to remain with the most of his force through August and September. As it was, just apprehension for the Niagara line compelled his return thither; and the same considerations that decided the place of the Commander-in-Chief, dictated also that of the mass of his troops. The command at Detroit and Malden was left to Colonel Procter, whose position was defensively secured by naval means; the ship *Queen Charlotte* and brig *Hunter* maintaining local control of the water. He was, however, forbidden to attempt operations distinctively offensive. "It must be explicitly understood," wrote Brock to him, "that you are not to resort to offensive warfare for the purposes of conquest. Your operations are to be confined to measures of defence and security."[473] Among these, however, Brock included, by direct mention, undertakings intended to destroy betimes threatening gatherings of men or of stores; but such action was merely to secure the British positions, on the principle, already noted, that offence is the best defence. How far these restrictions represent Brock's own wishes, or reflect simply the known views of Sir George Prevost, the Governor General, is difficult to say. Brock's

---

472. Chauncey to Secretary, Nov. 26, 1812. Ibid.
473. Life of Brock, p. 293.

last letter to Procter, written within a week of his death, directed that the enemy should be kept in a state of constant ferment. It seems probable, however, that Procter's force was not such as to warrant movement with a view to permanent occupation beyond Detroit, the more so as the roads were usually very bad; but any effort on the part of the Americans to establish posts on the Maumee, or along the lake, must be promptly checked, if possible, lest these should form bases whence to march in force upon Detroit or Malden, when winter had hardened the face of the ground.[474]

The purpose of the Americans being to recover Detroit, and then to renew Hull's invasion, their immediate aim was to establish their line as far to the front as it could for the moment be successfully maintained. The Maumee was such a line, and the one naturally indicated as the advanced base of supplies upon which any forward movement by land must rest. The obstacle to its tenure, when summer was past and autumn rains had begun, was a great swamp, known locally as the Black Swamp, some forty miles wide, stretching from the Sandusky River on the east to the Indiana line on the west, and therefore impeding the direct approach from the south to the Maumee. Through this Hull had forced his way in June, building a road as he went; but by the time troops had assembled in the autumn progress here proved wholly impossible.

On account of the difficulties of transportation, Harrison divided his force into three columns, the supplies of each of which in a new country could be more readily sustained than those of the whole body, if united; in fact, the exigencies of supply in the case of large armies, even in well-settled countries, enforce "dissemination in order to live," as Napoleon expressed it. It is of the essence of such dissemination that the several divisions shall be near enough to support each other if there be danger of attack; but in the case of Harrison, although his dispositions have been

---

474. In the Canadian Archives frequent mention is made of expeditions by Procter's forces about the American lines, as of the British shipping on the Lake front during the autumn of 1812.

severely censured on this score, south of the Maumee no such danger existed to a degree which could not be safely disregarded. The centre column, therefore, was to advance over the road opened by Hull; the right by the east of the Sandusky River to its mouth on Lake Erie, east of the swamp, whence it could move to the Maumee; while the left, and the one most exposed, from its nearness to the Indian country, was to proceed by the Auglaize River, a tributary of the Maumee navigable for boats of light draught, to Fort Defiance, at the junction of the two streams. Had this plan been carried out, the army would have held a line from Fort Defiance to the Rapids of the Maumee, a distance of about forty miles, on which fortified depots could be established prior to further operations; and there would have been to it three chains of supply, corresponding to the roads used by the divisions in their march. Fort Defiance, with a work at the Rapids, afterward built and called Fort Meigs, would sustain the line proper; while a subsidiary post, subsequently known as Fort Stephenson, on the Lower Sandusky, was essential to the defence of that road as it approached the lake, and thence westward, where it skirted the lake shore, and was in measure open to raids from the water. The western line of supplies, being liable to attack from the neighbouring Indians, was further strengthened by works adequate to repel savages.

Fort Defiance on the left was occupied by October 22, and toward the middle of December some fifteen hundred men had assembled on the right, on the Sandusky, Upper and Lower; but the centre column could not get through, and the attempt to push on supplies by that route seems to have been persisted in beyond the limits of reasonable perseverance. Under these conditions, Harrison established his headquarters at Upper Sandusky about December 20, sending word to General Winchester, commanding at Defiance, to descend the Maumee to the Rapids, and there to prepare sleds for a dash against Malden across the lake, when frozen. This was the substitution, under the constraint of circumstances, of a sudden blow in place of regulated advance; for it abandoned, momentarily at least, the plan of establishing a permanent line. Winchester moved as directed, reaching the Rapids January 10, 1813, and fixing himself in position with thirteen hundred men on the north bank, opposite Hull's road. Early in the month the swamp froze over, and quantities of supplies were hurried forward. The total disposable force now under Harrison's command is given as sixty-three hundred.

Preparations and concentration had progressed thus far, when an impulsive outburst of sympathy evoked a singularly inconsiderate and rash movement on the part of the division on the Maumee, the commander of which seems to have been rather under the influence of his troops than in control of them. Word was brought to the camp that the American settlement of Frenchtown, beyond the River Raisin, thirty miles away toward Detroit, and now within British control, was threatened with burning by Indians. A council of war decided that relief should be attempted, and six hundred and sixty men started on the morning of January 17. They dispossessed the enemy and established themselves in the town, though with severe losses. Learning their success, Winchester himself went to the place on the 19th, followed closely by a re-enforcement of two-hundred and fifty. More than half his command was now thirty miles away from the position assigned it, without other base of retreat or support than the remnant left at the Rapids. In this situation a superior force of British and Indians under Procter crossed the lake on the ice and attacked the party thus rashly advanced to Frenchtown, which was compelled to surrender by 8 a.m. of January 22.

Winchester had notified Harrison of his proposed action, but not in such time as to permit it to be countermanded. Receiving the news on the morning of January 19, Harrison at once recognized the hazardous nature of the step, and ordered forward troops from Upper and Lower Sandusky; proceeding himself to the latter place, and thence to the Rapids, which he reached early on the 20th, ahead of the re-enforcements. There was nothing to do but await developments until the men from

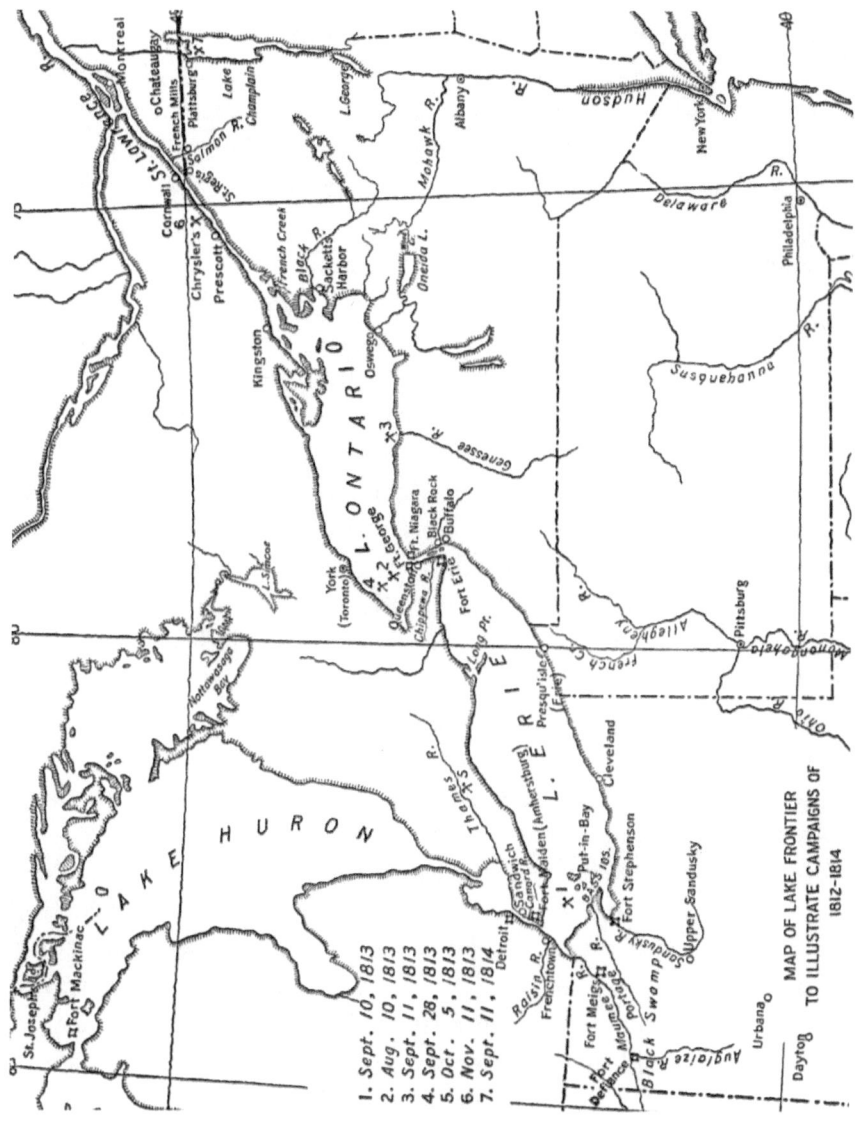

Sandusky arrived. At noon of the 22nd he received intelligence of the surrender, and saw that, through the imprudence of his subordinate, his project of crossing the ice to attack the enemy had been crushed by Procter, who had practically annihilated one of his principal divisions, beating it in detail.

The loss of so large a part of the force upon which he had counted, and the spread of sickness among the remainder, arrested Harrison's projects of offensive action. The Maumee even was abandoned for a few days, the army falling back to Portage River, toward the Sandusky. It soon, however, returned to the Rapids, and there Fort Meigs was built, which in the sequel proved sufficient to hold the position against Procter's attack. The army of the Northwest from that time remained purely on the defensive until the following September, when Perry's victory, assuring the control of the lake, enabled it to march secure of its communications.

Whatever chance of success may attend such a dash as that against Malden, planned by Harrison in December, or open to Hull in August, the undertaking is essentially outside the ordinary rules of warfare, and to be justified only by the special circumstances of the case, together with the possibility of securing the results obtained. Frenchtown, as a particular enterprise, illustrates in some measure the case of Malden. It was victoriously possessed, but under conditions which made its tenure more than doubtful, and the loss of the expeditionary corps more than probable. Furthermore, if held, it conferred no advantage. The position was less defensible than the Maumee, more exposed because nearer the enemy, more difficult to maintain because the communications were thirty miles longer, and, finally, it controlled nothing. The name of occupation, applied to it, was a mere misnomer, disguising a sham. Malden, on the contrary, if effectually held, would confer a great benefit; for in the hands of an enemy it menaced the communications of Detroit, and if coupled with command of the water, as was the case, it controlled them, as Hull found to his ruin. To gain it, therefore, justified a good deal of risk; yet if seized, unless control of the water were also soon established, it would, as compared with Detroit, entail upon the Americans the additional disadvantage that Frenchtown incurred over the Maumee,—an increase of exposure, because of longer and more exposed lines of communication. Though Malden was valuable to the British as a local base, with all the benefits of nearness, it was not the only one they possessed on the lakes. The loss of it, therefore, so long as they possessed decided superiority in armed shipping, though a great inconvenience, would not be a positive disability. With the small tonnage they had on the lake, however, it would have become extremely difficult, if not impossible, to transport and maintain a force sufficient seriously to interrupt the road from the Maumee, upon which Detroit depended.

In short, in all ordinary warfare, and in most that is extraordinary and seems outside the rules, one principle is sure to enforce itself with startling emphasis, if momentarily lost to sight or forgotten, and that is the need of secured communications. A military body, land or sea, may abandon its communications for a brief period, strictly limited, expecting soon to restore them at the same or some other point, just as a caravan can start across the desert with food and water which will last until another base is reached. There is no surrender of certainty in such a case; but a body of troops thrown into a position where it has no security of receiving supplies, incurs a risk that needs justification, and can receive it only from special circumstances. No position within striking distance of the lake shore was permanently secure unless supported by naval power; because all that is implied by the term "communications"—facility for transporting troops, supplies, and ammunition, rapidity of movement from point to point, central position and interior lines—all depended upon the control of the water, from Mackinac to the rapids of the St. Lawrence.

This truth, announced before the war by Hull and Armstrong, as well as by Harrison somewhat later, and sufficiently obvious to any thoughtful man, was recognized in act by Harrison and the Government after the Frenchtown disaster. The general was not responsible for the blunder of his subordinate, nor am I able to see that his general plans for a land campaign, considered independent of the water, lacked either insight, judgment, or energy. He unquestionably made very rash calculations, and indulged in wildly sanguine assurances of success; but this was probably inevitable in the atmosphere in which he had to work. The obstacles to be overcome were so enormous, the people and the Government, militarily, so ignorant and incapable, that it was scarcely possible to move efficiently without adopting, or seeming to adopt, the popular spirit and conviction. Facts had now asserted themselves through the unpleasant medium of experience, and henceforth it was tacitly accepted that nothing could be done except to stand on the defensive, until the navy of Lake Erie, as yet unbuilt, could exert its power. Until that day came, even the defensive positions taken were rudely shaken by Procter, a far from efficient officer, but possessed still of the power of the lakes, and following, though over-feebly, the spirit of Brock's instructions, to attack the enemy's posts and keep things in a ferment.

With the Frenchtown affair hostilities on the Canada frontier ceased until the following April; but the winter months were not therefore passed in inactivity. Chauncey, after laying up his ships at Sackett's Harbour, and representing to the Government the danger to them and to the navy yard, now that frost had extended over the waters the solidity of the ground, enabling the enemy to cross at will, departed to visit his hitherto neglected command on Lake Erie. He had already seen cause to be dissatisfied with Elliott's choice of a navy yard, known usually by the name Black Rock, a quarter of a mile above Squaw Island. The hostile shores were here so close together that even musketry could be exchanged; and Elliott, when reporting his decision, said "the river is so narrow that the soldiers are shooting at each other across." There was the further difficulty that, to reach the open lake, the vessels would have to go three miles against a current that ran four knots an hour, and much of the way within point-blank range of the enemy. Nevertheless, after examining all situations on Lake Erie,

Elliott had reported that none other would answer the purpose; "those that have shelters have not sufficient water, and those with water cannot be defended from the enemy and the violence of the weather."[475] Here he had collected materials and gathered six tiny vessels; the largest a brig of ninety tons, the others schooners of from forty to eighty. These he began to equip and alter about the middle of October, upon the arrival of the carpenters sent by Chauncey; but the British kept up such a fire of shot and shell that the carpenters quitted their work and returned to New York, leaving the vessels with their decks and sides torn up.[476]

They were still in this condition when Chauncey came, toward the end of December; and although then hauled into a creek behind Squaw Island, out of range, there were no workmen to complete them. He passed on to Presqu'Isle, now Erie, on the Pennsylvania shore, and found it in every way eligible as a port, except that there were but four or five feet of water on the bar. Vessels of war within could reach the lake only by being lightened of their guns and stores, a condition impracticable in the presence of a hostile squadron; but the local advantages were much superior to those at Black Rock, and while it could be hoped that a lucky opportunity might insure the absence of the enemy's vessels, the enemy's guns on the Niagara shore were fixtures, unless the American army took possession of them. Between these various considerations Chauncey decided to shift the naval base from Black Rock to Erie; and he there assembled the materials for the two brigs, of three hundred tons each, which formed the backbone of Perry's squadron nine months later.[477] For supplies Erie depended upon Philadelphia and Pittsburgh, there being from the latter place water communication by the Alleghany River, and its tributary the French River, to within fifteen miles, whence the transportation was by good road. Except timber, which grew upon the spot, the materials—iron, cordage, provisions, and guns—came mainly by

---

475. Elliott to Chauncey, Sept. 14, 1812. Captains' Letters, Navy Department.
476. Chauncey to the Secretary, Oct. 22, 1812. Captains' Letters, Navy Department.
477. Chauncey to the Secretary, Dec. 25, 1812; Jan. 1 and 8, and Feb. 16, 1813. Captains' Letters.

this route from Pennsylvania; a number of guns, however, being sent from Washington. By these arrangements the resources of New York, relieved of Lake Erie, were concentrated upon Lakes Ontario and Champlain.

Chauncey further provided for the defence of Black Rock by its own resources against sudden attack; the army, except a local force of three hundred men, having gone into winter quarters ten miles back from the Niagara. He then returned to Sackett's Harbour January 19, where he found preparations for protection even less satisfactory than upon Lake Erie,[478] although the stake was far greater; for it may safely be said that the fall of either Kingston or Sackett's would have decided the fate of Lake Ontario and of Upper Canada, at once and definitively. It had now become evident that, in order to decide superiority on the water, there was to be between these neighbouring and hostile stations the race of ship-building, which became and continued the most marked feature of the war on this lake. Chauncey felt the increasing necessity thus entailed for his presence on the scene. He was proportionately relieved by receiving at this time an application from Commander Oliver H. Perry to serve under him on the lakes, and immediately, on January 21, applied for his orders, stating that he could "be employed to great advantage, particularly on Lake Erie, where I shall not be able to go so early as I expected, owing to the increasing force of the enemy on this lake." This marks the official beginning of Perry's entrance upon the duty in which he won a distinction that his less fortunate superior failed to achieve. At this time, however, Chauncey hoped to attain such superiority by the opening of spring, and to receive such support from the army, as to capture Kingston by a joint operation, the plan for which he submitted to the Department. That accomplished, he would be able to transfer to Lake Erie the force of men needed to destroy the enemy's fleet there.[479] This expectation was not fulfilled, and Perry remained in practically independent command upon the upper lakes.

---

478. See Chauncey's letters of Dec. 1, 1812, and Jan. 20, 1813. Captains' Letters.
479. Chauncey to the Secretary, Jan. 21, Feb. 22, 1813. Captains' Letters.

The season of 1812 may be said, therefore, to have closed with the American squadron upon Lake Ontario concentrated in Sackett's Harbour, where also two new and relatively powerful ships were building. Upon Lake Erie the force was divided between Black Rock, where Elliott's flotilla lay, and Erie, where the two brigs were laid down, and four other gunboats building. The concentration of these two bodies could be effected only by first taking possession of the British side of the Niagara River. This done, and the Black Rock vessels thus released, there still remained the bar at Erie to pass. The British force on Ontario was likewise divided, between Toronto and Kingston, the vessels afloat being at the latter. Neither place, however, was under such fetters as Black Rock, and the two divisions might very possibly be assembled despite the hostile fleet. On the upper lake their navy was at Amherstburg, where also was building a ship, inferior in force, despite her rig, to either of the brigs ordered by Chauncey at Erie. The difficulties of obtaining supplies, mechanics, and seamen, in that then remote region, imposed great hindrances upon the general British preparations. There nevertheless remained in their hands, at the opening of the campaign, the great advantages over the Americans—first, of the separation of the latter's divisions, enforced by the British holding the bank of the Niagara; and secondly, of the almost insuperable difficulty of crossing the Erie bar unarmed, if the enemy's fleet kept in position near it. That the British failed to sustain these original advantages condemns their management, and is far more a matter of military criticism than the relative power of the two squadrons in the battle of September 10. The principal business of each commander was to be stronger than the enemy when they met. That the American accomplished this, despite serious obstacles, first by concentrating his force, and second by crossing the bar unimpeded, so that when he encountered his opponent he was in decisively superior force, is as distinctly to his credit as it would have been distinctly to his discredit had the odds been reversed by any fault of his. Perry by diligent efficiency overcame his difficulties, combined his divisions, gained the lake, and, by commanding it, so cut off his enemy's supplies that he compelled him to come out, and fight, and be destroyed. To compare the force of the two may be a matter of curious interest; but for the purpose of making comparisons of desert between them it is a mere waste of ink, important only to those who conceive the chief end of war to be fighting, and not victory.

* * * * * * * *

The disaster at Frenchtown, with the consequent abandonment of all project of forward movement by the Army of the Northwest, may be regarded as the definite termination of the land campaign of 1812. Before resuming the account of the ocean operations of the same period, it is expedient here to give a summary of European conditions at the same time, for these markedly affected the policy of the British Government towards the United States, even after war had been formally declared.

The British Orders in Council of 1807, modified in 1809 in scope, though not in principle, had been for a long while the grievance chiefly insisted upon by the United States. Against them mainly was directed, by Jefferson and Madison, the system of commercial restrictions which it was believed would compel their repeal. Consequently, when the British Government had abolished the obnoxious Orders, on June 23, 1812, with reservations probably admissible by the United States, it was unwilling to believe that war could still not be avoided; nor that, even if begun in ignorance of the repeal, it could not be stopped without further concession. Till near the end of the year 1812 its measures were governed by this expectation, powerfully re-enforced by momentous considerations of European events, the effect of which upon the United States requires that they be stated.

In June, 1812, European politics were reaching a crisis, the issue of which could not then be forecast. War had begun between Napoleon and Russia; and on June 24 the Emperor, crossing the Niemen, invaded the dominion of the Czar. Great Britain, already nine years at war with France, had just succeeded in detaching Russia from her enemy, and ranging her on her own side. The accession of Sweden to this alliance conferred complete control of the Baltic, thus releasing a huge British fleet hitherto maintained there, and opening an important trade, debarred to Great Britain in great measure for four years past. But on the other hand, Napoleon still, as during all this recent period, controlled the Continent from the Pyrenees to the Vistula, carrying its hosts forward against Russia, and closing its ports to British commerce to the depressing injury of British finance. A young Canadian, then in England, in close contact with London business life, wrote to his home at this period:

> There is a general stagnation of commerce, all entrance to Europe being completely shut up. There was never a time known to compare with the present, nearly all foreign traders becoming bankrupt, or reduced to one tenth of their former trade. Merchants, who once kept ten or fifteen clerks, have now but two or three; thousands of half-starved discharged clerks are skulking about the streets. Customhouse duties are reduced upwards of one half. Of such dread power are Bonaparte's decrees, which have of late been enforced in the strictest manner all over the Continent, that it has almost ruined the commerce of England.[480]

A month before the United States declared war the perplexities of the British Government were depicted by the same writer, in terms which palpably and graphically reflect the contemporary talk of the counting-house and the dinner-table:

> If the Orders in Council are repealed, the trade of the United States will flourish beyond all former periods. They will then have the whole commerce of the Continent in their hands, and the British, though blockading with powerful armaments the hostile ports of Europe, will behold fleets of American merchantmen enter in safety the harbours of the enemy, and carry on a brisk and lucrative

---

480. Ridout, "Ten Years in Upper Canada," pp. 52, 58, 115.

trade, whilst Englishmen, who command the ocean and are sole masters of the deep, must quietly suffer two thirds of their shipping to be dismantled and lie useless in little rivers or before empty warehouses. Their seamen, to earn a little salt junk and flinty biscuits, must spread themselves like vagabonds over the face of the earth, and enter the service of any nation. If, on the contrary, the Government continue to enforce the Orders, trade will still remain in its present deplorable state; an American war will follow, and poor Canada will bear the brunt.

Cannot one see the fine old fellows of the period shaking their heads over their wine, and hear the words which the lively young provincial takes down almost from their lips? They portray truly, however, the anxious dilemma in which the Government was living, and explain concisely the conflicting considerations which brought on the war with the United States. From this embarrassing situation the current year brought a double relief. The chance of American competition was removed by the declaration of war, and exclusion from the Continent by Napoleon's reverses.

While matters were thus in northern and central Europe, in the far southwest the Spanish peninsula had for the same four dreary years been the scene of desolating strife, in which from the beginning Great Britain had taken a most active part, supporting the insurgent people with armies and money against the French legions. The weakening effect of this conflict upon the Emperor, and the tremendous additional strain upon his resources now occasioned by the break with Russia, were well understood, and hopes rose high; but heavy in the other scale were his unbroken record of success, and the fact that the War in the Peninsula, the sustenance of which was now doubly imperative in order to maintain the fatal dissemination of his forces between the two extremities of Europe, depended upon intercourse with the United States. The corn of America fed the British and their allies in the Peninsula, and so abundantly, that flour was cheaper in Lisbon than in Liverpool. In 1811, 802

American vessels entered the Tagus to 860 British; and from all the rest of the outside world there came only 75. The Peninsula itself, Spain and Portugal together, sent but 452.[481] The merchants of Baltimore, petitioning against the Non-Intercourse Act, said that $100,000,000 were owing by British merchants to Americans, which could only be repaid by importations from England; and that this debt was chiefly for shipments to Spain and Portugal.[482] The yearly export thither, mainly for the armies, was 700,000 barrels of flour, besides grain in other forms.[483] The maintenance of this supply would be endangered by war.

Upon the continuance of peace depended also the enjoyment of the relatively tranquil conditions which Great Britain, after years of vexation, had succeeded at last in establishing in the western basin of the Atlantic, and especially in the Caribbean Sea. In 1808 the revolt of the Spanish people turned the Spanish West Indies once more to her side; and in 1809 and 1810 the conquest of the last of the French islands gave her control of the whole region, depriving French privateers of every base for local operations against British commerce. In 1812, by returns to September 1, the Royal Navy had at sea one hundred and twenty ships of the line and one hundred and forty-five frigates, besides four hundred and twenty-one other cruisers, sixteen of which were larger and the rest smaller than the frigate class—a total of six hundred and eighty-six.[484] Of these there were on the North American and West India stations only three of the line, fifteen frigates, and sixty-one smaller—a total of seventy-nine.[485] The huge remainder of over six hundred ships of war were detained elsewhere by the exigencies of the contest, the naval range of which stretched from the Levant to the shores of Denmark and Norway, then one kingdom under Napoleon's control; and in the far Eastern seas extended to the Straits of Sunda, and beyond. From Antwerp to Venice, in various ports,

---

481. *Niles' Register*, vol ii. p. 42.
482. Ibid., p. 119.
483. Ibid., p. 303.
484. Naval Chronicle, vol. xxviii. p. 248.
485. Quoted from Steele's List (British) by Niles' Register, vol. ii. p. 356.

when the Empire fell, Napoleon had over a hundred ships of the line and half a hundred frigates. To hold these in check was in itself a heavy task for the British sea power, even though most of the colonial ports which might serve as bases for their external action had been wrested from France. A hostile America would open to the French navy a number of harbours which it now needed; and at the will of the Emperor the United States might receive a division of ships of a class she lacked entirely, but could both officer and man. One of Napoleon's great wants was seamen, and it was perfectly understood by intelligent naval officers, and by appreciative statesmen like John Adams and Gouverneur Morris, that a fleet of ships of the line, based upon American resources, would constitute for Great Britain a more difficult problem than a vastly larger number in Europe. The probability was contemplated by both the British Commander-in-Chief and the Admiralty, and was doubtless a chief reason for the comparatively large number of ships of the line—eleven—assigned on the outbreak of hostilities to a station where otherwise there was no similar force to encounter.[486] To bring the French ships and this coast-line together was a combination correct in conception, and not impracticable. It was spoken of at the time—rumoured as a design; and had not the attention and the means of the Emperor been otherwise preoccupied, probably would have been attempted, and not impossibly effected.

To avert such a conjuncture by the restoration of peace was necessarily an object of British policy. More than that, however, was at stake. The Orders in Council had served their turn. In conjunction with Napoleon's Continental System, by the misery inflicted upon all the countries under his control, they had brought about the desperation of Russia and the resistance of the Czar, who at first had engaged in the Emperor's policy. Russia and France were at war, and it was imperative at once to redouble the pressure in the Peninsula, and to recuperate the financial strength of Great Britain, by opening every possible avenue of supply and

---

486. Croker to Warren, Nov. 18, 1812, and March 20, 1813. British Admiralty MSS. Out-Letters.

of market to British trade, in order to bring the whole national power, economical and military, to bear effectively upon what promised to be a death struggle. The repeal of the Orders, with the consequent admission of American merchant ships to every hostile port, except such, few as might be effectively blockaded in accordance with the accepted principles of International Law, was the price offered for the preservation of peace, and for readmission to the American market, closed to British manufacturers and merchants by the Non-Importation Acts. This extension of British commerce, now loudly demanded by the British people, was an object to be accomplished by the same means that should prevent the American people from constituting themselves virtually the allies of Napoleon by going to war. Should this dreaded alternative, however, come to pass, not only would British trade again miss the market, the loss of which had already caused widespread suffering, but, in common with it, British navigation, British shipping, the chief handmaid of commerce, would be exposed in a remote quarter, most difficult to guard, to the privateering activity of a people whose aptitude for such occupation had been demonstrated in the fight for independence and the old French wars. Half a century before, in the years 1756-58, there had been fitted out in the single port of New York, for war against the French, forty-eight privateers, carrying six hundred and ninety-five guns and manned by over five thousand men.[487]

The conditions enumerated constituted the principal important military possibilities of the sea frontier of the United States, regarded as an element in the general international situation when the year 1812 opened. Its importance to France was simply that of an additional weight thrown into the scale against Great Britain. France, being excluded from the sea, could not be aided or injured by the United States directly, but only indirectly, through their common enemy; and the same was substantially true of the Continent at large. But to Great Britain a hostile seaboard in America meant the possibility of all that has been stated; and therefore, slowly and unwillingly, but surely, the ap-

---

487. *Niles' Register*, vol. iii. p. 111. Quoted from a publication of 1759.

prehension of war with its added burden forced the Government to a concession which years of intermittent commercial restrictions by the United States, and of Opposition denunciation at home, had not been able to extort. The sudden death of Spencer Perceval, the prime minister identified with the Orders in Council, possibly facilitated the issue, but it had become inevitable by sheer pressure of circumstances as they developed. It came to pass, by a conjuncture most fortunate for Great Britain, and most unfavourable to the United States, that the moment of war, vainly sought to be avoided by both parties, coincided with the first rude jar to Napoleon's empire and its speedy final collapse; leaving the Union, weakened by internal dissension, exposed single-handed to the full force of the British power. At the beginning, however, and till toward the end of 1812, it seemed possible that for an indefinite period the efforts of the Americans would receive the support derived from the inevitable preoccupation of their enemy with European affairs; nor did many doubt Napoleon's success against Russia, or that it would be followed by Great Britain's abandoning the European struggle as hopeless.

For such maritime and political contingencies the British Admiralty had to prepare, when the near prospect of war with America threatened to add to the extensive responsibilities entailed by the long strife with Napoleon. Its measures reflected the double purpose of the Government: to secure peace, if possible, yet not to surrender policies considered imperative. On May 9, 1812, identical instructions were issued to each of the admirals commanding the four transatlantic stations,—Newfoundland, Halifax, Jamaica, and Barbados,—warning them of the imminent probability of hostilities, in the event of which, by aggressive action or formal declaration on the part of the United States, they were authorized to resort at once to all customary procedures of war; "to attack, take or sink, burn or destroy, all ships or vessels belonging to the United States or to the citizens thereof." At the same time, however, special stress was laid upon the urgent wish of the Government to avoid occasions which might induce a collision.

You are to direct the commanders of his Majesty's ships to exercise, except in the events hereinbefore specified, all possible forbearance toward the United States, and to contribute, as far as may depend upon them, to that good understanding which it is his Royal Highness's[488] most earnest wish to maintain.[489]

The spirit of these orders, together with caution not to be attacked unawares, accounts for the absence of British ships of war from the neighbourhood of the American coast noted by Rodgers' cruising squadron in the spring of 1812. Decatur, indeed, was informed by a British naval agent that the admiral at Bermuda did not permit more than two vessels to cruise at a time, and these were instructed not to approach the American coast.[490] The temper of the controlling element in the Administration, and the disposition of American naval officers since the *Chesapeake* affair, were but too likely to afford causes of misunderstanding in case of a meeting.

---

488. The Prince Regent. George III. was incapacitated at this time.
489. Admiralty Out-Letters, British Records Office.
490. Rodgers to the Secretary, April 29, 1812. Decatur, June 16, 1812. Captains' Letters.

CHAPTER 8

Privateering & Naval Actions

In anticipation of war the British Admiralty took the military measure of consolidating their transatlantic stations, with the exception of Newfoundland. The Jamaica, Leeward Islands, and Halifax squadrons, while retaining their present local organizations, were subordinated to a single chief; for which position was designated Admiral Sir John Borlase Warren, an officer of good fighting record, but from his previous career esteemed less a seaman than a gallant man. This was apparently his first extensive command, although he was now approaching sixty; but it was foreseen that the British minister might have left Washington in consequence of a rupture of relations, and that there might thus devolve upon the naval commander-in-chief certain diplomatic overtures, which the Government had determined to make before definitely accepting war as an irreversible issue. Warren, a man of courtly manners, had some slight diplomatic antecedents, having represented Great Britain at St. Petersburg on one occasion. There were also other negotiations anticipated, dependent upon political conditions within the Union; where bitter oppositions of opinion, sectional in character, were known to exist concerning the course of the Administration in resorting to hostilities. Warren was instructed on these several points.

It was not until July 25, 1812, that a despatch vessel from Halifax brought word to England of the attack upon the *Belvidera* by Rodgers' squadron on June 24. By the same mail Admiral

Sawyer wrote that he had sent a flag of truce to New York to ask an explanation, and besides had directed all his cruisers to assemble at Halifax.[491] The Government recognized the gravity of the news, but expressed the opinion that there was no evidence that war had been decided upon, and that the action of the American commodore had been in conformity with previous orders not to permit foreign cruisers within the waters of the United States. Some colour was lent to this view by the circumstance that the "*Belvidera*" was reported to have been off Sandy Hook, though not in sight of land.[492] In short, the British Cabinet officially assumed that facts were as they wished them to continue; the course best adapted to insure the maintenance of peace, if perchance not yet broken.

On July 29, however, definite information was received that the United States Government had declared that war existed between the two countries. On the 31st the Cabinet took its first measures in consequence.[493] One order was issued forbidding British merchant vessels to sail without convoy for any part of North America or the West Indies; while another laid an embargo on all American merchant ships in British ports, and directed the capture of any met at sea, unless sailing under British licenses, as many then did to Continental ports. No other hostile steps, such as general reprisals or commercial blockade, were at this time authorized; it was decided to await the effect in the United States of the repeal of the obnoxious Orders in Council. This having taken place only on June 23, intelligence of its reception and results could not well reach England before the middle of September. When Parliament was prorogued on July 30, the speech from the throne expressed a willingness still "to hope that the accustomed relations of peace and amity between the two countries may yet be restored."

It is a coincidence, accidental, yet noteworthy for its signifi-

---

491. Naval Chronicle, vol. xxviii. p. 73.
492. Ibid.
493. Ibid., pp. 138, 139.

cance, that the date of the first hostile action against the United States, July 31, was also that of the official promulgation of treaties of peace between Great Britain, Russia, and Sweden.[494] Accompanied as these were with clauses embodying what was virtually a defensive alliance of the three Powers against Napoleon, they marked that turn of the tide in European affairs which overthrew one of the most important factors in the political and military anticipations of the United States Administration. "Can it be doubted," wrote Madison on September 6, "that if, under the pressure added by our war to that previously felt by Great Britain, her Government declines an accommodation, it will be owing to calculations drawn from our internal divisions?"[495] Of the approaching change, however, no sign yet appeared. The reverses of the French were still in the far future. Not until September 14 did they enter Moscow, and news of this event was received in the United States only at the end of November. A contemporary weekly, under date of December 5, remarked: "Peace before this time has been dictated by Bonaparte, as ought to have been calculated upon by the dealers (*sic*) at St. Petersburg, before they, influenced by the British, prevailed upon Alexander to embark in the War. . . . All Europe, the British Islands excepted, will soon be at the feet of Bonaparte."[496] This expectation, generally shared during the summer of 1812, is an element in the American situation not to be overlooked. As late as December 4, Henry Clay, addressing the House of Representatives, of which he then was Speaker, said:

> The British trade shut out from the Baltic—excluded from the Continent of Europe—possibly expelled the Black Sea—perishing in South America; its illicit avenue to the United States, through Canada, closed—was this the period for throwing open our own market by abandoning our restrictive system? Perhaps at this moment the fate of

---

494. Naval Chronicle, vol. xxviii. p. 139.
495. Writings of Madison (ed. 1865), vol. ii. p. 545.
496. *Niles' Register*, vol. iii. p. 220

the north of Europe is decided, and the French Emperor may be dictating the law from Moscow.[497]

The following night Napoleon finally abandoned his routed army and started on his return to Paris.

War having been foreseen, the British Government took its first step without hesitation. On August 6 the Foreign Office issued Warren's secret instructions, which were substantially the repetition of those already addressed on July 8 to its representative in Washington. It being probable that before they could be received he would have departed in consequence of the rupture, Warren was to submit the proposition contained in them, that the United States Government, in view of the revocation of the Orders in Council, so long demanded by it, should recall the hostile measures taken. In case of acceptance, he was authorized to stop at once all hostilities within his command, and to give assurance of similar action by his Government in every part of the world. If this advance proved fruitless, as it did, no orders instituting a state of war were needed, for it already existed; but for that contingency Warren received further instructions as to the course he was to pursue, in case "a desire should manifest itself in any considerable portion of the American Union, more especially in those States bordering upon his Majesty's North American dominions, to return to their relations of peace and amity with this country." The admiral was to encourage such dispositions, and should they take shape in formal act, making overtures to him for a cessation of hostilities for that part of the country, he was directed to grant it, and to enter into negotiations for commercial intercourse between the section thus acting and the British dominions. In short, if the General Government proved irreconcilable, Great Britain was to profit by any sentiment of disunion found to exist.[498]

---

497. Annals of Congress, 1812-13, p. 301.
498. Castlereagh to the Admiralty, Aug. 6 and 12, 1812. British Record Office MSS. Warren's Letter to the United States Government and Monroe's reply are in American State Papers, vol. iii. pp. 595, 596.

Warren sailed from Portsmouth August 14, arriving in Halifax September 26. On the 30th, he despatched to the United States Government the proposal for the cessation of hostilities. Monroe, the Secretary of State, replied on October 27. The President, he said, was at all times anxious to restore peace, and at the very moment of declaring war had instructed the *chargé* in London to make propositions to that effect to the British Ministry. An indispensable condition, however, was the abandonment of the practice of impressment from American vessels. The President recognized the embarrassment under which Great Britain lay, because of her felt necessity to control the services of her native seamen, and was willing to undertake that hereafter they should be wholly excluded from the naval and merchant ships of the United States. This should be done under regulations to be negotiated between the two countries, in order to obviate the injury alleged by Great Britain; but, meanwhile, impressing from under the American flag must be discontinued during any armistice arranged.

> It cannot be presumed, while the parties are engaged in a negotiation to adjust amicably this important difference, that the United States would admit the right, or acquiesce in the practice of the opposite party, or that Great Britain would be unwilling to restrain her cruisers from a practice which would have the strongest tendency to defeat the negotiation.

The Orders in Council having been revoked, impressment remained the only outstanding question upon which the United States was absolute in its demand. That conceded, upon the terms indicated, all other differences might be referred to negotiation. Upon this point Warren had no powers, for his Government was determined not to yield. The maritime war therefore went on unabated; but it may be mentioned here that the President's undertaking to exclude British-born seamen from American ships took effect in an Act of Congress, approved by him March 3, 1813. He had thenceforth in hand a pledge which he considered a full guarantee against whatever Great Britain feared to lose by ceasing to take seamen from under the American flag. It was not so regarded in England, and no formal agreement on this interesting subject was ever reached.

The conditions existing upon his arrival, and the occurrences of the past three months, as then first fully known to Warren, deeply impressed him with the largeness of his task in protecting the commerce of Great Britain. He found himself at once in the midst of its most evident perils, which in the beginning were concentrated about Halifax, owing to special circumstances. Although long seemingly imminent, hostilities when they actually came had found the mercantile community of the United States, for the most part, unbelieving and unprepared. The cry of "Wolf!" had been raised so often that they did not credit its coming, even when at the doors. This was especially the case in New England, where the popular feeling against war increased the indisposition to think it near. On May 14, Captain Bainbridge, commanding the Boston navy yard, wrote:

> I am sorry to say that the people here do not believe we are going to war, and are too much disposed to treat our national councils with contempt, and to consider their preparations as electioneering.[499]

The presidential election was due in the following November. A Baltimore newspaper of the day, criticising the universal rush to evade the embargo of April 4, instituted in order to keep both seamen and property at home in avoidance of capture, added that in justice it must be said that most people believed that the embargo, as on former occasions, did not mean war.[500]

Under the general sense of unpreparedness, it seemed to many inconceivable that the Administration would venture to expose the coasts to British reprisals. John Randolph, repeating in the House of Representatives in secret session a conversation between the Committee on Foreign Relations and the Secretary of State, said:

---

499. Captains' Letters. Navy Department MSS.
500. *Niles' Register*, vol. ii. p. 101.

He was asked whether any essential changes would be made in the sixty days (of the proposed embargo) in the defence of our maritime frontier and seaports. He replied, pretty considerable preparations would be made. He said New York was in a pretty respectable state, but not such as to resist a formidable fleet; but that it was not to be expected that that kind of war would be carried on.

The obvious reply was:

We must expect what commonly happens in wars. . . . As to the prepared state of the country, the President, in case of a declaration, would not feel bound to take more than his share of the responsibility. The unprepared state of the country was the only reason why ulterior measures should be deferred.[501]

Randolph's recollections of this interview were challenged by members of the Committee in other points, but not in these. The Administration had then been in office three years, and the causes of war had been accumulating for at least seven; but so notorious was the unreadiness that a great part of the community even now saw only bluster.

For these reasons the first rush to privateering, although feverishly energetic, was of a somewhat extemporized character. In consequence of the attempt to elude the embargo, by a precipitate and extensive export movement, a very large part of the merchant ships and seamen were now abroad. Hence, in the haste to seize upon enemy's shipping, anything that could be sent to sea at quick notice was utilized. Vessels thus equipped were rarely best fitted for a distant voyage, in which dependence must rest upon their own resources, and upon crews both numerous and capable. They were therefore necessarily directed upon commercial highways near at hand, which, though not intrinsically richest, nor followed by the cargoes that would pay best in the United States, could nevertheless adequately reward enterprise. In the near vicinity of

---

501. Annals of Congress, 1811-12, p. 1593.

Halifax the routes from the British West Indies to New Brunswick, Nova Scotia, and the St. Lawrence, met and crossed the equally important lines of travel from the British Islands to the same points. This circumstance contributed to the importance of that place as a naval and commercial centre, and also focussed about it by far the larger part of the effort and excitement of the first privateering outburst from the United States. As Rodgers' bold sortie, and disappearance into the unknown with a strong squadron had forced concentration upon the principal British vessels, the cruisers remaining for dispersion in search of privateers were numerically inadequate to suppress the many and scattered Americans. Before Warren's arrival the prizes reported in the United States were one hundred and ninety, and they probably exceeded two hundred. An analysis of the somewhat imperfect data which accompany these returns indicates that about three fourths were seized in the Bay of Fundy and in the off-lying waters from thence round to Newfoundland. Of the remainder, half, probably, were taken in the West Indies; and the rest out in the deep sea, beyond the Gulf Stream, upon the first part of the track followed by the sugar and coffee traders from the West Indies to England.[502] There had not yet been time to hear of prizes taken in Europe, to which comparatively few privateers as yet went.

One of the most intelligent and enterprising of the early privateers was Commodore Joshua Barney, a veteran of the American Navy of the Revolution. He commissioned a Baltimore schooner, the *Rossie*, at the outbreak of the war; partly, apparently, in order to show a good example of patriotic energy, but doubtless also through the promptings of a love of adventure, not extinguished by advancing years. The double motive kept him an active, useful, and distinguished public servant throughout the war. His cruise on this occasion, as far as can be gathered from the reports,[503] conformed in direction to the quarters in which the enemy's merchant ships might

---

502. These data are summarized from Niles' Register, which throughout the war collected, and periodically published, lists of prizes.
503. A synopsis of the *Rossie*'s log is given in Niles' Register, vol. iii p. 158.

most surely be expected. Sailing from the Chesapeake July 15, he seems to have stood at once outside the Gulf Stream for the eastern edge of the Banks of Newfoundland. In the ensuing two weeks he was twice chased by an enemy's frigate, and not till July 31 did he take his first prize. From that day, to and including August 9, he captured ten other vessels—eleven in all. Unfortunately, the precise locality of each seizure is not given, but it is inferable from the general tenor of the accounts that they were made between the eastern edge of the Great Banks and the immediate neighbourhood of Halifax; in the locality, in fact, to which Hull during those same ten days was directing the *Constitution*, partly in pursuit of prizes, equally in search of the enemy's ships of war, which were naturally to be sought at those centres of movement where their national traders accumulated.

On August 30 the *Rossie*, having run down the Nova Scotia coast and passed by George's Bank and Nantucket, went into Newport, Rhode Island. It is noticeable that before and after those ten days of success, although she saw no English vessels, except ships of war cruising on the outer approaches of their commerce, she was continually meeting and speaking American vessels returning home. These facts illustrate the considerations governing privateering, and refute the plausible opinion often advanced, that it was a mere matter of gambling adventure. Thus Mr. Gallatin, the Secretary of the Treasury, in a communication to Congress, said:

> The occupation of privateers is precisely of the same species as the lottery, with respect to hazard and to the chance of rich prizes.[504]

Gallatin approached the subject from the standpoint of the financier and with the abstract ideas of the political economist. His temporary successor, the Secretary of the Navy, Mr. Jones, had been a merchant in active business life, and he viewed privateering as a practical business undertaking.

---

504. Gallatin, Dec. 8, 1812. American State Papers, Finance, vol. ii. p. 594.

The analogy between privateering and lotteries does not appear to me to be so strict as the Secretary seems to consider it. The adventure of a privateer is of the nature of a commercial project or speculation, conducted by commercial men upon principles of mercantile calculation and profit. The vessel and her equipment is a matter of great expense, which is expected to be remunerated by the probable chances of profit, after calculating the outfit, insurance, etc., as in a regular mercantile voyage.[505]

Mr. Jones would doubtless have admitted what Gallatin alleged, that the business was liable to be overdone, as is the case with all promising occupations; and that many would engage in it without adequate understanding or forethought.

The elements of risk which enter into privateering are doubtless very great, and to some extent baffle calculation. In this it only shares the lot common to all warlike enterprise, in which, as the ablest masters of the art repeatedly affirm, something must be allowed for chance. But it does not follow that a reasonable measure of success may not fairly be expected, where sagacious appreciation of well-known facts controls the direction of effort, and preparation is proportioned to the difficulties to be encountered. Heedlessness of conditions, or recklessness of dangers, defeat effort everywhere, as well as in privateering; nor is even the chapter of unforeseen accident confined to military affairs. In 1812 the courses followed by the enemy's trade were well understood, as were also the characteristics of their ships of war, in sailing, distribution, and management.[506] Regard being had to these conditions, the pecuniary venture, which privateering essentially is, was sure of fair returns—barring accidents—if the vessels were thoroughly well found, with superior speed and nautical qualities, and if directed upon the centres of ocean travel, such as the approaches to the English Channel, or, as before

---

505. Jones, July 21, 1813. American State Papers, Finance, vol. ii. p. 645.
506. In the memoir of Commodore Barney (p. 252), published by his daughter, it is said that, successful though the *Rossie's* cruise was in its issue, he was dissatisfied with the course laid down for him by his owners, who did not understand the usual tracks of British commerce.

noted, to where great highways cross, inducing an accumulation of vessels from several quarters. So pursued, privateering can be made pecuniarily successful, as was shown by the increasing number and value of prizes as the war went on. It has also a distinct effect as a minor offensive operation, harassing and weakening the enemy; but its merits are more contestable when regarded as by itself alone decisive of great issues. Despite the efficiency and numbers of American privateers, it was not British commerce, but American, that was destroyed by the war.

From Newport the *Rossie* took a turn through another lucrative field of privateering enterprise, the Caribbean Sea. Passing by Bermuda, which brought her in the track of vessels from the West Indies to Halifax, she entered the Caribbean at its northeastern corner, by the Anegada Passage, near St. Thomas, thence ran along the south shore of Porto Rico, coming out by the Mona Passage, between Porto Rico and Santo Domingo, and so home by the Gulf Stream. In this second voyage she made but two prizes; and it is noted in her log book that she here met the privateer schooner *Rapid* from Charleston, fifty-two days out, without taking anything. The cause of these small results does not certainly appear; but it may be presumed that with the height of the hurricane season at hand, most of the West India traders had already sailed for Europe. Despite all drawbacks, when the *Rossie* returned to Baltimore toward the end of October, she had captured or destroyed property roughly reckoned at a million and a half, which is probably an exaggerated estimate. Two hundred and seventeen prisoners had been taken.

While the *Rossie* was on her way to the West Indies, there sailed from Salem a large privateer called the *America*, the equipment and operations of which illustrated precisely the business conception which attached to these enterprises in the minds of competent business men. This ship-rigged vessel of four hundred and seventy-three tons, built of course for a merchantman, was about eight years old when the war broke out, and had just returned from a voyage. Seeing that ordinary commerce was likely to be a very precarious undertaking, her owners spent the months of July and August in preparing her deliberately for her new occupation. Her upper deck was removed, and sides filled in solid. She was given larger yards and loftier spars than before; the greatly increased number of men carried by a privateer, for fighting and for manning prizes, enabling canvas to be handled with greater rapidity and certainty. She received a battery of very respectable force for those days, so that she could repel the smaller classes of ships of war, which formed a large proportion of the enemy's cruisers. Thus fitted to fight or run, and having very superior speed, she was often chased, but never caught. During the two and a half years of war she made four cruises of four months each; taking in all forty-one prizes, twenty-seven of which reached port and realized $1,100,000, after deducting expenses and government charges. As half of this went to the ship's company, the owners netted $550,000 for sixteen months' active use of the ship. Her invariable cruising ground was from the English Channel south, to the latitude of the Canary Islands.[507]

The United States having declared war, the Americans enjoyed the advantage of the first blow at the enemy's trade. The reduced numbers of vessels on the British transatlantic stations, and the perplexity induced by Rodgers' movement, combined to restrict the injury to American shipping. A number of prizes were made, doubtless; but as nearly as can be ascertained not over seventy American merchant ships were taken in the first three months of the war. Of these, thirty-eight are reported as brought under the jurisdiction of the Vice-Admiralty Court at Halifax, and twenty-four as captured on the Jamaica station. News of the war not being received by the British squadrons in Europe until early in August, only one capture there appears before October 1, except from the Mediterranean. There Captain Usher on September 6 wrote from Gibraltar that all the Americans on their way down the Sea—that is, out of the Straits—had been taken.[508] In like manner, though with somewhat better fortune,

---

507. Account of the Private Armed Ship *America*, by B.B. Crowninshield. *Essex* Institute Historical Collections, vol. xxxvii.
508. Naval Chronicle, vol. xxviii. p. 431.

thirty or forty American ships from the Baltic were driven to take refuge in the neutral Swedish port of Gottenburg, and remained war-bound.[509] That the British cruisers were not inactive in protecting the threatened shores and waters of Nova Scotia and the St. Lawrence is proved by the seizure of twenty-four American privateers, between July 1 and August 25;[510] a result to which the inadequate equipment of these vessels probably contributed. But American shipping, upon the whole, at first escaped pretty well in the matter of actual capture.

It was not in this way, but by the almost total suppression of commerce, both coasting and foreign, both neutral and American, that the maritime pressure of war was brought home to the United States. This also did not happen until a comparatively late period. No commercial blockade was instituted by the enemy before February, 1813. Up to that time neutrals, not carrying contraband, had free admission to all American ports; and the British for their own purposes encouraged a licensed trade, wholly illegitimate as far as United States ships were concerned, but in which American citizens and American vessels were largely engaged, though frequently under flags of other nations. A significant indication of the nature of this traffic is found in the export returns of the year ending September 30, 1813. The total value of home produce exported was $25,008,152, chiefly flour, grain, and other provisions. Of this, $20,536,328 went to Spain and Portugal with their colonies; $15,500,000 to the Peninsula itself.[511] It was not till October, 1813, when the British armies entered France, that this demand fell. At the same time Halifax and Canada were being supplied with flour from New England; and the common saying that the British forces in Canada could not keep the field but for supplies sent from the United States was strictly true, and has been attested by British commissaries. An American in Halifax in November, 1812, wrote home that within a fortnight twenty thousand barrels of flour had arrived

---

509. *Niles' Register*, vol. iii. p. 320.
510. Naval Chronicle, vol. xxviii. p. 257.
511. American State Papers, Commerce and Navigation, vol. i. p. 992.

in vessels under Spanish and Swedish flags, chiefly from Boston. This sort of unfaithfulness to a national cause is incidental to most wars, but rarely amounts to as grievous a military evil as in 1812 and 1813, when both the Peninsula and Canada were substantially at our mercy in this respect. With the fall of Napoleon, and the opening of Continental resources, such control departed from American hands. In the succeeding twelvemonth there was sent to the Peninsula less than $5,000,000 worth.

Warren's impressions of the serious nature of the opening conflict caused a correspondence between him and the Admiralty somewhat controversial in tone. Ten days after his arrival he represented the reduced state of the squadron: "The war assumes a new, as well as more active and inveterate aspect than heretofore." Alarming reports were being received as to the number of ships of twenty-two to thirty-two guns fitting out in American ports, and he mentions as significant that the commission of a privateer officer, taken in a recaptured vessel, bore the number 318. At Halifax he was in an atmosphere of rumours and excitement, fed by frequent communication with eastern ports, as well as by continual experience of captures about the neighbouring shores; the enemies' crews even landing at times. When he went to Bermuda two months later, so many privateers were met on the line of traffic between the West Indies and the St. Lawrence as to convince him of the number and destructiveness of these vessels, and "of the impossibility of our trade navigating these seas unless a very extensive squadron is employed to scour the vicinity." He was crippled for attempting this by the size of the American frigates, which forbade his dispersing his cruisers. The capture of the *Guerrière* had now been followed by that of the *Macedonian*; and in view of the results, and of Rodgers being again out, he felt compelled to constitute squadrons of two frigates and a sloop. Under these conditions, and with so many convoys to furnish, "it is impracticable to cut off the enemy's resources, or to repress the disorder and pillage which actually exist to a very alarming degree, both on the coast of British America and in the West Indies, as will be seen by the copies of letters enclosed," from colonial and naval officials. He goes on to speak, in terms not carefully weighed, of swarms of privateers and letters-of-*marque*, their numbers now amounting to six hundred; the crews of which had landed in many points of his Majesty's dominions, and even taken vessels from their anchors in British ports.[512]

The Admiralty, while evidently seeing exaggeration in this language, bear witness in their reply to the harassment caused by the American squadrons and private armed ships. They remind the admiral that there are two principal ways of protecting the trade: one by furnishing it with convoys, the other by preventing egress from the enemy's ports, through adequate force placed before them. To disperse vessels over the open sea, along the tracks of commerce, though necessary, is but a subsidiary measure. His true course is to concentrate a strong division before each chief American port, and they intimate dissatisfaction that this apparently had not yet been done. As a matter of fact, up to the spring of 1813, American ships of war had little difficulty in getting to sea. Rodgers had sailed again with his own squadron and Decatur's on October 8, the two separating on the 11th, though this was unknown to the British; and Bainbridge followed with the *Constitution* and *Hornet* on the 26th. Once away, power to arrest their depredations was almost wholly lost, through ignorance of their intentions. With regard to commerce, they were on the offensive, the British on the defensive, with the perplexity attaching to the latter role.

Under the circumstances, the Admiralty betrays some impatience with Warren's clamour for small vessels to be scattered in defence of the trade and coasts. They remind him that he has under his flag eleven sail of the line, thirty-four frigates, thirty-eight sloops, besides other vessels, making a total of ninety-seven; and yet first Rodgers, and then Bainbridge, had got away. True, Boston cannot be effectively blockaded from November to March, but these two squadrons had sailed in October.

---

512. Warren to Croker, Dec. 28 and 29, 1812. Records Office MSS.

(Even). . . . in the month of December, though it was not possible perhaps to have maintained a permanent watch on that port, yet having, as you state in your letter of November 5, precise information that Commodore Bainbridge was to sail at a given time, their Lordships regret that it was not deemed practicable to proceed off that port at a reasonable and safe distance from the land, and to have taken the chance at least of intercepting the enemy. . . . The necessity for sending heavy convoys arises from the facility and safety with which the American navy has hitherto found it possible to put to sea. The uncertainty in which you have left their Lordships, in regard to the movements of the enemy and the disposition of your own force, has obliged them to employ six or seven sail of the line and as many frigates and sloops, independent of your command, in guarding against the possible attempts of the enemy. Captain Prowse, with two sail of the line, two frigates, and a sloop, has been sent to St. Helena. Rear-Admiral Beauclerk, with two of the line, two frigates, and two sloops, is stationed in the neighbourhood of Madeira and the Azores, lest Commodore Bainbridge should have come into that quarter to take the place of Commodore Rodgers, who was retiring from it about the time you state Commodore Bainbridge was expected to sail. Commodore Owen, who had preceded Admiral Beauclerk in this station, with a ship of the line and three other vessels, is not yet returned from the cruise on which the appearance of the enemy near the Azores had obliged their Lordships to send this force; while the *Colossus* and the *Elephant* (ships of the line), with the *Rhin* and the *Armide*, are but just returned from similar services. Thus it is obvious that, large as the force under your orders was, and is, it is not all that has been opposed to the Americans, and that these services became necessary only because the chief weight of the enemy's force has been employed at a distance from your station.[513]

---

513. Croker to Warren, Jan. 9, Feb. 10, and March 20, 1813. Records Office MSS.

The final words here quoted characterize exactly the conditions of the first eight or ten months of the war, until the spring of 1813. They also define the purpose of the British Government to close the coast of the United States in such manner as to minimize the evils of widely dispersed commerce-destroying, by confining the American vessels as far as possible within their harbours. The American squadrons and heavy frigates, which menaced not commerce only but scattered ships of war as well, were to be rigorously shut up by an overwhelming division before each port in which they harboured; and the Admiralty intimated its wish that a ship of the line should always form one of such division. This course of policy, initiated when the winter of 1812-13 was over, was thenceforth maintained with ever increasing rigor; especially after the general peace in Europe, in May, 1814, had released the entire British navy. It had two principal results. The American frigates were, in the main, successfully excluded from the ocean. Their three successful battles were all fought before January 1, 1813. Commodore John Rodgers, indeed, by observing his own precept of clinging to the eastern ports of Newport and Boston, did succeed after this in making two cruises with the *President*; but entering New York with her on the last of these, in February, 1814, she was obliged, in endeavouring to get to sea when transferred to Decatur, to do so under circumstances so difficult as to cause her to ground, and by consequent loss of speed to be overtaken and captured by the blockading squadron. Captain Stewart reported the *Constitution* nearly ready for sea, at Boston, September 26, 1813. Three months after, he wrote the weather had not yet enabled him to escape. On December 30, however, she sailed; but returning on April 4, the blockaders drove her into Salem, whence she could not reach Boston until April 17, 1814, and there remained until the 17th of the following December. Her last successful battle, under his command, was on February 20, 1815, more than two years after she captured the *Java*. When the war ended the only United States vessels on the ocean were the *Constitution,* three sloops—the *Wasp, Hornet* and *Peacock*—

and the brig *Tom Bowline*. The smaller vessels of the navy, and the privateers, owing to their much lighter draft, got out more readily; but neither singly nor collectively did they constitute a serious menace to convoys, nor to the scattered cruisers of the enemy. These, therefore, were perfectly free to pursue their operations without fear of surprise.

On the other hand, because of this concentration along the shores of the United States, the vessels that did escape went prepared more and more for long absences and distant operations. On the sea "the weight of the enemy's force," to use again the words of the Admiralty, "was employed at a distance from the North American station." Whereas, at the first, most captures by Americans were made near the United States, after the spring of 1813 there is an increasing indication of their being most successfully sought abroad; and during the last nine months of the war, when peace prevailed throughout the world except between the United States and Great Britain, when the Chesapeake was British waters, when Washington was being burned and Baltimore threatened, when the American invasion of Canada had given place to the British invasion of New York, when New Orleans and Mobile were both being attacked,— it was the coasts of Europe, and the narrow seas over which England had claimed immemorial sovereignty, that witnessed the most audacious and successful ventures of American cruisers. The prizes taken in these quarters were to those on the hither side of the Atlantic as two to one. To this contributed also the commercial blockade, after its extension over the entire seaboard of the United States, in April, 1814. The practically absolute exclusion of American commerce from the ocean is testified by the exports of 1814, which amounted to not quite $7,000,000;[514] whereas in 1807, the last full year of unrestricted trade, they had been $108,000,000.[515] Deprived of all their usual employments, shipping and seamen were driven to privateering to earn any returns at all.

---

514. American State Papers. Commerce and Navigation, vol. i. p. 1021.
515. American State Papers. Commerce and Navigation, vol. i. p. 718.

From these special circumstances, the period from June, 1812, when the war began, to the end of April, 1813, when the departure of winter conditions permitted the renewal of local activity on sea and land, had a character of its own, favouring the United States on the ocean, which did not recur. Some specific account of particular transactions during these months will serve to illustrate the general conditions mentioned.

When Warren reached Halifax, there were still in Boston the *Constitution* and the ships that had returned with Rodgers on August 31. From these the Navy Department now constituted three squadrons. The *Hornet*, Captain James Lawrence, detached from Rodgers' command, was attached to the *Constitution,* in which Captain William Bainbridge had succeeded Hull. Bainbridge's squadron was to be composed of these two vessels and the smaller 32-gun frigate *Essex*, Captain David Porter, then lying in the Delaware. Rodgers retained his own ship, the *President,* with the frigate *Congress*; while to Decatur was continued the *United States* and the brig *Argus*. These detachments were to act separately under their several commodores; but as Decatur's preparations were only a few days behind those of Rodgers, the latter decided to wait for him, and on October 8 the two sailed in company, for mutual support until outside the lines of enemies, in case of meeting with a force superior to either singly.

In announcing his departure, Rodgers wrote the Department that he expected the British would be distributed in divisions, off the ports of the coast, and that if reliable information reached him of any such exposed detachment, it would be his duty to seek it. "I feel a confidence that, with prudent policy, we shall, barring unforeseen accidents, not only annoy their commerce, but embarrass and perplex the commanders of their public ships, equally to the advantage of our commerce and the disadvantage of theirs." Warren and the Admiralty alike have borne witness to the accuracy of this judgment. Rodgers was less happy in another forecast, in which he reflected that of his countrymen generally. As regards the reported size of British re-enforcements to America—

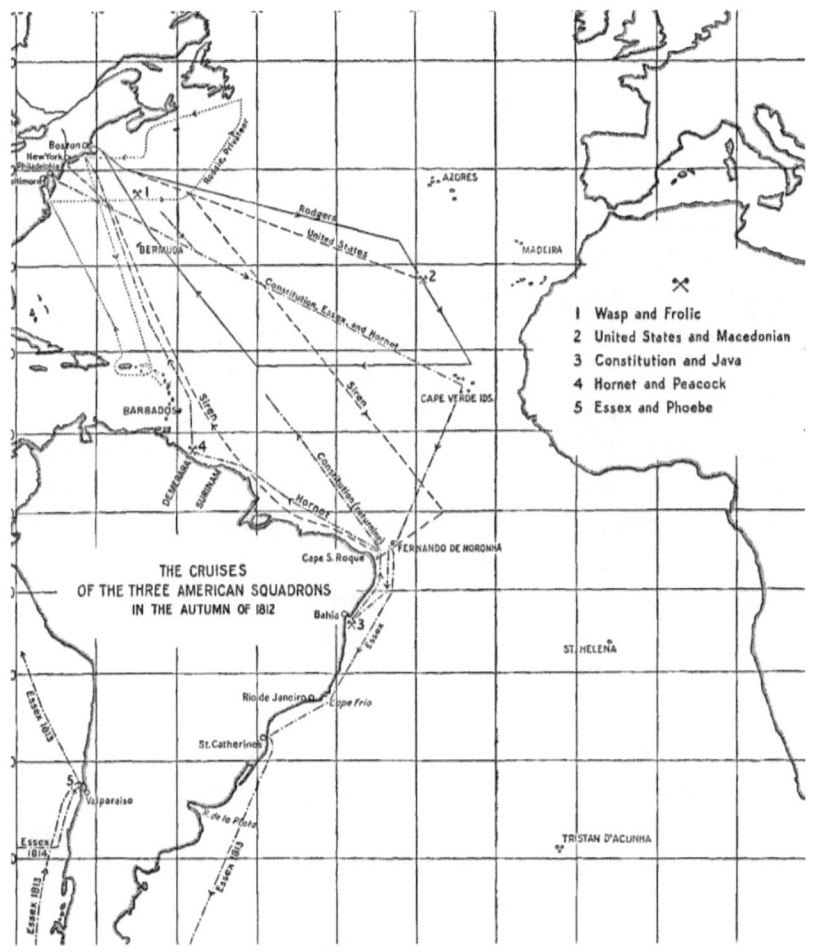

THE CRUISES OF THE THREE AMERICAN SQUADRONS
IN THE AUTUMN OF 1812

I do not feel confidence in them, as I cannot convince myself that their resources, situated as England is at present, are equal to the maintenance of such a force on this side of the Atlantic; and at any rate, if such an one do appear, it will be only with a view to bullying us into such a peace as may suit their interests.[516]

The Commodore's words reflected often an animosity, personal as well as national, aroused by the liberal abuse bestowed on him by British writers.

On October 11 Decatur's division parted company, the *President* and *Congress* continuing together and steering to the eastward. On the 15th the two ships captured a British packet, the *Swallow*, from Jamaica to Falmouth, having $150,000 to $200,000 *specie* on board; and on the 31st, in longitude 32° west, latitude 33° north, two hundred and forty miles south of the Azores, a Pacific whaler on her homeward voyage was taken. These two incidents indicate the general direction of the course held, which was continued to longitude 22° west, latitude 17° north, the neighbourhood of the Cape Verde group. This confirms the information of the British Admiralty that Rodgers was cruising between the Azores and Madeira; and it will be seen that Bainbridge, as they feared, followed in Rodgers' wake, though with a different ulterior destination. The ground indeed was well chosen to intercept homeward trade from the East Indies and South America. Returning, the two frigates ran west in latitude 17°, with the trade wind, as far as longitude 50°, whence they steered north, passing one hundred and twenty miles east of Bermuda. In his report to the Navy Department Rodgers said that he had sailed almost eleven thousand miles, making the circuit of nearly the whole western Atlantic. In this extensive sweep he had seen only five enemy's merchant vessels, two of which were captured. The last four weeks, practically the entire month of December, had been spent upon the line between Halifax and Bermuda, without meeting a single enemy's ship. From this he concluded that "their trade is at present infinitely more limited than peo-

---

516. Captains' Letters. Navy Department, Oct. 3, 1812.

ple imagine."⁵¹⁷ In fact, however, the experience indicated that the British officials were rigorously enforcing the Convoy Law, according to the "positive directions," and warnings of penalties, issued by the Government. A convoy is doubtless a much larger object than a single ship; but vessels thus concentrated in place and in time are more apt to pass wholly unseen than the same number sailing independently, and so scattered over wide expanses of sea.

Shortly before his return Rodgers arrested and sent in an American vessel, from Baltimore to Lisbon, with flour, sailing under a protection from the British admiral at Halifax. This was a frequent incident with United States cruisers, national or private, at this time; Decatur, for example, the day after leaving Rodgers, reported meeting an American ship having on board a number of licenses from the British Government to American citizens, granting them protection in transporting grain to Spain and Portugal. The license was issued by a British consular officer, and ran thus:⁵¹⁸

> To the commanders of His Majesty's ships of war, or of private armed ships belonging to subjects of His Majesty.
>
> Whereas, from the consideration of the great importance of continuing a regular supply of flour and other dried provisions, to the allied armies in Spain and Portugal, it has been deemed expedient by His Majesty's Government that, notwithstanding the hostilities now existing between Great Britain and the United States, every degree of encouragement and protection should be given to American vessels laden with flour and other dry provisions, and *bonâ fide* bound to Spain or Portugal, and whereas, in furtherance of the views of His Majesty's Government, Herbert Sawyer, Esq., Vice Admiral and commander-in-chief on the Halifax station, has addressed to me a letter under

---

517. Captains' Letters, Navy Department, Dee. 31, 1812, and Jan. 2, 1813.
518. From the file of Captains' Letters, Jan. 1, 1813. Found in the American licensed brig *Julia*, captured by United States frigate *Chesapeake*, Captain Samuel Evans. The vessel was condemned in the United States Courts.

the date of the 5th of August, 1812 (a copy whereof is hereunto annexed) wherein I am instructed to furnish a copy of his letter certified under my consular seal to every American vessel so laden and bound, destined to serve as a perfect safeguard and protection of such vessel in the prosecution of her voyage: Now, therefore, in obedience to these instructions, I have granted to the American ship ———, ———, Master, etc.

To this was appended the following letter of instructions from Admiral Sawyer:

Whereas Mr. Andrew Allen, His Majesty's Consul at Boston, has recommended to me Mr. Robert Elwell, a merchant of that place, and well inclined toward the British Interest, who is desirous of sending provisions to Spain and Portugal for the use of the allied armies in the Peninsula, and whereas I think it fit and necessary that encouragement and protection should be afforded him in so doing. These are therefore to require and direct all captains and commanders of His Majesty's ships and vessels of war which may fall in with any American or other vessel bearing a neutral flag, laden with flour, bread, corn, and pease, or any other species of dry provisions, bound from America to Spain or Portugal, and having this protection on board, to suffer her to proceed without unnecessary obstruction or detention in her voyage, provided she shall appear to be steering a due course for those countries, and it being understood this is only to be in force for one voyage and within six months from the date hereof.
Given under my hand and seal on board His Majesty's Ship *Centurion*, at Halifax this fourth day of August, one thousand eight hundred and twelve.
H. Sawyer
Vice-Admiral

This practice soon became perfectly known to the American Government, copies being found not only on board vessels stopped for carrying them, but in seaports. Nevertheless, it went on, apparently tolerated, or at least winked at; although, to say the least, the seamen thus employed in sustaining the enemies' armies were needed by the state.[519] When the commercial blockade of the Chesapeake was enforced in February, 1813, and Admiral Warren announced that licenses would no longer enable vessels to pass, flour in Baltimore fell two dollars a barrel. The blockade being then limited to the Chesapeake and Delaware, the immediate effect was to transfer this lucrative traffic further north, favouring that portion of the country which was considered, in the common parlance of the British official of that day, "well inclined towards British interests."

On October 13, two days after Rodgers and Decatur parted at sea, the United States sloop of war *Wasp*, Captain Jacob Jones, left the Capes of the Delaware on a cruise, steering to the eastward. On the 16th, in a heavy gale of wind, she lost her jibboom. At half-past eleven in the night of the 17th, being then in latitude 37° north, longitude 65° west, between four and five hundred miles east of the Chesapeake, in the track of vessels bound to Europe from the Gulf of Mexico, half a dozen large sail were seen passing. These were part of a convoy which had left the Bay of Honduras September 12, on their way to England, under guard of the British brig of war *Frolic*, Captain Whinyates. Jones, unable in the dark to distinguish their force, took a position some miles to windward, whence he could still see and follow their motions. In the morning each saw the other, and Whinyates, properly concerned for his charges chiefly, directed them to proceed under all sail on their easterly course, while he allowed the *Frolic* to drop astern, at the same time hoisting Spanish colours to deceive the stranger; a ruse prompted by his having a few days before passed a Spanish fleet convoyed by a brig resembling his own.

---

519. Besides the obvious impropriety, the practice was expressly forbidden by law. It was reprobated in strong terms by Justice Joseph Story, of Massachusetts, of the Supreme Court of the United States, affirming the condemnation of the "Julia." His judgment is given in full in Niles' Register, vol. iv. pp. 393-397.

It still blowing strong from the westward, with a heavy sea, Captain Jones, being to windward, and so having the choice of attacking, first put his ship under close-reefed topsails, and then stood down for the *Frolic*, which hauled to the wind on the port tack—that is, with the wind on the left side—to await the enemy. The British brig was under the disadvantage of having lost her main-yard in the same gale that cost the American her jib-boom; she was therefore unable to set any square sail on the rearmost of her two masts. The sail called the boom mainsail in part remedied this, so far as enabling the brig to keep side to wind; but, being a low sail, it did not steady her as well as a square topsail would have done in the heavy sea running, a condition which makes accurate aim more difficult.

The action did not begin until the *Wasp* was within sixty yards of the *Frolic*. Then the latter opened fire, which the American quickly returned; the two running side by side and gradually closing. The British crew fired much the more rapidly, a circumstance which their captain described as "superior fire;" in this reproducing the illusion under which Captain Dacres laboured during the first part of his fight with the *Constitution*. Whinyates wrote in his official report:

> The superior fire of our guns gave every reason to expect a speedy termination in our favour.

Dacres before his Court Martial asked of two witnesses, "Did you understand it was not my intention to board whilst the masts stood, in consequence of our superior fire and their great number of men?" That superior here meant quicker is established by the reply of one of these witnesses: "Our fire was a great deal quicker than the enemy's." Superiority of fire, however, consists not only in rapidity, but in hitting; and while with very big ships it may be possible to realize Nelson's maxim, that by getting close missing becomes impossible, it is not the same with smaller vessels in turbulent motion. It was thought on board the *Wasp* that the enemy fired thrice to her twice, but the direction of their shot was seen in its effects; the American losing within ten minutes her main topmast with its yard, the mizzen-topgallant-mast, and spanker gaff. Within twenty minutes most of the running rigging was also shot away, so as to leave the ship largely unmanageable; but she had only five killed and five wounded. In other words, the enemy's shot flew high; and, while it did the damage mentioned, it inflicted no vital injury. The *Wasp*, on the contrary, as evidently fired low; for the loss of the boom mainsail was the only serious harm received by the *Frolic*'s motive power during the engagement, and when her masts fell, immediately after it, they went close to the deck. Her loss in men, fifteen killed and forty-three wounded, tells the same story of aiming low.

The *Frolic* having gone into action without a main-yard, the loss of the boom mainsail left her unmanageable and decided the action. The *Wasp*, though still under control, was but little better off; for she was unable to handle her head yards, the main topmast having fallen across the head braces. There is little reason therefore to credit a contemporary statement of her wearing twice before boarding. Neither captain mentions further manoeuvring, and Jones' words, "We gradually lessened the space till we laid her on board," probably express the exact sequence. As they thus closed, the *Wasp*'s greater remaining sail and a movement of her helm would affect what followed: the British vessel's bowsprit coming between the main and the mizzen rigging of her opponent, who thus grappled her in a position favourable for raking. A broadside or two, preparatory for boarding, followed, and ended the battle; for when the Americans leaped on board there was no resistance. In view of the vigorous previous contest, this shows a ship's company decisively beaten.[520]

Under the conditions of wind and weather, this engagement may fairly be described as an artillery duel between two vessels of substantially equal force. James' contention of inferior numbers in the *Frolic* is true in the letter; but the greater rapidity of her firing shows it irrelevant to the issue. The want of

---

520. Captain Jones' Report of this action can be found in Niles' Register, vol. iii. p. 217; that of Captain Whinyates in Naval Chronicle, vol. xxix. p. 76.

the main-yard, which means the lack of the main topsail, was a more substantial disadvantage. So long as the boom mainsail held, however, it was fairly offset by the fall of the *Wasp*'s main topmast and its consequences. Both vessels carried sixteen 32-pounder carronades, which gave a broadside of two hundred and fifty-six pounds. The *Wasp* had, besides, two 12-pounder long guns. The British naval historian James states that the *Frolic* had in addition to her main battery only two long sixes; but Captain Jones gives her six 12-pounders, claiming that she was therefore superior to the *Wasp* by four 12-pounders. As we are not excusing a defeat, it may be sufficient to say that the fight was as nearly equal as it is given to such affairs to be. The action lasted forty-three minutes; the *Frolic* hauling down her colours shortly after noon. Almost immediately afterward the British seventy-four *Poietiers* came in sight, and in the disabled condition of the two combatants overhauled them easily. Two hours later she took possession of both *Wasp* and *Frolic*, and carried them into Bermuda. The *Wasp* was added to the British navy under the name of *Loup Cervier (Lynx)*.

When Rodgers and Decatur separated, on October 11, the former steered rather easterly, while the latter diverged to the southward as well as east, accompanied by the *Argus*. These two did not remain long together. It is perhaps worth noticing by the way, that Rodgers adhered to his idea of co-operation between ships, keeping his two in company throughout; whereas Decatur, when in control, illustrated in practice his preference for separate action. The brig proceeded to Cape St. Roque, the easternmost point of Brazil, and thence along the north coast of South America, as far as Surinam. From there she passed to the eastward of the West India Islands and so toward home; remaining out as long as her stores justified, cruising in the waters between Halifax, Bermuda, and the Continent. These courses, as those of the other divisions, are given as part of the maritime action, conducive to understanding the general character of effort put forth by national and other cruisers. Of these four ships that sailed together, the *Argus* alone encountered any considerable force of the enemy; falling in with a squadron of six British vessels, two of them of the line, soon after parting with the *United States*. She escaped by her better sailing. Her entire absence from the country was ninety-six days.

Decatur with the *United States* kept away to the southeast until October 25. At daybreak of that day the frigate was in latitude 29° north, longitude 29° 30' west, steering southwest on the port tack, with the wind at south-southeast. Soon after daylight there was sighted a large sail bearing about south-southwest; or, as seamen say, two points on the weather bow. She was already heading as nearly as the wind permitted in the direction of the stranger; but the latter, which proved to be the British frigate *Macedonian*, Captain John S. Carden, having the wind free, changed her course for the "United States," taking care withal to preserve the windward position, cherished by the seamen of that day. In this respect conditions differed from those of the *Constitution* and *Guerrière*, for there the American was to windward. Contrary also to the case of the *Wasp* and *Frolic*, the interest of the approaching contest turns largely on the manoeuvres of the antagonists; for, the "United States" being fully fifty per cent stronger than the *Macedonian* in artillery power, it was only by utilizing the advantage of her windward position, by judicious choice of the method of attack, that the British ship could hope for success. She had in her favour also a decided superiority of speed; and, being just from England after a period of refit, was in excellent sailing trim.

When first visible to each other from the mastheads, the vessels were some twelve miles apart. They continued to approach until 8.30, when the "United States," being then about three miles distant, wore—turned round—standing on the other tack. Her colours, previously concealed by her sails, were by this manoeuvre shown to the British frigate, which was thus also placed in the position of steering for the quarter of her opponent; the latter heading nearer the wind, and inclining gradually to cross the *Macedonian*'s bows (1). When this occurred, a conversation was going on between Captain Carden, his first lieutenant, and the master;[521] the latter being the officer who usually worked the ship in battle, under directions from the captain. These officers had been in company with the *United States* the year before in Chesapeake Bay; and, whether they now recognized her or not, they knew the weight of battery carried by the heavy American frigates. The question under discussion by them, before the *United States* wore, was whether it was best to steer direct upon the approaching enemy, or to keep farther away for a time, in order to maintain the windward position. By the first lieutenant's testimony before the Court, this was in his opinion the decisive moment, victory or defeat hinging upon the resolution taken. He favoured attempting to cross the enemy's bows, which was possible if the *United States* should continue to stand as she at the moment was—on the port tack; but in any event to close with the least delay possible. The master appears to have preferred to close by going under the enemy's stern, and hauling up to leeward; but Captain Carden, impressed both with the advantage of the weather gage and the danger of approaching exposed to a raking fire, thought better to haul nearer the wind, on the tack he was already on, the starboard, but without bracing the yards, which were not sharp. His aim was to pass the *United States* at a distance, wear—turn round from the wind, toward her—when clear of her broadside, and so come up from astern without being raked. The interested reader may compare this method with that pursued by Hull, who steered down by zigzag courses. The Court Martial censured Carden's decision, which was clearly wrong, for the power of heavy guns over lighter, of the American 24's over the British 18's, was greatest at a distance; therefore, to close rapidly, taking the chances of being raked—if not avoidable by yawing—was the smaller risk. Moreover, wearing behind the *United States*, and then pursuing, gave her the opportunity which she used, to fire and keep away again, prolonging still farther the period of slow approach which Carden first chose.

---

521. *Macedonian* Court Martial. British Records Office MSS.

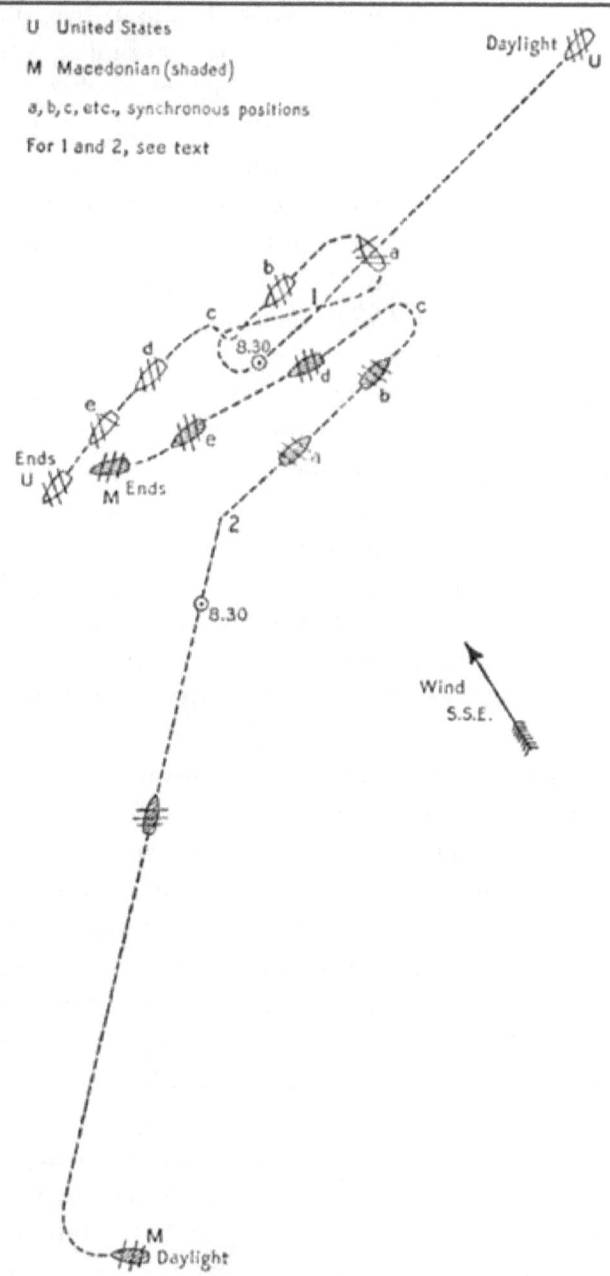

PLAN OF THE ENGAGEMENT BETWEEN THE
UNITED STATES AND MACEDONIAN

The *United States* wearing, while this conversation was in progress, precipitated Carden's action. He interpreted the manoeuvre as indicating a wish to get to windward, which the *Macedonian*'s then course, far off the wind, would favour. He therefore hurriedly gave the order to haul up (2), cutting adrift the topmast studdingsail; a circumstance which to seamen will explain exactly the relative situations. That he had rightly interpreted Decatur's purpose seems probable, for in fifteen or twenty minutes the *United States* again wore (*a*), resuming her original course, by the wind on the port tack, the *Macedonian* continuing on the starboard; the two now running on lines nearly parallel, in opposite directions (*b b*). As they passed, at the distance of almost a mile, the American frigate discharged her main-deck battery, her spar-deck carronades not ranging so far. The British ship did not reply, but shortly afterward wore (*c*), and, heading now in the same general direction as the *United States*, steered to come up on her port side. She thus reached a position not directly behind her antagonist, but well to the left, apparently about half a mile away. So situated, if steering the same course, each ship could train its batteries on the opponent; but the increased advantage at a distance was with the heavier guns, and when the *Macedonian*, to get near, headed more toward the *United States*, most of hers ceased to bear, while those of her enemy continued their fire. A detailed description of the *United States*'s manoeuvres by her own officers has not been transmitted; but in the searching investigation made by Carden's Court Martial we have them probably well preserved. The master of the British ship stated that when the *Macedonian* wore in chase, the United States first kept off before the wind, and then almost immediately came back to it as before (*c*), bringing it abeam, and immediately began firing. By thus increasing her lateral distance from the line of the enemy's approach, she was able more certainly to train her guns on him. After about fifteen minutes of this, the *Macedonian* suffering severely, her foresail was set to close (*e*), upon which the *United States*, hauling out the spanker and letting fly the jib-sheet, came up to the wind and backed her mizzen-topsail, in order not to move too fast from the advantageous position she had, yet to keep way enough to command the ship (*e*).

Under these unhappy conditions the *Macedonian* reached within half musket-shot, which was scarcely the ideal close action of the day; but by that time she had lost her mizzen-topmast, main-yard, and main topsail, most of her standing rigging was shot away, the lower masts badly wounded, and almost all her carronade battery, the principal reliance for close action, was disabled. She had also many killed and wounded; while the only visible damage on board the *United States* was the loss of the mizzen-topgallant-mast, a circumstance of absolutely no moment at the time. In short, although she continued to fight manfully for a half-hour more, the *Macedonian*, when she got alongside the *United States*, was already beaten beyond hope. At the end of the half-hour her fore and main topmasts fell, upon which the *United States* filled her mizzen-topsail and shot ahead, crossing the bows of the *Macedonian*,[522] and thus ending the fight. Surprise was felt on board the British vessel that a raking broadside was not at this moment poured in, and it was even believed by some that the American was now abandoning the contest. She was so, in the sense that the contest was over; a ship with all her spars standing, "in perfect condition," to use the expression of the enemy's first lieutenant, would be little less than brutal to use her power upon one reduced to lower masts, unless submission was refused. Upon her return an hour later, the *Macedonian*'s mizzenmast had gone overboard, and her colours were hauled down as the *United States* drew near.

This action was fought by the *United States* with singular wariness, not to say caution. Her change to the starboard tack, when still some three miles distant, seems to indicate a desire to get the weather gage, as the *Macedonian* was then steering free. It was so interpreted on board the British vessel; but as Carden also

---

[522.] James states that this was in order to fill fresh cartridges, which is likely enough; but it is most improbable that the movement was deferred till the last cartridge ready was exhausted—that the battery could not have been fired when crossing the bows.

CAPTAIN STEPHEN DECATUR FROM THE PAINTING BY
GILBERT STUART, IN INDEPENDENCE HALL, PHILADELPHIA

at once hauled up, it became apparent that he would not yield the advantage of the wind which he had, and which it was in his choice to keep, for the *United States* was a lumbering sailer. Decatur, unable to obtain the position for attacking, at once wore again, and thenceforth played the game of the defensive with a skill which his enemy's mistake seconded. By the movements of his ship the *Macedonian*'s closing was protracted, and she was kept at the distance and bearing most favourable to the American guns. But when her foresail was set, the *United States*, by luffing rapidly to the wind—flowing the jib-sheet and hauling out the spanker to hasten this movement—and at the same time backing the mizzen-topsail to steady her motions and position, was constituted a moving platform of guns, disposed in the very best manner to annihilate an opponent obliged to approach at a pretty broad angle.

This account, summarized from the sworn testimony before the British court, is not irreconcilable with Decatur's remark, that the enemy being to windward engaged at his own distance, to the greatness of which was to be ascribed the unusual length of the action. Imbued with the traditions of their navy, the actions of the *United States* puzzled the British extremely. Her first wearing was interpreted as running away, and her shooting ahead when the *Macedonian*'s topmasts fell, crossing her bows without pouring a murderous broadside into a beaten ship, coupled with the previous impression of wariness, led them to think that the American was using the bad luck by which alone they could have been beaten, in order to get away. Three cheers were given, as though victorious in repelling an attack. They had expected, so the testimony ran, to have her in an hour.[523] Judged by this evidence, the handling of the *United States* was thoroughly skilful. Though he probably knew himself superior in force, Decatur's object necessarily should be to take his opponent at the least possible injury to his own ship. She was "on a cruise"; hence haste was no object, while serious damage might cripple her further operations. The

---

523. *Macedonian* Court Martial.

result was, by his official statement, that "the damage sustained was not such as to render return to port necessary; and I should have continued her cruise, had I not deemed it important that we should see our prize in."[524]

In general principle, the great French Admiral Tourville correctly said that the best victories are those which cost least in blood, timber, and iron; but, in the particular instance before us, Decatur's conduct may rest its absolute professional justification on the testimony of the master of the British ship and two of her three lieutenants. To the question whether closing more rapidly by the *Macedonian* would have changed the result, the first lieutenant replied he thought there was a chance of success. The others differed from him in this, but agreed that their position would have been more favourable, and the enemy have suffered more.[525] Carden himself had no hesitation as to the need of getting near, but only as to the method. To avoid this was therefore not only fitting, but the bounden duty of the American captain. His business was not merely to make a brilliant display of courage and efficiency, but to do the utmost injury to the opponent at the least harm to his ship and men. It was the more notable to find this trait in Decatur; for not, only had he shown headlong valour before, but when offered the new American *Guerrière* a year later, he declined, saying that she was overmatched by a seventy-four, while no frigate could lie alongside of her. "There was no reputation to be made in this."[526]

The *United States* and her prize, after repairing damages sufficiently for a winter arrival upon the American coast, started thither; the *United States* reaching New London December 4, the *Macedonian*, from weather conditions, putting into Newport. Both soon afterward went to New York by Long Island Sound. It is somewhat remarkable that no one of Warren's rapidly increasing fleet should have been sighted by either. There was as yet no commercial blockade, and this, coupled with the numbers of American vessels protected by licenses, and the fewness of the

---

524. Decatur's Report. Niles' Register, vol. iii. p. 253.
525. *Macedonian* Court Martial.
526. Captains' Letters, April 9, 1814. Navy Department MSS.

American ships of war, may have indisposed the admiral and his officers to watch very closely an inhospitable shore, at a season unpropitious to active operations. Besides, as appears from letters already quoted, the commander-in-chief's personal predilection was more for the defensive than the offensive; to protect British trade by cruisers patrolling its routes, rather than by preventing egress from the hostile ports.

ALSO FROM LEONAUR
AVAILABLE IN SOFTCOVER OR HARDCOVER WITH DUST JACKET

CAPTAIN OF THE 95th (Rifles) *by Jonathan Leach*—An officer of Wellington's Sharpshooters during the Peninsular, South of France and Waterloo Campaigns of the Napoleonic Wars.

BUGLER AND OFFICER OF THE RIFLES *by William Green & Harry Smith* With the 95th (Rifles) during the Peninsular & Waterloo Campaigns of the Napoleonic Wars

BAYONETS, BUGLES AND BONNETS *by James 'Thomas' Todd*—Experiences of hard soldiering with the 71st Foot - the Highland Light Infantry - through many battles of the Napoleonic wars including the Peninsular & Waterloo Campaigns

THE ADVENTURES OF A LIGHT DRAGOON *by George Farmer & G.R. Gleig*—A cavalryman during the Peninsular & Waterloo Campaigns, in captivity & at the siege of Bhurtpore, India

THE COMPLEAT RIFLEMAN HARRIS *by Benjamin Harris as told to & transcribed by Captain Henry Curling*—The adventures of a soldier of the 95th (Rifles) during the Peninsular Campaign of the Napoleonic Wars

WITH WELLINGTON'S LIGHT CAVALRY *by William Tomkinson*—The Experiences of an officer of the 16th Light Dragoons in the Peninsular and Waterloo campaigns of the Napoleonic Wars.

SURTEES OF THE RIFLES *by William Surtees*—A Soldier of the 95th (Rifles) in the Peninsular campaign of the Napoleonic Wars.

ENSIGN BELL IN THE PENINSULAR WAR *by George Bell*—The Experiences of a young British Soldier of the 34th Regiment 'The Cumberland Gentlemen' in the Napoleonic wars.

WITH THE LIGHT DIVISION *by John H. Cooke*—The Experiences of an Officer of the 43rd Light Infantry in the Peninsula and South of France During the Napoleonic Wars

NAPOLEON'S IMPERIAL GUARD: FROM MARENGO TO WATERLOO *by J. T. Headley*—This is the story of Napoleon's Imperial Guard from the bearskin caps of the grenadiers to the flamboyance of their mounted chasseurs, their principal characters and the men who commanded them.

BATTLES & SIEGES OF THE PENINSULAR WAR *by W. H. Fitchett*—Corunna, Busaco, Albuera, Ciudad Rodrigo, Badajos, Salamanca, San Sebastian & Others

AVAILABLE ONLINE AT
www.leonaur.com
AND OTHER GOOD BOOK STORES

ALSO FROM LEONAUR
AVAILABLE IN SOFTCOVER OR HARDCOVER WITH DUST JACKET

WELLINGTON AND THE PYRENEES CAMPAIGN VOLUME I: FROM VITORIA TO THE BIDASSOA by *F. C. Beatson*—The final phase of the campaign in the Iberian Peninsula.

WELLINGTON AND THE INVASION OF FRANCE VOLUME II: THE BIDASSOA TO THE BATTLE OF THE NIVELLE by *F. C. Beatson*—The second of Beatson's series on the fall of Revolutionary France published by Leonaur, the reader is once again taken into the centre of Wellington's strategic and tactical genius.

WELLINGTON AND THE FALL OF FRANCE VOLUME III: THE GAVES AND THE BATTLE OF ORTHEZ by *F. C. Beatson*—This final chapter of F. C. Beatson's brilliant trilogy shows the 'captain of the age' at his most inspired and makes all three books essential additions to any Peninsular War library.

NAVAL BATTLES OF THE NAPOLEONIC WARS by *W. H. Fitchett*—Cape St. Vincent, the Nile, Cadiz, Copenhagen, Trafalgar & Others

SERGEANT GUILLEMARD: THE MAN WHO SHOT NELSON? by *Robert Guillemard*—A Soldier of the Infantry of the French Army of Napoleon on Campaign Throughout Europe

WITH THE GUARDS ACROSS THE PYRENEES by *Robert Batty*—The Experiences of a British Officer of Wellington's Army During the Battles for the Fall of Napoleonic France, 1813.

A STAFF OFFICER IN THE PENINSULA by *E. W. Buckham*—An Officer of the British Staff Corps Cavalry During the Peninsula Campaign of the Napoleonic Wars

THE LEIPZIG CAMPAIGN: 1813—NAPOLEON AND THE "BATTLE OF THE NATIONS" by *F. N. Maude*—Colonel Maude's analysis of Napoleon's campaign of 1813.

BUGEAUD: A PACK WITH A BATON by *Thomas Robert Bugeaud*—The Early Campaigns of a Soldier of Napoleon's Army Who Would Become a Marshal of France.

TWO LEONAUR ORIGINALS

SERGEANT NICOL by *Daniel Nicol*—The Experiences of a Gordon Highlander During the Napoleonic Wars in Egypt, the Peninsula and France.

WATERLOO RECOLLECTIONS by *Frederick Llewellyn*—Rare First Hand Accounts, Letters, Reports and Retellings from the Campaign of 1815.

AVAILABLE ONLINE AT
www.leonaur.com
AND OTHER GOOD BOOK STORES

ALSO FROM LEONAUR
AVAILABLE IN SOFTCOVER OR HARDCOVER WITH DUST JACKET

THE JENA CAMPAIGN: 1806 *by F. N. Maude*—The Twin Battles of Jena & Auerstadt Between Napoleon's French and the Prussian Army.

PRIVATE O'NEIL *by Charles O'Neil*—The recollections of an Irish Rogue of H. M. 28th Regt.—The Slashers— during the Peninsula & Waterloo campaigns of the Napoleonic wars.

ROYAL HIGHLANDER *by James Anton*—A soldier of H.M 42nd (Royal) Highlanders during the Peninsular, South of France & Waterloo Campaigns of the Napoleonic Wars.

CAPTAIN BLAZE *by Elzéar Blaze*—Elzéar Blaze recounts his life and experiences in Napoleon's army in a well written, articulate and companionable style.

LEJEUNE VOLUME 1 *by Louis-François Lejeune*—The Napoleonic Wars through the Experiences of an Officer on Berthier's Staff.

LEJEUNE VOLUME 2 *by Louis-François Lejeune*—The Napoleonic Wars through the Experiences of an Officer on Berthier's Staff.

FUSILIER COOPER *by John S. Cooper*—Experiences in the 7th (Royal) Fusiliers During the Peninsular Campaign of the Napoleonic Wars and the American Campaign to New Orleans.

CAPTAIN COIGNET *by Jean-Roch Coignet*—A Soldier of Napoleon's Imperial Guard from the Italian Campaign to Russia and Waterloo.

FIGHTING NAPOLEON'S EMPIRE *by Joseph Anderson*—The Campaigns of a British Infantryman in Italy, Egypt, the Peninsular & the West Indies During the Napoleonic Wars.

CHASSEUR BARRES *by Jean-Baptiste Barres*—The experiences of a French Infantryman of the Imperial Guard at Austerlitz, Jena, Eylau, Friedland, in the Peninsular, Lutzen, Bautzen, Zinnwald and Hanau during the Napoleonic Wars.

MARINES TO 95TH (RIFLES) *by Thomas Fernyhough*—The military experiences of Robert Fernyhough during the Napoleonic Wars.

HUSSAR ROCCA *by Albert Jean Michel de Rocca*—A French cavalry officer's experiences of the Napoleonic Wars and his views on the Peninsular Campaigns against the Spanish, British And Guerilla Armies.

SERGEANT BOURGOGNE *by Adrien Bourgogne*—With Napoleon's Imperial Guard in the Russian Campaign and on the Retreat from Moscow 1812 - 13.

AVAILABLE ONLINE AT
www.leonaur.com
AND OTHER GOOD BOOK STORES

ALSO FROM LEONAUR
AVAILABLE IN SOFTCOVER OR HARDCOVER WITH DUST JACKET

LIGHT BOB by *Robert Blakeney*—The experiences of a young officer in H.M 28th & 36th regiments of the British Infantry during the Peninsular Campaign of the Napoleonic Wars 1804 - 1814.

NAPOLEON'S RUSSIAN CAMPAIGN by *Philippe Henri de Segur*—The Invasion, Battles and Retreat by an Aide-de-Camp on the Emperor's Staff

SWORDS OF HONOUR by *Henry Newbolt & Stanley L. Wood*—The Careers of Six Outstanding Officers from the Napoleonic Wars, the Wars for India and the American Civil War. Illustrated.

HUSSAR IN WINTER by *Alexander Gordon*—A British Cavalry Officer during the retreat to Corunna in the Peninsular campaign of the Napoleonic Wars.

THE LIFE OF THE REAL BRIGADIER GERARD VOLUME 1 THE YOUNG HUSSAR 1782 - 1807 by *Jean-Baptiste De Marbot*—A French Cavalryman Of the Napoleonic Wars at Marengo, Austerlitz, Jena, Eylau & Friedland.

THE LIFE OF THE REAL BRIGADIER GERARD VOLUME 2 IMPERIAL AIDE-DE-CAMP 1807 - 1811 by *Jean-Baptiste De Marbot*—A French Cavalryman of the Napoleonic Wars at Saragossa, Landshut, Eckmuhl, Ratisbon, Aspern-Essling, Wagram, Busaco & Torres Vedras.

THE LIFE OF THE REAL BRIGADIER GERARD VOLUME 3 COLONEL OF CHASSEURS 1811 - 1815 by *Jean-Baptiste De Marbot*—A French Cavalryman in the retreat from Moscow, Lutzen, Bautzen, Katzbach, Leipzig, Hanau & Waterloo.

RIFLEMAN COSTELLO by *Edward Costello*—The adventures of a soldier of the 95th (Rifles) in the Peninsular & Waterloo Campaigns of the Napoleonic wars.

WITH THE LIGHT DIVISION by *John H. Cooke*—The Experiences of an Officer of the 43rd Light Infantry in the Peninsula and South of France During the Napoleonic Wars.

COLBORNE: A SINGULAR TALENT FOR WAR by *John Colborne*—The Napoleonic Wars Career of One of Wellington's Most Highly Valued Officers in Egypt, Holland, Italy, the Peninsula and at Waterloo.

A VOICE FROM WATERLOO by *Edward Cotton*—The Personal Experiences of a British Cavalryman Who Became a Battlefield Guide and Authority on the Campaign of 1815.

AVAILABLE ONLINE AT
www.leonaur.com
AND OTHER GOOD BOOK STORES

ALSO FROM LEONAUR
AVAILABLE IN SOFTCOVER OR HARDCOVER WITH DUST JACKET

CAMP-FIRE AND COTTON-FIELD by *Thomas W. Knox*—A New York Herald Correspondent's View of the American Civil War.

SERGEANT STILLWELL by *Leander Stillwell*—The Experiences of a Union Army Soldier of the 61st Illinois Infantry During the American Civil War.

STONEWALL'S CANNONEER by *Edward A. Moore*—Experiences with the Rockbridge Artillery, Confederate Army of Northern Virginia, During the American Civil War.

CONFEDERATE BLOCKADE RUNNER by *John Wilkinson*—The Personal Recollections of an Officer of the Confederate Navy.

THE SIXTH CORPS by *George Stevens*—The Army of the Potomac, Union Army, During the American Civil War.

THE RAILROAD RAIDERS by *William Pittenger*—An Ohio Volunteers Recollections of the Andrews Raid to Disrupt the Confederate Railroad in Georgia During the American Civil War.

CITIZEN SOLDIER by *John Beatty*—An Account of the American Civil War by a Union Infantry Officer of Ohio Volunteers Who Became a Brigadier General.

COX: PERSONAL RECOLLECTIONS OF THE CIVIL WAR--VOLUME 1 by *Jacob Dolson Cox*—West Virginia, Kanawha Valley, Gauley Bridge, Cotton Mountain, South Mountain, Antietam, the Morgan Raid & the East Tennessee Campaign.

COX: PERSONAL RECOLLECTIONS OF THE CIVIL WAR--VOLUME 2 by *Jacob Dolson Cox*—Siege of Knoxville, East Tennessee, Atlanta Campaign, the Nashville Campaign & the North Carolina Campaign.

THE RELUCTANT REBEL by *William G. Stevenson*—A young Kentuckian's experiences in the Confederate Infantry & Cavalry during the American Civil War.

KERSHAW'S BRIGADE VOLUME 1 by *D. Augustus Dickert*—Manassas, Seven Pines, Sharpsburg (Antietam), Fredricksburg, Chancellorsville, Gettysburg, Chickamauga, Chattanooga, Fort Sanders & Bean Station.

KERSHAW'S BRIGADE VOLUME 2 by *D. Augustus Dickert*—At the wilderness, Cold Harbour, Petersburg, The Shenandoah Valley and Cedar Creek.

AVAILABLE ONLINE AT
www.leonaur.com
AND OTHER GOOD BOOK STORES

www.ingramcontent.com/pod-product-compliance
Lightning Source LLC
Chambersburg PA
CBHW030814190426
43197CB00035B/151